THE LIFE OF SIR STAMFORD RAFFLES

H. S. del.

Institution
Madeley lith. 3, Wellington St. Strand.

Demetrius Charles Boulger

THE LIFE OF SIR STAMFORD RAFFLES

With a preface by Dr. John Bastin

THE PEPIN PRESS
Amsterdam & Kuala Lumpur

Originally published in 1897, reprinted in the present format in 1899.

ISBN 90 5496 029 9

The Pepin Press
P.O. Box 10349 / 1001 EH Amsterdam / The Netherlands
Tel 31 20 4202021 / Fax 31 20 4201152
E-mail: mail@pepinpress.com

CONTENTS

THE EASTERN ARCHIPELAGO

LIST OF ILLUSTRATIONS

W. Jones & Co

XIV

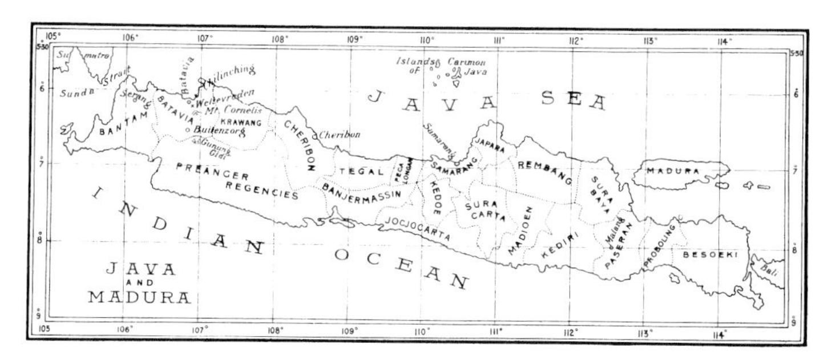
JAVA AND MADURA
JAVA SEA
INDIAN OCEAN
Sumatra
Sunda Strait
Islands of Carimon Java
Batavia
Tjilinching
Serang
Weltevreden
Mt. Cornelis
Buitenzorg
Gunung Gidi
Cheribon
Samarang
BANTAM
BATAVIA
KRAWANG
CHERIBON
PREANGER REGENCIES
TEGAL
PECA LONGAN
BANJERMASSIN
SAMARANG
JAPARA
KEDOE
SURA CARTA
JOCJOCARTA
REMBANG
MADIOEN
KEDIRI
SURA BAYA
Malang
PASERAN
PROBOLING
BESOEKI
MADURA
Bali
105° 106° 107° 108° 109° 110° 111° 112° 113° 114°

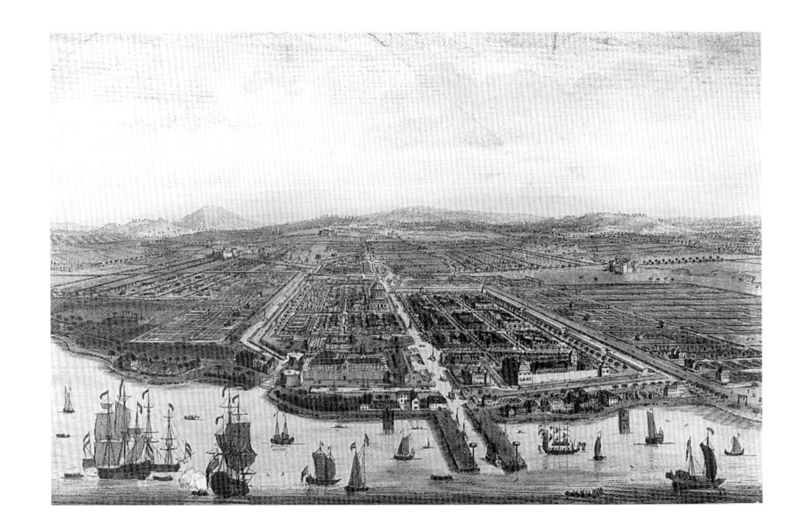

Singhapour

波架星

SINGAPORE
DISPENSARY
RAFFLES SQUARE S. 212.

BAR
&
BILLIARD ROOM
Raffles Hotel

PREFACE

THIS book was published in 1897, the year of Queen Victoria's Diamond Jubilee. The 60th anniversary of the Queen's reign was marked by services of thanksgiving and by processions throughout Great Britain, the most important being in London when thousands of representatives of the Queen's 300 million overseas subjects marched in a colourful parade prior to a service in St. Paul's Cathedral. Maori riflemen, Borneo Dyaks, Hong Kong Chinese, Canadian Hussars, Australian cavalrymen, Bengal Lancers, artillerymen from Sierra Leone, policemen from British Guiana and Malta, and a host of others, dazzled the London crowds who, in a frenzy of excitement and enthusiasm, shouted and waved their Jubilee flags for the Empire and the Queen, the two by now having become synonymous in the public mind. It was a celebration of empire the like of which had never been seen since the days of Rome.

Inevitably, a biography of one of Britain's greatest proconsuls, written at the high noon of empire, reflects the values of the age. Indeed, Raffles's claim to fame is stated in the opening sentence of the book: 'Among the men who have established the political and commercial power of this country in the seas of India and China, no one would deny a foremost place to Stamford Raffles'. Yet, apart from common assumptions, and a conclusion which contemplates a limited future for the British Empire without the independence and assertiveness of imperialists like Raffles, the book gives an extremely balanced account of his life. The reason for this is not hard to find, for Demetrius Charles

Boulger was far from being a parochial writer. He possessed an extensive knowledge of Asia, and was the author of works on Central Asia and India, as well as a three-volume *History of China*, which was published between 1881 and 1884. He was, moreover, the founder, with Sir Lepel Griffin, of *The Asiatic Quarterly Review*, and was its editor during the first four years of its existence. Like most of his contemporaries, he was a firm believer in the benefits of British rule in Asia; but this belief was qualified by a deep understanding of Asian history.

In the Introduction to his book, Boulger explains how in 1885-86, while classifying manuscript records in the India Office, he came across a considerable number of Raffles's letters and despatches. He approached two publishers with offers to write a book dealing with his career but was turned down. It was only while he was recovering from diphteria in a London Fever Hospital ten years later, and met the Revd. Robert Blanchard Raffles, that he was encouraged to reconsider the project. The Revd. Raffles had also contemplated writing a biography of his forbear, having himself also gone through the records in the India Office making extensive extracts from them. These materials he agreed to place at Boulger's disposal on the latter's undertaking to write the biography after completing his *Life of Gordon*. The climate for publishing such a book had changed markedly in ten years, and arrangements were soon made with Horace Marshall & Son, London, to undertake the work.

In confronting his task, Boulger was fortunate in having the assistance of the Revd. R.B. Raffles, who had spent much time mastering the details of Raffles's administrations in Java and Sumatra. He was the grandson of Raffles's first cousin, the Revd. Dr. Thomas Raffles, the independent minister of Great George Street Chapel, Liverpool, and like his grandfather was an excellent preacher; but although being a well read theologian, he did not attain any particular degree of prominence, and when Boulger met him he was Chaplain of the London Fever Hospital. He died at Camberly in 1905, his obituary notice declaring that in 'everything else retiring, he had one fixed and dominant purpose that filled his mind to the last hour of his life, and about which he strove with equal energy and discretion. This was to obtain in every way full recognition by the British people at home and beyond the seas for the services as a statesman, and for the character as a man, of his cousin, Sir Stamford Raffles, Governor of Java and Sumatra, and founder of Singapore and the Zoological Society'. It is singularly appropriate that Boulger dedicated his book to him.

The Revd. R.B. Raffles also obtained for Boulger the extant correspondence of Sir Stamford Raffles with his cousin, the Revd. Dr. Thomas Raffles, during the years he was in the East. This correspondence was in the possession of the Revd. R.B. Raffles's aunt, widow of the Liverpool Police Magistrate who also bore the name Thomas Stamford Raffles. When he examined this correspondence, and the manuscript 'Reminiscences' of the Revd. Dr. Thomas Raffles from the same source, Boulger decided to use these materials as the structure of his book. Portions of the letters had already been cited by Lady Raffles in her *Memoir of the Life and Public Services of Sir Thomas Stamford Raffles* (London, 1830), but the transcription of the letters was often inaccurate and the passages highly selective. One of the great virtues of Boulger's biography is that it reproduces these letters in full, including the long and autobiographical letter which Raffles wrote to his cousin in 1819 (pp. 21-32, 81-2).

The book was written in the short space of a year, and exhibits the fluent and polished style of a professional writer. It was issued by Horace Marshall & Son in royal octavo format in alternative olive green and maroon coloured cloth, with Raffles's coat of arms stamped in gilt on the upper cover. It was a handsome looking book by any standards, and obviously proved popular since it was reissued in 1899 in a slightly smaller format with Raffles's arms stamped in blind.

The book firmly fixed Raffles in the British imperial firmament as is evident by the decision of the London publisher T. Fisher Unwin to plave Raffles's name foremost among the biographies which were to make up his series 'Builders of Great Britain' in 1898. This short biography was undertaken by the editor of the series, H.F. Wilson of the Colonial Office, but he eventually handed over the task to the Oxford historian, Hugh E. Egerton, whose *Sir Stamford Raffles: England in the Far East* appeared in 1900. It is interesting that when the Revd. R.B. Raffles learned of this projected biography he wrote to Wilson offering his material on

Raffles on condition that he should be co-author of the book. This offer was politely declined, but in the course of correspondence between the two men the Revd. Raffles set down his criticism of Boulger's biography. Much of this criticism related to Boulger's treatment in Chapter *vii* of the Gillespie Charges levelled against Raffles's administration in Java. It is not possible to examine the subject here, but it certainly has to be recognized that there are some errors of fact in Boulger's book.

One of these errors, pointed out by the Revd. R.B. Raffles to H.F. Wilson, was that Raffles was born on 6 July 1781, and not 5 July as stated by Boulger. But the latter is correct in a strict sense as Raffles was born at sea, and by sea reckoning his date of birth was 5 July. Boulger wrongly states (p. 2) that Raffles's mother's name was Lindeman, when in fact it was Lyde. He states (p. 16) that a witness at Raffles's first marriage in 1805 was a cousin, Charles Hamond, whereas he was Raffles's uncle, a tea-merchant who sponsored his employment with the East India Company. There are other blemishes of this kind in this book, but they are to be found in all the biographies of Raffles. Boulger's *The Life of Sir Stamford Raffles* remains one of the best of them, a major biography written in the Victorian manner at the height of the British Empire.

John Bastin

INTRODUCTION

THE remarks which it is alone necessary to make as introductory to this work come under two heads. I may explain, first, how I came to write this biography; and, secondly, I must record my sense of obligation to the many persons who, in one way or another, have contributed to its completeness.

In 1885–86 I examined and classified a large quantity of the Manuscript Records in the India Office, and among them I noted a considerable number of the letters and despatches of Sir Stamford Raffles, whose example had inspired Rajah Brooke at the outset of his career, so that he said on first proceeding to the East in 1838—"I go to carry Sir Stamford Raffles' views in Java over the whole archipelago." At that moment two of the leading publishers were each bringing out a series of monographs on distinguished English public men, amongst whom Stamford Raffles was entitled to a place. I made offers to both of these firms of a volume describing his career, with special reference to the unutilised material in the India Office. The first publishers would not admit Raffles into their gallery; the second, favourable to his claims, had concluded too many arrangements to allow of a definite agreement until the series had justified its existence, which, unfortunately, it never did. Other subjects supervened to occupy my time; but the possibility of writing a new life of Sir Stamford Raffles, and the desire to do so, were never absent from my mind.

In 1895 a terrible illness, diphtheria, befell me, and in the first stage of the attack I was an inmate of a London Fever

Hospital, where I met, and had the privilege of gaining the friendship of, two men, actively and zealously engaged in the discharge of difficult and delicate duties, but practically unknown to the outer world. One was employed in the cure of bodies, and the other, if I may say so without irreverence, in the cure of souls. Dr. William Gayton has, in nearly thirty years of the unceasing direction of several of the fever hospitals of the metropolis, battled with the most destructive epidemics of that period, and to his skill and assiduous attention, I, in common with many hundreds of the community, undoubtedly owed my recovery to health. The other was the Rev. R. B. Raffles, then chaplain in the same hospital.

When I learnt the name of the clergyman, on reaching that stage in the illness which is the deceptive convalescence between the worst stage of the fever and its after-consequences, I asked him, "Are you any relative of one of my heroes, Stamford Raffles?" Having received the information that he was, being the grandson of Sir Stamford's most intimate cousin, the subject of his career naturally formed a great part of our conversation during the remainder of my brief stay in the hospital. I then found that Mr. Raffles had, in 1887–88, gone through the same records at the India Office as I had inspected two years earlier; but in his case he had examined and copied many of them with the special object of writing a biography of his cousin, whereas I had only noted their existence in the course of my work of classification. At the time stated Mr. Raffles fully intended writing his cousin's Life, but several years before our meeting he had abandoned it in order to devote all his time to the reading necessary for taking orders. When we met, he had finally laid aside the intention of writing a biography, although he none the less deplored the want of a complete and effective Life of Sir Stamford Raffles, which the Memoir by Lady Raffles is certainly not, although it contains much of permanent value.

At that time I was engaged on my *Life of Gordon*, and, much delayed as that book was by my protracted illness, it was impossible even for me to discuss the acceptance of any fresh task until it had been completed. But a tacit understanding was come to that, if after finishing that work, I could arrange for any publisher to take up the subject, I could rely on receiving all the documents in the possession of the family and such co-operation as I might desire. Delays from various causes followed, and it was not for a year and nine months after the convention in the hospital that it was possible to conclude the definite understanding preliminary to this work. I had the matter so much at heart from long association with the subject, that I made every effort to overcome those preliminary difficulties arising from the deficiency of means of my friend, Rev. R. B. Raffles, which had operated against the speedier realisation of his own wishes.

The task once begun, I found that I had secured an able ally for its completion, and that Mr. Raffles was not only master of all the details of the many intricate questions connected with his cousin's career, but that he also possessed a sound and critical judgment, which never went astray. Of his literary style the reader can judge, for, besides the two passages in the Java Expedition and Singapore chapters where his name is given, he is the writer of the scenic descriptions of Penang, Malacca, and Sumatra on pp. 34, 59, and 263 respectively. These passages justify regret that he did not adhere to his intention ten years ago of being his cousin's biographer; but he preferred to give to the Church that ability, and natural gift of style which would have found less fettered outlet in literature. However, what was his loss provides my gain, but it is due to myself as well as to him to say that the views taken of every transaction in this life are my views, and that the responsibility is mine alone. They are views I held before I knew Mr. Raffles; his main part with regard to them has been in providing much of the information and many of the documents strengthening their force. I conclude this part of the story with the expression of the hope that now that he has, however indirectly, made a commencement, he will not refrain from turning to useful account the happy literary gift he has evidently inherited from his grandfather, the Rev. Dr. Raffles, so frequently quoted in the following pages.

I may now come to the second portion of my task, the

return of my grateful thanks to those who have assisted me in the production and illustration of this volume.

In the first place, I must express my indebtedness for the loan of Dr. Raffles's Reminiscences of his Cousin, and of several rare printed documents, including the whole of the reply and appendices on Gillespie's Charges, to Mrs. Raffles, widow of the late Thomas Stamford Raffles, Esquire, Police-Magistrate of the city of Liverpool, and heir male and representative of Sir Stamford Raffles. At Mr. Raffles's death the representation of the family devolved upon his only son, the Rev. T. Stamford Raffles, Rector of Langham, near Colchester, who has two sons, named Stamford Cecil and Reginald Lovett Stamford, to perpetuate the name of the subject of this biography.

I am indebted to W. Hargreaves Raffles, Esquire, brother of my friend, for preparing the sketch-plan of Java, and to the Misses Raffles for much copying, and for assistance in the preparation of the Index of Subjects.

Sir Arthur Godley, Under-Secretary of State for India, kindly granted me permission to inspect and make such extracts from the Records in the India Office as related to Sir Stamford Raffles; and for assistance in the execution of that purpose I am under great obligations to the gentlemen in the "Record" and "Secret and Political" Departments of that Office. It may interest the reader if I mention that, in the course of my researches, I read through documents, written or recorded by Sir Stamford Raffles, which would fill four or five volumes such as this; and that many of these documents are of undoubted historical value.

With regard to the various portraits and other illustrations in this volume, I have in the first place to thank the present Earl of Minto for his kindness in providing the photograph from which the portrait of the Governor-General is taken. The photograph is taken of the copy in Minto House of Chinnery's painting which is in Government House, Calcutta. It represents the first Earl in his robes as Governor-General, with his hand on the map of Java.

My friend Mr. Raffles has provided the originals of his grandfather, of the second engraving of Sir Stamford, and of the view of the ceremony of unveiling the statue at Singapore.

I am under very special obligations to W. M. Sandison, Esquire, of Highlaws, Aytoun, Berwickshire, for the very generous manner in which he has provided me with the photographs of Olivia Raffles's tomb and monument. To him also I am directly indebted for the photographs of Penang and Chilingching, the landing-place of the British troops in Java. To his efforts I am as well under great obligations for the portrait of Leyden, which is taken, with the permission of the owner of the picture, John Blair, Esquire, W.S., Edinburgh, from a print of Sir David Wilkie's painting supplied by George G. Napier, Esquire, of Orchard, West Kilbride. Through Mr. Sandison's kind mediation I received from his friend, D. Richmond, Esquire, of 23 Queen Mary's Avenue, Glasgow, the four photographs of modern Singapore. While expressing my deep sense of obligation to Mr. Sandison for the very considerable trouble—the desire to help the work involved him in a heavy correspondence, of which many letters to myself were I fear only the smaller half—I think the reader will be interested in reading what he says in one of them describing his discovery of the tombs of Olivia Raffles and John Leyden :—

"Before closing I may as well mention the somewhat curious way in which I was led to take an interest in the matter. I happened to be sailing in a small Chinese steamer in the Straits of Banca, and, being almost the only European on board, the captain let me have the use of his cabin and the run of his library, which comprised a medicine-book and a volume of the Minstrelsy of the Scotch Border, from which I noticed that Dr. Leyden died in Batavia. Having some leisure when in Batavia, I thought I would hunt out his resting-place, and went over some old Dutch burial-places without success, as the inscriptions were barely decipherable. I then went to the large cemetery of Tanabang, still in use, and spent some hours strolling amongst the thousands of tombs, but without success, until, being tired out with the search and the strong heat, I sat down on the nearest flat tombstone for a smoke. In striking my first match the head came off, and with the second one I looked at the part of the stone when I was striking it and found it to be on the word Teviotdale, which at once apprised me that I had unconsciously come to the stone I had been hunting for, and looking round about I noticed Olivia Raffles's tomb as well." That is how the neighbouring graves of Olivia Raffles and John Leyden were discovered. As a remarkable indication of the quick literary instinct possessed by Sir Stamford Raffles, I would mention that he caused to be placed on the commemoration slab over Olivia Raffles the four lines of Leyden's poem beginning—

"But chief that in this Eastern Isle";

and over that to Leyden the concluding four lines of reference from Scott's *Lord of the Isles.*

DEMETRIUS C. BOULGER.

Nelson's Day, 1897.

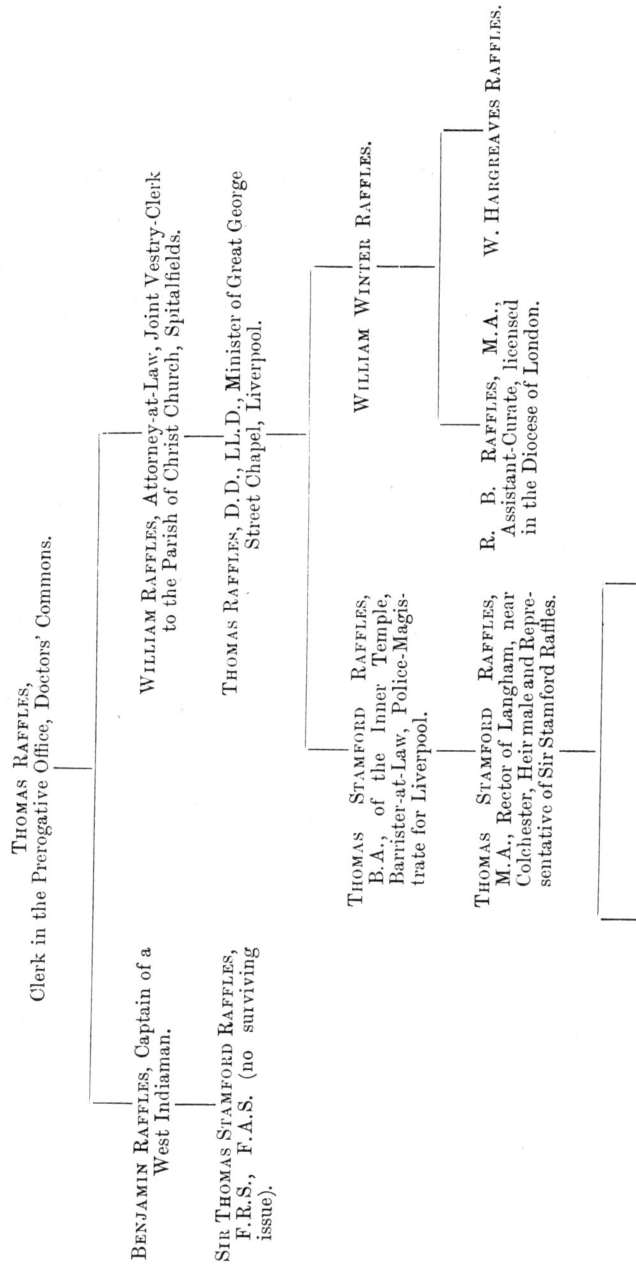
THOMAS RAFFLES,
Clerk in the Prerogative Office, Doctors' Commons.
BENJAMIN RAFFLES, Captain of a West Indiaman.
WILLIAM RAFFLES, Attorney-at-Law, Joint Vestry-Clerk to the Parish of Christ Church, Spitalfields.
SIR THOMAS STAMFORD RAFFLES, F.R.S., F.A.S. (no surviving issue).
THOMAS RAFFLES, D.D., LL.D., Minister of Great George Street Chapel, Liverpool.
THOMAS STAMFORD RAFFLES, B.A., of the Inner Temple, Barrister-at-Law, Police-Magistrate for Liverpool.
WILLIAM WINTER RAFFLES.
THOMAS STAMFORD RAFFLES, M.A., Rector of Langham, near Colchester, Heir male and Representative of Sir Stamford Raffles.
R. B. RAFFLES, M.A., Assistant-Curate, licensed in the Diocese of London.
W. HARGREAVES RAFFLES.
STAMFORD CECIL RAFFLES.
REGINALD LOVETT STAMFORD RAFFLES.

the reach of the Senior Naval Officer - and
fortunately it was acted upon - On the
4th of August 1811 - the whole of the fleet
consisting of upwards of Ninety Vessels arrived
off the Coast of Java, without the loss of a
single Spar or the slightest accident -
having passed by a Route previously
almost unknown, and accomplished a
Passage declared to be impracticable - I
will not attempt to say what my
feelings were on the occasion - We had
separated from the fleet for a few days
and it was only when we again joined
them that we saw all the divisions
united, at the close of one of the finest
Days I ever recollect, and this in sight
of the land of Promise - Lord Minto while
at Malacca had communicated his
Intention of appointing me to the Govt
in case of Success, and as I had nothing
to do with the Military Operations,
I now looked upon my part as
completed

IN SIGHT OF JAVA—"THE LAND OF PROMISE."

A Facsimile of a page in the Autobiographical Letter from Sir Stamford to Dr. Rafflès.

LIFE OF SIR STAMFORD RAFFLES

CHAPTER I

EARLY LIFE AND FIRST MARRIAGE

AMONG the men who have established the political and commercial power of this country in the seas of India and China, no one would deny a foremost place to Stamford Raffles. This silent acquiescence is the tribute paid by national gratitude to the greatness of a name, when the precise nature of the man's work has been consigned to oblivion, or perhaps never appreciated. But the work in this case was an achievement well worth description for its own value, and not less noteworthy because accomplished by a humble individual in the teeth of personal prejudice and official opposition. Raffles owed nothing to favour or fortune; he was the architect of his own position and reputation; while the breadth of his views and the boldness of his deeds often brought him the censure of his narrow-minded and faint-hearted superiors. But the difficulties and malice which nearly crushed him during life enhance his posthumous fame, and to him will ever be given the chief, if not the sole, credit of instituting the measures which permanently assured our hold on the sea route to the Far East.

Thomas Stamford Bingley Raffles, to give him his full name, was the only son of Benjamin Raffles, who, at the time of his famous son's birth, was captain of a merchant vessel trading between London and the West Indies. As was the practice of that age, Benjamin Raffles was accompanied on some of his voyages by his wife, and, during one of these, Stamford Raffles was born on the 5th July 1781, on board the ship *Ann*, off the harbour of Port Morant in the island of Jamaica. A ship and the West Indies were no inappropriate birthplace for a man destined to increase the maritime power of his country, and to accomplish the great work of his life amid the no less lovely islands of the Eastern Archipelago. Mrs. Raffles's family name was Lindeman, and her brother, the Rev. John Lindeman, held the living of Eaton Bishop in Herefordshire. On her return from Jamaica she took the child to her brother's parish to be baptized. His first name, Thomas, was derived from his father's father, who, the *Gentleman's Magazine* informs us, had spent an honourable life as a clerk, latterly one of the principal clerks, during forty years in the Prerogative Office, Doctors' Commons. It is not clear whence he obtained the name Stamford, by which he was to become best known; and the third name of Bingley was never used, and has been practically forgotten. Up to a certain period in his career Raffles was only known, and signed his name, as Thomas, but after the appointment as Lieutenant-Governor of Java he used the name of Stamford. Dr. Raffles, in his reminiscences, suggests that this was done to distinguish himself from Sir Thomas Sevestre; but it is far more probable that it was really adopted to avoid his being confused with the other Thomas Raffles, the reverend and learned doctor himself.

The family of Raffles, although its representatives occupied at the close of the last century a position of neither affluence nor social importance, was undoubtedly of gentle origin. The name itself is one of the modern forms of the surnames originating in the fine Norman name of Ralph or Raufe. Yorkshire was one of the chief homes of this great family,—an early record of the thirteenth century gives the name of Sir Robert Fitz Raufe of Everwyke vel Yorkeshire as present in Henry the Third's camp,—and it is in that county that the name Raffles first makes its appearance.

The registers of the two oldest churches at Beverley contain repeated entries of the name, and one member of the family officiated as mayor of that town in the reign of Queen Elizabeth, dying during his mayoralty. It appears that another, in the seventeenth century, Sir Benjamin Raffles, attained the dignity of a knight-banneret. The memory of the antiquity of his family exercised, it may be conjectured, some influence on Stamford Raffles in his upward struggle. In his private and public character and actions may be traced the influence of a gentle and honourable descent through many generations. The evidence that Raffles, even when a young man, was not indifferent to the question of his ancestry, is provided in the following letter to his uncle, Mr. William Raffles, attorney-at-law, the father of Dr. Thomas Raffles, enclosing an extract from a book of heraldry, and requesting him to ascertain the correct arms of the family :—

"My dear Sir,—The above extract will in part show the purport of this letter. The only circumstance relative to our family to be traced in the Heralds' College is, as far as I could learn, that about the time of James the First, or Second, there was a Sir Benjamin Raffles created Knight-Banneret, and I recollect to have heard you mention that, after some troublesome search for the arms of the family, this information could alone be obtained.

"Now, as Knights-Banneret were next to Barons in dignity, as appears by statute made in the fifth year of King Richard II., statute 2, chap. 4, and by the foregoing extract, their heirs male are entitled to precedence, and consequently the title, it is of some importance to me to trace this more particularly, not that I am anxious at present to obtain the title, but I have reason to think that hereafter it may be of consequence. I have therefore to request of you, as a particular favour, that you will make the most diligent enquiry for me into *every particular* to be found in the Heralds' Office, and communicate the same to me with *every particular* you know respecting the family of my grandfather, and back from him to the date in which the glorious Knight-Banneret, Sir Benjamin, strutted his hour.

"Whatever expense may attend the inquiry will be cheerfully defrayed by my friend Mr. R. S. Taylor of Gray's Inn. If you are successful, send out attested copies of every particular in duplicate by the first opportunity, and oblige, your affectionate nephew,

"THO. RAFFLES.

"PRINCE OF WALES'S ISLAND,
24th Feb. 1809.

"*P.S.*—At all events get the arms drawn and emblazoned with their supporters, etc."

Thomas Raffles of the Prerogative Office, the grandfather, died in 1784, and the loss of his pension was no doubt one cause of the straitened circumstances which compelled young Raffles to make an early start in facing the grim realities of life. After undergoing some preliminary training in a school kept by a Dr. Anderson at Hammersmith, which, so far as is known, constituted the only regular education he ever received, he was compelled by his father's want of means to seek remunerative work, and in 1795, when he was little more than fourteen years of age, he obtained temporary employment in the Secretary's office of the East India Company. The pay for this work seems to have been very scanty, but it opened to the youth a vista of improvement, which was all he asked for. As he was not on the establishment of the office, a diligent search has failed to reveal any mention of his name in the Company's records, until there appears in the Court Minutes, under the date 16th July 1800, his appointment as "the junior clerk in the Secretary's office on the usual terms." On the following 7th April his name again appears as the recipient of a gratuity of £20 a year, with the arrears from midsummer 1800, but the amount of his regular salary is not specified. On 21st July 1802, he was given a further gratuity of £30, and his salary was fixed at £70 a year; and, so far as can be traced, that was his position when, in the spring of 1805, he was sent out to the East.

The autobiographical letter with which I close this chapter gives some particulars of his early life, but we owe the information as much to the tradition of his family as to any specific source that he displayed unusual thoughtfulness and diligence in his work, giving himself up to serious pursuits, and taking no part in the innocent frivolities of youth. During his school days his garden was his delight; and as Lady Raffles, his second wife, observes in her Memoir, "it was perhaps peculiar to himself to be able to remark on his last return to England, that he had never seen a horse-race, and never fired a gun;" while, on the other hand, he displayed from his earliest youth an enthusiastic love of natural history and of animals, which never deserted him. He "spent hours in fondling and domesticating those objects of his care and attention." The references to the death of his animal pets are frequent throughout his correspondence, and with regard to one of them, a fine Siamang, nicknamed Mr. Silvio, he said, "I am often accused of paying more attention to the monkey than the children." His early love of gardening continued to the end of his life. He was also fond of drawing and poetry, and it was written of him many years later, that "a mountain scene would bring tears into his eyes, a flower would call forth a burst of favourite poetry." These fragmentary indications will show that he was a man of quick impressions and a sympathetic nature, and such he proved himself to be in regard to the most important and critical undertakings, as well as in trivial matters.

When he entered the India House the Secretary was Mr. William Ramsay, a gentleman of much intelligence and a kindly disposition, who soon took a warm interest in the boy struggling to make a way for himself, and to mitigate the troubles of his "family, at this time suffering in obscurity and distress." There is no doubt that Mr. Ramsay did everything he could to assist young Raffles; but he was able to do so without showing favouritism or injustice to others, because Raffles helped himself and proved that he was worthy of any patronage or promotion. The evidence is clear that Mr. Ramsay did not know his youthful assistant's family, pride keeping them in the background.

The biography by his widow has some reminiscences of this early office life in England, which are not without interest in view of the character and energy displayed by Raffles in later years. "His attention," she writes, "to his dull routine of duty was unremitting; he worked early and late; he studied, as he himself says, in stolen moments; by his extra labour at his office he obtained an addition to his salary, which was not appropriated to any selfish purpose; but all he earned was carried home to his parents, as they were at this time in difficulties. . . . Such a sedentary life of labour was, however, ill adapted to the delicacy of his frame; and it was feared that symptoms of consumption were becoming confirmed; he was ordered to relax his exertions, and to leave his office for a time; he obeyed, and obtained a fortnight's leave of absence. The use which he made of this short period of recreation is very characteristic; he seized on the moment to indulge that love of mountain scenery so strong in most youthful minds, so happily undying and unfading in its exciting joyous feeling. He resolved to go into Wales, set off on foot, and *walked at the rate of thirty and forty miles a day*, accomplished his object, and returned to his desk with restored health."

In connection with this walking tour, his long rides in Java of sixty or seventy miles a day, in order to make himself personally acquainted with the native chiefs and all local peculiarities with special regard to the land revenue, may be referred to as providing evidence of his capacity to undergo physical exertion notwithstanding his want of physical strength. His spirit and energy carried him along.

The autobiographical letter referred to will show the reader how hard Raffles worked to improve himself, and to supply the deficiencies of his education, at the same time that he was diligent in the discharge of his office duties. He was only nineteen when he was placed on the establishment, and less than twenty-four when the great turn came in his fortunes, but before the latter event he had indulged in some literary work, and, according to his own statement, he was to take a conspicuous part in carrying on the *Asiatic Annual Register* on an enlarged and improved principle. How important his share in the matter was, can be judged from the fact that the whole scheme fell to the ground in consequence of his quitting England. There is no reason for believing Raffles's statement to be exaggerated or over-coloured, and it shows that the junior clerk in the Secretary's office at the India House had exercised a considerable influence on those brought into contact with him. His views even then were not confined by the office walls.

It was during this period that Raffles acquired the knowledge of French which afterwards proved of very considerable practical use to him while governing Java; and it speaks much for the tenacity of his memory that when, many years later, a lady sang at Government House, Bencoolen, Moore's melody, "Rich and rare were the gems she wore," in the presence of two French gentlemen, the naturalists Diard and Duvancel, who regretted that they did not understand the words, he was able at once to translate the poem into French verse. This incident is only one of many testifying to his natural aptitude in acquiring a knowledge of languages. At all times of his career he endeavoured to devote a portion of his day to study or reading, and on one occasion he laid it down as a rule for himself that he should "appropriate eight hours in each day to study, reading, or writing, and that the loss of time on any day should be made up on another. My object in making this memorandum is that I may hold the rule as inviolable as I can, and by frequently recurring to it revive my sleeping energies should I at any time be inclined to indolence. I should not, however, omit to add that all reading and study on a Sunday is to be confined to the Bible and religious subjects. The Greek and Hebrew, however, as connected, may nevertheless form a part of the study of that day."

The harsh mistress, necessity, compelled his early departure from school, and his first earnings were devoted to the mitigation of his parents' necessities. When he obtained a higher salary, which only began on his arrival at Penang in September 1805, he hastened to make them share in his improved fortune, and the last five years of his father's life—he died in 1812—were thus passed under brighter circumstances. The only evidence I have obtained as to his father's death is indirect, and as it is contained in a letter to his uncle, Mr. William Raffles, already mentioned, it will be best to quote it, because it furnishes proof of Stamford Raffles's natural courtesy and appreciation of the smallest act of kindness. The letter is written from Government House, Buitenzorg, Java, under date 29th October 1812 :—

"My dear Sir,—My mother informs me that she is much indebted to you for your kind attention to her in the hour of trouble and at the time of my poor father's death, and I should not do justice to my feelings did I not avail myself of the earliest opportunity to express my acknowledgments.—Believe me affectionately yours,

"Thomas S. Raffles."

For his mother, who died during his home voyage in 1824, and to whom he was tenderly attached, he was able to do much more. The correspondence which he carried on with her while he was harassed by the labours of his responsible position, by ill-health, and by the attacks of jealous colleagues, breathes the tenderest affection and the liveliest concern for her happiness and comfort. He set apart a portion of his salary for the benefit of his parents, and, when the suitable occasion arrived, he took his three sisters off their hands. In letters which still exist, and which denote the strongest filial devotion, there occur at frequent intervals such passages as these: "Spare nothing to make yourself comfortable."—"I hope to hear good accounts of Ann. She will now be your only resource, and it would make me truly happy to hear she was a comfort. Give my love to her, and tell her how much I look to her for, and how deeply I shall estimate all her kindness to you."—"Such is the dispensation of Providence that we should be separated for a time, and we must be content; but we live in hope, and my only comfort is that I know you can want for nothing."—"If you have any wants or wishes tell them to me that I may attend to them; you could not confer on me a greater delight than the power of contributing to your happiness and comfort to the extent of my means."—"Sophia unites with me, my dearest mother, in every prayer for your happiness and comfort; pray neglect nothing that will add to either. My agents have instructions to attend to your wishes in all respects."—" God, of his infinite mercy, preserve you, my dearest mother, and grant that we may once more meet in happiness, to part no more. The hope that I may reach England in time to keep up your spirits and give you a new lease of this life is ever present, and will be my first inducement to turn my steps homeward the moment my public duty admits."

These several extracts, taken from letters spread over a period of twelve years, and written not by a young man under the first impulse of home-leaving, but by the father of, at times, a large family, and with many outside responsibilities, will serve to show the reader how warm and how constant was the affection of Stamford Raffles for his mother. John and Henry Lawrence were rightly praised by the former's biographer because they never rested until they had provided sufficient means to enable their mother to keep a carriage. Raffles put before himself a still higher object, and that was to place his mother in a position of independence quite apart from the continuance of his own life. He was only thirty-six years of age when he wrote, " My friend and agent Mr. John Taylor will take care you want for nothing. Should any accident happen to me your £400 a year is still secure, therefore you can never, I hope, be again distressed for money." During the earlier years of his career, when little more than a boy, he had done what he could to alleviate the difficulties of his parents, and when he himself succeeded in the world he finally removed them.

In all these inner relations and higher duties of family life his actions were guided by the lofty motives and the disregard of personal advantage which characterised his public measures. His amiable and affectionate disposition, his literary and scientific enthusiasm, first displayed when cramped in leisure and opportunity by the office duties of a very subordinate position, but subsequently revealed publicly by his remarkable volumes on Java, and the founding of the Zoological Society, together with the sympathy he always manifested towards schemes that promised benefit to humanity, as well as to his own country, these were his chief characteristics. His was an essentially simple, clear, childlike, and enthusiastic nature. Nothing was too great or too small to attract his attention and awake his sympathies. He was intensely interested in all life as well as in nature. The gambols of a monkey, the play and prattle of his own children,—all of whom, with one exception, died in infancy or early youth,—the discovery of a rare plant, gave him as much pleasure and satisfaction, when a man, as the successful accomplishment of those schemes which promoted the power and realised the destiny of his country. If Raffles possessed that element of simplicity which seems to be the one essential accompaniment of true greatness, it was to his energy, hopefulness, and courage that he owed his success in life. Those qualities made him able to emancipate himself from the humble position he occupied in the India House, and to display on the wide platform of imperial administration a dignity, capacity, and boldness which proved him a born dictator. He had anticipated the advice of Tennyson, and made his past the stepping-stone to higher things; but the grace with which he played his new and prominent part before the eyes of a world filled with great names, and witnessing daily events of tragic and historical importance, was due to his own kindly, unaffected, and sincere disposition, which revealed itself under the most severe and cruel trials.

It is not surprising that the bright intelligent youth, who was so evidently superior to the routine duties of an office, but who performed them in a most exemplary manner, should have attracted the favourable notice of his official chief, and Mr. William Ramsay, then and for many years the Secretary of the East India Company, was by all accounts a man of great discernment and a genial temperament. He took much interest in Raffles from his first entry into his office as a temporary assistant. It was by his recommendation that he was placed on the establishment, and it was to him alone that the otherwise friendless, but promising, assistant owed his first appointment in the East. To the end of his life Mr. William Ramsay was the staunch friend of Stamford Raffles, who always gave his first chief the credit of having launched him on his successful career. Moreover, William Brown Ramsay, the son of the Secretary, was the companion and close friend of Raffles in the India House, and their affectionate relations were only terminated by the latter's death. In the light of certain malicious and slanderous statements about Stamford Raffles that will be referred to and examined later on in this chapter, it is desirable to make clear what were the relations between him and the Ramsay family.

In the early part of 1805 the East India Company decided to send out a fresh establishment to Penang or Prince of Wales's Island, an account of which Settlement can be more conveniently given in the next chapter. Raffles apparently expressed a desire to Mr. Ramsay to go to the East, for we find that gentleman recommending his claims to the Chairman of the Company, Sir Hugh Inglis, although he said that "in parting with so useful an assistant in his department he should suffer the greatest inconvenience, and that it would be like the loss of a limb to him." Sir Hugh Inglis seems to have satisfied himself that Raffles deserved these encomiums, for when Mr. Philip Dundas was appointed Governor of Prince of Wales's Island, Raffles was nominated Assistant-Secretary, and on 8th March 1805 this appointment was ratified, at the Court meeting, by ballot. The salary of the post was £1500 a year, and it carried with it the rank of Junior Merchant in the East India Company's service. The circumstances under which young Raffles got this post before he was twenty-four years of age rest on conclusive and unimpeachable evidence. The only element of fortune in them was the coincidence of a new establishment being required at Penang, which allowed of a draft, as it were, of recruits being sent out from Leadenhall Street. But the eyes of Raffles had for some time been steadily turned towards India as the only sphere that would procure for him a sufficient salary to relieve his family, and a sufficient field to realise his ambition. If Penang had not offered the opportunity, some delay would have followed, but none the less he would sooner or later have directed his steps eastward.

It was only natural that a young man about to leave his country for many years, and placed in possession of a salary which secured his first object, namely, the relief of his family, and which also provided him with an adequate income, should have turned his thoughts, on the eve of what might be a protracted exile, to marriage, and here we come to the romance of Raffles's life. Even on that ground the story might detain us a little, but there are other and important reasons why, at this preliminary stage, all the facts bearing on this matter should be carefully examined, and the truth laid bare. To do that we must anticipate some events, and glance much farther ahead in the career of Stamford Raffles than his appointment to Penang in March 1805.

The simple and sufficient explanation of his appointment to Penang at a salary large in comparison with that he earned in Leadenhall Street, but still in accordance with the Company's scale, has been given. It was the reward of merit, the expression of confidence on the part of his superiors in an interesting and striking personality, and no one can deny that their judgment was fully justified by the result. But there was a certain mystery and suddenness about Raffles's first marriage which gave his unscrupulous detractors and enemies long years afterwards a weapon, as they thought, that would vilify his character and disparage his success. Such mystery as there was, let it at once be stated, was due to a very simple and harmless cause, to the fact that the lady's age was greater than that of her husband, while such suddenness as attended the event was caused by Raffles's hurried departure for the East. But these natural circumstances did not commend themselves to General Gillespie and his satellites, who, to judge from their methods of procedure against the head of the British Government in Java, considered a masked assault no less permissible in civil than it is allowed to be in military operations. When beaten in their avowed attacks on Sir Stamford Raffles they resorted to an unworthy device, and sent the following account of his career to Colburn's *Biographical Dictionary of the Living Authors of Great Britain and Ireland*, in the supplement of which, on page 445, appears the following paragraph:—

"Raffles, T. S., Esq., Lieutenant-Governor of Batavia (*sic*), to which situation he was appointed by Lord Minto on the conquest of the island of Java in 1812 (*sic*). Mr. Raffles went out to India in an inferior capacity, through the interest of Mr. Ramsay, Secretary to the Company, and in consequence of his marrying a lady connected with that gentleman."

That statement did not come under the notice of Sir Stamford Raffles for some time after it was published, and it was this allegation which drew from him the autobiographical letter given in full at the end of this chapter. The indignant passages in that letter, disclaiming the charge and asserting that Mr. Ramsay never so much as saw his first wife, and that his marriage, far from benefiting him in a pecuniary sense, entailed some pecuniary sacrifices, will claim the reader's special attention. They are now published for the first time, as Lady Raffles, the second wife, with the exception of a single brief footnote, and that erroneous, carefully eliminated in the Memoir published after Sir Stamford's death everything referring to her predecessor. That studied and ostentatious omission, due to petty but intelligible motives, has strengthened the original theory as to the first wife, and the silence of the widow, the suppression of the husband's indignant and passionate denial of the statement the instant it came under his notice, have led to a far too prevalent belief that Raffles placed his foot on the first rung of the ladder of success by conveniently relieving his superior of a mistress of whom he had grown tired or who had become too exacting. It is time, and this is the place, to dispose of this libel once and for ever. It originated in the malice of a thwarted enemy, it has been strengthened by the unfortunate and misjudged silence of Sir Stamford's widow and first biographer, and, it must be allowed, by the reticence of Sir Stamford himself, who, although he records that the first marriage "gave me domestic enjoyment, and thus contributed to my happiness," omits to supply any particulars as to his first wife's history. Yet there was nothing to conceal beyond the simple fact that his wife was some years older than himself, while the admiration and respect she obtained from men of distinction like Lord Minto and John Leyden, and the grace and dignity with which she played the part of chief lady at Government

House in Java required only to be cited in order to discomfit the libellers.

But an answer has now to be given to the question, Who was Sir Stamford's first wife? In a footnote on page 234 (edition of 1830) of Lady Raffles's Memoir it is stated that she was "the widow of W. Fancourt, Esq., of Lanark." I will not go so far as to say that such a person never existed, but I am enabled to state, as the result of careful and laborious researches in the various registers of Lanark back to the year 1750,—most kindly undertaken and completed by Mr. Hugh Davidson of Braedale, Lanark,—that there is no record of the name Fancourt, and that no one connected with that place ever heard of it. The designation "of Lanark" is therefore as erroneous as the "W. Fancourt, Esq." If there ever was such an individual, he was certainly not the husband of Olivia Raffles, and those who have attempted to trace her through "W. Fancourt, Esq., of Lanark," have been on a wrong track and in pursuit of a chimera. Who, then, was Olivia Raffles?

In the month of August or September 1804, there appeared in the Secretary's office of the India House a tall, distinguished-looking lady, with flashing black Italian eyes, as a petitioner. Young Raffles saw her, and it may even have been part of his duty to receive her petition, to instruct her as to the correct form in which it should be drafted, and, perhaps, even to add some literary flourish of his own. Her application was not an uncommon one. It was the petition of the widow of an officer on the Military Establishment of Madras for assistance from the compassionate fund, which was long known by the name of Clive, who founded it out of Mir Jaffir's gift. The record still exists which sets forth the petition of Olivia Mariamne, widow of Jacob Cassivelaun Fancourt, assistant-surgeon on the Madras Establishment, who had died at Ryacotta in May 1800. It is quite certain that Jacob Fancourt had no connection with Lanark, but it is possible, and even probable, that he was a relative of Samuel Fancourt, the originator of the circulating library, who died at a great age in the year 1768. Olivia's petition was presented on 5th September 1804. In accordance with custom, it lay on the table for a week, and on the 12th of September Olivia Fancourt was granted a pension of one shilling and threepence a day, and in addition the sum of twenty-five guineas. This was entirely according to rule. The matter followed a prescribed course. If she had been any other assistant-surgeon's widow, old or young, remarkable for her plainness instead of for her beauty, the result would have been precisely the same.

The next question that arises is, Who was this Mrs. Olivia Fancourt? Jacob Cassivelaun Fancourt, when he died in May 1800, must still have been a young man, for his commission as assistant-surgeon only dates from the year 1791. It is probable that his age at the time last mentioned was not more than twenty-four, and it may have been less. The announcement of his death in the *Madras Courier* gives no particulars. On searching the Madras register of marriages, I found, however, the entry of the marriage of Jacob Cassivelaun Fancourt and Olivia Mariamne Devenish, under the date 26th of May 1793. Most unfortunately there are no other particulars, and the volume of the *Madras Courier* for the year 1793 in the India Office Library is deficient for the months April to September, while the British Museum Library cannot supply the missing numbers, although it possesses a few of the same period. From the inscription on her tomb in Java we learn that Olivia Mariamne Raffles was forty-three years of age when she died, so that she was born in 1771. Mrs. Olivia Fancourt was therefore ten years the senior of Stamford Raffles. She was something more than thirty-three when she appeared at the India House, while Raffles had just passed the age of twenty-three.

I have no positive information to offer as to Olivia Devenish's family. The name, although of English origin, has for three centuries been most closely connected with Ireland, and the family of that name located at Mount Pleasant, Roscommon, is well known. I think it is highly probable that the future Mrs. Raffles, or, at all events, her father, came from Ireland, and they may even have been members of that particular family, for Lord Minto, whose description of the lady I am about to give, and who is the only authority to refer directly or indirectly to her earlier life in India, states that he had heard that she was the object of some of the odes of Anacreontic Moore. This is highly improbable, for Moore was only fourteen when Olivia married Fancourt in India, and when he was scandalising the Dons of Trinity with his version of Anacreon, she was resident with her first husband in Madras. The germ of truth in Lord Minto's statement, which he makes merely as gossip, may well have been that Olivia Devenish, or her father, came from Ireland. I am also informed by the Rev. William Devenish of Abbey-Lara, the present head of the family, that in 1770 or 1771 two members of the family named Godfrey and George left Ireland, and were never afterwards heard of, but I have not been able to establish a connection between either of them and Olivia.

The Court passed Raffles's appointment on 8th March 1805; on the 13th of the same month he obtained a licence of marriage at the Vicar-General's office. In that document it is stated that the marriage was to be between "Thomas Raffles, Esq., of the parish of St. George, Bloomsbury, in the county of Middlesex, a bachelor, aged twenty-three years, and Olivia Mariamne Fancourt, of the same parish, widow," and that the ceremony was to take place "in the Parish Church of St. George, Bloomsbury, aforesaid." On the following day, 14th March 1805, the marriage was duly celebrated by the Rev. A. P. Poston, in the presence of Richard S. Taylor, Charles Hamond, Mariamne Etherington, and Maria Walthew. We know that Mr. Taylor was Raffles's friend and business agent in London, and his name will recur in these pages. Charles Hamond was a cousin, and the ladies probably were the friends of the bride. Beyond the bare facts recorded in the certificate, the only interesting point is that the signature Olivia Mariamne Fancourt is traced in delicate but firm characters. It is a piece of really pretty caligraphy.

The passage in Lord Minto's letters, which were published sixty years after his premature death, and constitute one of the most interesting works about India, referring to Mrs. Raffles, reads as follows, and is dated 31st May 1811:—

"Mrs. Raffles is the great lady with dark eyes, lively manner, accomplished and clever. She had a former husband in India, and I have heard, but am not sure of the fact, that she was one of the beauties to whom Anacreontic Moore addressed many of his amatory elegies." After these words occurs an hiatus, and this left room for the insinuation that something followed of a disparaging nature. With a view to removing this last loophole of misrepresentation, my friend the Rev. R. B. Raffles addressed a letter of inquiry in 1887 to the late Earl of Minto, and received a reply that there was no further reference to Mrs. Raffles. In order to render misconceptions impossible, Lord Minto very kindly copied out the suppressed passage, which related not to Mrs. Raffles but to Mr. Raffles's three sisters. After "amatory elegies" the letter proceeds: "The sisters are all fair, one a very pretty woman. You need not smile, Anna Maria, for George says so. She is the wife of Captain Flint of the Royal Navy; the other two, to avoid sneering, I shall say, are honest-like. I have exchanged dinners with them, have breakfasted and visited there." Then follows the next sentence in the book, "I have mustered the whole," etc.

The evidence given establishes for all necessary purposes the early record of the first Mrs. Raffles, and effectually disposes of the cruel charge through which a beaten adversary sought to damage for all time the memory of the victor by a secret stab at the reputation of an innocent woman. Colburn's *Biographical Dictionary of Living Authors* is not a work of any merit or much utility. No second edition was ever called for to furnish the opportunity of correcting by removal the slanderous statement to which reference has been made; but it still stands in a convenient position for reference in our chief libraries, and for eighty years this libel has held possession of the field, although at the very time of its utterance Raffles penned his indignant and powerful refutation. The additional facts I have cited amply corroborate his statement that his first wife never so much as saw Mr. Ramsay, and that his marriage did not bring him the smallest pecuniary or official advantage.

Having thus effectually, and, as I hope, finally, disposed

of this base charge, made with the express object of injuring the reputation of Stamford Raffles, and of lowering the standard of honour and moral principle to which he might lay claim, it will not be out of place to give some positive evidence as to the character and qualifications of the lady whom Raffles selected as his partner when he went out to seek a brighter fortune in the Eastern world. I have cited the competent and weighty opinion of Lord Minto. Mrs. Raffles was worthy of doing the honours of Government House at Batavia when the Governor-General of India was present in person. That fact speaks for itself, but there is other evidence besides that of Lord Minto. There is Stamford Raffles's own noble tribute to her, paid on his leaving Java eighteen months after her death. What said the bereaved husband to his own personal staff who had lived under the same roof? "You have been with me in the days of happiness and joy—in the hours that were beguiled away under the enchanting spell of one of whom the recollection awakens feelings which I cannot suppress. You have supported and comforted me under the affliction of *her* loss, you have witnessed the severe hand of Providence in depriving me of those whom I held most dear, snatched from us and the world ere we could look around us!"

The statement that Moore made the future Olivia Raffles the subject of his muse has been referred to, but although we cannot accept it, there is no doubt that another poet was inspired by the qualities of her mind and the attractions of her person. There will be much more to tell of John C. Leyden and of his relations with the Raffles family; but here I give the substance of the poem on "The Departed Year," which referred to the period when he was staying at Penang in 1805–6 as the guest of Raffles and his wife. During much of that time Leyden was seriously ill. The verses will give the reader some idea of the true Olivia libelled by implication in Colburn's *Dictionary*.

It may not be out of place to record before this excerpt that the Rev. James Morton, editor of Leyden's poems, and also his biographer, from whose work our quotation is taken, goes out of his way to describe Mrs. Raffles in the following sentence:—"Olivia, remarkable for her benevolence and the richer endowments of her mind."

DIRGE OF THE DEPARTED YEAR.

To OLIVIA.

OLIVIA, ah! forgive the bard,
If sprightly strains alone are dear;
His notes are sad, for he has heard
The footsteps of the parting year.

For each sweet scene I wander'd o'er,
Fair scenes that shall be ever dear,
From Curga's hills to Travancore—
I hail thy steps, departed year!

But chief that in this eastern isle,
Girt by the green and glistening wave,
OLIVIA's kind, endearing smile
Seem'd to recall me from the grave.

When far beyond Malaya's sea,
I trace dark Soonda's forests drear,
Olivia! I shall think of thee—
And bless thy steps, departed year!

Each morn or evening spent with thee
Fancy shall mid the wilds restore
In all their charms, and they shall be
Sweet days that shall return no more.

Still may'st thou live in bliss secure
Beneath that friend's protecting care,
And may his cherish'd life endure
Long, long, thy holy love to share.

That poetical tribute does not stand alone. It is matched and completed by the following letter from Leyden, written on 7th January 1806, on board the Portuguese ship *St. Antonio*, when a few days out from Penang, on his return to Calcutta. The MS. from which it is taken is in the British Museum:—

"MY DEAR MADAM,—We have now lost sight of Pooloo Penang, more, I am sorry to say, from the darkness than from the distance, and while our Portuguese friends are recommending themselves with great fervency of devotion to their patron saint, I have retired to pay the devoirs which I owe to her whom I have chosen my patroness for the voyage. I cannot help congratulating myself a good deal on the superiority of my choice of a living saint to a dead one, and am positive if you choose to exert yourself a little you have a great chance of rivalling his sublimest miracles, among which none of the least is his preaching on a certain day with great zeal and fervour to divers asses till their long ears betrayed powerful symptoms of devotion. Now, without wishing to cast any reflections on the wisdom of the islanders of the modern Barataria, I am perfectly of opinion that this miracle, doughty as it is, may be rivalled in Penang.

"There is, however, another miracle which I should be glad you would first try your hand at to enliven the dreariness of a voyage which bids fair to be one of the most tedious and insipid I was ever engaged in, as, if Providence do not send some French privateers or others to our assistance, we have not the least chance of an adventure. Most travellers by land or sea are of a different way of thinking, and maintain that no adventure is a lucky adventure, just as no news are reckoned good news by all our insipid, half-alive, half-vegetable acquaintance. I confess honestly I like to see some fun, and to see every possible variety of situations as well as of men and manners. However, if it be possible to overcome the irksomeness of light gales, a heaving cradle of a sea, and a barren, sweltering, tropical voyage, I flatter myself that I have adopted the best possible method by associating with all the pleasant recollections which I hoarded up at Penang in the society of you and your amiable husband. It is a terrible circumstance, after all, that there is little real difference between the recollections of past pleasures and of past sorrows. Perhaps the most we can make of it is that the memory of past pleasures is pleasant and mournful, and the memory of past sorrows is mournful and pleasant. I remember to have read of some such distinction in a volume of sermons, but I will by no means vouch for the accuracy of the quotation, as on second thoughts the epithets, I imagine, might be reversed with equal propriety. However this may be, the recollection of the pleasure I enjoyed in your society is by no means so vivid as my distress at losing it, and the little prospect I have of soon recovering it I need not now request you, my dear sister Olivia, to think of me kindly, and never to believe any evil you may hear of me till you have it under my own hand, for whenever I have the courage to become a villain,—scoundrel and rascal are too pitiful to be mentioned,—but I say, whenever it shall be possible for me to become a villain, I shall have the courage to subscribe myself one, which I am in no danger of doing while I have the honour of subscribing myself your sincere friend."

Enough has been said to prove that in the lady who could inspire these sentiments and win the respectful admiration, not merely of the members of her husband's staff, but of the Malay chiefs and Dutch officials before whom she had to play the part of mistress in Government House, Stamford Raffles had made a good choice of a helpmate, and found one who would grace whatever position he should attain. Only those who have felt their steps clogged and hindered by an unfortunate or ill-judged marriage can fully appreciate the benefit and help that the subject of this biography must have derived from the intelligent and gifted co-operation of Olivia Raffles. To her, if to anyone, he owed a large portion of his success.

When the Penang Establishment sailed in the ship *Ganges*[1] for their destination in April 1805, Stamford Raffles was accompanied by his eldest sister, Mary Anne, as well as by his wife. The voyage was a good one, for the party having exchanged into another ship, the *Warley*, at Madras, reached the harbour of Penang on 19th September, and the young Assistant-Secretary began that public career which was to be marked by experiences widely differing from the regular routine, and by signal services of national importance.

The following autobiographical letter was written at sea on 14th October 1819, and addressed to Sir Stamford's cousin, Dr. Raffles of Liverpool:—

"My dear Cousin,—I have just observed a very incorrect and unpleasant account of my progress in life, published in the supplement to the *Biographical Dictionary of*

[1] The *Ganges* was wrecked on her return voyage off the Cape of Good Hope.

Living Authors, etc.; a work printed for Henry Colburn, Public Library, Conduit Street, Hanover Square, London. This work, from its nature, must be in general circulation; and the mention it makes of one who is no more, as well as the general tendency of the article altogether, is as disagreeable to my feelings as discreditable to my character. My first wife was in no manner connected with Mr. Ramsay; they never saw each other; neither could my advancement in life possibly be accelerated by that marriage. It gave me no new connections, no wealth, but, on the contrary, a load of debt which I had to clear off. It increased my difficulties, and thus increased my energies. It gave me domestic enjoyment, and thus contributed to my happiness; but in no way can my advancement in life be accounted owing to that connection. My resolution to proceed to India and my appointment to Prince of Wales's Island were made before the marriage took place; and, when I was about to quit all other ties and affections, it was natural that I should secure one bosom friend, one companion on my journey who would soothe the adverse blasts of misfortune and gladden the sunshine of prosperity—but what have the public to do with this? What right have they to disturb and animadvert on my domestic arrangements? What right have they to conclude that interest and not affection was consulted by me? The account must, I think, have been inserted by some pitiful enemy. I suspect the individual, and his object must have been to lower my general pretensions in order to set those of a rival (Gillespie) more conspicuously forward.

"Successful as my career may be considered to have been, my advancement has been entirely owing to my own personal exertions, and to what I have always called my good fortune. Family, friends, and connections have done nothing for me. At a very early age, before I had attained my fourteenth year, I was withdrawn from school and admitted as an extra clerk in the India House. In this capacity I might have remained, drudging at a guinea a week, had not my own exertions and the kindness of friends, whom those exertions had created, interested itself in my favour. A vacancy happened in the establishment, and my peculiar qualifications for once set aside the pretensions of those who were supported by the usual patronage. I succeeded; and a continuance of the same exertions on a larger scale increased the circle of my friends and widened my prospects in life; but these friends were entirely unknown to my family, at this time suffering in obscurity and distress. My earnings went for their relief, but it was insufficient. Long-standing debts, and a want of the means to prevent still further involvement, caused me many a bitter moment.

"At length a new establishment at Prince of Wales's Island was contemplated. India seemed to open a field for my ambition, at the same time that it promised the means of relieving my family; but so far from my going out in an *inferior* capacity, I obtained the appointment of Assistant-Secretary, with a salary of £1500 a year, the rank of a junior merchant, and an eventual succession to Council.

"I had not been many months at Prince of Wales's Island before I was called upon to act as Secretary to the Government. In this appointment I was shortly after confirmed, with the rank of senior merchant and a salary of £2000 a year. While holding this office the Commander-in-Chief of the Navy solicited that I would act as Agent for the Navy. This office I also filled as long as it was convenient.

"In these conspicuous situations the diligence, and perhaps fitness, which I evinced attracted considerable attention. Shortly after my arrival at Prince of Wales's Island I had also paid considerable attention to the Malay and other languages in the Archipelago; and an intimacy with the late Dr. Leyden led me to contemplate with him extensive plans for the elucidation and improvement of the various interests in the Eastern Archipelago. As a reward for my labours, and on account of my peculiar qualifications for the office, I was appointed Malay translator to Government; and the Earl of Minto, then Governor-General of Bengal, thought fit to honour my name and exertions with notice in one of his anniversary addresses to the College of Calcutta. This was the origin of my acquaintance with Lord Minto, and the commencement of that intimacy and confidence to which I am proud to say that I owe the whole of my subsequent advancement and prosperity in life.

"Encouraged by the flattering notice thus unexpectedly taken of my humble exertions by the first authority in India, and by a nobleman whose attainments and virtues had never been surpassed, I was induced to submit to him the considerations which occurred to me on the impolicy of the measures pursued by the Government of Prince of Wales's Island towards Malacca, once the emporium of the East, and still a place of great commercial intercourse. This policy went to raze to the ground every public edifice, and to drive from the land of their forefathers every remnant of population. The object was, of course, to aggrandise Prince of Wales's Island, a small and insignificant spot, which in its greediness to devour the resources of this more important neighbour reminded me, in some degree, of the fable of the frog and the ox. In these considerations I took a general view of the nature of the Eastern trade, and the conclusions were so obvious that the Governor-General in Council, without waiting for any explanation on the part of the subordinate Government, at once put a stop to the devastating and desolating system which had been adopted, and acted without reserve on the propositions I had submitted.

"It happened that, not long after this interference on the part of the Supreme Government, the conquest of the Moluccas was unexpectedly achieved by a small naval force which had been merely sent to plunder them. The Governor-General refused to take charge of these islands on account of the Company, and the Naval Commander hardly felt himself warranted in establishing a king's government; but as the decision was left with him, he proposed to the Governor-General, who was then at Madras, that I should be nominated to the charge, and a provisional administration established pending a reference to Europe. Lord Minto immediately replied that I was not unknown to him, that he was perfectly satisfied of my fitness and claims, and that he would immediately appoint me if the Admiral would undertake that I should accept the office; for it occurred to Lord Minto that, being a family man, and of high pretensions, I might be unwilling to sacrifice a certainty for an uncertainty. My advancement at Prince of Wales's Island was secure, but the Moluccas were only a war dependency, and it was not known what measures regarding them might be taken by the Government at home. The Admiral did not like to take the responsibility, and the arrangement dropped on an understanding that my assent was alone wanting; but, as the Governor-General was about to return to Bengal, he would, of course, feel himself at perfect liberty to bestow the office on another, should an immediate arrangement or the claims of others require an early attention. Lord Minto went to Bengal, and the Admiral despatched a vessel to give me the earliest intimation of what had occurred, hoping he had acted for the best in declining to take on himself the responsibility. Some months had now elapsed, and it was to be feared that arrangements for the administration of the Moluccas were already in progress. Yet the chance of being in time, and the expectation of still further advancing my interests with Lord Minto, weighed with me in the resolution I took of proceeding in person to Bengal.

"My attention had long been directed to the state of the Dutch possessions to the eastward; and, as rumours were afloat of a projected armament going against the Isle of France, it occurred to me that the information I possessed respecting Java might be useful, and possibly turn the attention of our Government in that direction. I accordingly left my family, and proceeded to Calcutta in a small and frail vessel—the only one which offered, but in which all my future prospects had well-nigh perished. This was in the month of June 1810. On my arrival in Bengal, I met with the kindest reception from Lord Minto. I found that, though the appointment to the Moluccas had not actually taken place, it was promised to another. I, in consequence, relinquished all idea of it, and at once drew his Lordship's attention to Java by observing that there were other islands worthy of his Lordship's consideration besides the Moluccas,—Java, for instance. On the mention of Java, his Lordship cast a look of such scrutiny, anticipation, and kindness upon me that I shall never forget.

"'Yes,' said he, 'Java is an interesting island. I shall be happy to receive any information you can give me concerning it.'

"This was enough to encourage me, and, from this moment, all my views, all my plans, and all my mind were devoted to create such an interest regarding Java as should lead to its annexation to our Eastern Empire; although I confess that I had never the vanity to expect that, when this object was accomplished, so important an administration would have been entrusted to my individual charge; that I should be entrusted with what Mr. Marsden emphatically observes was 'as great a charge as a nation could entrust to an individual.'

"It is unnecessary to enter on the detail which followed. The fall of Bourbon, and the anticipation of success at the Isle of France, encouraged a plan for the conquest of Java. As it in a great measure originated with me, and as it was almost entirely on my information that the decision was taken, I naturally took a conspicuous part, although little or nothing met the public eye—perhaps no secret was ever better kept than the projected scheme against Java; for, until it was publicly announced, and the intention of the Governor-General to proceed in person was made known, not a word was surmised or whispered on the subject.

"As an *avant courier*, and to prepare the way for the expedition, I was appointed Agent to the Governor-General with the Malay States, and took up my headquarters at Malacca, where the rendezvous was fixed. I remained here, as Representative to the Governor-General, until his Lordship's arrival, when, instead of the designation of agent, I was styled Secretary to the Governor-General. In this capacity I accompanied his Lordship to Java. Various doubts and difficulties, and, I might say, insurmountable obstacles, had been started to prove the impossibility of the expedition proceeding to Java during the present season. The opinion of the Naval Commander-in-Chief, and, indeed, of all competent authorities, was decidedly against it. It was, in fact, pronounced impracticable. Lord Minto alone stood firm, and placed his entire and unreserved reliance on the opinion which I had given him on the subject.

"I had ascertained the practicability by an experiment in a small vessel, the *Minto*, commanded by Captain Greigh, a most intelligent and zealous officer, who had been placed under my orders, and to whom I am indebted for the discovery of the passage by the coast of Borneo. At the period that the expedition sailed from Malacca, it was uncertain by which route it would proceed. I really believe no fixed route was determined on, and Lord Minto had too much judgment and precaution to interfere. He placed the information he possessed within the reach of the senior naval officer, and, fortunately, it was acted upon.

"On the 4th of August 1811 the whole of the fleet, consisting of upwards of ninety vessels, arrived off the coast of Java without the loss of a single spar, or the slightest accident, having passed by a route previously almost unknown, and accomplished a passage declared to be impracticable. I will not attempt to say what my feelings were on the occasion. We had separated from the fleet for a few days, and it was only when we again joined them that we saw all the divisions united at the close of one of the finest days I ever recollect, and this in sight of the Land of Promise. Lord Minto, while at Malacca, had communicated his intention of appointing me to the government in case of success; and, as I had nothing to do with the military operations, I now looked upon my part as completed—perhaps a greater responsibility was never for so long on the head of a single individual, and the relief which I felt was proportionate.

"In October 1811 I was appointed Governor of Java, and continued to hold this post until March 1816, a period of nearly five years. I had then the option of proceeding to Fort Marlborough, to which I had, before the departure of Lord Minto, been appointed as a *retreat* in the event of any circumstances occasioning my removal from Java. Ill-health, however, occasioned partly by a domestic affliction, and partly from the severe duties of my station and a desire to supply the blank which the melancholy and sudden death of my friend and patron Lord Minto had occasioned in the accounts received at home respecting my administration, and the nature and importance of our interests in the Eastern seas, induced me to proceed at once to Europe. Here, with the exception of the time occupied during our tour on the Continent, my almost undivided attention was directed to the public object of my voyage, and my *History of Java*, imperfect as it is, will evince that I was not idle.

"As an acknowledgment for my services, and as the best appointment within their reach in the line which I had chalked out for myself, the Court of Directors confirmed my appointment to Bencoolen, and conferred upon me the personal rank and title of Lieutenant-Governor. I arrived at Bencoolen in March 1818, and immediately set about a thorough reform in all the establishments. The alarming and unqualified proceedings of the Dutch soon attracted my attention. I did not hesitate to oppose their pretensions, and although some doubts may exist how far it was prudent to risk as much as I did on my personal responsibility, the necessity and obvious advantage of such an interference are indisputable; the important measures of reform and reduction introduced by me at Bencoolen have met the unqualified approval of the higher authorities, and I have since been appointed Agent and Representative of our Governor-General, first, for settling the affairs of the distracted kingdom of Achen, and secondly, for establishing the Port of Sincapore at the extremity of the Malay Peninsula. Complete success attended both these important measures, and ensured the navigation and command of the Straits of Malacca, which secures us against all attempts at exclusion on the part of the Dutch, and places our intercourse with China beyond risk or annoyance. Of the value and importance of these measures I will not say more. They are recent, and have obtained publicity; but, while speaking of myself, I may observe that the full confidence of successive governor-generals is no small satisfaction and encomium on what I may consider my deserts, particularly when it is considered how adverse one of them, the Marquess of Hastings, at first appeared to all my plans and purposes. I shall say nothing respecting the attempts made to sully the purity of my character and administration by General Gillespie and a party whose envy and disappointment were combined with all wickedness and uncharitableness.

You know the particulars of the charges, the delay of justice, and how far it was eventually obtained with a liberality proportioned to that delay. I will only add that, as I have at length presented my defence to the consideration of the noble Marquess himself, who was the first to take up arms against me, I have obtained the greatest of all triumphs, and have been benefited rather than injured by the whole course of the proceeding. It is no easy matter for a man to come out of such a fire unhurt, but, having done so, it is some proof of the purity of the metal of which he is composed.

"With regard to the attention which may be considered to have been paid by me to objects of a still more general and interesting nature, whether literary, scientific, or benevolent, I have only a few words to say. The deficiency of my early education has never been fully supplied, and I have never ceased to deplore the necessity which withdrew me so early from school. I had hardly been two years at a boarding-school when I was withdrawn and forced to enter on the busy scenes of public life, then a mere boy. My leisure hours, however, still continued to be devoted to favourite studies; and, with the little aid which my allowances afforded, and which was not completely swallowed up by the wants of my family, I contrived to make myself master of the French language, and to prosecute inquiries into some of the various departments of literature and science. This was, however, in stolen moments, either before the office hours in the morning, or after them in the evening; and I shall never forget the mortification I felt when the penury of my family once induced my mother to complain of my extravagance in burning a candle in my room. And yet I look back to those days of misery, difficulty, and application with some degree of pleasure. I feel that I did all I could, and I have nothing to reproach myself with.

"This statement will account for my deficiencies in education; and all I ever presumed to consider myself was a lover and admirer of all that I could reach in literature and science. The varied, important, and incessant duties of my public life have always deprived me of that calm and retirement which I have desired, and to which I alone look as the ultimate end of my ambition on earth. To qualify myself for the enjoyment of such a state I omit no opportunity. The high stations I have held have enabled me to foster and encourage the pursuits of others; and, if I have any merit, it has rather been as the patron than in any other capacity. I will, however, recapitulate all that I can set down to my favour on this head.

"Before I left England in 1805, I had occasionally assisted in some periodical publications, and a plan was formed, in which I was to take a conspicuous part, for continuing the *Asiatic Annual Register* on an enlarged and improved principle. The plan fell to the ground in consequence of my quitting England. One or two volumes were published on the old plan, and the work, to the regret of everyone, has since been discontinued. While in Bengal in 1810 I read a paper to the Asiatic Society in Calcutta on the "Maritime Laws of the Malays." This paper the Society has done me the honour to publish in their *Transactions*, and I was admitted a member of the Institution. This account comprised only a portion of a work on which I had then been long engaged for elucidating the laws and usages of the Malayan tribes. My subsequent removal to Java placed me in a new scene, and, for a time, broke in on this intended work, and it is now a question with me how far I shall still prosecute it. My removal, however, to Java was important in other respects; and, though the first and fairest blossoms were blasted, I have reason to believe some good was done. Many of my views regarding the Malayan islands had been taken with my intimate friend Dr. Leyden. We had but one soul on the subject, and the expedition against Java was no sooner resolved upon than he required of me to exert all my influence with Lord Minto that he should accompany it. His Lordship regretted the desire, but complied with it, and Leyden had the promise from me that when I was Governor he should be my private secretary. In this capacity he would have had every advantage; but, alas! it was not ordained that he should enjoy it. He had hardly set foot on Java ere he fell a sacrifice to his zeal and devotion. Thus left alone, and deprived of more indeed than my right arm, I could do but little—that, however, was as follows: I raised the Literary Society of Batavia, which had almost become extinct, into credit and importance. Two volumes of its *Transactions* were published while I was president, to which I prefixed prefatory discourses, which I believe have not been read without interest. I encouraged and assisted the labours of Dr. Horsfield, an eminent naturalist, who, through that assistance, was able to prosecute his studies and researches to their final accomplishment, and to proceed to England with a body of information and a collection of interesting objects more extensive, perhaps, than have ever passed the Cape of Good Hope from the Eastern world. I also take some credit to myself for the establishment of the Benevolent Society at Batavia, the object of which was the abolition of slavery and the improvement of the condition of the islanders, to say nothing of the Bible Society, of which I was president, and to which I gave all the aid which, in such a heathenish land, could be brought to avail. Before I quitted Java the Bombay Literary Society had conferred upon me the distinction of an honorary member, and on my arrival in England I was almost immediately elected a Fellow of the Royal and Antiquarian Societies. I have published my *History of Java.* The statistical account alluded to in the *Dictionary of Living Authors* is, I suppose, the substance of my Minute on the Land Revenue.

"To the above I may add that the leisure of the outward-bound voyage and the society of my friend Dr. Arnold, who accompanied me as a naturalist, have contributed essentially to quicken my zeal and to give an additional stimulus in my pursuits of natural history and general knowledge. Ardent in these pursuits, and desirous of ascertaining the resources and character of the country I had to govern, I lost no time in penetrating into the interior of Sumatra; and the result of the different journeys I have taken has added much to the general stock of information. The discovery of a populous and fertile country at Menangkabu, if not, at the present, important in a political point of view, is interesting to the philanthropist, and may lead to important results. I have been unfortunate in the death of Dr. Arnold before he had time to expand or regulate his views, but my subsequent visit to Calcutta has enabled me to command the assistance of several able naturalists, who are now engaged in the discovery of all that is important.

"But it is to man, and the state in which he is found, that my attention is at this moment directed, and among other measures for the improvement of his condition, the most important and, perhaps, the most certain of eventual success, has been the establishment of schools on the Lancastrian plan. On what I have done, am doing, and anticipate from this measure you will hear further; and, in the meantime, you may be assured that I let no opportunity escape of placing the foundation of my public character on the broadest basis—that is to say, on the happiness and improvement of those I am destined to govern. The inward satisfaction which such a principle affords is beyond the reach of worldly praise or censure. I will not say that these are indifferent to me, but I covet them not, and give them but their *just* value and estimation.

"I have now, my dear cousin, passed an hour or two in giving you a sketch of my public life. I know not what for, or for what purpose, or what tempted me to do it, but idleness. I have not stopped on the way to make a single reflection; but many occurred, and if, from this outline, you feel yourself authorised to correct the misstatement and rather *degrading* account of the *Biographical Dictionary*, I shall be obliged. Perhaps if you were to call upon the publisher to strike out the whole article, and simply to insert my name and that of my book, it would answer my purpose; but I leave this to your discretion. Adieu! Remember me most affectionately to your Mary, and tell your little one or ones that they have an uncle who does not forget them.—Yours,

"T. S. RAFFLES."

CHAPTER II

PRINCE OF WALES'S ISLAND

WHEN the East India Company decided in 1805 to constitute Penang, or Prince of Wales's Island, "a regular Presidency with a Governor and Council," and sent out for that purpose a staff of twenty-six Englishmen,—whose salaries amounted to the aggregate of £43,500 a year, from the Governor, Mr. Philip Dundas, brother of the Chief Baron of Scotland, with his salary of £9000 a year, to the schoolmaster, Thomas Cullum, whose pay was £225 per annum,—that possession had been in the hands of the English for twenty years. In 1786 the Rajah of Quedah, or Kedah, as the modern orthographer has it, handed over the island of Pulo Penang—that is, Areca Nut Island—to Captain Francis Light, a naval officer in the East India Company's service. The motive and the consideration for this cession are equally obscure. The story goes that Captain Light married the Rajah's daughter, and received the island as her dowry; but, after being accepted as history for nearly a century, the statement was challenged by a friend of Captain Light's eldest son, Colonel Light, who served on Wellington's staff in the Peninsula and at Waterloo, and who took a prominent part in the founding of the Australian Colonies. It may be pointed out that there would have been nothing out of the practice of his time if the elder Light had married a Malayan princess, or any other native lady, and his second son unquestionably did marry a native of Java nearly thirty years afterwards. It seems clear, however, that Light had to pay a rent of 10,000 dollars a year for Penang, which, in consequence of his taking possession on the birthday of the heir-apparent, Prince George, namely, 12th August 1786, he renamed Prince of Wales's Island; while the town was also named after the same personage, George Town. While speaking of Penang nomenclature it will not be out of place to add that the Fort was called Cornwallis, after the Governor-General at the date of its construction, that the strip of territory on the mainland, added after the composition for the rent, was named Wellesley Province in honour of another Indian ruler, and that the chief mountain of the dependency was designated Mount Olivia after Mrs. Raffles.

The newly-formed Presidency comprised then, besides Pulo Penang, a strip of territory called Province Wellesley, extending for some forty-five miles along the adjacent coast of the Malay Peninsula. The island of Penang itself lies in the sunlight and the sea at a distance of seven miles from the mainland. It is some fifteen miles in length from north to south, and about nine miles in breadth, covering an area of rather more than one hundred square miles. Along its western and south-western coasts, regularly watered by the fertilising monsoons, are rich plantations of spices, grain, and timber; while a thickly populated and productive tract, cultivated for the most part in gardens, stretches along its eastern shores. A mountain range, diversified with granite rocks and mica schist, and beautifully clothed with woods, runs from one end of the island to the other, rising in the north, at the health resort of Strawberry Hill, to a height of 2922 feet. The temperature near the sea-level averages from 80° to 90° F.; but inasmuch as rain falls all the year round except in January and February, and a cool breeze from the sea sweeps day by day refreshingly across the island, while at Strawberry Hill on its northern heights the thermometer seldom rises above 75° or falls below 62°, the settlement had acquired, at the time of which we write, a high but little-deserved reputation as a health resort. George Town, the capital, is situated at the north-eastern end of the island, and its harbour, protected then as now by Fort Cornwallis, is so safe and convenient that, in Raffles's time, the British Government had it in contemplation to make the island one of their regular naval stations for the refitting and refreshment of His Majesty's fleet in the Eastern seas. In erecting Penang into a Presidency, the Court had not been uninfluenced by such ideas on the part of His Majesty's ministers; but the hopes thus originated were doomed to disappointment. In this spot, then, Raffles was to pass the first years of his life in the East.

I will not attempt to assert positively how the colony came into our hands, but Francis Light, the first Superintendent of Trade at Prince of Wales's Island, died there on 21st October 1794. Although the connection was maintained, and the rental compounded for a sum of money in 1800, Penang languished in the hands of a Lieutenant-Governor, who was also Agent to the Governor-General with the Malay States. It was to restore the fortunes of this place that the Company raised it to the rank of a Presidency in 1805, and Colonel, afterwards Sir R. T. Farquhar, then Lieutenant-Governor, not to be confounded with Colonel William Farquhar, of whom we shall hear much more in connection with Singapore, handed over the government to Mr. Dundas and his Council on arrival. The early days of the new Government do not seem to have been altogether happy. In almost their first communication home, the Governor and Council complain of "the very great inconvenience suffered since their arrival from the want of offices and proper assistants," and hope any irregularity will be excused. A more serious matter is dealt with in the alleged expense of living in the place, house rent in particular being mentioned; and to show that this was no exaggeration, it may be stated that Raffles paid £330 a year, or more than one-fifth of his salary, for "Runnymede," his home on the island. On the junior members of the establishment this pressed with such severity, that in order to enable them to live a house had to be taken for their accommodation. In the first general letter home the Governor and his Council wrote:—"We must observe that the duties to be performed by your different servants herein mentioned will not leave them any time to devote to trade or other employment; and we are sorry to state as our opinion that they can never look to the possibility of acquiring independence on the smallest scale from the allowances which your Honourable Court have been pleased to attach to their respective situations, which will barely subsist them and their families, unless the price of house rent and the common necessaries of life are very materially reduced." The whole situation was summed up in one pathetic sentence from a letter written by a secretary, "a dollar here does not go as far as a rupee in the other Presidencies." This will explain the statement made in one of Raffles's letters, that he was not as well off as immediately before he left England, but then it must be admitted he had taken a good deal more on his hands.

Such was the place to which fate had called Raffles, and such were the conditions under which he began his official work in the East. But before he actually arrived there he had begun the training which distinguished him from every other member of the staff, in the study of the Malay language on board the *Ganges*. When he landed he had already mastered the grammar, and within a very brief period he had sufficiently qualified himself to act as interpreter. At that time there was a regular interpreter on the island, Mr. Thomas Hutton, a member of the old administration, who employed a certain number of natives to do the work. Doubts seem very reasonably to have occurred to Mr. Dundas and his Council as to Mr. Hutton's qualifications, and as to how far it would be safe to employ Malays in translating important documents without proper supervision. This led to the gradual employment of Raffles, not only as occasional interpreter, but also as general supervisor of Malay translations, and in 1807 he succeeded to the office. It was a compliment to the young student, and he soon showed that he thoroughly deserved it; but none the less it signified a considerable addition to his already heavy labours.

The most important event in the first few months of Raffles's life at Penang was undoubtedly the arrival of John Caspar Leyden. It stimulated his Malay studies, but in the outcome it did a great deal more in procuring for Raffles a friend and advocate at the seat of the Supreme Government. But for Leyden, Raffles might never have had the chance of winning the ear of a sympathetic Governor-General, or of moulding to his own views the policy of India on an important external question. Leyden was a remarkable man,—a statesman not less than a poet and a polyglot,—and it was a happy chance that threw two such kindred spirits as his and Raffles's into friendly communion and alliance on the remote shores of the Malay Peninsula. The reader could not have better evidence of the attractive and striking personality of Raffles than the promptness with which Leyden, an older and better educated man, already distinguished as the friend and colleague of Scott, admitted him to the very first place in his friendship. The appreciation was the more gratifying and exceptional when we remember that Leyden's qualities have been truthfully portrayed in the following sentences:—"He was distinguished for the manly simplicity and independence of his character. He could suppress, but knew not the art of disguising his emotion. In his judgment of men, and his value for their society and acquaintance, he was guided solely by his opinion of their moral and intellectual worth, and never paid any regard to claims founded merely upon the adventitious circumstances of rank and fortune."

John Caspar Leyden is not the only representative of a striking type of character given to the world by the peasant class of Scotland; but he will rank as such with Burns and Carlyle. He was born on 8th September 1775, at Denholm, a village on the banks of the Teviot, in the parish of Cavers and the county of Roxburgh. His father, also John Leyden, was a virtuous and industrious peasant of that class which in Scotland is totally unlike the same grade of society in any other country unless it be Norway, and the story is told of him that after Leyden's death, when Colonel Malcolm wished to explain some facts to him about the property left by his son, he interrupted him with the proud remark that "although he was a poor man he did not want to hear about his son's money, but about his son's fame." Young John Leyden was educated in the village school, where he laid the sound foundation of his future extensive linguistic achievements. In November 1790, when little more than fifteen years of age, he proceeded to Edinburgh University, where he studied Hebrew, Arabic, theology, and medicine. He was intended for the presbytery, but medicine had an early fascination for him. At college he astonished his tutors by the rapidity with which he acquired knowledge, and the thoroughness with which he retained it. As Lockhart says in his *Life of Sir Walter Scott*: "Few can need to be reminded that this extraordinary man, born in a shepherd's cottage in one of the wildest valleys of Roxburghshire, and of course almost entirely self-educated, had before he attained his nineteenth year confounded the doctors of Edinburgh by the portentous mass of his acquisitions in almost every department of learning. He had set the extremest penury at utter defiance, or rather he had never been conscious that it could operate as a bar; for bread and water and access to books and lectures comprised all within the bound of his wishes, and thus he toiled and battled at the gates of science after science until his unconquerable perseverance carried everything before it; and yet with this monastic abstemiousness and iron hardness of will, perplexing those about him by manners and habits in which it was hard to say whether the mosstrooper or the schoolman of former days most prevailed, he was at heart a poet."

From Edinburgh he went on to St. Andrews, where in May 1798 he was licensed to preach, but his thoughts were not in the pulpit. They turned to literature, and his early love, medicine, for the practice of which he had qualified himself with an M.D. degree at St. Andrews. He wrote the *Complaynt of Scotland*, he contributed to the *Scots Magazine*, he became the collaborator of Scott in his *Border Minstrelsy*. What permanent result might have flowed from these literary efforts, need not be inquired into, for in 1803 Leyden came to London, with his certificates and testimonials, to knock at the doors of the India House as a candidate for employment on its Medical Establishment in the East. An appointment on the Madras Establishment was secured for him through the influence of Mr. George Ellis, who had taken a deep interest in the *Border Minstrelsy*, and to whom Scott introduced Leyden. On 7th April 1803 he sailed for Madras, which he reached on 19th August in the same year. Scott, it will be remembered by readers of his biography, rushed up to London to see him once more before his departure, but arrived a few days too late. That alone was no slight tribute to Leyden's character and power of influencing men. Scott and he were never to meet again.

Leyden reached Madras in ill-health, and he was at first employed in the general hospital at that town, of which he had sole charge during four months; and he employed all his leisure in the study of languages. In January 1805 he was attached to the Commission of Survey in Mysore as assistant-surgeon and naturalist. His health was still bad, and for some months he was seriously ill in the hospital at Seringapatam. In the autumn he was moved down to the coast, and embarked at Quilon, on the Malabar coast in Travancore, for Penang, on a Parsee vessel. Penang was then supposed, but very erroneously, to be a healthy station, and Leyden gives the following description of his arrival there on 22nd October 1805:—

"Eight o'clock. With the utmost difficulty we have at last got into the harbour between five and six o'clock in the evening. The hills on both sides of the bay remained almost completely concealed by the haze, but the bay is wide and spacious, and extremely well sheltered on every side. The entrance is wide, open, and safe. The fort [Fort Cornwallis] and Government House are the first objects which present themselves to attract the attention. The town lies low, and is in a great measure concealed by wood. We found a considerable number of ships in the harbour, and among the rest two line-of-battle ships commanded by Sir Thomas Trowbridge, namely, the *Rattlesnake* and the *Dedaigneuse*. The town is full of strangers, and of persons who have been superseded by the erection of Puloo Penang into a Presidency, and who are consequently ready to take their departure, so that there is not only a great deal of confusion, but a sort of interregnum."

During the nearly three months of his stay at Penang, Leyden was more or less an invalid. To use his own words: "In Penang, being confined entirely to the house, and having abundance of time on my hands, to get rid of the *ennui* of a tedious convalescence, I applied vigorously to the acquisition of the Malay, the Hindustani of the East." In those studies he was helped by Raffles, who had already made some progress with the language. Leyden remained as the guest of Raffles during the greater part of his stay on the island. He was nursed by Mrs. Raffles, and he pursued linguistic studies with her husband. A common pursuit strengthened their sympathy, and each discovered the other to be a man after his own heart. Leyden's *Dissertation on the Language and Literature of the Indo-Chinese Nations*, and his translation of the *Malay Annals*, show that these labours were not unprofitable, and they were lightened because, Leyden says, he was "happy in the enjoyment of agreeable society." When Leyden quitted Penang in January 1806 the basis of a great and enduring friendship had been laid. Leyden invoked Olivia Raffles to inspire his muse. Under the pseudonym of "Amicus," Raffles recorded his feelings towards his friend; and the words he wrote formed no unfitting frame for Leyden's poem already quoted, when it was reproduced in the Government *Gazette* of Prince of Wales's Island for 22nd March 1806:—

"The following lines on the departed year have too much merit not to find an acceptable place in your paper. They were written by a friend who, after travelling far and near in pursuit of knowledge, was at last driven to our Eastern Isle for the recovery of his health. He has now quitted our shores, but his distinguished talents and enthusiastic feeling must ever endear him to those who knew him sufficiently to estimate his worth and value his friendship. 'The stranger is gone, but we cannot forget.'"

There is no doubt that the intimacy with a man of such energy and genius as Leyden, whose tastes in at least linguistic studies were very similar to his own, acted as a great stimulant and encouragement to Raffles. He was seized with the spirit of emulation. He prosecuted his Malay studies with increased ardour, and he wrote home for Hebrew and Greek dictionaries and grammars. But in Leyden he had found much more than a co-worker, he had discovered that rare possession, a staunch and loyal friend. We may glance a little ahead and see how it was that Leyden acquired the means of showing his friendship in a practical form, and of influencing the fortunes of Raffles, who was then in a far superior official position to himself. During the remainder of 1806 Leyden's health prevented his performing any regular duties; but in the first few months of the following year he was elected Professor of Hindustani at Calcutta University. His Malay studies had already made him a prominent member of the Asiatic Society. He was in this academic position when Lord Minto arrived as Governor-General in July 1807, and a change at once took place in Leyden's fortunes. Lord Minto was the chief of the great Elliot family of Teviotdale, which has played its part in border war and song for centuries. Leyden had helped to make the epics of the locality world-known. He came from Teviotdale, and might almost be termed a clansman of the Elliots. He was also the foremost, if not the only scholar—Marsden having gone home—in Calcutta. There was nothing strange or incomprehensible in Lord Minto's taking an interest in Leyden, nor in the fact that the statesman received the scholar into high favour on discovering what manner of man he was.

Before the end of 1807, Leyden, the assistant-surgeon and humble professor, was appointed Judge of the Twenty-four Pergunnahs—Mir Jaffir's old jaghir—at Calcutta, and in 1809 he resigned this post to become a Commissioner of the Court of Requests, which kept him busy on three days in the week, and left him the others for his own studies. His great and wide knowledge of Eastern languages justified those appointments, and was indispensable for the discharge of the judicial duties assigned to him. In 1810 he resigned the Commissionership, and was appointed Assay Master at the Calcutta Mint, with a large salary and easy work. The enumeration of these posts, which made Leyden an official of the first rank at Calcutta, is only intended to show how he acquired the opportunities to help Raffles, and to obtain for his work and views the direct personal knowledge of the Governor-General. Leyden himself gained Lord Minto's confidence and esteem. Having done this by his own merit, he bethought him of his best friend; and that is why the visit of the invalid to Penang in the autumn of 1805 must be regarded as having exercised a powerful influence on the career of Stamford Raffles.

It is time now to turn to the less interesting features of life in Prince of Wales's Island at the beginning of this century. Raffles had gone out as Assistant-Secretary at a salary of £1500 a year. Before he had been there four months he reported in a letter, dated 26th February 1806, to the Governor in Council that, "having paid considerable attention to the acquisition of the Malayee language, he felt himself competent not only to detect any error or misrepresentation made in translating or transcribing letters from the English into the Malayee, but, when necessary, to translate or transcribe such letters himself"; and he also went on to make the following characteristic statement:—"I have been at much expense in retaining in my service several natives whom I have selected as persons whose ability, and perhaps integrity, might be depended upon from their not being engaged in trade or other pursuits wherein the occasional knowledge they might obtain of the affairs of Government might be improper. These men were engaged by me, and have hitherto been maintained at my expense." The rest of this letter runs as follows:—

"But I have now to regret the narrow limits of my income will not longer admit of continuing so expensive an establishment on my own account, and more particularly so as I had reason to expect from them considerable assistance in explaining and commenting upon the customs and laws of the adjacent States, which I am endeavouring to collect, in the hope of laying a fair translation thereof before your Honourable Board.

"I cannot, however, omit adding that I was in a great measure induced to engage those men, from the circumstance of the *full* appointment of Translator to Government not having been yet granted to any person at this Presidency, conceiving that it was thereby intended to leave an opening for such who might prove themselves best qualified for the situation. And I trust that whenever the Honourable the Governor and Council shall take this appointment under consideration that I shall be honoured with their favourable notice, being willing to undertake, if necessary, to write all letters in the Malayee language that may be deemed of a secret nature in my own hand, and in many other respects to prevent, by my personal application, the affairs and interests of Government being intrusted in the hands of a native.—I have the honour to be, with the greatest respect, honourable sir and sirs, your obedient, humble servant, THOMAS RAFFLES.

"FORT CORNWALLIS, *the 20th February* 1806."

"Resolved that Mr. Raffles be informed that we are sorry we have not at present any opportunities of rewarding him for his very meritorious exertions in acquiring a knowledge of the Malay language, but that we shall transmit a copy of his letter, a number in the first packet, to the Honourable Court of Directors, when we shall take that opportunity of recommending him to the favourable consideration of the Honourable Court. That in the meantime Mr. Raffles be requested to state to the Board the expense likely to be incurred by the employment of the natives alluded to in his letter, as employed by him in explaining and commenting upon the customs and laws of the adjacent States, in order that we may judge how far it will be in our power to render him the assistance he requires in compiling so useful a work."

As the subject is of great interest, I give Raffles's reply to these questions :—

"At a Council, Fort Cornwallis, 6th March 1806. (Present: Dundas, Oliphant, Gray.) Read the following letter from Mr. Raffles, namely :—

"To H. S. PEARSON, Esq., Secretary to Government.

"SIR,—I have the honour to acknowledge the receipt of your letter of the 27th ultimo, conveying to me the flattering opinion entertained by the Honourable the Governor and Council of my acquisitions in the Malayee language, and I beg you will assure them that I feel very sensible of the honour they intend me in forwarding to the Honourable Court a copy of my letter favourably recommended by Government. In reply to that part of your letter requesting that I will state for their information the expense incurred in maintaining my present establishment of natives, I beg leave to represent that for the last two months I have employed six natives, namely, four Malays, one native of Mecca, and one native of the Coromandel coast, at the monthly expense of about eighty dollars, but as these men were principally employed in copying fair, several old and valuable manuscripts from the Malayee, the chief of which are now completed, I intended from this month to discharge two, and, if my circumstances would [allow], to have continued the remainder. The establishment, therefore, that I could wish to continue for a few months is as follows, namely :—

2 Head Malay Natives of Vuddah at 20ds. each . . .	40 dollars.
1 Malay to transcribe	15 ,,
1 Arab	10 ,,
Total Sp. dollars,	65

"The last I consider as absolutely necessary wherever any accurate translation is to be made from any Malayee work, that language, like those of most countries where the Mahomedan faith is professed, abounding not only with many words, but sentences and frequently passages of pure Arabic.

"In collecting several books containing accounts of the manners, particular customs, and laws of the Malays, I must necessarily be led into frequent expenses, but it will be impossible for me to state any exact sum as likely to be incurred, as much must depend upon the facility with which I obtain the books from the natives, and the time I am able to devote for the purpose of translating them. —I have the honour to be, sir, your most obedient, humble servant,

"THOMAS RAFFLES.

"FORT CORNWALLIS, *the 6th March* 1806."

"Resolved that Mr. Raffles be allowed the natives he requires, the Board relying on his not keeping them longer than is necessary for the completion of the work on which he is employed."

The outcome of this offer was that when the incompetence of the Government Translator, Mr. Hutton, was fully exposed, Raffles was appointed to his post and duties. For this work he does not appear to have ever received the least remuneration, but the native staff he had organised was taken into Government pay at the total cost of sixty dollars a month.

In a General Letter, dated the 20th of March 1806, the Penang Government brought the linguistic proficiency of Raffles before the Court in the following paragraph:—"Mr. Thomas Raffles, whom your Honourable Court was pleased to appoint our Deputy-Secretary, having, by studious application, united to great natural talent for the acquisition of knowledge in languages, notwithstanding every attention was at the same time bestowed to his other more immediate duties, attained for the time he studied it a wonderful proficiency in that of the Malays, we beg leave strongly to recommend his very praiseworthy exertions to the notice of your Honourable Court, by whom merit is sure to be rewarded."

The Court of Directors, in their despatch of 18th February 1807, replied as follows:—"We have derived much satisfaction from the representation made of the conduct of Mr. Thomas Raffles, your Deputy-Secretary, in the great proficiency he has acquired of the Malay language, in the short period of five months after his arrival at Prince of Wales's Island, and desire he be informed, that we entertain a high sense of his laudable exertions, and that a perseverance in that line of conduct will ensure our approbation and support. The establishment of natives at an expense of sixty dollars per month, which you have allowed Mr. Raffles to employ, and from whom he expects to derive great assistance in explaining and commenting upon the laws of the adjacent States (a work which Mr. Raffles has commenced), has our entire approbation. We trust, however, the establishment will be abolished on the completion of the work."

Illness soon made gaps in the ranks of the original establishment at Penang. Two of the writers died on the journey out, and only a brief experience was needed to show that the place did not deserve the high character it had been given for healthiness. On 28th August 1806 the Secretary, Mr. H. S. Pearson, was compelled to leave for a six months' holiday and change of air; and Raffles, who had been doing the work of the office for some time, was appointed Acting Secretary from that date. The reader must not suppose that the clerical work was light. Four sets of all correspondence had to be made, two for the Court in London, one for the Supreme Government at Calcutta, and one for the office at Penang. The correspondence had also got very much into arrears, and Raffles not only undertook to make up the copies in default, but also that "no exertion on his part should be wanting to prevent the records from falling into arrear." Some blame seems to have attached to the junior writers and clerks for the manner in which they did their work, for the Governor refers to their neglect and remissness as having compelled him to engage extra clerks, and he concludes by declaring his determination to compel them to do their duty. It is only fair to note that Raffles himself gives a more satisfactory explanation. He said: "The arrears are due, not to idleness, but to illness and being undermanned, to ignorance of writers on arrival, and to absence of paper for one month, etc." He then recommended an increased staff, and payment by section, or, in other words, by piecework, for copying diaries.

In March 1807, Mr. J. H. Oliphant, senior member of Council, died, and in the following month Governor Dundas also died. Mr. Pearson returned with recruited health at this juncture, and succeeded to the vacancy in the Council caused by Oliphant's death. Raffles was then appointed full Secretary; a post which carried with it the higher salary of 8000 dollars, or £2000 a year. He was quite qualified for the post, and indeed he had practically filled it for a long period. Liberal as the salary may appear at a cursory examination,—for in reality none of these salaries were quite as large as they seemed, owing to the cost of living,—the Governor and his Council seized the opportunity to benefit their energetic and accomplished Secretary. They were, no doubt, encouraged to take the step they did by the manner in which he discharged all his duties, and took upon himself additional work without pay. A further tribute to his good qualities was sent home a few months later by Governor Macalister, the successor to Dundas, and as it affords the justification for the proposed increase of salary, I cite it here:—

"To the services and merits of Mr. Raffles, as well as in duty to my employers, I should feel alike wanting were I to omit this opportunity of pointing out to the favourable notice of your Honourable Committee the unwearied zeal and assiduity with which he has, since the formation of the establishment, devoted his talents to the furtherance of the Company's interests, his unremitting attention to the duties of the most laborious office under this Government, added to those of Registrar to the Recorder's Court, which at the period of its establishment he voluntarily and gratuitously undertook."

Sir Edward Stanley, the Recorder, added his own testimony to the value of his semi-legal co-operation in the following words:—"I must never forget to mention the cheerful disposition Mr. Raffles has manifested to aid the Court in its operations as far as it was possible for him, consistent with his other occupations, to do."

The arrangement proposed by the Penang Government is explained in the following correspondence, but it was, briefly, by a readjustment of the salaries in the office, to give the Secretary 200 dollars a month extra pay; and the justification put forward for it was not merely the superior merit of Raffles, but the inferior rank of the new Assistant-Secretary, who was a writer of only two years' standing. It is worth noting that Mr. Pearson, the ex-Secretary, strongly supported the proposal, which is thus set forth in a letter of 8th July 1807:—

"Having on the succession of Mr. Pearson to a seat in Council, appointed Mr. Thomas Raffles to succeed him as Secretary to this Government, we have to solicit your Honourable Court's favourable attention to an arrangement which we have deemed it our duty to make in appointing Mr. William Armstrong Clubley, a writer on this establishment, to the office of Assistant-Secretary.

"Adverting to the very great responsibility and labour attached to the office of Secretary at this Presidency, and conceiving from our local knowledge of the duties of the two situations, that it would be a much more equitable distribution of the salaries annexed to the offices of Secretary and his Assistant, if 200 dollars per month were deducted from that of the Assistant and made over to the Secretary, we have fixed the salaries as follows, viz. :—

To the Secretary—Sp. Dollars, 866·66 per month.
To the Assistant— ,, ,, 300 ,,

"This arrangement, by which no additional expense will attach to the Honourable Company, and which will prove equally beneficial to the Assistant in the event of his succession to the Secretaryship, will, we trust, meet with your Honourable Court's approbation and confirmation.

"The salary which we have now taken upon ourselves to fix for the Secretary we deem to be no more than a fair remuneration for the laborious duties and responsibility of the office, whilst that now annexed to the situation of Assistant is, we conceive, fully equal to any office which your Honourable Court would be desirous a young man of not two years' standing in your service should be appointed to, unless under very particular circumstances; and we recommend to your Honourable Court's consideration the propriety of reducing in like manner the salary of the Assistant-Accountant and Auditor on any alteration taking place in that office; the allowances granted by your Honourable Court to the Assistants when these offices were bestowed upon experienced persons selected from your service in England to whom a superior rank has been attached, not appearing to us to apply to the case of the young men sent out as writers on this establishment, who, without their age or experience warranting much responsibility, would otherwise, from the necessity of the offices of Assistants being filled by them, hold situations as writers nearly equal in emolument to Senior Merchants, on whom all responsibility must attach as Chiefs of Departments."

The Court, notwithstanding the testimonial they had passed on Raffles's Malay studies, did not see the matter in the same light, but they were somewhat slow in expressing their disapprobation of the arrangement and their refusal to sanction the necessary payments. In the first instance they even called upon Raffles to refund the sums he had received on this head. The following extracts, which were their first protest against the increase, are from a letter dated 28th April 1809, nearly two years after the alteration, and certainly more than a year after news of the step had reached them :—

"We are not aware of any objection to the appointments of Mr. Thomas Raffles and Mr. W. Clubley to the offices of Secretary and Assistant-Secretary to your Government, in consequence of the succession of Mr. Pearson to a seat at your Council Board; we, however, highly disapprove the arrangements you have adopted with regard to the salary of the former.

"The salary established by our Orders of the 18th April 1805, for the Secretary to your Government, namely, dollars 8000 per annum, we consider in every respect sufficient; and although the addition you have granted is to be provided by a corresponding reduction in the salary of the Assistant-Secretary, by which no additional expense was to attach to the Company, yet we can never admit that because the salary of one office will bear reduction, another is therefore to be increased in a proportionate degree.

"Mr. Clubley being a writer of only two years' standing, you very properly restricted his allowances to dollars 2000 per annum; but upon the expiration of three years' residence in India, we agree with you that 3600 dollars per annum will be an adequate allowance, which we accordingly authorise you to allow to him.

"With respect to the salary of the Secretary to your Government, we desire that it be reduced to the sum originally fixed by us, and that Mr. Raffles be called upon to refund the amount which he may have received over and above the sum of dollars 8000 per annum."

When this despatch reached Penang, Raffles had already drawn under this head, as extra salary, 6500 dollars, or £1625, and the order to refund this large amount filled him with consternation, and was practically impossible. By that time he had rendered, and was still rendering, great services; and the Governor and Council of the Presidency, knowing him to be at that juncture simply indispensable, stood by him and made representations on his behalf. Perhaps the strongest advocacy was furnished by his own letter, dated 8th February 1810, which he wrote when the Court's decision had been first intimated to him. The following is the text of this letter, and indicates the steps taken by the local authorities in the matter:—

"HONOURABLE SIRS,—In respectfully soliciting your favourable consideration of the peculiar and distressing circumstances in which I am placed by the receipt of the Honourable Court's Orders of the 28th April last, I trust I am justified in presuming that on a subject so seriously affecting my interests and future prospects your liberal attention will be afforded.

"On the decease of Mr. Oliphant and the consequent succession of Mr. Pearson to a seat in Council, your Honourable Board were pleased to appoint me to the office of Secretary to Government, and on the 1st April 1807, in nominating one of the writers of this establishment to be Assistant, thought proper for reasons then assigned to fix the salaries of those offices for the future, the former at Spanish dollars 866·66, and the latter at Spanish dollars 300 per month, being the total amount authorised by the Court of Directors, though differently portioned.

"This arrangement, made with the entire approbation and sanction of the Honourable Philip Dundas, then Governor, was proposed by Mr. Pearson to the Board (Mr. Dundas' indisposition preventing his attendance then and subsequently), and met the unanimous approval of the members.

"My salary being thus established by Government in the year 1807, and given to me (as then stated) as a fair remuneration for the laborious and responsible duties I had to perform, has naturally been considered at my free disposal, until the receipt on the 15th ultimo of the Honourable Court's

Orders directing that I should be called on to refund any sum received beyond Spanish dollars 8000 per annum.

"Had the arrangement been expressed or understood to have been in any way provisional or conditional, or had it been made in consequence of any representation, or effected by any act of my own, I should of course have held myself liable to refund what the Honourable Court might disapprove of, but in receiving what was voluntarily authorised by your Honourable Board, I felt that I might justly avail myself of its advantages in discharging the heavy incumbrances which necessarily devolved on me in my first establishment in this country, and in aiding such parts of my family as stood in need of my support and assistance; and at this moment most solemnly do I assure your Honourable Board of my total inability to comply with the heavy and unexpected demand now made—nearly three years subsequent to my appointment.

"The circumstances of the office devolving on me as it did at the time, without the aid of an experienced Assistant, of which my predecessor had the advantage, added to the serious illnesses under which I have laboured, brought on chiefly from close attention to duty and a constant anxiety to benefit the public service as far as lay in my power, will, I hope, meet with your favourable consideration; and when the increased demands on my earnings in consequence of the death of a near relative, which has left a widowed sister and three infant children entirely dependent on my support, are adverted to as connected with this statement, I hope that I may not be deemed improperly intrusive on your time.

"With every desire to obey to their fullest extent the Orders of the Honourable Court of Directors, I trust the peculiar circumstances under which I have taken the liberty to solicit your consideration will be sufficient to justify my respectful representation on the present instance.—I have, etc.,

(Signed) "THO. RAFFLES."

"Mr. Raffles having submitted the above letter to me in order that I might state to the Board whether he was correct or not in his representation of the facts relative to the increase of the Secretary's salary and decrease of that of his Assistant, I have to state for the information of the Honourable the Governor and Council that a day or two previous to the departure of Mr. Dundas from the Presidency he sent for me to his chamber, where he was lying extremely ill, when he informed me that he was totally unable to attend to the duties of the Government, and therefore intended to leave it and proceed to sea with Captain Byng in the *Belliqueux*, desiring me at the same time to take charge of the Government. I then consulted Mr. Dundas on several points relating to the Government, and among other propositions, to which he gave his entire acquiescence, suggested to him the propriety of decreasing the salary of the Assistant-Secretary, he being a very young man, who had just entered the service, and adding the amount of decrease to the salary of the Secretary, who in fact had all the responsibility attached to the office, which at that period (before the establishment of the Court of Judicature), I will venture to say from my own experience and knowledge, was one of the most troublesome and laborious offices in India. (Signed) "H. S. PEARSON."

"Having as your Honourable Board will perceive submitted this representation to Mr. Pearson, I humbly trust that, under all the circumstances of the case, your Honourable Board will be induced to permit the Orders of the

Honourable Court to lie over until this statement with such opinion as you may be pleased to form thereon is transmitted to the Honourable Court, holding myself of course liable to the amount ordered to be refunded.

(Signed) "THO. RAFFLES."

"Resolved that in consideration of the peculiar circumstances stated by Mr. Raffles, and of the increased allowance in question having been given to him unconditionally as the spontaneous act of the Board, and not in consequence of any representation whatever on his part, the subject be again referred to the Honourable Court of Directors, and the representation now made by Mr. Raffles recommended in the strongest manner to their favourable consideration.

"Ordered that in the meantime the retrospective effect of the Honourable Court's Orders, as contained in paragraphs 93 and 96 of the Company's General Letter under date the 28th April 1809, be postponed."

Having exempted Raffles from the obligation to refund the arrears of the excess salary he had received, the Governor made the following answer to the Court on 15th March 1810:—

"We are sorry to have met the disapprobation of your Honourable Court in the adoption of the arrangement herein referred to, and shall be particular in future in avoiding the recurrence of similar occasions.

"By the separate despatch to your Honourable Court of the 1st ultimo, you were informed that in consequence of your Orders of the 21st April 1809 your wishes with respect to the future allowances of the Secretary and his Assistant had been fixed as follows:—

Secretary . . .	666·66 dollars per month,
Assistant-Secretary . .	300 ,, ,,

thereby effecting a saving on the salaries originally fixed for this department of Sp. dollars 200 per month.

"We have at the same time to refer your Honourable Court to a representation recorded on our proceedings from Mr. Raffles, our Secretary, detailing the circumstances attending his original appointment to that office, and the distressing situation in which he must be placed by the effect of your Orders as contained in the 96th paragraph of your despatch.

"Aware of the correctness of the statement, and being impressed with the peculiarity of the case, we have felt it incumbent on us to give the subject the most serious consideration, and under all circumstances to postpone enforcing your Orders retrospectively until the whole might be again brought under your Honourable Court's consideration by a further representation from us.

"The arrangement that took effect on the 1st April 1807 for the future division of the salaries attached to the offices of the Secretary and his Assistant was adopted, as your Honourable Court will perceive on reference to the statement of Mr. Pearson, at the recommendation of the Honourable Philip Dundas, then Governor, which meeting the approbation of other members of the Board, the increased allowances authorised to be drawn by Mr. Raffles were therefore given to him as the spontaneous act of the Board unsolicited by him, and had your Honourable Court's disapprobation of the measure been received in the usual course of time for such replies, your Orders could not have had the serious tendency that would inevitably arise under the present circumstance of his being called on to refund the increased allowances for a period of near three years.

"Adverting therefore to the duties performed by Mr. Raffles as Secretary previous to the establishment of the Court of Judicature, and the circumstances under which he was authorised to draw the increased allowances in question, and being aware of the many serious calls that have lately been made on him in consequence of misfortunes in his family; we respectfully solicit your reconsideration of this subject, under the hope that as the arrangement by which Mr. Raffles's increased allowances were effected did not subject the Honourable Company to any additional expense whatever, you will not see occasion to enforce a retrenchment so ruinous in its effects to that gentleman."

The consequence of this step was that Raffles, having enjoyed for two years an extra salary of £600 a year, was in January 1810 reduced to the lower scale, while the question of the arrears due for 1807–9 was not finally settled in his favour till 1817, when on the occasion of his first return to England the Court was graciously pleased to waive its claims for the £1625 under discussion. The loss of salary, to say nothing of the mental anxiety caused by the claim of the Company, which hung over him for many years, was the more serious, because he had taken upon himself many fresh duties that did not appertain to his office, and for which he got scanty recognition and less tangible reward. As Secretary, it was his duty to represent the Company in all cases that arose with its debtors, and he thus picked up a smattering of legal phraseology and procedure, which led to his being appointed first, a Registrar of the Court, and, then, one of the Commissioners of a new Court of Requests—an institution, by the way, which did not find favour with the directors, as they absolutely refused to allow any salaries for it. He also held the office of Licenser or Censor of the Press, and a Judge Dickens at the end of 1806 calls notice to "the inattention of Mr. Raffles to what the Governor and Council must have expected from him when they made him Licenser of the Press." This inattention was most trivial. He had omitted to scratch out an underlining!

Our notice of his official position at Penang may be concluded with his elevation from the rank of Junior Merchant to Senior Merchant in 1809–10. In the early part of the former year, he and two of his colleagues on the establishment presented a petition to rise to the higher grade, and, after twelve months' consideration of the matter, it was decided that this claim was in conformity with rule, and that the step should be accorded the applicants subject to the confirmation of the Court. Speaking of Mr. Raffles, the Governor said: "His conduct throughout entitles him to my fullest approbation as well as it did to that of Mr. Dundas when Governor, and will, I trust, obtain for him the approbation of the Honourable Court of Directors." The confirmation of his elevation to the rank of Senior Merchant was of course given, but already there were signs that the Company thought mainly of economy in regard to its establishments in the Malay Peninsula and the Eastern Archipelago. Raffles, without any participating act on his part, had come into collision with them on the subject of his extra pay as Secretary. It was unfortunately to be the precursor of more serious differences on financial topics during the later passages of his career, but, even at this early stage, it will not be out of place to point out that the views of the Court were based on the failure of any of these possessions to be remunerative. They resented any proposition to add a farthing to the cost of the establishment, and the good services or particular merit of any single individual in any one of these languishing stations could not affect their general decision. With regard to Penang they were specially disappointed, not only in the result, but in the promises they alleged they had received from the Home Government when despatching the new establishment in 1805. They accordingly ordered in 1809 the reduction of the establishment there, because "the Ministers of the Crown had not fulfilled their intention of making the island an important naval station where an arsenal and docks should be constructed to render it commodious for the resort and repair of British ships of war and other ships employed in the Eastern seas, and also for building ships both for the Royal Navy and for the purposes of commerce."

The reader must not suppose that the attention of the little colony at Prince of Wales's Island was entirely engrossed in official work and the serious task of keeping down the expenses of the establishment to the lowest point, under the fear of the displeasure and more unpleasant measures of the august assembly in Leadenhall Street. Captain Travers, a prominent member of the staff in Java, whose acquaintance with Sir Stamford Raffles began in 1806, has left on record in his journal the following account of his chief's mode of life and popularity at this early period. "It is due to Mr. Raffles to state that he was respected and consulted by every member of it (the Government). In his official capacity he gave most general satisfaction, whilst the settlers looked up to him for assistance and advice in every difficulty; and when he afterwards became chief secretary the most general satisfaction was evinced throughout the Settlement. Being of a cheerful, lively disposition, and very fond of society, it was surprising how he was able to entertain so hospitably as he did and yet labour so much as he was known to do at the time, not only in his official capacity, but in acquiring a general knowledge of the history, government, and local interests of the neighbouring states, and this he was greatly aided in doing by conversing freely with the natives who were constantly visiting Penang at this period, many of whom were often found to be sensible, intelligent men, and greatly pleased to find a person holding Mr Raffles's situation able and anxious to converse with them in their own language."

There is some detailed information procurable from the contemporary records as to Raffles's hospitality. In the local paper there is an account of "the elegant dinner given by Mr. Raffles" on the occasion of the King's Birthday,—4th June 1807,—which was followed by "a subscription assembly at the Navy House, attended by all the beauty and fashion of the island." In the following account of a ball that took place in November 1807, the reporter of *The Prince of Wales's Island Gazette* gives us a glimpse of Mrs. Raffles. It would be a pity to curtail the description in any way.

"THE BEAU MONDE.

"We have the pleasure to congratulate our numerous readers upon the happy return of the gaieties of Penang.

"On Thursday, being Lord Mayor's Day, Mr. Robinson entertained a select party of friends to dinner at his mansion on the north beach. In the evening a most elegant *fête* was given by Messrs. Clubley and Phipps. It is impossible for us to convey any idea of the style and manner in which everything was concluded.

"The Honourable the Governor, together with the whole of the beauty and fashion of the island, assembled at an early hour.

"The ball commenced between eight and nine. Mr. Clubley had the honour of leading Mrs. Raffles down the first dance to the tune of "Off she goes."

"The supper rooms were thrown open precisely at twelve o'clock. The tables were covered with every delicacy that India can produce. The wines were of the most delicious quality; and that nothing might be wanting to render gratification perfect, several ladies and gentlemen entertained the company with songs, displaying on the one part the utmost delicacy of taste, and on the other true original comicality.

"Dancing recommenced with increased life immediately after supper, and continued until an early hour in the morning, when the party separated with every appearance of regret,

> "'That time should steal the night away
> And all their pleasures too—
> That they no longer there could stay,
> And all their joys renew.'

"In addition to the musicians of the island, Captain Harris was so good as to allow his band to attend. They played several pieces in a very superior style. One of the performers danced a hornpipe *à la tamborina*, which bore strong marks of his being a perfect adept in the art, and called forth loud and reiterated bursts of applause from his fair beholders."

Reference was made in the last chapter to Raffles's affection for his mother and the warmth of his family feeling. He had taken out with him to Penang his eldest sister, Mary Anne Raffles, and before he had been there many months he had the pleasure of seeing her well married from his own house to Mr. Quintin Dick Thompson, a gentleman holding the post of Sub-Warehouseman and Deputy-Paymaster on the island, at a salary of £1500 a year. Mr. Thompson died quite suddenly on 29th June 1809, leaving three children, one of whom, Charlotte Raffles Drury,—her godfathers being Raffles and Admiral Drury,—married long afterwards the fourth Earl of Castle Stuart. Raffles refers in his letter, on the subject of the claim made against him for the extra pay, to his sister and her family as having become dependent on him, but this charge did not remain on him very long, for Mrs. Thompson was married again in 1811, at Malacca, to Captain Flint of the Royal Navy, then commanding H.M.S. *Teign-*

mouth. Before the death of Mr. Thompson, Raffles had incurred another responsibility. In his desire to benefit his family he had sent home for his two other sisters, and on 2nd March 1810 the Court sanctioned the departure of the Misses Harriet and Leonora Raffles to join their brother. It will thus be seen that at the very moment that the East India Company cut down his salary and threatened to enforce the return of the extra payment he had received, Raffles, out of the kindness of his heart, had taken on himself the responsibility for two of his sisters, and a great misfortune had thrown on him a third sister and her children.

In a wider circle than his own immediate family he showed the kindliness and sympathy of his disposition. With his cousin, Thomas Raffles, afterwards of Liverpool, he began immediately after his arrival at Penang a correspondence that throws fresh light on many passages in his career, and much of which is now published for the first time. They had been comrades together in London, and the first letter from Penang, in April 1806, shows that he had not forgotten his younger cousin, who was then prosecuting his studies for the Congregational ministry. The principal passages read as follows:—"The very heavy press of business here which falls almost entirely on my shoulders has prevented my writing you before; and even now the packet is closing, and I have several persons on business waiting in the hall. Believe me, you have no surer friend than myself, and no one will be more happy to hear of your success in the world. I hope you will frequently write, not short letters, for they are abominable from such a distance, but such as will take up a morning to peruse. You will no doubt think us all heathens and sinners here, and will give me some morality. This, you know, can easily fill a page or two, and for you who are young will be a pleasant exertion on a *frosty* morning. I entreat you make every kind remembrance in your power to your father, mother, and sister. Tell them I hope to *tiff*, or what you call *munch* or *lunch*, with them in about four or five years, and sooner if I have the good luck to be ill."

I may close this chapter with two further letters, one to

Mr. William Raffles, Sir Stamford's uncle, and father of the last-named correspondent, and the second again to the same son. They both deal more or less directly with the important question of Raffles's religious views. If he could scarcely be termed from them a theologian, or even a sound Churchman, they at least show him to have been a man of broad views and earnest in the desire to live up to a high standard of duty. Considering the narrowness of English life in his day, his views on the merit of the Mahomedan religion, and on its suitability to many of the races of the East, are quite remarkable.

"PENANG, 15*th January* 1807.

"To Mr. WM. RAFFLES.

"MY DEAR SIR,—I had the pleasure to receive a letter from you some months back, and beg leave to return you my sincere thanks for its contents. Be assured I shall ever be happy to hear from you. The accounts of your son Thomas are very satisfactory. By this time I imagine him firmly fixed in the pulpit, and expect shortly to hear of his continued success. I must confess to you that I should have been much better pleased if his inclination had turned towards the Church of England; but as he has taken that path which the light of the gospel pointed out to him as the best, he must ever be respected for the choice he has made. Tell him that I shall be very happy to receive letters from him, and that I look forward to receive much benefit and instruction from his correspondence. He need not be afraid of writing on religious topics, although he looks upon me as a heathen; it was the *cant* of Methodism that I detested, and that only. Wherever there is cant there must be hypocrisy. I respect the religious of every persuasion, and am sorry my experience draws from me a wish that Christians did as much justice to their Redeemer as Mahometans do to their Prophet.

"As I know that religious topics are those principally brought forward in the society which you have selected for yourself, it may be more entertaining to dwell upon them in this letter than any other. Of the Christian religion I fear there is more said than done, and therefore shall not add to the numerous useless and foolish remarks upon it. I ever considered it as the simplest religion on earth, and for that reason the best. But of the Mahometan religion, on the contrary, as much, if not more, is done than said. We are here surrounded with Mussulmen, and I find them very good men, and by far more attentive to the duties and observances of their religion than the generality of Christians—even *Methodists*. No religion on earth is so extensive, and though in many instances it has been extended by fire and sword, it has in equally many others found its way without such means. Their religion, which you know is called Islâm (faith), would, in its general principles, be very good if divested of its corruptions, superstitions, and ridiculous observances. The great doctrine of the Koran is the Unity of God—to restore which point was the main object of Mahomed's mission, and to be candid, I think Mahomed has done a great deal of good in the world. I amuse and instruct myself for hours together with the Mahometans here, who to a man all believe in the Scriptures. They believe Jesus Christ a prophet, and respect Him as such. Mahomed's mission does not invalidate our Saviour's. One has secured happiness to the Eastern and one to the Western world, and both deserve our veneration.

"I wish you would instruct Thomas to send me out a Hebrew grammar and dictionary, as well as a Greek dictionary. I am applying myself close to the Eastern languages, and must obtain a general knowledge of these ancient languages before I can finally decide on many points."

(Left unfinished in the original.)

"MALACCA, *15th September* 1808.

"DEAR THOMAS,—I have had much pleasure in perusing some of your poetical effusions inserted in the European magazine, and they appear to me to evince much genius. In my letters from home I have been informed of your favourable progress in the profession you have undertaken, and I beg you will accept my warmest wishes for your success. I believe I am a letter in your debt, but you should not stand upon such ceremonies. I am in general taken up with my important duties during the whole day, and when I take a few hours to myself I find my correspondents so numerous that I am often obliged to omit some. To add to this, I find many of my most particular letters have miscarried, and therefore I am obliged to submit to the drudgery of writing duplicates of all letters of consequence. By this time I imagine you must nearly have finished your studies at Homerton. I shall be happy to hear of your future prospects, and if it is ever in my power to assist you in any way, I need not repeat how happy I shall be to render you any service. I suppose you are calculating that by this time I am rolling in riches, a perfect Nabob, reviling religion, and glorying in immorality; in this, however, you will be mistaken. I am poorer than I was three months before I left England, and as to splendour or luxury, we have nothing of the kind in our little island. Some of the necessaries with very few of the comforts are alone afforded us. I must acknowledge that we cannot say much for our general appearance of religion. We have a clergyman, but no church, and though a very good man, like most others of the Church, too careless of the eternal interests of his flock. The Mahometans, and in short every sect on the island have a place of worship but the English Protestants. We have Romish missionaries, but none Protestants. Of course, religion may be said to be at a low ebb here. Men seem to look to their worldly interests only. I shall be happy to second any plan that can be adopted for making the gospel more generally known, and although I have some doubts of its good effects on particular classes of the natives of India, I think it might with others be easily introduced and attended with the happiest effects.—Yours very sincerely, THOS. RAFFLES.

"*P.S.*—To ensure your correspondence, I trouble you with a trifling commission. I will thank you to purchase and send out to me by the first fleet the following book, and shall be obliged by any observations you may make on it: *Hebrew Characters, or Elements of the Hebrew Language*, in 2 parts, etc. etc., by Hyman Hurwitz, Master of the Jewish Academy at Highgate. 8vo, price 5s. 6d. Mr. Taylor of Gray's Inn will reimburse you the expense."

CHAPTER III

MALACCA

IN spite of the diligence and attention with which Raffles performed his secretarial duties and prosecuted his Malay studies at Penang, the opportunity would never have come there for him to display any conspicuous merit as either an administrator or a scholar. The place was foredoomed to commercial and political insignificance, and but for the measures to the accomplishment of which Raffles devoted his life, a study and mastery of the Malay language would never have procured for him a reputation beyond the narrowest circles of Eastern pundits. That he was an admirable superintendent of an office, that his active mind rested satisfied with nothing short of a mastery of surrounding conditions for which a knowledge of the language and the locality was the indispensable preliminary, these were the signs that he was worthy of better things, but unless he had known how to " take occasion by the hand," and, still more than that, to turn the thoughts of statesmen and the policy of Government into the channel he had marked out for himself and his country as the true path of greatness, his ability and admirable qualities would never have formed the theme of a biographer. The turning-point in his career came in 1808, and it came, strangely enough, through illness.

The extent of his official and other duties, the thorough spirit of self-sacrifice in which he devoted himself to them, and the unhealthiness of the island—an unhealthiness which carried off three Governors and several members of Council in the first few years—all told on his health. He had never been robust. At last he completely broke down, and, as the only means of saving his life, he was ordered to take a sea-trip, and enjoy, however briefly, a change of scene. He decided on visiting the not far distant and older station of Malacca, which was at that moment of special interest to everyone connected with the Penang administration, because the orders to abandon it, originally issued in 1805, but temporarily suspended, had just been renewed by the Company in a more peremptory form. To an active intelligence such as Raffles possessed the prospect of a holiday without a motive or object seemed a depressing blank. He filled up the void by selecting as the goal of his journey Malacca, the ancient seat of Malay power and lore, the mart of trade whose vitality had surprised and embarrassed the very administration of which he was a humble member.

Malacca is a district about 25 miles in breadth, and stretching for a distance of some 40 miles along the south-western coast of the Malay Peninsula. The town of the same name is picturesquely placed; and as the voyager in 1808 approached it, he saw the buildings to whose varied architecture Malays and Portuguese, Dutch, English, and Chinese had all contributed, clustering beyond the shallow harbour, on the banks of a small river also called Malacca. The river separates the old Dutch town to the northward from the bazaars on its southern banks. South also of the river, Flagstaff Hill, ever brilliantly green, and girt with the massive, freshly-ruined walls of the fortress built by Albuquerque, bears on its higher slopes a spot consecrated through the labours of S. Francis Xavier in the 16th century as the site of the first Christian Church ever reared on Malay territory. To the north stands S. John's Hill with its Dutch redoubt; while as a background to the town are masses of fair and thickly clustering fruit trees, which almost bury beneath their dense foliage the native quarter. Behind, again, rises the rich verdure of another hill; and beyond, lining the lowlands to the eastward like a wall, stretches a blue mountain range, from which Mount Ophir in the farthest distance uplifts its "jagged cone," "blue as a sapphire," to the height of well-nigh 4000 ft. The country round the town is "flat and jungly." Dense and far-spreading masses of fruit trees and tall timber in its nearer neighbourhood are succeeded at last by an "open country," where fields of rice and tapioca, marsh and fen, reach away to thickets of "virgin forest" underneath the eastern hills. Although the town of Malacca lies some 300 miles down the Straits, to the southward of Penang, its climate is said to be very healthy, and cooler by several degrees than that of its northern neighbour.

Malacca only came into the hands of the English in 1795, when it was captured from the Dutch by a small force under Major Brown and Captain Newcome. As the possession of a European State its history went back as far as 1511, in which year the Portuguese took the place from the Malays and built a fort there. They, in turn, lost it to the Dutch in 1641, and then, in the year named, it passed into our hands. With the exception of the brief period 1818–24, during which it was restored to the Dutch, it has remained under the British flag ever since. But when the East India Company decided to make Penang a place of increased importance, it was also arranged that Malacca should be abandoned, and that the staff, stores, and population should be removed to the former place. Orders were sent out in 1805 to demolish the fort, and the intention of the Penang authorities was "to gradually transfer to Prince of Wales's Island the trade and capital of Malacca, together with the most valuable part of the population." The Commandant, Captain William Farquhar, protested, as has been stated, but, none the less, he was compelled to obey his orders to the extent of razing the old fort, on which task a sum of three or four thousand pounds was expended in the course of the year 1807, when final peremptory orders were issued for "the destruction of Malacca." In August of that year Farquhar sent a petition against the measures in progress from the principal European and native inhabitants, and he supported this petition with his own opinion; but he did not dare to ignore his instructions as to the works of the fort, which he "levelled so as to render them of the least possible use to any European Power hereafter in possession of that Settlement." It was well for him that he did not disobey, for the Board sharply censured him for even sending in the petition; and this letter was signed by Raffles, who was destined himself the very next year to save Malacca from impending destruction. It was the irony of fate!

Such was the place to which, in 1808, Raffles proceeded in search of health. He was accompanied by his wife. As soon as he had somewhat recovered, he applied himself to the investigation of the history, resources, and present condition of the doomed Settlement, and he speedily formed the conclusion that Malacca was a possession that should not be abandoned, and that the policy pursued towards it was a mistaken one. He also devoted much of his time to personal inquiries among the Malays who consorted there. He took into his employment several Malay scholars as readers and translators. His intercourse with them was of a very cordial character, and his courtesy and consideration made a deep impression on their sensitive natures. Evidence of this was afforded by the case of the young man Abdulla bin Abdulkada, son of Marsden's old tutor. Abdulla's uncle was Raffles's chief interpreter at Malacca, while he himself assisted in the office. Abdulla's reminiscences were published in London in 1874, under the title of *Hakayit Abdulla*, and they give a curiously interesting picture, from a native point of view, both of the situation during the whole of this period in the Malay Peninsula, and of Raffles's work there. Indirectly there is much to support the statement made by one of his English staff at a later date that "Raffles undoubtedly had the faculty of attaching his subordinates closely to him." Before passing on, the following description of Raffles and his wife at this time, drawn up by this young Malay of Arab descent who watched them very closely, will not be out of place, and will serve to bring out not merely the individuality of each, but the harmony with which they worked together, thus affording another unsought-for tribute to the merit and the charm of Olivia Raffles.

"When I first saw Mr. Raffles he struck me as being of middle stature, neither too short nor too tall. His brow was broad, the sign of large-heartedness; his head betokened his good understanding; his hair being fair, betokened courage; his ears being large, betokened quick hearing; his eyebrows were thick, and his left eye squinted a little; his nose was high; his cheeks a little hollow; his lips narrow, the sign of oratory and persuasiveness; his mouth was wide; his neck was long; and the colour of his body was not purely white; his breast was well formed; his waist slender; his legs to proportion, and he walked with a slight stoop. I observed his habit was to be always in deep thought. He was most courteous in his intercourse with all men. He always had a sweet expression towards European as well as native gentlemen. He was extremely affable and liberal, always commanding one's best attention. He spoke in smiles."

Abdulla's account of Mrs. Raffles reads as follows:—

"Then as to his wife, she was not an ordinary woman, but was in every respect co-equal with her husband's position and responsibilities; bearing herself with propriety, politeness, and good grace. She was very fond of studying the Malay language, saying, What is this in Malay? and what that? Also whatever she saw she wrote down, and, whatever her husband intended to undertake, or when buying anything, he always deferred to her. Thus, if it pleased his wife, it pleased him. Further, her alacrity in all work was apparent; indeed she never rested for a moment, but she was always busy day after day. In this diligence which I observed there is a very great distinction between the habits of the natives (of Malayan countries) and the white people. For it is the custom of the Malayan women on their becoming the wives of great people to increase their arrogance, laziness, and habitual procrastination. . . . But to look at Mrs. Raffles, her hands and feet were in continual motion like chopping one bit after another. Then there was sewing, which was succeeded by writing, for it is a real truth that I never saw her sleep at mid-day, or even reclining for the sake of ease, but always at work with diligence, as day follows day. This the Almighty knows also. And if I am not wrong in the conclusion that I have arrived at, these are the signs of good sense and understanding, which qualify for the undertaking of great deeds. Thus her habits were active, so much so, that in fact she did the duty of her husband; indeed, it was she that taught him. Thus God had matched them as king and counsellor, or as a ring with its jewels."

Brief as was the holiday Raffles proposed to take, and serious as was the illness which obliged him to seek a change at all, he was not allowed to complete the leave accorded him. The Penang Government could not get on without him, and found it impossible to draft their correspondence for England in his absence. The Governor, Colonel Macalister, wrote him an urgent letter, and sent him a special ship, in the "hope you will find yourself well enough to come back to us" in it. The writer goes on to say, "It is distressing to me, my dear sir, to be under the necessity of stating in this pointed manner the unavoidable exigence of the case, but such is the case that we shall not be able to make up any despatches for the Court without your assistance. This is truly hard upon you under the present circumstances of your delicate state of health, but I trust you will believe that nothing else would induce me to press so hard upon you at this time." Raffles had anticipated his chief's wish, for hearing that the China ships would arrive sooner than was expected, and realising the dilemma of the Board at Penang without its Secretary, he embarked on a country boat,—Captain Travers states that it was "a pleasure boat, formerly the long-boat of an Indiaman,"—and reached Prince of Wales's Island, much to the relief of his superiors. Immediately after his return he drew up his report on Malacca, which was sent under cover of the following despatch to the Governor-General, as well as with an equally complimentary letter to the Court in London:—

"MY LORD,—The fortifications at Malacca having been destroyed under the Orders received from the Supreme Government, it is our intention at an early opportunity to address your Lordship in Council upon the subject, and to request your further instructions respecting that Settlement.

"The reference made by this Government, with the final Orders of the Honourable Court of Directors, are before your Lordship on our Proceedings, from which you will have perceived the difficulties apprehended in withdrawing the garrison, and I have now the honour to transmit for your Lordship's information a clear and comprehensive report from the hands of our Secretary, Mr. Raffles, explanatory of the present circumstances of the Settlement of Malacca, drawn up there, and the dangers that must inevitably result in the full execution of the Honourable Court's Orders, relative to the final abandonment of that Settlement by the English. Every information that I have otherwise collected during a long residence in this quarter, confirms the observations in this report, and I am fully convinced of the policy, if not necessity, of continuing an establishment there, the charges of which may be fully provided for by the revenues of the place.

"In the Orders issued by the Court of Directors for the removal of the garrison, and the final abandonment of the Settlement, it appears that considerable weight must have been given to the representation made by Mr. Farquhar, the late Lieutenant-Governor, of the facility with which the inhabitants might be removed and remunerated for the loss they would sustain in their fixed and immovable property.

"From the most correct information procurable, I can take upon myself to say that if double the sum estimated by Mr. Farquhar were disbursed on this account, the inhabitants would be far from considering themselves adequately remunerated for their losses.

"Admitting, however, that the sum of 300,000 dollars were disbursed, and that this sum proves adequate for the purpose, Malacca, on the garrison being withdrawn, must be possessed by some native Power, who would not long be able to support his authority there without occasional assistance from us, equally expensive perhaps with the charges incurred on account of the present establishment.

"Were Malacca in the hands of a native prince, however respectable, the check that has hitherto existed there to the alarming depredations of the Eastern pirates, would not only be lost, but fleets of piratical vessels would be fitted out even from its shores, whose lawless attacks upon the regular trader, the enterprise of our cruisers would find it difficult to keep under ; and in the event of that Settlement ever falling into the hands of a foreign European Power, it would not only from its facilities in trade, [and] command [within] the Straits, destroy the best interests of this island, but materially endanger the China and Eastern trade as now carried on from Bengal.

"The inhabitants seem perfectly satisfied with the security afforded by the present garrison, and as the civil disbursements there are chiefly confined to members and officers of the College of Justice, and others, who may be considered in the light of prisoners, it is fair to calculate that further reductions therein will be gradually made, while the revenues may be expected to increase on its being understood that the Settlement is to remain under the protection of the British flag.

"As, however, the consideration of the subject will thoroughly come before our Board, with the view of forwarding to your Lordship such suggestions as may be expected from our local observation, I shall not now press further on your Lordship, referring you, in the meantime, to the accompanying report and the papers already before your Lordship."

"To the Honourable the Governor and Council.

"Honourable Sirs,—Having lately had an opportunity of noticing the destruction of the works at Malacca as well as the general effect of the measures taken towards reducing and eventually abandoning that Settlement, I have been led to pay particular attention to the subject, and being impresssed with a conviction that the future prosperity of Prince of Wales's Island is materially involved in the impending fate of Malacca, I feel it a duty incumbent on me respectfully to submit to your Honourable Board the result of my observations.

"The fortifications may be considered as completely demolished, the convicts being principally employed in removing the ruins, but the storehouses and some of the public buildings, such as the Government House, church, gaol, etc., still remain entire, in consequence, I believe, of a wish expressed on the part of His Excellency Sir Edward Pellew, and of the recommendation of the Honourable the Governor. As, however, the destruction of the latter must, under the Commandant's present instructions, be almost immediately proceeded on, and the last appearance of a respectable Government annihilated, I am induced to hope that a faithful report at this time of the actual state of Malacca and the dangers to be apprehended in eventually withdrawing the garrison, will be acceptable to your Honourable Board.

"On the political expediency of destroying the permanent fortifications it does not become me to remark. My observations are intended wholly to apply to the Settlement as it at present stand[s].

"The object of the measures taken with regard to Malacca, appears to have been twofold—to discourage, by the destruction of the works, any European

Power from setting a value on the place or turning it to account in the event of its falling into their hands ; and to have improved the Settlement at Prince of Wales's Island by the transfer of its population and trade. These objects were, undoubtedly, highly desirable and of great political importance. The former, perhaps, may, in some degree, have been effected by the destruction of the works and removal of the ordnance and stores to Penang; but with respect to the latter much remains to be done.

"Very incorrect information appears to have been received by the Honourable Court of Directors respecting the trade and advantages of the Settlement of Malacca. It has by them been considered as a place possessing no natural advantages in product or trade, and involving great expense without corresponding benefit, either in its revenues or commerce. Under such a representation it is not surprising that the destruction and abandonment of Malacca should have been determined on, the more particularly as it was stated, from personal knowledge, that the population and trade of the place might with ease be removed to Penang, a Settlement likely to unite every advantage desired by the British Government.

"The inaccuracy of the above statement will, I doubt not, fully appear in the course of this paper.

"The inhabitants resident within the territory of Malacca are estimated at 20,000 souls, of which the majority reside in the town and its neighbourhood. They consist chiefly of Europeans (few in number and mostly Dutch), the descendants of such (principally half-castes) born in the place, Chinese and their descendants by Malay women, Malays, Portuguese, Arabs, Javanese, and Chuliahs [Chuliahs, men of the Kaling country].

"More than three-fourths of the above population were born in Malacca, where their families have been settled for centuries. The Chinese appear to have emigrated to this place at a very early period, as is evident from the remarks of Albuquerque, when it fell into the hands of the Portuguese in 1511, and the antiquity and extent of their tombs and burial-places, which occupy the base of the different hills in the neighbourhood.

"The Malays, a class of people not generally valued as subjects, are here industrious and useful members of society ; attached to the place from their birth, they are accustomed to the local regulations ; and in the bosom of their family feel that they are at home. Their peculiarities are attended to, their rank respected, and their necessities easily supplied.

"Independent of the fixed population above mentioned, there is a continual resort of native traders from the eastward and the countries in the vicinity, Malacca being the centre of the native commerce within the Straits.

"From the antiquity and former celebrity of the place it follows that the country is well cultivated, and that valuable buildings, public and private, have been erected by the inhabitants ; to which they must be attached, as well on account of their comforts as of their more absolute necessities. The prejudices of the natives are too well known to require comment here ; and it is no common advantage that will induce them to quit the tombs of their ancestors, their temples sacred to the Deity, their independence, and estates on which they depend for their livelihood aud respectability.

"The inhabitants of Malacca are very different from what they appear to have been considered. Three-fourths of the native population of Prince of Wales's Island might, with little encouragement, be induced to remove, having no fixed or permanent property ; adventurers, ready to turn their hands to any

5

employment. But the case is very different with the native inhabitants of Malacca. Those answering the above description appear to have removed long ago, in consequence of the measures taken by the Government of Prince of Wales's Island. The inhabitants that remain are mostly proprietors of property or connected with those that are; and those possessing independence from their gardens, fishing, and the small traffic of the place. The more respectable, and majority, accustomed to respect and independence from their childhood, would ill brook the difficulties of establishing themselves at a new settlement. They are not men that can easily be converted into artificers or artisans. The few of these now resident at Malacca obtain an easy livelihood in supplying the comforts of their superiors.

"The present population must therefore be considered as attached to the soil; and, from every appearance, it seems they have determined to remain by Malacca, let its fate be what it will. Into whatever hands it falls it cannot be much more reduced than at present, and they have a hope that any change must be for the better. The offer made by Government of paying the passage of such as would embark for Penang was not accepted by a single individual.

"Malacca, although it has ever been discouraged in raising its own supplies, produces sufficient rice for six months' consumption, and, from the constant resort of prows from Java and its vicinity (commanded by Arabs or other neutrals), has never required any supply from Bengal till very lately, when, in consequence of the expected abandonment of the settlement, and the conduct of some of our vessels to the Eastward, some trifling assistance has occasionally been required from Bengal.

"During a scarcity of rice, sago—always cheap, and received in the greatest quantities from the opposite coast of Siak—may always be substituted. The country abounds in cattle, poultry, etc., which, notwithstanding the constant supplies to His Majesty's and other ships passing up and down the Straits, are always in plenty, and at the same price.

"The coast abounds with the finest fish,—salted fish and fish roes, first imported from Siak, form an extensive export. Of the soil, and its produce in sugar, fruits, etc. etc., it is unnecessary to make any observations; its superiority being universally admitted.

"Thus situated, the population of Malacca is, in a great degree, independent; and when it is considered that no corresponding benefit can be offered to them at Penang, it cannot be expected that they will remove. Admitting even that they are indemnified for the loss of their fixed property, they would feel but little inclination to adventure at Penang, where they must either purchase land and houses from others, or undertake the clearing of an unhealthy jungle.

"The natives consider the British faith as pledged for their protection. When the settlement fell into the hands of the English, they were invited to remain; protection and even encouragement were offered them. The latter has long ago ceased; and they are in daily expectation of losing the former. For our protection they are willing to make great sacrifices; and they pay the heavy duties imposed on them, with the cheerfulness of faithful and obedient subjects. The revenues of Malacca are never in arrear.

"With respect to the European inhabitants, it appears admitted that they should, in some measure, be indemnified for the loss of their property on the garrison being withdrawn. The estimate that has been formed of the fixed and immovable property of individuals, amounts to the sum of dollars

300,000 (at 5s. a dollar, £75,000), a principal part of which, it appears, must be paid before Penang can reap the expected advantage from the destruction of Malacca. No doubt many deductions might be made from the above estimate: and, by a liberal policy in the commencement, the few might follow the majority obtained by such means; but I am apprehensive that it would be neither fair nor honourable to indemnify one, and not the whole. Prince of Wales's Island would, of course, derive the benefit of an increase of population by these means, as the indemnifications would only be granted conditionally on their removal, and that condition strictly enforced; but whether so great an outlay of the public money can, for attaining such an object, at the present time be authorised, is, perhaps, very doubtful; and, admitting it were granted, and the population actually removed, what check could be placed over emigration? Malacca, the abode of their fathers and of the ancestors of their fathers, would alone be considered as their home.

"The trade of Malacca is now principally carried on with the Bugguese and Javanese (neutrals), with Rhio, Lingin, and the ports in the immediate neighbourhood; the Indian and China trade having, with the exception of the resort of a few merchants from the coast and Surat, been annihilated by the superior advantages afforded at Penang in duties, etc.

"The Bugguese or Eastern trade, which now forms so important and valuable a branch of the commerce of Penang, appears originally to have entered at Malacca; but on an attentive observation of the share now enjoyed by it, it will be found that Penang cannot expect much further advantages, or that its remaining trade can be forced further up the Straits, whatever may be the fate of Malacca.

"The Bugguese prows are from Macassar, Passeir, Banjarmassin, but mostly from Bally, Mandar, Sambava, etc., which ports they leave at the commencement of the south-west monsoon, and arrive in the Straits in the month of July, increasing in number during August, September, and October, and declining with the year. Having touched on the coasts of Borneo and Java on their way, their cargoes generally consist of Bugguese sarangs, mats, and birds' nests; from their own country inferior spices, and diamonds clandestinely procured from the Dutch, gold dust, and dollars; and from the ports at which they touch occasionally, of rice, tobacco, oil, etc. In return they take away opium and cloths, mostly coarse Indian. Of these prows the whole touch at Malacca, but the rich and well-equipped proceed on to Penang for the advantage of obtaining opium at a better rate than the duties at Malacca will admit of. These endeavour to arrive early in the season to avoid the north-west winds that often set in in September, but are always uncertain; they are often driven back after leaving Malacca for Penang by the north-west winds setting in earlier than expected, and are in consequence forced to end their adventure at Malacca. The best equipped of their prows can only sail before the wind, and the voyages of the whole must be made with the favourable monsoons. The smaller Bugguese prows and other[s] arriving late in the season, and those badly equipped, find it impossible to weather the north-west winds, and, of necessity, stop at Malacca. Of these there are many, but they are not so rich as those which proceed to Penang; they mostly bring sarangs, in constant demand by the Malays at Malacca and its neighbourhood, and of which only a certain quantity will obtain a favourable sale at Penang. The superior advantage in the sale of this article at Malacca and its neighbourhood, added to the quicker return they make to the Eastward, counterbalances, in some degree, the advantage of the lower duties at Penang, by enabling them to anticipate the return to the Eastward of their greater rivals who had extended their voyage; the prows first returning enjoying the readiest and most profitable sale. They time their voyages so well as generally to avoid adverse winds, except in the Straits; in which, from the uncertainty of the seasons, they can never be depended on. The delay in proceeding on to Penang frequently lengthens their voyage for months, and always for many weeks, an object of the first importance to these traders, sailing but with the fair monsoon, and obliged to perform their voyages periodically.

"Besides those denominated Bugguese prows, there are also a few with birds' nests, camphor, pepper, and sago from Borneo proper, one with pepper from Tringano, and one or two from Pahan with gold dust for opium.

"From the nature of this trade it is apparent that, if the duties of Malacca were lowered to the standard of Penang, very few prows would proceed further up the Straits; and that the portion now stopping at Malacca is not of a description to be forced further on, but on being driven out of Malacca, if it is possible to do so by still heavier duties, would either cease altogether, or attain its object at a less advantage, at the native port of Rhio, or of the Dutch at Java.

"The average exports of opium at Malacca by means of this trade may now be estimated at from one hundred to one hundred and fifty chests per annum. This is obtained, in the first instance, either by commission from Bengal, or by purchase from Bengal ships returning from an unsuccessful voyage to the Eastward. The Sultan of Rhio has lately been more settled in his Government, and may in like manner obtain opium from returning ships; while the Dutch Government at Batavia, notwithstanding every effort on our part, appear to obtain supplies by neutrals and others. It is stated that last year, from captures taken by these and other means, they obtained opium at the rate of from seven hundred to eight hundred dollars per chest; but, as they hold the monopoly of this article in their own hands, they, of course, sell it at a very different price.

"The great object in fixing the commerce of Prince of Wales's Island, is to establish it as an entrepôt between Eastern and Western India; and if the regulations and interests of the Bengal Government would have admitted of it, perhaps it might have been of the greatest advantage for the Company to have imported into Penang a quantity of opium on their own account, or, indeed, to have held the monopoly of it themselves, thereby forcing the Eastern prows to come up to Penang for the whole of their supplies of this article. Great delicacy is requisite in keeping the duties at Penang (and, perhaps, at Malacca, for the smaller prows) sufficiently low to prevent the merchants in Bengal from fitting out vessels direct for the Eastward. It should be more to their interest to be satisfied in leaving it at Penang; and the uncertainty and length of an Eastern voyage will always induce them to put up with less profit there. This trade from Bengal (which is now occasionally carried on) not only deprives Penang of its advantages as an entrepôt, but, in many instances, from overstocking the market to the Eastward at different seasons of the year, deprives the Bugguese prows on their return from Penang of that advantage they calculated upon; and finding themselves thus anticipated in the Eastern market, some are ruined, while others are discouraged in further voyages, trusting to future supplies being in the same way received from Bengal ships, which can always afford to undersell them.

"The Javanese trade is carried on by Java prows (commanded by Arabs, Malays, or Chinese, as neutrals), bringing rice, sugar, arrack, coffee, spices (cloves), and a little tin which they pick up on their way. They take in return Pulicat[1] and Nagore cloths, gambier,[2] salted fish and fish roes, putchuk,[3] tutenague (when it is to be procured), a few Surat piece goods, etc.

"This trade may be said properly to belong to Malacca, and were it driven out from thence, is not likely to find its way to Penang. The vessels are, in general, but badly equipped, and not calculated for a voyage up the Straits. The ancient connection subsisting between Java and Malacca gave rise to it, and, with the decline of the latter, it has gradually decreased. The great supply of rice is obtained by means of this trade, and Malacca can always command through this channel the quantity it may require. The uncertain footing on which Malacca is at present held discourages the prows from coming until they ascertain what is to be done, now the works are demolished ; but it will rapidly resume its former extent as soon as it may be settled and understood that the garrison is not to be withdrawn.

"Next to this trade may be ranked that from Rhio, Lingin, Palembang, and the countries in the more immediate neighbourhood of Malacca.

The Palembang and Lingin vessels import about 1500 peculs[4] of tin annually, which, with what is brought from other quarters, may be estimated at from 2000 to 3000 peculs annually. Rumbo,[5] a Malay country in the interior of the Peninsula at the back of Malacca, formerly, under a contract with the Dutch Government, supplied of itself 2000 peculs, but now only sends about 400 peculs annually, and this is obtained at some risk by advances. The remainder might, perhaps, be obtained in the same way, but, at present, seems to take its course down the Pahan River on the other side of the Peninsula, from whence it is transported in small prows to Rhio, etc. etc.

"The interior produce of the Malacca territory in pepper is but trifling, having ever been discouraged, but considerable quantities are constantly imported from Rhio, where it is produced in great abundance.

"A considerable trade was formerly carried on with Siak on the East coast of Sumatra, nearly opposite Malacca. At this place the Dutch once had a

---

[1] "Pulicat, a town on the Madras coast which was long the seat of an important Dutch factory."—*A Glossary of Anglo-Indian Words*. Yule & Burnell.

[2] "*Gambier*, the extract of a climbing shrub which is a native of the regions about the Straits of Malacca, and is much grown in plantations in Singapore and the neighbouring islands. The substance in chemical composition and qualities strongly resembles *cutch*." It is used in mastication with the betel-nut. Cutch is "an astringent extract from the wood of several species of acacia."—*Glossary of Anglo-Indian Words*. Yule & Burnell.

[3] "*Putchock*. This is the trade name for a fragrant root, a product of the Himālaya in the vicinity of Kashmir, and forming an article of export from both Bombay and Calcutta to the Malay countries and to China, where it is used as a chief ingredient in the Chinese pastille-rods, commonly called jostick."

[4] *Pecul, Pikol*, "a man's load" (Malay and Javanese) = $133\frac{1}{3}$ lbs. avoirdupois. *Glossary, etc.* Yule & Burnell.

[5] *Rumbo* = "Rumbowe (correctly Râmbau)," in Crawfurd's *Descriptive Dictionary of the Indian Islands, etc.*

factory and derived advantages ; but for many years this trade has been on the decline owing to our settlements on the West coast,[1] and the subsequent usurpation of the government by the present Rajah ; and it is now almost annihilated.

"The traders from the populous countries in the interior of Sumatra have turned their course to the other side ; but, in the event of the English settlements there being reduced, there seems no doubt but it might with ease be again brought into its original channel by an enterprising Government at Malacca. The trade from Malacca to Siak formerly consisted of raw silk, coast and other cloths, and opium, in return for which was received gold, wax, sago, salted fish and fish roes, elephants' teeth, gambier, hogslard, camphor, rattans,[2] etc. The Dutch Company were also in the habit of sending annually from Siak to Java several rafts of spars for masts ; and we have lately had an opportunity of knowing its capability in the produce of frame timbers for shipbuilding.[3]

"The Dutch had also a factory at Jamby[4] on the same coast, and kept up a similar intercourse ; but at present the trade with Malacca is very trifling. The returns are nearly the same as from Siak, with the addition of coarse benjamin[5] and dragon's blood. The smaller ports to the northward of Siak, as far as Assahan[6] and Batta Bara,[7] still send their small produce in rattans, wax, and rice, mostly to Malacca.

"The only Indian trade now carried on with Malacca is by a few Pulicat merchants freighting annually on the Indiaman from eighty to one hundred and fifty bales of cloth to the value of 80,000 to 140,000 dollars ; by three or

---

[1] The British Settlements at this time (1808) on the West coast of Sumatra were Bencoolen (Fort Marlborough) and its dependencies, including Padang, the island of Little Ponchong in the bay of Tapanuly, etc. Bencoolen was occupied by the British from 1685 till 1825. The second fort, constructed in 1714, was built a mile and a half from the river, and called Fort Marlborough. The abandoned fort had been on the banks of the river.—CRAWFURD.

[2] "Rattan : the long stem of various species of Asiatic climbing palms . . . of which canes are made, . . . and which, when split, are used to form the seats of cane-bottomed chairs and the like. . . . Some of these attain a length of several hundred feet, and are used in the Himalāya and Kāsia Hills for making suspension-bridges, etc., rivalling rope in strength."—*Glossary, etc.* Yule & Burnell.

[3] The Government of Prince of Wales's Island were, at this time, making efforts to prove practically that great facilities for shipbuilding existed at their Presidency.—*Records, Straits Settlements, passim.*

[4] Jamby : "Jambi is the name of a Malay State on the north-eastern side of Sumatra."—CRAWFURD.

[5] "Benjamin, Benzoin, etc. : a kind of incense derived from the resin of the *Styrax benzoin*, Dryander, in Sumatra. . . . It got from the Arab traders the name of lubān-Jāwī, *i.e.* 'Java Frankincense,' corrupted in the Middle Ages into such forms as we give." "The terms Jāwā, Jāwī, were applied by the Arabs to the Malay countries generally (especially Sumatra), and their products." —*Glossary, etc.* Yule & Burnell.

[6] *Assahan* : "Asahan, . . . the name of a river and Malay State on the north-eastern side of Sumatra."—CRAWFURD.

[7] *Batta Bara* : "Batubara. A river and district of the eastern side of Sumatra, subject to the Malay State of Siak."—CRAWFURD.

four Chuliah vessels, every monsoon bringing coarse cloths (blue), coir[1] and seeds, etc., for the native bazaar ; and by a few Surat merchants, passengers on the Bombay and China ships, and two annual native vessels from Surat, touching on their way to Siam and other ports, bringing silks and chintzes.

"Of the above trade almost the whole first goes to Penang, but the articles, being exclusively adapted for the Malacca market, or that of Penang being, perhaps, overstocked, cannot find a sale there. The finer, or Pulicat cloths, are taken away from Malacca in Javanese prows, as well as part of the coarse, and the silks and chintzes generally by the Eastern prows. Three or four Siamese junks arrive at Malacca in the course of the year, coming round the Peninsula, bringing rice, salt, salt fish, sticklack,[2] sappan-wood,[3] etc., and take cloths, opium, etc. ; and, until the last three years, a large annual junk came from China, bringing raw silk, coarse China ware, paper, tobacco, and supplies of various kinds required by the inhabitants of Malacca and the neighbouring States. On the arrival of the vessel the native prows from the adjacent States crowded to Malacca, and, each bringing the produce of its country, were of some importance to the trade of the place. The junk, on its return, carried away tin, fish roes, beche-de-mer, rattans, birds' nests, camphor, etc., to a great amount ; the savings of the Chinese inhabitants of Malacca and the neighbouring countries invested in the above articles ; and such of the Chinese as were desirous of returning to Macao. The savings of the Chinese inhabitants are also sent on in pepper and similar articles by the Macao Portuguese ships.

"The surplus arrack, sugar, etc., imported in the Javanese prows, is generally sent on to Penang, as opportunities offer ; and, in addition to the trade carried on by the means of native vessels, as above mentioned, there are a few brigs and other small craft belonging to the inhabitants of Malacca, but mostly navigated by natives.

"I have deemed it necessary to be thus particular respecting the trade of Malacca, as it does not appear to be generally understood ; and the nature of the population and trade being made known, I feel confident that I shall not stand alone in the opinion that Penang cannot expect much more of either than it already possesses ; and, with regard to the latter, that it is now a trade almost exclusively belonging to Malacca from its natural advantages.

"Thus far it has been my object to explain the difficulties that will arise in transferring the present population and trade. It is now necessary to view the subject as to the dangerous consequences likely to ensue to Penang in the event of the garrison being withdrawn.

---

[1] "Coir : the fibre of the cocoa-nut husk, from which rope is made."—*Glossary*. Yule & Burnell.

[2] *Sticklack* : "1727. It (the Siam coast) produces good store of Sapan and Agala woods, with Gumlack and Sticklack, and many drugs that I know little about."—Captain Alexander Hamilton, *A New Account of the East Indies.* Edinburgh, 1727 ; London, 1744. (Quoted in the article on Sappan-wood, *Glossary, etc.* Yule & Burnell.)

[3] "Sappan-wood . . . the tree appears to be indigenous in Malabar, the Deccan, and the Malay Peninsula." Sappan-wood is a red dye-wood, formerly called brazil-wood. Since the discovery of the same dye-wood in South America, in Brazil, the name brazil-wood has only been given to the South American product.—*Glossary, etc.* Yule & Burnell.

"Malacca, having been in the possession of a European Power for three centuries, and even previously to that period considered as the capital of the Malay States, has obtained so great an importance in the eyes of the native princes, that they are ever anxious to obtain the friendship of the nation in whose hands it may be. Its name carries more weight to a Malay ear than any new settlement, whatever its importance. This pre-eminence ensures constant respect from the traders to and from the neighbouring ports: at least it has done so till very lately; and by this means affords a considerable check to piracy. Were Malacca in the hands of a native prince, however respectable, or supported by us, this check would not only be lost, but fleets of piratical vessels and prows would be fitted out, even from its shores, whose depredations the enterprise of our cruisers would find it difficult to keep under.

"From the trade of Rhio,—since it was given up to Sultaun Mahomed in 1795, to be attributed to the exactions being less there than at Malacca,—and the advantages which Rhio seems likely to derive, now that its government is more settled and the conduct of the Rajah more steady, it is but fair to infer that Malacca, in the hands of a native prince, would, with its superior population and extent of resources, adopt a similar conduct, and obtain an equal, and in all probability a far superior advantage. It would still afford its usual facilities and accommodations to traders, and there is but too much reason to believe that Penang would be deprived of that great advantage she has hitherto derived in the Eastern trade.

"But, to look at the subject in a more serious point of view still,—for I am far from thinking it would ever remain in the hands of a native Power,—although the permanent fortifications and public works of every description may be effectually destroyed, the possession of Malacca will ever be a most desirable object to a European Power and to our enemy. Prince of Wales's Island, though advantageously situated for commanding the bay and the northern entrance of the Straits, has by no means the same advantage and command within the Straits that Malacca possesses. Every ship that passes up or down must be observed from the latter place, and should this station ever be held by an enterprising enemy, not only Penang, but our more important China trade, would be materially endangered. We have now the command. Why give it up, unless we are forced? and I trust we are not reduced to that extremity.

"Waiving the great advantages that might be derived from encouraging Malacca, or rather allowing it to have fair play, let the subject only be considered as it relates to the interests of Penang.

"It is well known that the Dutch Government had in contemplation to make Malacca a free port, with the view of destroying the English settlement at Penang. Should the place ever fall into their hands again, or into that of their now superior authority, which it no doubt will if evacuated by the English, a similar, or more active policy must be expected. This alone, independent of every other consideration, should, I think, be a sufficient inducement for the British Government to retain it in support of their settlement at Prince of Wales's Island. The Eastern trade, now so lucrative a source of commerce and revenue at Penang, would at once be destroyed, while passing vessels would never find it worth their while to submit to the delay of stopping at Penang. Trade must ever flourish most where the greatest advantages are afforded. Malacca has greater natural advantages than Penang, and these can only be counterbalanced by the policy of the Penang Government in exacting heavier duties there.

"The fortifications of Malacca were extensive but irregular and badly constructed, more formidable in appearance than in reality, and were of more use in inspiring awe in the natives than they ever would have been in resisting any regular force. Whoever is acquainted with the difficulty of clearing and settling a Malay country, knows well the value of the place upon cleared and cultivated [land]; [and] in what estimation it is held in respect to the extent of cleared lands, its orchards and plantations, the value of brick and other buildings, etc. etc. Malacca possesses an advantage in this respect beyond every other Malay settlement. The houses, etc. etc., constructed after the style of the Dutch, are of brick and stone, and likely to resist the effects of ages. The public works may be demolished, the principal buildings levelled with the earth from which they sprang, but Malacca in its facilities for trade, its extent of cultivation, its permanent style of native buildings, must remain the same. Fortifications can in a short time be destroyed by the *fiat* of man, but who shall direct the forests to reassume their former extent, or the country of Malacca at once to become an impenetrable forest and unhealthy swamp? The industry of ages has been too effectually and too successful[ly] exerted to be effaced with common trouble. Time and the exterminating sword alone will ever be able to reduce it to its original state: and when it is so reduced, it will always be an object of importance to our European enemy, as well on account of superior advantages in trade and produce, as of its capability of annoying, and effectually destroying the English interests at Penang.

"It does not fall within my line to submit the actual advantages of Malacca as to its natural defences, or to set forth the various plan[s] that might be adopted for supporting them. They can be professionally and better pointed out by Captain Farquhar, the Engineer officer now in charge of the government. For the present purpose it is sufficient to say that from that source and my own observation, I am enabled to assert with correctness that any European Power possessing Malacca would, in a very short time, be able to intrench themselves nearly as securely as they could have done within the old walls, and that we should find the greatest difficulty in again obtaining possession of the place.

"To evince more clearly the actual state of Malacca in regard to its revenues and disbursements, I take the liberty of referring to the official documents lately furnished by the Commandant, by which it will appear that the estimated revenues of the present year exceed the disbursements, the former being estimated at 83,000 and the latter at 79,000 dollars,[1] including military and all other charges.

"The foregoing statement will afford a more satisfactory proof than any I could offer of the settlement being [maintained] at no expense to the Company; and if the actual annual cost of the settlement were calculated on the same principle as that of Penang has been, by leaving out the military as chargeable to other Presidencies, a surplus revenue, after paying every charge, would arise to the amount of a lac of rupees.

"It should, however, be stated that, while Malacca continues to be discouraged as it has been, the revenues cannot be expected materially to increase, although they have annually done so, in a trifling degree, for the last five years. Some relaxation in the very heavy duties now imposed may, perhaps,

---

[1] At 5s. for a dollar; revenues = £20,750, disbursements = £19,750, surplus = £1000.

be deemed advisable, as they not only affect the inhabitants very seriously, but may be the means of forcing [a] considerable part of the trade to Rhio and other ports. Great care should be observed in fixing the extent of the duties, so as to insure to Penang the whole of the trade that may be forced out of Malacca.

"The garrison and establishment at Malacca appear to have been reduced to the very lowest state consistent with the honour of the British Flag and the internal safety of the place; and no further reduction can, I think, with safety, be attempted. It may, however, be deemed sufficient; and if the Commandant is authorised to lay out a very small sum in repairing the works at Bookis China and on the hill of St. John's, and in erecting some temporary works near the town, the settlement may be considered as secure against any predatory force of the enemy, being defended by nature from any attack by shipping. It is at the same time fair to infer that, if the above temporary works are erected, and it is determined to continue the present garrison and government, the superior advantages that may be derived from the revenues in consequence of the safety of the place, will fully reimburse any trifling expense incurred on that account.

"The policy of, at any rate, keeping Malacca in our possession until we are actually obliged to give it up, is, I must presume, made apparent in the remarks I have taken the liberty to submit, not only on account of the difficulty of doing justice to the inhabitants, but as such a measure can be of no real service to Penang, but in all probability [will be] most injurious. Notwithstanding our utmost efforts the settlement will be an object of importance to our enemies, whenever they have the power to settle in it.

"It is unnecessary to dwell on the advantages of Malacca as a port of refreshment for His Majesty's and other ships. His Excellency, the Commander-in-Chief, I have reason to believe, is fully convinced of this, and has represented to the Supreme Government the advantage of holding the settlement on this account alone; but I trust, and confidently hope, that enough has been said to prove the policy, not to say necessity, of continuing the present garrison till the conclusion of this war;[1] and that, on a review of the actual importance of Malacca in its relation to Prince of Wales's Island, your Honourable Board will be induced to call the attention of the Supreme Government to the subject. Should the Right Honourable the Governor-General be inclined to interest His Majesty's Ministers in retaining it, on a peace, and eventually establishing it as a British settlement, a more detailed statement can be drawn up, and from the memoranda I deemed it my duty to make while at Malacca, I may probably be able to furnish further information as to the real advantages that might be expected from Malacca as a permanent settlement. Malacca ceded to the English, its rivalship with Penang would cease. No longer the oppressor and oppressed, they would mutually assist each other. The revenues of Malacca would immediately increase, while the Dutch law might be abolished by proclamation from His Majesty, and the jurisdiction of the Court at Prince of Wales's Island[2] with ease extended in its room.

---

[1] *This war*, *i.e.* the war with Napoleon.

[2] "The Court of Judicature at Prince of Wales's Island in the East Indies" was established by "Letters Patent," bearing date the twenty-fifth day of March, in the forty-seventh year of the reign of George III., *anno Domini*

"With the assistance of Malacca the whole of the Malay rajahs in the Straits and to the Eastward might be rendered not only subservient, but, if necessary, tributary. But to dwell on the permanent advantages to Penang that, on a more extended and political point of view, might be derived from the possession of Malacca, under an enlightened and liberal policy, is not the object of this paper. Facts evincing the impracticability of destroying the settlement, and the danger to be apprehended from any further attempts to effect such a measure, are simply stated. If I am wrong in the conclusions I have drawn, I trust to the Honourable Board's favourable construction of my intentions. Actuated from a sense of duty alone, I have presumed thus unasked to intrude on the time of your Honourable Board, and a consciousness of the correctness of my statement flatters me with the hope of your approbation.—I have the honour to remain, with great respect, honourable sirs, your most obedient and faithful servant,

"THOS. RAFFLES.

"PRINCE OF WALES'S ISLAND,
the 31*st October* 1808."

The effect of this report was marked and immediate. It led to a complete reversal of the policy that was being pursued, and both the Governor-General and the Company hastened to follow the lead of this youthful official, and to order the suspension of all the measures for the evacuation of Malacca. Lord Minto and his Council wrote: "The circumstances represented in that report appear to us to render it highly inexpedient to withdraw the garrison and inhabitants from the Settlement at Malacca. We do not hesitate in recommending to you that the measure be suspended until a further reference can be made on the subject to the Honourable the Court of Directors." The decision of the Court was of similar purport, and is contained in the following paragraphs from their despatch of 1st November 1809. It will not fail to be noted that the determining argument with the Company was that it would put them to no expense:—

"We have also perused with much attention the report prepared by your Secretary, Mr. Raffles, and forwarded to us by your Governor, Colonel Macalister, in his letter to the Chairman and Deputy-Chairman under date the 7th November 1808. This document has in so comprehensive a manner laid open to our view the present circumstances of the Settlement of Malacca, and the dangers which

---

one thousand eight hundred and seven. [A printed copy, dated London, April 1807, of these Letters Patent is in vol. 8 of the *Straits Settlement Records.*] Sir Edward Stanley was the first Recorder.

may arise by the total abandonment of it, that we agree as a temporary measure to the continuance of the present establishment there; and the more readily, as we find by the above-quoted letter, that the charges, including every possible contingency, are fully provided for by the revenues of the place.

"We, however, desire that no expense be incurred in the erection of any buildings or fortifications. We understand that the Settlement is defended by nature from any predatory attack which can be made by shipping; and we therefore do not conceive that there can, in the present state of the enemy's navy, be any danger of an attack from them by a regular force equal to the present detachment at Malacca. Besides, as it cannot at present be absolutely determined that we shall always retain that Settlement, it would be very impolitic to incur any expense in public works of any denomination, excepting such as are absolutely necessary.

"We have derived much satisfaction from the perusal of Mr. Raffles's report, and we desire that you will communicate to that gentleman that we entertain a favourable sense of the talents he has evinced upon that occasion."

In this manner did Stamford Raffles save Malacca from its impending fate. It was long afterwards said and "generally allowed that by a timely representation of some circumstances till then unknown, or not duly considered, he prevented the alienation of Malacca from the British Crown." But it must be admitted that the arguments and facts put forward in the report carried special weight on account of the favourable manner in which Raffles's study of the Malay language had impressed both Lord Minto and his superiors at home. During a Public Disputation at the Calcutta College in February 1808, Lord Minto had called attention to his efforts in the following words:—"The Malay language has been successfully cultivated by Mr. Raffles, Secretary to the Government of Prince of Wales's Island, who, much to his honour, has long been employed in compiling a code of Addat Malaya or Malay Laws from the best authorities in the Malay and Bugguese languages." The following extracts from a correspondence with Mr. Marsden, the greatest Malay scholar of the day, and the author of the standard *History of Sumatra*, bear upon the same subject, and it will be noted that the first letter was written within a very brief period after Raffles's first arrival at Penang:—

"PENANG, *6th July* 1806.

"To the HON. P. DUNDAS.

"DEAR SIR,—I should have taken an earlier opportunity of communicating with you on the subject of Mr. Marsden's letter, which you are pleased to refer to me, if I had not expected a few leisure hours, in which I could have given sufficient attention to his queries to reply to them with the satisfaction I desired.

"Another reason prevented my replying to your flattering reference. I had planned a short excursion of a few days to Queda, and expected from the observations I might make there to have confirmed several particulars respecting the Malays which I could have communicated to Mr. Marsden. In this also I have been disappointed, from the circumstance of Mr. Pearson's having obtained leave of absence. The length of time Mr. Pearson may be absent, and the little prospect I now have of the leisure which I so anxiously desire, can only induce me at this time to hazard my inexperienced opinions on any subject connected with Oriental literature.

"On the interesting subject of the chronology of the Malays I fear but little light will be thrown from the discovery of their using a cycle in their dates. I am convinced of the justness of Mr. Marsden's conclusion that the cycle amongst the Malays has been adopted from the Siamese. I have not, however, observed in any of their books that the cycle alluded to is used with the religion of Mahomed; the epoch of the Hegira has been introduced, and with the Arabian months and days is universally used in their manuscripts. The first I knew of their using a cycle or particular names for their years was from a very old MS., half in Bugguese, half in the Malay or Arabic character, in which were inserted the Relika or times (lucky and unlucky) with tables for computing time according to the Mahomedan calendar. The Siamese, I believe, in conformity with the Indians in general, as well as the Chinese, have a cycle of sixty years containing five lesser cycles of twelve years each. Of the Menangkabus, after a good deal of inquiry, I have not yet been able decidedly to ascertain the relation between those of that name in the Peninsula and the Menangkabus on Pulo Percha. The Malays I have met affirm without hesitation that they all come originally from Pulo Percha; the circumstance of the nation of that name in Sumatra being so great and ancient leaves but little doubt, however, in my mind that the nation (if any), hardly known on the Peninsula, must have emigrated from thence, although the contrary may, as we are at a loss to account for the former, appear at first sight most probable.

"I hope I may hereafter have it in my power to furnish Mr. Marsden with still further additions to his *Semang* vocabulary, although I am not much inclined to think that from this nation, or rather race of men, much interesting information can be derived beyond that of their actual existence and extent. They are decidedly Caffres, or people with woolly hair—to appearance a distinct race in every respect from the Malays, from whom they cannot have in any probability descended. Those inhabiting the skirts of the woods have considerable intercourse with the Malays, and speak their language tolerably well, but the Malays consider it a perfect jargon. Their talking is looked upon by the Malays as the chattering or chirping of large birds, and bears no similitude whatever to their own. I have not yet met with any of these Caffres. I observe Mr. Marsden, in his *History of Sumatra*, speaks of the Caffres of the Philippines, who appear to resemble those alluded to in the Malay Peninsula. These last are called by the Spaniards *Negritos del Monte* and are many of them as black as the natives of Guinea.

"With respect to Mr. Marsden's query on the terms used by the Malays for the different pieces in the game of chess, I will state the results of my inquiries among the Malays themselves. The chatter or chess board is avowedly and evidently received by the Malays from the Chuliahs, or men of the Kaling country. The terms which they could understand they soon altered to their own fashion. . . . All I can learn respecting the term *ter* is that it is a name given by the Hindus to a small temple. I regret that I have not a complete Sanscrit vocabulary by me, but in referring to Forster's *Bengallee Vocabulary*, which is, I believe, almost pure Sanscrit, I am enabled to state something satisfactory. The word *ter* there signifies 'border, verge, utmost,' a sufficient proof, I think, that the term used for the chessman is borrowed from the Sanscrit, the place of the *ter* on the board being at the border, etc. . . . I take the liberty of annexing a Javanese alphabet. I also add a Bugguese alphabet. I have never been able to trace one before, and if it is new to Mr. Marsden I shall be much gratified. I have hitherto learnt but little about this nation. . . . Should you deem the replies to Mr. Marsden's queries in any way satisfactory and worthy of communication, I hope you will at the same time state them as coming from a young man who never made Oriental literature his study, and is but lately arrived in the place which furnishes the means of his observations."

"RUNEMEDE, PENANG, *March* 1809.

"To W. MARSDEN, Esq.

"MY DEAR SIR,—Two very long and severe illnesses, during which I was under the necessity of denying myself the use of the pen and all kinds of study, and from the effects of which I am hardly recovered even at this time, must plead my excuse for not answering, or indeed acknowledging, the receipt of your polite and friendly letters of the 18th of June and 15th of November last, both of which arrived when I was confined to my room. With respect to the Menangkabus, I am more than ever confident that those in the Peninsula derive their origin from the country of that name in Sumatra. Inland of Malacca, about sixty miles, is situated the Malay kingdom of Rumbo, of which you have no doubt heard. The Sultan and all the principal officers of state hold their authority immediately from Menangkabu, and have even written commissions for their respective offices. This shows the extent of its power even now, reduced as it must be in common with that of the Malay States in general. In the *Asiatic Researches* you will perceive a long disquisition on the Indo-Chinese nations by my friend Dr. Leyden, which will no doubt interest you very much. I wish we had the good fortune of his local information. He was to the Eastward but a few months, during which time he lived with me; you will see what use he made of his time. I have by me a sketch of a grammar which I have drawn up, and which I will send you as soon as I get time to correct and copy it; and I am gradually compiling a dictionary, which you shall be welcome to, if it can be of any service to you. I must apologise for the hasty style in which this is written. You, my dear sir, have been a Secretary yourself, and will make due allowances."

At the same time that Raffles drew up his official report on Malacca, he prepared a paper on the Malay nation, with a translation of their maritime institutions. This he sent to his friend Leyden at Calcutta, and in due course it was read before the Bengal Asiatic Society. The paper is a striking one, and was remarkable as the first serious attempt to regard the scattered fragments of the Malay race as one nationality. Lord Minto did not happen to be in Bengal at the moment this lecture was presented to the Asiatic Society, but, as has been shown, he had seen and acted upon the earlier report on the Malacca question. The following letter from Leyden to his friend refers to both:—

"CALCUTTA, *9th October* 1809.

"MY DEAR RAFFLES,—I have received both your letters, and with great vexation have to inform you that Lord Minto is at present gone to the unfortunate Presidency of Madras, where I believe he has got his hands full. I laid before him without delay the MS. concerning Malacca, with which he was greatly pleased [from this we may infer that Raffles had sent a copy personally in addition to that from the Governor of Penang], and desired me to say he should be gratified in receiving immediately from yourself any communications respecting the Eastern parts of a similar nature. I shall not fail to write to him as soon as I am a little recovered, for I have been for some time (days I mean) confined to bed by a smart attack of fever. However, I am to-day up for the first time, but not at all able to write letters, so you must excuse me for the present. My literary studies were quite knocked on the head for some time by the duties of a magistrate in so large a district as the Twenty-four Pergunnahs, and I was afterwards for some months also magistrate of Nadeah, where I was constantly engaged in bush-fighting in the jungles. I have now more time, and have again begun my literary avocations with vigour ; nor have I given up my Eastern researches quite. Now, pray do contrive to tell me what you are doing in the literary way, and to get me a few copies of the best Malay MSS. Above all, try and get me the works of the famous Bugis bard Saveri-yading, and anything you can in Bali and Siamese. You have never, I presume, been able to get the *Batavian Researches* into your clutches, but do try and get me the best alphabets of all the Eastern tribes. Have you no *Batta* that can read the lingo of the man-eaters? I have got a book, but cannot read it. I must be done, however, and go to bed, or encrease my fever.—Yours ever truly,

"J. LEYDEN."

The autobiographical letter at the end of the first chapter gives a clear account of the circumstances that followed. As a result of operations conducted in the first place by Sir Thomas Trowbridge in 1806, and afterwards by Sir Edward Pellew in the following year, the Dutch fleet was driven from the sea, and so close a blockade of the Javan ports was instituted that even native craft were not allowed to come out, to the considerable injury of the trade of Penang. These operations were carried out by the King's vessels, and not by those of the East India Company, and whenever they interfered with trade they caused the Company's representatives much annoyance, and sufficient loss to arouse criticism. Raffles, however, was officially connected with the Royal Navy as well as with the Company. He was Naval Agent for His Majesty's fleet at Penang, but when his work became too heavy for him he transferred this task to his brother-in-law, Mr. Thompson. Two letters are in existence, one from Admiral Drury, and the other from Captain Christopher Cole, of H.M.S. *Doris*, requesting him, as a personal favour, and in order to prevent the King's service from being seriously embarrassed, to continue to discharge the duties after Mr. Thompson's death. His relations with all the naval commanders were excellent, and it was probably from their actions and views that his attention was first seriously turned towards Java. Among those actions the two most important were a descent on the Eastern coast of Java, described in the following paragraph from the official paper, *The Prince of Wales's Island Gazette*, dated 6th February 1808, and the unexpected capture of the Moluccas:—

"We are authorised to state that the object of the expedition to the Eastward, under His Excellency Sir Edward Pellew, has been completely successful, and that the undermentioned Dutch men-of-war were destroyed in the harbour of Griessie, at the eastern extremity of Java, by the squadron under His Excellency's command, without the loss of a man. The batteries at that place having surrendered on the approach of the English, were occupied during the time the squadron continued in the harbour by the Grenadiers of His Majesty's 30th Regiment, disembarked for that purpose.

"The Government of the Chief Settlement of Sourabaya having supplied His Excellency, by treaty, with refreshments, and pilots to conduct the squadron out of the harbour, His Excellency quitted the place accordingly on the 16th December 1807; the guns, military and naval stores in the garrison of Griessie, as well as the batteries at Sambelangan, on the island of Madura, having been previously destroyed under the orders of Lieutenant-Colonel Lockhart, commanding the detachment co-operating with the naval forces.

"Dutch men-of-war destroyed in the harbour of Griessie by the squadron under the command of His Excellency Sir Edward Pellew, on the 11th December 1807:—

Revolutie	70 guns.
Pluto	70 ,,
Kortenam	68 ,,
(No name)	Hulk.
Rustoff, Indiaman	of 1000 tons."

Raffles, we may feel assured, was no indifferent observer of that military success on the mainland of Java. The account of the capture of the Moluccas, as it bore on the career of our subject, had better be told in his own words:—

"It happened that not long after this interference (*re* Malacca) on the part of the Supreme Government the conquest of the Moluccas, was unexpectedly achieved by a small naval force which had been merely sent to plunder them. The Governor-General refused to take charge of these islands on account of the Company, and the Naval Commander hardly felt himself warranted in establishing a King's Government; but, as the decision was left with him, he proposed to the Governor-General, who was then at Madras, that I should be nominated to the charge, and a provisional administration established pending a reference to Europe. Lord Minto immediately replied that I was not unknown to him; that he was perfectly satisfied of my fitness and claims, and that he would immediately appoint me if the Admiral would undertake that I should accept the office—for it occurred to Lord Minto that, being a family man and of high pretensions, I might be unwilling to sacrifice a certainty for an uncertainty. My advancement at Prince of Wales's Island was secure; but the Moluccas were only a war dependency; and it was not known what measures regarding them might be taken by the Government at home. The Admiral did not like to take the responsibility, and the arrangement dropped on an understanding that my assent was alone wanting; but, as the Governor-General was about to return to Bengal, he would, of course, feel himself at perfect liberty to bestow the office on another, should an immediate arrangement or the claims of others require an early attention. Lord Minto went to Bengal, and the Admiral despatched a vessel to give me the earliest intimation of what had occurred, hoping he had acted for the best in declining to take on himself the responsibility.

"Some months had now elapsed, and it was to be feared that arrangements for the administration of the Moluccas were already in progress. Yet the chance of being in time, and the expectation of still further advancing my interests with Lord Minto, weighed with me in the resolution I took of proceeding in person to Bengal [on 7th June 1810 he was granted two months' leave from Penang]. My attention had long been directed to the state of the Dutch possessions to the Eastward, and as rumours were afloat of a projected armament going against the Isle of France, it occurred to me that the information I possessed respecting Java might be useful, and possibly turn the attention of our Government in that direction. I accordingly left my family, and proceeded to Calcutta in a small and frail vessel, the only one which offered, but in which all my future prospects had well-nigh perished. On my arrival in Bengal I met with the kindest reception from Lord Minto. I found that, though the appointment to the Moluccas had not actually taken place, it was promised to another. I, in consequence, relinquished all idea of it, and at once drew his Lordship's attention to Java, by observing that there were other islands worthy of his Lordship's consideration besides the Moluccas: Java, for instance. On the mention of Java his Lordship cast a look of such scrutiny, anticipation, and kindness upon me, as I shall never forget. 'Yes,' said he, 'Java is an interesting island; I shall be happy to receive any information you can give me concerning it.' This was enough to encourage me; and from this moment all my views, all my plans, and all my mind were devoted to create such an interest regarding Java as should lead to its annexation to our Eastern Empire; although I confess that I had never the vanity to expect that, when this object was accomplished, so important an administration would have been intrusted to my individual charge."

The departure for Calcutta in the summer of 1810 marks the true turning-point in the career of Stamford Raffles. It was the beginning of his more public life, for which all that had gone before furnished the training and preliminary setting. During the five years he had resided in the Malay peninsula he had mastered the language of the people, and he had acquired a thorough grasp of the political situation in the Archipelago. Among the local officials he was the only man with any pretensions to that knowledge. His zeal on the spot, in the discharge of a daily task that was never interesting and soon became monotonous, had made him the most popular, as well as the most active, member of the Penang administration. Captain Travers, a member afterwards of his personal staff in Java, says that at this period " he was respected and consulted by every member of it," and " that the settlers looked up to him for assistance and advice in any difficulty." His study of the language, history, and customs of the Malay race obtained for him three valuable friends in Minto, Leyden, and Marsden, and the recognition of his merit by his superiors. Yet his success, astonishing as it was for so young a man, and for one who carried on his back the burdens of so many persons, had not spoilt him. He was entirely free from envy or little-mindedness. His generous tribute to Leyden in his letter to Mr. Marsden, his modest description of himself in the same document, the scrupulousness with which he continued to discharge the trifling clerical duties of his post while his mind was turned on questions of magnitude that would have engrossed the attention of most men, even if they did not conceive their daily duties to have thereby become beneath their notice, together with the tolerance with which he regarded the creeds and customs of alien and semi-civilised races, all showed the ready sympathy and the breadth of a mind highly gifted by nature.

At Penang or Malacca, however, he might never have

become famous. Commercial prosperity shunned those stations, and the East India Company had no love or regard for places that did not contribute to its coffers. Malacca was doomed to exalt Penang; Penang itself did not realise the expectations formed of it, and was accordingly reduced. The Company had no policy at all in the Malay peninsula and the Archipelago, where a knowledge of the Malay language was alone of practical use. Nor had any of the Governor-Generals who wielded its power any clearer views in this direction, with one exception; and that was the very ruler whose notice Raffles had attracted, and whose close confidence and favour he was now about to obtain. Lord Minto was the one Governor-General who had grasped fully the secret of maritime supremacy, and who believed that security in India depended as much on the control of the seas and the possession of the isles along our ocean highway as on military achievements within the peninsula itself. Raffles must be pronounced supremely fortunate in the fact that such a statesman held the reins of power at the moment of his going to Calcutta with the set purpose of inducing the Government to conquer Java. It may even be said that if he had come in the time of any other ruler than Lord Minto, his errand would have been bootless; but the recent conqueror of the isles of Bourbon and France was naturally sympathetic to a scheme which would entail the expulsion of French influence and authority from the one remaining island east of the Cape where they still survived.

In everything he had undertaken Raffles had shown an earnestness and elevation of spirit which gave him a title to success. His uppermost feeling must have been one of benefiting his country rather than himself, for he could not have foreseen that his personal reward would have been as great as it proved. All that need be said is that he threw himself into this task with the energy that had characterised his other proceedings; while the recompense he obtained was fully and fairly earned by his own efforts, and by the care and thoroughness with which he directed the course of a critical national undertaking, and piloted it to a brilliant and successful end.

CHAPTER IV

THE JAVA EXPEDITION

BEFORE following Stamford Raffles on his journey to Calcutta, it will be convenient to take a brief view of the general political situation, as it affected the Dutch colonies in the Eastern Archipelago and the action of the British authorities in India with regard to them. The reader should remember that the period of which we are writing was no ordinary one. It was not merely the Napoleonic era, but that particular moment of the great international struggle when England was left alone to uphold the cause of liberty. This country was only able to fulfil her part because she commanded the seas, and because she wrested from her rival the islands that Napoleon's genius would have made the base of his designs on our Eastern possessions. It must not be supposed that these designs exist only in the imagination of English writers, or that Napoleon accepted his defeat in Egypt in 1798–99 as the termination of his dreams of Asiatic dominion. His embassies to Persia, the convention of Tilsit with the Russian emperor, but, still more, his measures in the Mauritius and in Java, prove the contrary. He only abandoned the hope of their success as, one after another, the islands of the Indian Ocean passed into the hands of the English.

But the French claim to have a voice in the affairs of Java began before the time of Napoleon. Holland had, almost simultaneously with France, shown a desire to possess a Republican form of Government; and an abortive insurrection against the House of Orange occurred in 1787. One of the leaders in that movement was General Daendels, then a young man of twenty-five, and undoubtedly a brave and capable officer. He escaped to France, entered her military service with the rank of general, and took part with Pichegru in the several campaigns between 1794 and 1797. On the success of the French arms, and the deposition of the House of Orange, Daendels was appointed to the supreme command of the Dutch Republican army. Holland then became one of the republics dependent on France, and its colonial possessions passed under the same influence. Even in 1797, Daendels, whose interest in Java dated from that early period, proposed that the island should be made the base of operations against the English in the East. This project would have formed a concomitant of the Egyptian expedition under Bonaparte but for the destruction of part of the Dutch fleet at the battle of Camperdown, and the surrender of the remainder at the Texel two years later. The English ministry was acquainted with this scheme, for among the subjects pressed by Pitt on the Marquis Wellesley, when he went out as Governor-General, was the conquest of Java. Sir Arthur Wellesley, the future Duke of Wellington, was even designated for the command of such an expedition; but the Maratha war broke out, and put an end to the possibility of any external operations.

In 1795 England had made a descent on the Dutch island of Ceylon; and, in the next year, the local authorities definitely ceded this possession to the English by a convention signed at Colombo. The Treaty of Amiens assigned that colony as a permanent possession to England, but there are authorities who affirm that she might then have had the choice of either Java or Ceylon. If this statement really represents what took place during the *pourparlers* between Lord Hawkesbury and M. Otto, we can only say that the Addington ministry made a bad selection. Ceylon could never be anything but an appendage of India, whereas Java might be made the seat of a formidable and rival empire. During the war we had, also in 1795, seized the Cape of Good Hope; but, on the conclusion of peace, we evacuated it, and the Dutch authority was restored. In India, France retained her old stations of Pondicherry and Chandernagore, and, in the Indian Ocean, the isles of France and Bourbon.

Napoleon availed himself of the opportunity afforded by the Peace of Amiens to strengthen the position of France and her allies, the Dutch, in all their colonies. He sent General Decaen, an able officer, to India; and he instructed him to take notes of the English position, to establish relations with the native princes, and, on the outbreak of war, to retire to the Mauritius. These preparations in time of peace foreshadowed renewed activity in the Indies on the resumption of hostilities, and the position was undoubtedly one of some anxiety for the authorities established at Madras and Calcutta.

When the struggle between England and France was resumed in the spring of 1803, Decaen, whose landing at Pondicherry with 1400 troops was prevented by the Anglo-Indian authorities, had reached the isles of France and Bourbon, both of which he placed in a position of defence. The rupture in Europe was not at once followed by hostilities in Asia, and the first blow was really struck when Sir David Baird and Sir Home Popham re-established our authority at the Cape of Good Hope on 10th January 1806, from which time to the present our supremacy in South Africa has been acknowledged and maintained. The Dutch governor, General Janssens, who signed the surrender, was destined to make, nearly six years later, a similar surrender in Java.

The interest in Franco-Dutch projects was much stimulated when, in 1806, Napoleon placed his brother Louis on the throne of Holland; and Lord Minto, who came out to India in the summer of 1807, was specially instructed to pay attention to the islands in the possession of the national enemies. He was fettered, however, by other conditions, of which the state of the Company's finances was not the least embarrassing. But, about the same time, the English fleet east of the Cape was very much strengthened, and at least three of Nelson's captains—Sir Thomas Trowbridge, Sir Edward Pellew, and William O'Brien Drury—were sent to seek fresh laurels under the tropics. They had not been inactive. A Dutch fleet was destroyed in Batavia harbour in November

1806. Sir Edward Pellew in the next year gained the signal success at Gressie, described in the last chapter, and all the islands were more or less closely blockaded.

When Louis Napoleon became king of Holland, Daendels was raised to the rank of a Dutch marshal, and sent to Java to carry out there defensive and offensive measures similar to those executed at the Mauritius by Decaen. He was accompanied by a considerable number of officers, and a few troops; and in the three years of his rule he reorganised the Dutch colonial forces, and greatly improved their military position in the island. By the energy of these two officers Napoleon had acquired, before he deposed his brother and annexed Holland to France in 1810, a strong and advantageous position in the Indian Ocean and the Eastern Archipelago for the embarrassment of England. He was induced, however, to recall Daendels at this juncture, superseding him by General Jan Willems Janssens, the officer who had surrendered the Cape, and whom it was deemed desirable to exile on account of the excessive favour shown him by Queen Hortense. On intrusting this command to Janssens, Napoleon is said to have observed to him, "Remember, a French general must not surrender twice."

Lord Minto had been in the first place instructed to watch these various movements; but, a few months after his arrival, he received, as stated in a letter to Sir Edward Pellew, printed in his interesting correspondence, entitled *Lord Minto in India* and published in 1880, "a positive prohibition of any expedition to Java and other places eastward of India"; and this prohibition was "transmitted," he adds, "to the Indian Government when Lord Castlereagh, at present War Minister, was Secretary of State for the Colonial and War Department, and also President of the Board of Control." Lord Minto goes on to say that he, however, intended to adopt this very policy whenever the condition of the Company's finances admitted of such action. After an interval of three years, the Governor-General found himself able to make a commencement on the ocean. In March 1810 Lord Minto wrote that he had decided to send a small expedition to occupy the island of Bourbon; and that, when that object was attained, he would reinforce it for the capture of the larger and more important island of the Mauritius. The first expedition consisted of 3000 men, and Admiral Bertie was in supreme command. In view of this peril, General Decaen concentrated all his resources on the defence of Mauritius; and Bourbon surrendered after a nominal resistance on 8th July 1810. The operations against the former island were then taken seriously in hand, and a preliminary repulse on 10th August, when four English ships were either sunk or captured in the harbour, warned the assailing commanders that General Decaen was a capable soldier. The expedition was raised to a strength of 10,000 men, with Sir John Abercrombie in command of the land forces; and then the French Governor agreed to surrender in the face of overwhelming force. The terms of the capitulation on 2nd December 1810 were honourable to both sides; and, although Mauritius was permanently retained by England at the general peace, Bourbon, now named Reunion, was restored to France. The first English Governor of the Mauritius was Sir Robert Farquhar, who, at an earlier period, had been Lieutenant-Governor of Penang. During the thirteen years he ruled the Mauritius, he gained a high reputation for ability, and a tactful courtesy which specially recommended him to the French planters.

The fall of the Mauritius, which was known at Calcutta before the end of January 1811, paved the way for the expedition eastward. The scheme foreshadowed by these operations required for its completion that Java should share the fate of the western islands, and Raffles employed his time so well that, as he afterwards wrote, he had every right to say that his representations fixed Lord Minto in his determination to expel French influence from its last stronghold in the East. These general observations on the political situation, and on Lord Minto's policy, will make the origin of the Java Expedition clearer for the reader.

When Raffles in the manner described reached Calcutta at the end of June 1810, attention was engrossed in the Bourbon affair; and, when he left it in October, it was known that the end there was certain, and could not be remote in the Mauritius. In those four months Raffles confirmed the good opinion Lord Minto had formed of him at a distance, and also gained his complete confidence. He supplied the Governor-General with such a mass of fresh and significant information about Java, that the conquest of that island came to be regarded as a matter of imperative necessity. Lord Minto's Council, however, were not all of this way of thinking, and the intentions of the Governor-General were consequently kept a close secret. As a preliminary measure, Lord Minto resolved to depute Mr. Raffles to proceed to the eastward as " Agent to the Governor-General with the Malay States," for the purpose of collecting information, and otherwise preparing the way for a military expedition. The date of his appointment to this special post was 19th October 1810, and he himself selected Malacca as the best point at which he could discharge his new duties. On his way he touched at Penang, and gave orders, as appears from an advertisement in the local gazette, for the sale of his house, " Runnymede," where he had dispensed an open hospitality to all comers, thus showing that he knew his association with that place had terminated. He reached Malacca on 4th December in the same year, and took up his residence in the Banda Illiar quarter of the town, where he opened a regular office for his Malay writers and translators, of whom the boy Abdulla, already mentioned in the last chapter, was one. He brought with him a large stock of guns, clocks, satin cloth, and other European goods, as presents for the Malay and Javanese princes. He was also provided with gorgeous letter paper, such as their souls would delight in, for his communications to the native rulers. A considerable amount of money was also placed at his disposal. Thus equipped Raffles began to carry out the objects of his secret political mission, which may be enumerated. He was to collect the fullest information possible about the so-called Malay States and islands in and around the Indian Archipelago; about the best route for the projected expedition to Java; about the numbers, disposition, and character of the enemy's forces on that island; and about its ports, roads, towns, and fortresses. The trade, resources, political and social conditions of those extensive and little-known regions of the East were to be examined into and described in a series of reports. Nor was he to neglect any other knowledge that might be conducive to success. He had also to enter into friendly communications with the sultans and chiefs of the various Malay and Javanese peoples embraced in that vast area, and to endeavour to obtain not only the co-operation of the native states, but the acquiescence of the Dutch themselves in the views of his government; for it was hoped that they felt no love for their new French masters, and also that the hoisting of the Tricolor in 1810 would have given them umbrage. It was a colossal task, and its accomplishment demanded and obtained his utmost energy. Native agents were despatched in all directions to the eastward, bearing letters in the Malay and Javanese languages; letters which were couched in such general terms of friendliness as left to the British administration, whose coming they foreshadowed, freedom of action and liberty for reform. In one of his letters to Lord Minto he points out how these communications had been materially impeded by the position taken off the Javan coast by the different ships of His Majesty's navy, whose presence had raised alarm and suspicion in the minds of the native chiefs.

To the Dutch he issued a short proclamation in their own language, and he had reason to believe, from the reports of M. Rochennot, a Swiss officer lately in their service, that their attitude would not be unfavourable to the invaders. To the Rajahs of Bali, an island at the eastern extremity of Java, he wrote in friendly terms; and these rajahs helped him to enter into communication with the Sultan of Mataram, on the southern coast of Java, and with the Sultan of the island of Madura, lying off its northern shores. By the same agency a good feeling towards the British was spread through Sumbawa, and onward along the chain of low islands stretching between Java and the Moluccas. The Sultan of Lombok, though unsolicited, offered his aid to the invaders. The chiefs of Bantam, in the western part of Java, and those of Lampong, on the southern shores of Sumatra, manifested a friendly disposition, which Raffles sought to cherish by the despatch of letters. He entered into an unsatisfactory negotiation with the cruel Sultan of Palembang. To the subject of piracy he devoted considerable attention, with the view of guarding against its sudden increase on the downfall of the Dutch, and of promoting its ultimate suppression under the British power. He protested in vain against the piratical acts of the Sultans of Rhio and Sambas; and corresponded on the same subject with the latter's neighbour, the friendly Sultan of Pontiana, on the south-western shores of Borneo.

In the Malay Peninsula itself he conceived it possible to render the British authority paramount by a timely alliance with Siam, in return for which that country might be induced to abstain from further interference. New settlements were to be formed in Borneo. A limited trade might be opened with Cochin-China; a more advantageous one with the almost unknown countries of Champa and Cambodia. A friendly correspondence was begun with the Sultan of Mindanao. Raffles suggested to Lord Minto that the Indian Government should take that large island under its protection, after giving to the Spaniards at Manilla such explanations as might be due. Celebes, torn by faction which the Dutch fomented, its lands blighted by their desolating slave-trade, was to be restored to peace with the consent of the native princes to whom he had written, and with the support of the British authority. The warlike Macassar and Bugis tribes in the same island were to be enrolled in the Company's army. Gilolo was also to be brought under British influence. Bali, Celebes, Gilolo, were to contain three strongholds of British power, each occupying a commanding position on the central island of three different groups, and each intended to survive the possible destruction by European diplomacy of the laborious achievements of Indian statesmen. Acheen was to be placed under British protection, with a resident and two hundred soldiers. Nor were Canton and Japan overlooked. The Dutch residents in Japan, and the corps of Japanese interpreters who knew Dutch, were to be brought over to English interests, however high the price might be. All these States and others, some weakened and impoverished by the ungenerous policy of the Dutch, and now under the dominion of the French, would pass on the fall of Java into the hands, or within the influence, of the Indian Government.

In ancient times all the Malay chiefs, while possessing full authority, each in his own dominion jealously cherishing his titles of sultan or rajah, had held sway in reality as the vassals of a suzerain or superior, the king of the powerful state of Majopahit, in the island of Java. In that capacity the king had been called Bitara. This title, equivalent to that of Lord-Protector, but dormant for three centuries, was to be revived in the person of the Governor-General of India. The Governor-General would be the head of a great confederacy of Malay States. The Confederated States were to be invited to send learned men, each state commissioning one or two, to a general congress, which was to be summoned for the revision of the Malay code of laws and usages. Piracy was to be suppressed; slavery put down or mitigated; slave-debtors relieved; trading monopolies regulated or abolished. Christianity, already known in parts, was to be widely diffused and universally protected. The extortions of Chinese tax-farmers, the oppressions of Arab and Chinese traders, were to be stopped, and their trade regulated, as well as that of the Americans, who were reckless importers of firearms. Privileged but fixed trading ports were to be established for foreigners, though the regulations were to be as liberal as, under existing circumstances, was possible. Between the manufactured products of the Western world and the raw produce of the East, a lively interchange would take place. The coffee of Java would spring from an annual weight of ten to that of fifty millions of pounds. England would derive vast supplies of teak and timber for her ships of war and her merchantmen. Everywhere would begin a reign of peace, of plenty, and of kindly civilisation; while over all would float the British flag, telling of justice and of freedom, and of the strong arm of British valour that rendered both secure.

Such was the vision of an island empire as it took shape in the mind of Raffles, and was laid by him before Lord Minto. And it might have reached accomplishment in fact, for the possession of Java rendered that accomplishment a possibility. But the time passed; and with it passed the opportunity. Happily the future veils its disappointments from the eye of hope. "The want of local information," he wrote in 1811, quoting Mr. R. T. Farquhar, once Lieutenant-Governor of Prince of Wales's Island, " is indeed the rock on which the infant settlements of the English have at all times been wrecked." He laboured hard to satisfy that want. He mentions in one of his despatches that he has a map of Java, " executed by Captain Farquhar from information in my possession." Every day, almost every hour, added to the mass of his information. Every successfully transmitted message seemed to weave another link in the bond that was to unite Java to the British Empire.

While Raffles was thus engaged at Malacca, his friend Leyden was doing everything he could at Calcutta to second his efforts. Leyden had thrown himself into the question with characteristic enthusiasm, and the following letter shows how warmly he had taken up the policy which Raffles had defined as the right one to be pursued in regard to Java and the Malays :—

" The military queries which I send you enclosed, I regret any delay in your receiving, but the letter itself was only to say that his Lordship was exceedingly well-disposed towards you, desirous of giving you every opportunity of distinguishing yourself, and rewarding you as highly as the imperious nature of circumstances would permit. This you knew very well before, and I was very glad that his Lordship thought it unnecessary to cause me to write you a formal letter on the subject. Indeed, Raffles, he has always talked of you to me with a kindness very uncommon in a Governor-General, and says that he is pleased with thinking he will be able to arrange matters very much to your satisfaction when he arrives. I am glad that I have been able to keep him tight up to this point. He is still fluctuating between the two old plans of keeping the country or rendering it independent. The orders which he has received from home are entirely and positively in favour of the last. He is required to expel the French and Dutch, and leave the country entirely to itself. This his own good sense directly saw to be impossible, from the shoals of half-castes at Batavia. Colebrooke and Lumsden have succeeded in making some impression on him by talking of accustoming the Malays to independence and all that, but may I never be a second Draco, nor write my laws in blood, if they succeed. Succeed they shall not, that is flat, for the Malays must neither be independent nor get very dependent ; but we must have a general Malay league, in which all the Rajahs must be united like the old Ban of Burgundy, or the later one of Germany, and these must all be represented in a general Parliament of the Malay States, like the Amphictyonic Council of the Greeks, and this council should meet in the island of Madura, or some celebrated ancient place, and under the protection of the Governor of Java. We ought to retain in some shape or other all the Dutch possessions at first, while we make ourselves known ; and you should write to all the Rajahs of the Malays, however far or wherever situated, to come in person to meet the *Good Maha Rajah of Bengal,* and state in your letters that the Malay States are expressly invited to send their most ancient and sagacious men to assist at a general meeting or congress, to take into consideration all their laws, institutions, government, religion, and policy. Publish broad and wide the coming of the *good Maha Rajah,* like another Secunder Zulkaram, to reign in Malacca and conquer Java, and drive out all the cruel Dutch and treacherous French, and take away all embargoes and restrictions on trade, abolish piracy, and bring peace and happiness to all the *anak Malayas.* In short, make a great and mighty noise, for we will compel his Lordship to be a greater man than he would wish to be if left alone."

Raffles required no stimulating or prompting in his own province, but it was gratifying to him to find that what he had already done had, in anticipation, commended itself to the judgment of his best friend. On the subject referred to by Leyden, viz. that of proclaiming Lord Minto to the Malays as a second national chieftain like Secunder Zulkaram, Raffles wrote in a fuller and more detailed manner to the Governor-General as follows :—

"In ancient times the Malay chiefs, though possessing the titles of Sultan or Rajah, and in full possession of authority within their own domains, yet all held of a superior or Suzerain, who was king of the ancient and powerful state of Majopahit on the island of Java, and who had the title of Bitara. . . . Though the present Malay chiefs are jealous and punctilious in a high degree about their own titles, they are by no means equally so respecting holding of a superior whose title would save their own dignity ; and I conceive they might easily be prevailed upon by suggestions to invest the Governor-General of India with the ancient title of Bitara, equivalent to Lord-Protector, which has become obsolete among them for nearly three centuries. . . . This would give a general right of superintendence over, and interference with, all the Malay States. . . . It is of importance, however, that this should appear to be the spontaneous and voluntary act of the Malay chieftains."

While thus actively engaged in the prosecution of his confidential mission, Raffles was not idle in literary and scientific pursuits. His house must have presented a busy scene. A vast store of Malay books and manuscripts, histories and poems, was collected: many were bought, many borrowed and copied, many read and translated. "The histories stored up in Malacca were nearly exhausted," says Abdulla. Meantime the surrounding country, the forests, and the seashore, were ransacked by persons eager to profit by the curious tastes of this impenetrable Englishman. Snakes and centipedes were laid in their last resting-place, coiled in bottles of arrack; flies and grasshoppers, moths, butterflies, and other insects, transfixed on pins, paid the last penalty of their beauty, rarity, or interest; flowers and leaves, seaweeds and fungi were pressed, or painted large as life; corals and shells labelled and stored up; beasts and birds imprisoned in cages, or killed and stuffed. He kept among these a young tiger and an ourang-outang; and, playful in the midst of so much care and labour, arrayed the latter in trousers, "with coat and hat complete." According to Abdulla, these varied occupations astonished—as well they might—the sleepy people of Malacca, and many profited by searching high and low for curiosities.

I have already quoted Abdulla's personal description of Raffles and his wife. To this may now be added the account of his employer's incessant work during this busy period when he was engaged in diplomatic preliminaries and the composition of the almost exhaustive despatches which he forwarded for the information of Lord Minto and his Council.

"Now I observed," says Abdulla, "his habit was to be always in deep thought. He also was an earnest inquirer into past history, and he gave up nothing till he had probed it to the bottom. He loved most to sit in quietude, when he did nothing else but write or read; and it was his usage, when he was either studying or speaking, that he would see no one till he had finished. He had a time set apart for each duty, nor would he mingle one with another. Further, in the evenings, after tea, he would take ink, pen, and paper, after the candles had been lighted, reclining with closed eyes, in a manner that I often took to be sleep; but in an instant he would be up, and write for a while, till he went to recline again. Thus would he pass the night, till twelve or one, before he retired to sleep. This was his daily practice. On the next morning he would go to what he had written, and read it while walking backwards and forwards, when, out of ten sheets, probably he would only give three or four to his copying clerk to enter into the books, and the others he would tear up. Such was his daily habit. Now Mr. Raffles took great interest in looking into the origin of nations, and their manners and customs of olden times, examining what would elucidate the same. He was especially quick in the uptake of Malay with its variations. He delighted to use the proper idioms as the natives do; he was active in studying words and their place in phrases, and not until we had told him would he state that the English had another mode. It was his daily labour to order post letters (*sic*) to various Malay countries to support their good understanding with his nation, and increase the bond of friendship—this with presents and agreeable words. This gained the goodwill of the various Rajahs.

"Now Mr. Raffles's disposition was anything but covetous, for, in whatever undertakings or projects he had in view, he grudged no expense, so that they were accomplished. Thus his intentions had rapid consummation. Thus loads of money came out of his chest daily in buying various things or in paying wages. I also perceived that he hated the habit of the Dutch who lived in Malacca of running down the Malays, and they detested him in return; so much so, that they would not sit down beside him. But Mr. Raffles loved always to be on good terms with the Malays—the poorest could speak to him; and while all the great folks in Malacca came to speak to him daily, whether Malays or Europeans, yet they could not find out his object of coming there—his ulterior intentions."

One evening Abdulla went with Raffles to see a Malay school near Malacca. Raffles asked why the schoolmaster taught the Arabic of the Koran and not Malay, and found that there was no demand for a school to teach Malay.

"If I live," said Mr. Raffles, "I shall have a school set agoing for teaching Malay. I am most anxious about this, as it is a beautiful language; further, it is of great utility."

It is now time to turn to Lord Minto, who had only been awaiting news of the result of the Mauritius expedition before assuming the personal direction of the Javan undertaking. News of the success of Admiral Bertie's attack reached him before the end of January 1811, and on 25th February he wrote as follows to his wife:—

"I am to embark in a few days for Madras. I shall then, I hope, proceed to Malacca on board the *Modestè*. . . . I have had Mr. Raffles, Secretary to the Government of Prince of Wales's Island, a very clever, able, active and judicious man, perfectly versed in the Malay language and manners, and conversant with the interests and affairs of the Eastern States, in advance for some months past, to collect recent intelligence, to open communications with the Javanese chiefs, and to prepare the way for our operations. I carry with me good assistance of every sort, though few in number. Among these are Mr. Hope, brother of Sir John Hope, a tolerable Dutchman, with excellent talents and habits of business; Dr. Leyden, a perfect Malay; Mr. Seton, now resident at Delhi, who is to be Governor of Prince of Wales's Island (in the room of poor Mr. Bruce, Lord Elgin's brother, lately dead), but who will go on with me to Java. Nothing can exceed his talents except the enthusiasm of benevolence which marks his character."

About the same date Lord Minto wrote from Calcutta to Raffles himself the following important letter:—

"The Mauritius and all the French islands being now in our possession, there is nothing to retard the execution of our further views to the eastward. The expedition, comprising 4000 European infantry with a suitable proportion of artillery, and 4000 native Bengal infantry with about 300 cavalry, will sail from India the beginning or middle of March. I am now to acquaint you with my own intention to proceed in person at least to Malacca, and eventually I may say probably to Java. The impossibility of your returning to Bengal in time with the information which can alone enable me to frame instructions for the conduct of this expedition and for settling the consequent arrangements, has been very obvious for some time. The expediency, not to say necessity, of my approaching the scene, and bringing the authority of Government, at least within reach of reference, is evident. That resolution is therefore taken. I count upon meeting you at Malacca, and then, in communication with yourself and Sir Samuel Achmuty, the final plans, military and political, will be settled. I have no doubt that the communications you will have opened with the island of Java and adjacent countries will have furnished authentic knowledge of the dispositions we shall meet there, and enable us to place our enterprise upon a footing which will ensure the concurrence and co-operation of the native states, if it does not procure the acquiescence of the Dutch themselves in our views. I must tell you in confidence that I have received the sanction of Government at home for this expedition, but that the views of the Directors do not go beyond the expulsion or reduction of the Dutch power, the destruction of their fortifications, the distribution of their arms and stores to the natives, and the evacuation of the island by our own troops. I conclude, however, that the destructive and calamitous consequences of this plan to so ancient and populous a European colony, the property and lives of which must fall a sacrifice to the vindictive sway of the Malay chiefs if transferred suddenly and defenceless to their dominion, have not been fully contemplated, and I have already stated my reasons for considering a modification of their orders as indispensable. The points on which I have been able to form a judgment with any confidence are: first, that we must establish provisionally an administration to supply the protection which will have been lost by the abolition of the Dutch authority—this applies more particularly to Batavia—That the Dutch may themselves be employed, in a great and principal proportion, in this new administration, under the control of a presiding British authority;

that the two principal ports of Samarang and Gressie must be retained with the territories dependent upon them, at least till we can form an adequate and informed judgment of the advantage or prejudice to be expected from abandoning them; that it may be considered as doubtful in the present state of the investigation whether any and what other stations should be kept in our possession: and these are points to be reserved for consideration when we meet, or when our information is more complete. To the native princes and people the abolition of Dutch power would alone afford a gratification of rooted passions, and a prospect of substantial relief and advantage which may be expected to withdraw them from the Dutch and unite them to our cause; and a system of connection between them and the English Government may be founded on principles so manifestly beneficial to the people of the island, as to attach them to our alliance, and ensure tranquillity between us. All this remains to be discussed when we meet; in the meanwhile, take this as a sketch and colour of my present views.—I am, sincerely and faithfully, MINTO."

This was the first intimation of Lord Minto's intention to take into his own hands the personal direction of the Javan expedition; and in one of his letters Leyden gives the following account of the surprise it caused at the seat of government in India:—

"All are utterly confounded by his Lordship's resolution, of which nobody had the slightest suspicion, and so completely were they all taken aback that nobody volunteered for service till the whole arrangements were settled. Indeed, more than the half are as yet thunderstruck, and are very far from believing that he has any real intention of visiting Java. 'No,' say they, 'to go and take such a little paltry place would not be decorous; no, no, there must be an insurrection breaking out again at Madras.' The selection of your humble servant is another very ominous circumstance, and I daresay has deterred a great many smart bucks from coming forward. The civilians of the Mint Committee have already discovered me to be a very devil incarnate, and the greatest mischiefmaker in the land. They will be very glad to see the back seams of *my* hose at all events. I volunteered of course, as soon as his lordship signified his desire of having me with him, to come off directly to join you; but he told me that he should prefer having me at his elbow. You may be sure no possible delay but will be avoided when I am of the party. We go first to Madras to see the whole force off from that quarter. The Bengal force will be shipped directly. In the *Modeste* go with his Lordship from Madras to Malacca, Mr. Seton, the present Resident at Delhi, who goes to be Governor of Penang. He is an excellent character; Mr. Elliot; Captain Taylor; Mr. Gordon, surgeon to the Body Guard; Mr. Hope, whom you saw when he came from the Mauritius when you were here; and your humble servant. Pray be most particular in your military queries against the time of our arrival, and be able to tell where the disposable force is stationed, for that will be of main utility. I have secured Greigh to be under your command, and that is giving you a fine fellow in every sense of the word, active and alert, and brother-in-law of Lord Rollo besides, and you owe not me, but a good many, for the circumstance."

With one more letter from Lord Minto the history of the preliminary arrangements for the Javan expedition can be closed. The letter was written from Calcutta in March 1811, on the eve of the departure from that place:—

"I still hope we may take our final departure from Malacca in April. The resolution will be taken there respecting the point to which we should first direct our operations; and this must greatly depend on what you tell us concerning the position of Daendels. If he remains in the west, we must no doubt begin there; and, under the circumstances of the season, I should not think that unfortunate, for, the affair once settled with him, and if he is either beat, capitulates, is deserted, or is driven to the hills, our game is won; and we are independent of the monsoon. If he is concentrated in the east our passage will be longer; but we shall have enough of the dry season left to spare. We shall also determine at Malacca what course to steer, whether to march up along the north coast of Java, to make the passage nearer to Borneo, or to go north about at once. You know that I am an Argonaut myself in this adventure.

"I bring also Mr. Seton, an admirable man. I shall probably install him at Penang; and then it is equally probable that he may accompany me to the eastward for counsel and general assistance. Not to alarm you, however, he will have no further relation with the Javanese affair, than as *amicus curiæ*; and as such he is invaluable in head, heart, and hand. . . . You will be glad to find my friend Greigh in this affair; he is placed at your disposal, and is peculiarly suited, as well as his ship, to many useful purposes. It is proposed to style you Secretary to the Governor-General when we come together: . . . secretary is the highest office below the Council. I hope you do not doubt the *prospective* interest I have always taken, and do not cease to take, in your personal views and welfare. I have not spoken distinctly on that subject, only because it has been from circumstances impossible for me to pledge myself to the fulfilment of my own wishes, and, I may add, intentions, if practicable. The best is, in truth, still subject to one contingency, the origin of which is earlier than my acquaintance with you; but I am happy to say that I do not expect an obstacle to my very strong desire upon this point; and if it should occur, the utmost will be done to make the *best attainable situation* worthy of your services, and of the high esteem I profess, with the greatest sincerity, for your person.—Yours very faithfully, MINTO."

Lord Minto sailed from Calcutta in the Company's ship *Mornington* on 11th March 1811, reaching Madras "after a very tedious passage of thirty days." He then exchanged to the *Modeste*, a fine and fast-sailing frigate, commanded by his son, Captain the Hon. George Elliot, and arrived at Penang on 18th April. Exactly one month later the Governor-General reached Malacca; whereupon Raffles ceased to be Agent for the Malay States, and assumed his new post as Principal Secretary. The manner in which Raffles had set himself to the task of obtaining the information required for the accomplishment of the expedition has been described. The information he obtained may be given in a paraphrase of the several voluminous reports he placed before Lord Minto immediately on his arrival at Malacca. Having described the result, as far as was known, of his friendly communications with the chiefs of the Archipelago, and mentioned that a supply of meat for the troops had been unexpectedly placed at his disposal by the voluntary act of a Sumatran princelet, he went on to point out that many of the Javan kings were actually embroiled with the Dutch authorities, and that their co-operation would be invaluable should the "war be carried on amid the mountains and jungles, to which all the operations of Marshal Daendels indicate an intention of transferring it." With regard to the strength of the garrison, Raffles computed it at a total of nearly 30,000 men, including a native contingent of several thousand pikemen. This estimate would give an effective total of about 20,000 men, which was practically correct. He had also ascertained that Batavia had been dismantled, that the seat of government had been removed to Buitenzorg, and that the Dutch commanders were fortifying a well-chosen position at Weltevreeden and Fort Cornelis. The accuracy of his information was demonstrated by the course of the campaign for the conquest of Java. It was typical of the thoroughness with which he did his work, and of the anxious care with which he scanned the future in search of all possible sources of danger, that he suggested an impressive appeal to the soldiers of the expedition, European and native, to take a higher view of the Malays and to act with due consideration towards them, "for a tame submission to personal injury is certainly not characteristic of either the Malays or Javanese."

I may quote here the passage in which Raffles describes the preparations made by Marshal Daendels. "The most active and unremitting exertions appear to have been made by Marshal Daendels towards securing his defences, and the fall of the Mauritius has no doubt fully confirmed his apprehensions of the nature of the intended attack. It seems currently believed in Java that the Marshal expects almost immediate assistance from France; and the circumstance of his being able to hoist the French flag at such a critical moment, and with so little opposition, strongly indicates that he relies on more than ordinary means of defence, and confides in resources which render the sentiments of the Dutch inhabitants of Java a circumstance of comparatively little importance. . . . With respect to the actual force of the enemy, it does not appear that any very considerable augmentation, beyond what might have been calculated upon, has been made since the date of the last accounts which I had the honour to transmit. The reinforcements which the Marshal has received, both in officers and men, from the different garrisons at the Moluccas, have no doubt enabled him to complete several of his defective corps; and as he appears still to retain a very considerable force in native Javanese, his number in this description of troops may exceed the former estimate, and perhaps a general estimate may be taken at about 30,000 men."

In the midst of these incessant political cares and the compilation of voluminous reports, which would alone fill a good-sized volume, Raffles did not forget his literary interests. Surrounded by the bustle of military preparations, and almost within sound of the clash of arms, a meeting of the Asiatic Society was held at Malacca under the personal auspices of Lord Minto and Raffles, and at the same time Raffles sent Mr. Marsden a paper for his periodical publication, *Asiatic Researches*. At the same juncture his mind was also relieved by the marriage of one sister, Mrs. Thompson, to Captain Flint of the Royal Navy, and of another, Leonora, to Mr. B. Loftie, a surgeon on the Madras establishment. His last associations with the Malacca which he had saved from destruction, were consequently of an eminently pleasing character.

But a still more urgent matter than the disposition of the Javanese and the military preparations of the defence was the question of the best and safest route to be followed by the British fleet. Raffles states that he applied to every person likely to possess information on the subject; and he employed Captain Greigh, so favourably mentioned by Lord Minto and

Dr. Leyden, in testing the accuracy of his information, and in reporting on the feasibility of the route which Raffles may be said to have himself discovered, or at least opened up for the use of the expedition. Captain Greigh seems to have been a very skilful mariner, and he did excellent service in this manner on his brig, the *Minto.* There was practically a choice of only two routes: one round the northern coast of Borneo, the other by its south-western coast. The objections to the former were many and weighty. Not the least of them was that it would take the fleet two months to accomplish it, and that the risks of navigation were numerous. Had it been necessary to follow that route, the expedition could not have sailed that summer, for the wet season would have begun before it could have reached its destination. On the other hand, nearly everyone said that the south-west passage was impracticable. Raffles was fortunately sceptical of this sweeping conclusion; and he sent Captain Greigh to report on it by personal examination. Time had now become so important that he could only give him twenty days to examine the channel and return with his report. The point to be settled was whether the expedition must sail by the Straits of Macassar, or whether the Caramata passage and the Strait of Billiton offered a feasible route.

Captain Greigh discharged his mission with perfect address and skill. "The report of Mr. Greigh," wrote Raffles in a despatch to Lord Minto, "sufficiently establishes the practicability of the Caramata passage, and he has likewise ascertained both the facility of working along the coast of Borneo, by the sea and land breezes, and likewise that of making Borneo through the Straits of Singapore." This is the first occasion on which, so far as can be traced, Sir Stamford Raffles wrote the name of Singapore, with which his name will be for ever associated. Within a few days of Lord Minto's arrival at Malacca, Raffles was able to report: "No doubt can now be reasonably entertained that the south-western passage may be effected, by the fleet sailing in divisions, in the space of a month, or six weeks at farthest." When some of the naval officers expressed their doubts on the subject, he went further, and "did not hesitate to stake his reputation on the success which would attend the expedition if the route he pointed out should be followed." Lord Minto declared himself in favour of this route, and his description of the result supplies the vindication of the choice: "The expectations which had been formed were verified in every part of the passage, and everything turned out precisely as had been foretold and proposed, with the exception of finding less difficulty than had been looked for, and the voyage proving shorter than could have been hoped. The whole fleet had assembled on the coast of Java by the 30th July, forty-two days, or exactly six weeks. The *Modeste*, if alone, would have done it a fortnight sooner."

The expedition being now ready to take its departure, it will be natural to pause here and review, however briefly, the nature and the condition of that island on which this, the most formidable Anglo-Indian expedition ever despatched from India up to that moment, was about to make a descent. With this object I introduce here the admirable description prepared some years ago by my friend, the Rev. R. B. Raffles. The literary merit of the description speaks for itself; but, although I reproduce the language of another, I do not devolve the responsibility for what is said on any other shoulders than my own. I associate myself to the fullest extent with the accuracy of the facts, and the tenor of the views, set forth in the remaining portion of this chapter, as in every other part of the book.

In area, Java is a little less than England, and contains about 45,700 square miles. The island is six hundred and fifty miles in length; its greatest breadth is one hundred and thirty-four miles, but in places the land does not exceed fifty miles across. Low plains, often swampy and overgrown with mangrove trees and bushes, lie along the northern coast, and behind Batavia, as they trend away inland for forty miles, rise by imperceptible gradations to the immediate base of the mountains. The southern coast is wilder. There the sea beats against a long wall of perpendicular rocks and cliffs, which rise to a great height, and afford but few anchorages, and fewer harbours, for passing ships. From east to west Java is traversed by a long chain of stupendous mountains.

among which are no less than forty-five volcanoes, some extinct, others shaking the earth from time to time with terrible eruptions, one towering to a height of over twelve thousand feet above the sea. From November till March the country is watered by warm and fertilising rain-clouds, which, drawn by westerly winds from the hot basin of the Indian Ocean, gather and break in the cooler air round the high summits of its mountains; but during the rest of the year the island lies under the dry, clear breath of the easterly monsoon. In the hot region of level plains, or rolling hills, which covers the larger part of the country, and attains an elevation of two thousand feet above the sea, the fields wave with a hundred varieties of rice, with maize, the indigo plant, the clove tree, and the pepper tree; while, in the temperate and delightful climate of the plateaus and valleys lying at a higher elevation, tea and coffee shrubs are massed in rich, green plantations. The great fertility of the island is largely due to its volcanic soil.

The cones of the volcanoes, when they rise above 4500 feet, are bathed in cool air, and on the loftiest mountains ice is sometimes formed at night; while, in the higher regions of the country, hoarfrost—called by the natives "the poisonous dew"—sometimes whitens the trees and vegetation. In fact, as Sir Stamford Raffles says in his standard work on Java, "between the tops of the mountains and the seashore, Java may be considered as possessing at least six distinct climates, each furnishing a copious indigenous botany." The following passage, descriptive of the scenery, is taken from that work:—

"Quitting the low coast of the north, in many parts unhealthy, the traveller can hardly advance five miles inland without feeling a sensible improvement in the atmosphere and climate. As he proceeds, at every step he breathes a purer air and surveys a brighter scene. At length he reaches the high lands. Here the boldest forms of nature are tempered by the rural arts of man: stupendous mountains clothed with abundant harvest, impetuous cataracts tamed to the peasant's will. Here is perpetual verdure; here are tints of the brightest hue. In the hottest season the air retains its freshness; in the driest, the innumerable rills and rivulets preserve much of their water. This the mountain-farmer directs in endless conduits and canals to irrigate the land, which he has laid out in terraces for its reception; it then descends to the plains, and spreads fertility wherever it flows, till at last, by numerous outlets, it discharges itself into the sea. . . An inland navigation is carried to a considerable extent, by means of small canals, in Demák and some of the neighbouring districts, where it is common even during the harvest, at the driest season of the year, to observe innumerable boats, with their light sails, crossing an extensive, flat, and highly cultivated country, and traversing the cornfields in various directions."

A splendid military road, eight hundred miles in length, constructed during the Dutch administration by the forced labour of the natives, and at an awful cost of life, skirts the northern coast from east to west, branching off at different points into the more important inland districts. With regard to the population Raffles wrote:—

"The total population of Java and Madura appears," from the census taken in 1815, "to amount to 4,615,270, of which about four millions and a half may be considered as the indigenous population of the country, and the rest as foreign settlers. Itinerants, who are principally found along the coast in the different maritime and commercial capitals, are not included; neither is the nautical population, which cannot be estimated at less than 30,000 souls; so that the whole population of these two islands may, perhaps, be taken in round numbers at not much less than five millions. . . Upwards of a million and a half" of these are "in the provinces of the native princes."

Since the year 1478 a superficial and tolerant Mahomedanism had been the religion of the country, except in the case of a very few secluded tribes, who, in the eastern parts, maintained some misty forms of the once prevalent Hinduism.

The following passages, selected from the *History of Java*, are interesting, as giving a pretty sketch of Javan life:—

"The cottages are never found detached or solitary; they always unite to form villages of greater or less extent, according to the fertility of the neighbouring plain, abundance of a stream, or other accidental circumstances. In some provinces the usual number of inhabitants in a village is about two hundred, in others less than fifty. In the first establishment or formation of a village on new ground, the intended settlers take care to provide themselves with sufficient garden ground round their huts for their stock, and to supply the ordinary wants of their families. The produce of this plantation is the exclusive property of the peasant, and exempted from contribution or burden; and such is their number and extent in some regencies (as in Kedú, for instance), that they constitute perhaps a tenth part of the area of the whole district. The spot surrounding his simple habitation the cottager considers his peculiar patrimony, and cultivates with peculiar care. He labours to plant and to rear in it those vegetables that may be most useful to his family, and those shrubs and trees which may at once yield him their fruit and their shade; nor does he waste his efforts on a thankless soil. The cottages, or the assemblage of huts, that compose the village, become thus completely screened from the rays of a scorching sun, and are so buried amid the foliage of a luxuriant vegetation that at a small distance no appearance of a human dwelling can be discovered, and the residence of a numerous society appears only a verdant grove or a clump of evergreens. Nothing can exceed the beauty or the interest which such detached masses of verdure, scattered over the face of the country, and indicating each the abode of a collection of happy peasantry, add to scenery otherwise rich, whether viewed on the sides of the mountains, in the narrow vales, or on the extensive plains. In the last case, before the grain is planted, and during the season of irrigation, when the ricefields are inundated, they appear like so many small islands rising out of the water. As the young plant advances, their deep rich foliage contrasts pleasingly with its lighter tints; and when the full-eared grain, with a luxuriance that exceeds a European harvest, invests the earth with its richest yellow, they give a variety to the prospect, and afford a most refreshing relief to the eye. The clumps of trees, with which art attempts to diversify and adorn the most skilfully arranged park, can bear no comparison with them in rural beauty or picturesque effect."

In the western districts "the framework of the cottages is generally made of timber, instead of bamboos, and the interior of them, as well as the front veranda, is raised about two feet from the ground. The accommodation consists of a room partitioned off for the heads of the family, and an open apartment on the opposite side for the children; there is no window either made or requisite. The light is admitted through the door alone; nor is this deficiency productive of any inconvenience in a climate where all domestic operations can be carried on in the open air, and where shade from the sun, rather than shelter from the weather, is required. The women perform their usual occupations of spinning or weaving on an elevated veranda in front, where they are protected from the rays of a vertical sun by an extended projection of the pitch of the roof."

" Much has been said of the indolence of the Javans, by those who deprived them of all motives for industry. I shall not again repeat what I have formerly on several occasions stated on this subject, but shall only enter a broad denial of the charge. The best refutation of the charge of indolence is to be found in the extent of their cultivation, the well-dressed appearance of their ricefields, and the abundant supplies of their harvests. They generally rise by daylight; at half-past six they go out to the ricefields, where they employ their buffaloes till ten, when they return home, bathe, and refresh themselves with a meal. During the violent heat of the noon they remain under the shade of their houses or village trees, making baskets, mending their implements of husbandry, or engaged in other necessary avocations, and at about four return to the sawahs to labour there, without buffaloes or other cattle. At six they return to their homes, sup, and spend the remainder of their time till the hour of rest (which is generally between eight and nine) in little parties for amusement or conversation, when the whole village becomes a scene of quiet content and pleasure. The same round of toil and relaxation is observed during the season for garden culture, dry field labour, or other employments.

" Under this system, the villagers seem to enjoy a greater degree of happiness than they could derive from those increased means that would result from increased exertion. I can bear testimony to their general cheerfulness, contentedness, and good humour; for, having visited their villages at all seasons, and often when least expected or entirely unknown, I have always found them either pleased and satisfied with their lot when engaged at their work, or social and festive in their hours of pleasure."

The following description of a Javanese scene, from a

lecture on Java written by the late Colonel Sir Henry Yule after a visit in 1860, may be introduced here:—"Now, every one of these great cones, covered, excepting perhaps a bare space near the summit, with a magnificent vegetation, stands up here attracting the benignant clouds from either ocean, and sucking in their moisture. Every one of these fire-born mountains thus becomes a great fountain of waters, sending down on every side hundreds of fertilising rills; whilst the very soil, which partakes of volcanic origin, is well known to be the most fertile of all when amply supplied with water. It is a glorious sight to see those mountains in Java, above all, perhaps, a naked cone, from which floats a white flag of smoke against the blue sky, their vast steeps of sombre forest succeeded by great masses of dark green conical shrub-like trees with white flowers, the regularity of which betrays the hand of man; these are the coffee gardens; then by the roots and spurs of the mountain radiating, spreading outward like the roots of a great tree, but all carved by the patient labour of centuries into beautiful terraces, hundreds and thousands of terraces forming giant staircases of the richest culture, and down every one of these staircases, cascading from terrace to terrace, gushes a stream of the purest water. When the rice crop is flooded, one of these hillsides I can compare to nothing but a staircase of looking-glasses."

Such was Java, a land on which nature, with ungrudging bounty, had heaped her choicest gifts; a climate varied and, for the most part, delightful; a volcanic soil, rich beyond the dreams of European agriculturists; a people naturally gentle, industrious, grateful, and often refined—an easy prey to brutal and rapacious strangers, till, when they had been goaded to desperation and revenge, the deadly kris was sheathed in the heart of the oppressor. The island might have been an earthly paradise; it became, wherever the contaminating power of the Dutch was felt, a long scene of misery and smothered discontent. Fair and fertile provinces, once peopled by a happy peasantry, were turned into vast farms or factories of sullen bondage, worked by a rapidly diminishing race of shrinking and famine-stricken paupers. Batavia, built in swamps, and steeped by night in the unhealthy vapours of creeping fogs, was a prison and a charnel-house, where in one short period of twenty-two years (1730–1752) more than a million lives had fallen a sacrifice to commercial monopoly.

It is impossible to follow the records of the Dutch Government in the East Indies without sharing the horror and detestation of the Commissioners appointed in 1790 by the States of Holland to ascertain the real cause of the Company's declining finances. They stood aghast before "the still increasing and exorbitant rate of the expenses, the incessant want of cash, the mass of paper money in circulation, the unrestrained peculations and faithlessness of many of the Company's servants, the consequent clandestine trade of foreign nations, the perfidy of the native princes, the weakness and connivance of the Indian Government, the excessive expenses in the military department and for the public defence."

But this Commission sat, and made its report, in the Netherlands. What would have been the feelings of the Commissioners had they proceeded to the East Indies in 1793 with the new Commission whose appointment they had recommended, and if they had seen, face to face, the suffering, the ruin, and the depopulation which lay behind the corrupt administration and the rotten finances upon which they had commented? Sent to inaugurate something like free trade, this last, the Company's Commission, proposed to restrict the little private trade there was. They were to loosen the grip of monopoly: they made that grip tighter. However wise the views entertained by the leading statesmen of the United States of Holland may have been, those views filtered down but slowly and in a weak solution, if at all, into the minds of the great majority of Dutch colonial administrators. Dutch colonists were traders, not statesmen. A country within the scope of their growing influence for more than two hundred years was not likely to rise in the scale of civilisation. Their conceptions might reach to the overgrown farm or the swollen factory; they could scarcely rise to that of an expanding state. Their empire widened; their sense of imperial responsibility slumbered. They provided almost nothing, and they cared less for the happiness of the native populations; the justice or injustice of their judicial systems; the protection afforded, or the cruelties inflicted, by the native rulers. Revenue was their only care; gain their dearest hope. There were some men of insight and humanity, both in the home country and in Java, but their efforts were powerless, and their theories abortive. Mr. Dirk Van Hogendorp, of Batavia, strenuously advocated the abolition of "the exclusive and oppressive trade of the Company, the forced deliveries, the feudal services—in short, the whole system of feudal government." But a committee, reporting to the Government of the Batavia Republic on the 31st of August 1803, declared that, "after long and laborious researches," they had been compelled to acknowledge the total impossibility of introducing property in the soil or abolishing the forced services.

Mr. H. W. Muntinghe, Member of Council during the British Administration, in a minute recorded in the Council Chamber, Batavia, on the 28th of July 1813, wrote as follows:—"The amelioration, however, of the natives of this island, though undoubtedly a consideration in the eyes of humanity, seems to me to become only a secondary object in a political point of view; and with the exception of every measure contrary to the principlès of justice and equity, it appears to me that the safest principle which can be adopted, to judge of the propriety of any colonial regulations, or of any changes and alterations to be introduced therein, is *that every colony does or ought to exist for the benefit of the mother-country.*"

If such, expressed in the restrained language of an official document, were the opinions of one of the most enlightened among Dutch statesmen, at a moment, too, when British authority was supreme, what must have been the sentiments of the coarse, selfish, and corrupt servant of the Company, removed from the influence of public opinion, and surrounded by a weaker and, in his eyes, an inferior race of people?

The great majority of mankind are wholly unfitted for the exercise of power and the right use of a position of ascendency. In their hands the reins of authority become the pitiless lash of brutal tyranny. Europe has but little cause to look back with pride on the early history of some of its colonial possessions. Race after race of free and ancient peoples, with many a noble trait and many a hopeful promise rooted in the national character, has gone down before the rush of European settlers—sometimes exterminated by fire and sword, sometimes devastated by the new and terrible curses of a corrupt civilisation. Even England is not free from this disgrace ; but in eastern lands the natives have, on the whole, fared better wherever her influence has been felt. In those hot countries there was no hunger for land gnawing at the white man's heart, and overpowering every moral consideration. There the white man came to trade rather than to settle ; he stayed to govern as well as trade, and, if at first he governed roughly, his government at least bore the marks of progressive and humane improvement. It is the chief glory of Sir Stamford Raffles to have been one of the pioneers in this work of kindly and beneficent administration, sometimes creating, sometimes remodelling the machinery of government, and by the force and brilliancy of his genius inspiring many of those around him with his own ardent and enthusiastic spirit. To make the people committed to his charge happier, better, and wiser by means of enlightened political and judicial institutions, by the patronage of literature and science, the protection and promotion of free commerce, and the advancement of religion—these were his guiding principles and aims.

It was far otherwise with the Dutch who preceded him in Java. After the dissolution of the misgoverned and bankrupt Company in 1795, the administration of the Dutch East Indies was, at one period (1808–1811), in the hands of Marshal Daendels, a man able, active, vigorous, "singularly unscrupulous," self-laudatory. He was recalled by the Emperor Napoleon only a few months before the British conquest of Java. Referring to the principles, or rather to the difficulties, by which his administration was guided, he says : "In the midst of such disastrous circumstances, and the failure of so many attempts to introduce reform and to maintain the dignity of government, I found it necessary to place myself above the usual formalities, and to disregard every law but that which enjoined the preservation of the colony intrusted to my management." The military training of the Marshal showed itself in his energetic and despotic sway. He deserved the title of "The Last of the Tyrants," given him by the late Sir Henry Yule. His predecessors had chastised the island with whips; the zealous and ferociously oppressive spirit of the Marshal led him to chastise it with scorpions. Territory and wealth, not men and human well-being, were the objects of his anxious solicitude. Revolting details, sad and hideous realities of cruelty and oppression lurk behind the measured language and the careful figures of the statesman, the commissioner, the historian, and the statistician, and fall like shadows on a screen.

Except in the district immediately round Batavia, the Dutch left the internal administration of their possessions entirely to the native chiefs. The country was divided into provinces, varying in size and population; and the ruler at the head of each, whatever his designation in the dialects of the island might be, was termed by the Dutch a Regent. To each Regent the Dutch Government apportioned a certain amount of rice or other produce, to be paid by him in kind yearly, together with a certain sum, as recognition-money, to be paid in coin. The Regent had at the same time to provide all the labour and necessaries which Government might from time to time require. The Regent, usually on the receipt of purchase-money, appointed certain subordinate officers under him, called Tumung'gungs, as District Officers, to farm the revenue throughout their several districts, collecting it from the heads of villages. These last sometimes obtained their posts by the patronage of their superiors, sometimes by purchase, sometimes by the free election of their fellow-villagers. It was the business of the head of a village to collect the rent from the actual cultivators, and to pass it on to his superiors.

The Regents obtained their offices from the Dutch by a contract binding them to pay this yearly rent in kind and money; a rent often exceeding the capacities of the soil.

The office was sold to the highest bidder, and the proceeds of these sales formed a principal part of the emoluments of the Dutch governor of the north-east coast. The man who was the chief Regent of Samarang in 1800 had, according to Mr. Hogendorp, paid 50,000 dollars, whether Spanish or not is unspecified, for the post he held. Purchase-money and rent were, of course, eventually extracted from the people.

A material change was, however, effected with regard to the Regents by Marshal Daendels. Previous to his organisation of the eastern districts, the Regents had been supposed to hold their authority of right, and their agreement with Government was considered as a contract; but the Marshal, by a very laudable stroke of policy, rendered them immediately dependent on the European Government, by giving them commissions and instructions as officers of Government.

In itself this measure, carried out apparently in the eastern districts only, did nothing to benefit the people; on the contrary, it only enabled the supreme tyranny to hold the instruments of oppression with a still firmer grasp. But the policy was good, because it brought the native authorities more within the control of a power which might be, and subsequently was, a merciful one.

When the Regent made a demand, the amount demanded at last reached the wretched cultivator, doubled twice over by the additional extortions of the intermediate officials. No cultivator had a written lease or any certain compensation for the improvements made by his own industry. The amount of rent exacted from him was, most frequently, as much as he could pay. The lands nearest the seat of the Regent, being the easiest to reach, had the most frequent demands made upon them. If the Regent was civil to the Resident, there was little inquiry into the conduct of the former. The people were the Regent's vassals, and he treated them as he pleased. All over the land the complaints of an unhappy peasantry were stifled by a host of petty tyrants before they reached the dull ears of the superior power. One remedy the poor had: they were not serfs, and could migrate to other territories. But the straits to which they had been reduced were desperate, before the home-loving Javanese left the old village and the deeply venerated tombs of his forefathers. When the Dutch were first established in the eastern parts of the island, inhabitants of whole districts at once migrated into the Native Provinces. Tracts were thus brought into cultivation which, in former times, had supported scarcely a family. In the years 1808–1810, during the administration of Marshal Daendels, nearly all the people in Demák, one of the richest of the eastern districts, took refuge under the less oppressive authority of the native princes. The population of Banyuwangi is said to have exceeded eighty thousand in 1750; in 1811 it had dwindled down to eight thousand. Bantam and Cheribon, once rich and populous, had been brought to poverty and insurrection by oppression and misrule; extensive tracts in the Priangen Regencies, once cultivated, had been turned into a wilderness.

The forced cultivation of coffee produced the most dreadful sufferings. In the Sunda districts the peasants were sometimes compelled to devote their energies so entirely to coffee that they were unable to grow food for themselves; and, while some perished from starvation, others fled to the mountains and lived chiefly on roots. The Dutch would pay a halfpenny for a pound of coffee delivered at the Government storehouses, after being carried, about a hundredweight between two men, for sixty miles over an almost impassable country. In Europe the coffee was never sold for less than elevenpence for a pound. The volcanic soil of Java was peculiarly adapted, like that of Italy, for the growth of the vine. The manufacture of wine from the grape was strictly prohibited, lest it should interfere with the profits of Dutch vine-culture at the Cape.

A typical picture of Dutch maladministration was furnished by the fertile province of Cheribon. This province was always financially disappointing to the Dutch. "The coffee and other produce exacted from the people was delivered by the Sultan, and paid for to him. Under this system the Resident of Cheribon enjoyed an annual income of from eighty to one hundred thousand dollars (£23,000), while the Sultans were every year more and more impoverished. At length an insurrection broke out in 1800," "the real cause" of which "was probably the great oppression of the common inhabitants, occasioned by the distress of the Sultans, and the indiscriminate admission of too many Chinese in the interior of the country."

Mr. John Crawfurd, Civil Commissioner, quoted in the *History of Java*, enumerated the following duties as exacted in Cheribon before the great land revenue settlement:—

1. The contingent: properly 15 per cent. of the rice crop, but arbitrarily assessed.

2. A poll-tax, or rather a tax on families; partly levied on account of Government, partly on account of the chiefs.

3. Market duties or tolls, literally levied on every article produced by agriculture, manufacture, or the petty arts.

4. A tax on the slaughter of buffaloes, which affected the price of food, and restricted the breeding of that useful animal.

5. The charge of lodging and feeding travellers, and transporting troops, baggage, and stores of all descriptions.

6. The obligation to construct and repair bridges, roads, and public buildings, throughout the country.

7. The obligation to cultivate and deliver, at inadequate rates, certain foreign and wholly unsuitable productions, chiefly coffee.

8. A nominal tithe, really less than one-twentieth of the rice crop, was allotted to religious purposes; a payment optional, but seldom withheld.

"Even the European authority did not escape the taint, but followed the track of corruption. Monopolies, unpaid services, licences, forced or, at least, expected presents, were but too common even in the best times."

The restrictions placed on foreign trade added to the general financial and commercial distress.

"Square-rigged vessels, navigated by Europeans, were excluded from all the minor ports; the little traffic of which was chiefly carried on by Bugguese and Malay prows," and on that traffic "the duties and charges amounted to more than forty-six per cent." And in the case of the three ports left open, "all goods paid at Batavia an import duty of six per cent., and at Samarang and Sourabaya, eleven per cent.; unless proceeding direct, in which case they paid fourteen," and " trade was virtually excluded from the minor ports."

" The trade carried on by native vessels along the coast with the neighbouring islands, and with the Peninsula of Malacca, has been even more shackled than that placed under the impolitic restraints of interior regulation." Not only was the peaceful trader exposed to numerous pirates, who annually swept the coast of Java, but " the various restrictions, penalties, and prohibitions established by the Dutch Government, in order to insure their own monopoly, closed all the minor ports against him."

Among these restrictions none operated more forcibly to prejudice the native trade than the rigid and enforced monopoly of the teak timber; an article of produce with which Java abounds, and of which the shipping of the Archipelago had, from time immemorial, been principally constructed. The facilities for building and repairing vessels along the coast, while the sale of this timber was unrestricted, not only allowed a more abundant supply of shipping at a cheap rate for the convenience of the native trader, but attracted the beneficial visits and the intercourse of foreigners, and encouraged a species of trade, which, under the recent system, had been lost. The Búgis, natives of Celebes, and Arabs of the different eastern ports, navigating in large vessels, were induced to give them an annual repair on Java ; and rather than depart in ballast, frequently carried out cargoes, the profits of which alone, independently of their refit, would not have been sufficient to tempt them to their speculation. These adventurers not only imported considerable quantities of gold dust to defray the expense of their repairs, but many other articles, the produce of the Malayan islands, for which they in return exported large quantities of salt and other bulky commodities, which would otherwise hardly repay their freight. In consequence of the stop put to this kind of intercourse, the Malayan States were principally supplied with salt from Siam and the Coromandel coast, or manufactured the article for themselves; while an accumulating undemanded surplus for many years remained on Java unsaleable.

Taxes similar to those described above in the case of Cheribon, "with still heavier and more vexatious duties and exactions, were levied on trade in other districts of the island. Constant requisitions were made by the Dutch Government for the services of native vessels, at rates far below a just compensation to the owner, and the native traders were forbidden to traffic in any of the articles of Dutch monopoly."

"The orders made in 1767, and strictly enforced throughout the Archipelago," say, in the first article, "All persons whatever are prohibited, under *pain of death,* from trading in the four fine kinds of spices, unless such spices shall be first bought of the Company." The traffic in opium was restricted by the same regulations and penalty.

Nor, at this early period, was Java free from the embarrassments of the Chinese question. "The favourite policy of the Dutch seems to have been to depress the native inhabitants, and give every encouragement to the Chinese, . . . who follow the almost universal practice of remitting the fruits of their industry to China, instead of spending them where they were acquired." The Chinese were good and stimulating traders, but bad and politically undesirable citizens. They lived generally under their own laws, administered by their own chiefs, but in certain cases came under European law.

Arriving at Batavia from China, to the amount of a thousand and more annually, in Chinese junks, a venal, crafty, unscrupulous, industrious, and heartless people, these Chinese immigrants, without resources on landing, soon acquired wealth. They either traded privately, or farmed the import and export duties, and the transport and other levies throughout the interior of the island. The internal transport duties sometimes amounted to forty-seven per cent. Independent of the personal taxes imposed on the cultivators, the taxes on the internal trade extended to every article of produce, manufacture, or consumption, passing through the country—they were levied by corrupt and extortionate agents, and in most instances were farmed out to the Chinese. A different mode of taxation existed in every district.

"To such an extent has this vexatious mode of taxation proceeded under the Chinese, and so numerous are the petty demands, that in many instances, on goods passing from one toll towards another, when the granting of something like a certificate of the last duty paid becomes necessary for the interest of the farmer, the chop or stamp is not marked on the goods transported, but on the body of the man who conveys them, who, on exhibiting the stamp at the next toll, has it effaced, and a new impression made in its room, to pass him further on."

When such expedients were resorted to for ensuring the collection of the revenue, it cannot be surprising that the Javanese abhorred the Chinese; and yet these were the only class of people intrusted by the former Government with the collection of these revenues.

As far as possible the Chinese got the markets and bazaars into their hands. "The bazaars," observes Mr. Hogendorp, "now produce a large, and even an incredible amount, which, however, is melted away in the hands of the native regents and also some European authorities; but the Chinese, to whom they are mostly farmed out, derive the greatest profits from them, both by the money which they extort from the Javans, and by the monopolies in all kinds of produce, and particularly of rice, which by these means they are enabled to secure to themselves. The abuses on this point are horrible, and almost induce me to recommend that the markets should be made free and open."

The Chinese farmed the public markets in Batavia and its vicinity, and, in consequence, the degeneracy and poverty of the lower orders became proverbial.

"Wherever the Chinese formed extensive settlements in Java, the native inhabitants had no alternative but that of abandoning the district or becoming slaves of the soil."

The manufacture of salt, an article incalculably necessary and precious in tropical countries, was farmed to the Chinese, who made their monopoly as oppressive and as lucrative as they could.

The forced and unpaid services exacted from the people weighed terribly upon them. The Tumung'gung and his family and all the petty chiefs had trains of unpaid followers: people were taken from the villages to wait without wages about the courts of sultans and regents. Chiefs of high and low degree, and the higher servants of the Government, when travelling for business or pleasure, quartered themselves and their followers freely on the people; so also did the officials of the post-carriages, the letter-carriers, and the police officers, the latter having no regular emoluments from Government.

The beating out of rice, together with the cutting of grass and firewood for Government, the transport of Government stores, the unpaid repair or construction of roads and public buildings, all added to the endless tale of oppression. These feudal services were rewarded solely "by the use of an assignment of ricefields, allotted either to individuals or to certain classes of workmen, but withdrawn from them as soon as the public duty ceased to be performed:" in other words, so far as the whole body of natives was concerned, they were not rewarded at all, the non-impressed labour of the country merely being compelled to support the impressed. For the cutting of teak timber and the planting of coffee, as well as their delivery, a similar reward was assigned, together with "a certain payment about equivalent to the expenses of transportation to the Government yards or storehouses."

"During the administration of Marshal Daendels, it has been calculated that the construction of public roads alone destroyed the lives of at least ten thousand workmen." "Their construction," instead of assisting trade or agriculture, "has, on the contrary, in many instances, been destructive to whole districts, and when completed by his own labour, or the sacrifice of the lives of his neighbours, the peasant was debarred from their use, and not permitted to drive his cattle along them, while he saw the advantages they were capable of yielding reserved for his European masters, that they might be enabled to hold a more secure possession of his country." Internal commerce was not, however, impeded by want of convenient roads, for "good inferior roads were often made by the side of these military roads, and bye-roads branched off through all parts of the country." The military roads were an additional safeguard recently made, in great part, during the blockade.

Unhealthy garrison stations, unnecessary hardships and

privations produced extraordinary casualties in the Dutch native army, which had to be constantly recruited by conscription. "The conscripts raised in the provinces were usually sent to the metropolis by water; and though the distance be but short between any two points of the island, a mortality, similar to that of a slave-ship in the middle passage, took place on board these receptacles of reluctant recruits. They were generally confined in the stocks till their arrival at Batavia, and it is calculated that for every man that entered the army and performed the duties of a soldier, several lives were lost. Besides the supply of the army, one-half of the male population of the country was constantly held in readiness for other public services; and thus a great portion of the effective hands were taken from their families, and detained at a distance from home, in labours which broke their spirit and exhausted their strength."

The forced services hitherto mentioned were more or less legalised injustice: but treatment, if it be possible, yet more cruel and lawless remains behind.

"The coasting vessels belonging to Chinese, Arabs, and others, navigate throughout the whole extent of the Archipelago, to Malacca and Acheen on one side, and to the Moluccas and New Guinea on the other. The class of common sailors on board these ships is almost exclusively composed of the natives of Java, who are known in the East under the general denomination of Malays. According to the maritime customs of the Malay peoples, all persons on board, from the captain downwards, including the petty officers, have an interest, however small, in the cargo, while the common sailors, Javans, are protected by these petty officers, their own countrymen." As the native traders "do not possess the authority to obtain crews by force, it is only by a character for good treatment, by attention to the usages, prejudices, and comfort of the crews, that they can insure an adequate supply of hands." As a consequence, "among themselves, the maritime population is distinguished for good faith and attachment," "and no instances occur of the crews rising either upon the Arab or Chinese commander: they are, on the contrary, found to be faithful, hardworking, and extremely docile." On the other hand, when so-called "Malays" are employed in vessels belonging to Europeans, they frequently mutiny, and massacre their officers. The reasons for this difference are given in the following passages from Raffles's paper on the "Maritime Institutions of the Malays":—

"The Javans are originally not a seafaring people; they have an aversion for distant voyages, and require the strongest inducements to quit the land, even for a coasting expedition in the smooth seas of their own Archipelago, beyond which, if they ever engage themselves on board a colonial vessel, they make an express agreement not to be carried. European vessels in want of hands for more distant voyages to Europe, India, and China, have been compelled therefore to resort to force or fraud, as the means of obtaining crews.

"The Dutch Government were in the habit of employing people as kidnappers, who prowled about at night, pounced upon the unwary peasant who might be passing alone, and hurried him on ship-board. When the direct influence of Government was not used, the native regents or chiefs were employed to obtain people for the crews of vessels: this they did sometimes in the same manner, though more frequently condemning to sea as many as were required, by an indiscriminate draft on the neighbouring population. The native chiefs were perhaps paid a certain head-money, on what may have been considered by the European commanders as nothing more than *crimpage*. The people who were seized were seldom of a seafaring class, but almost entirely landsmen, in many instances, perhaps, opium-smokers, or persons obtained from the lowest and most worthless part of the community. Once embarked, their fate was sealed for ever, and due care was taken that they never landed again on Java, as long as their services as sailors were required.

"In general, neither their language nor customs are in the least understood by their new master, for though most of the commanders in the eastern trade may speak the Malayan language and be accustomed to the Malayan character, they know nothing of the Javan language, and but little of the manners, habits, and prejudices of the Javan people."

On the subject of slavery in the island Raffles wrote as follows in one of his Reports to Lord Minto:—

"The Dutch had introduced slavery into Java on the ground that there did not exist in the island a class of people sufficiently adroit and docile for household service, and that they had therefore to create a class of domestic servants by rearing in their families children brought from other countries. But 'the Javans, during the residence of the British in Java,' were 'found perfectly trustworthy, faithful, and industrious; and the demand was alone wanting in this, as in most cases, to create a sufficient supply of competent domestics.' 'The native Javans were never reduced to slavery,' and the slave merchants drew their supplies in consequence from the neighbouring islands, particularly from Bali and Celebes. From returns obtained in 1814, it appeared that there were about 30,000 slaves in Java, of whom 27,142 were concentrated about the centres of Dutch life; the Samarang and Surabaya divisions containing

8170, while no less than 18,972 were crowded into either the Dutch capital, Batavia, or its environs. A few of these slaves worked for their masters at some handicraft or trade, or on their estates; but the majority were domestic servants.

"'These slaves are the property of the Europeans and Chinese alone; the native chiefs' (*i.e.* on Java itself) 'never require the services of slaves, or engage in the traffic of slavery.' 'Although they (the Dutch) adopted principles that admitted of the most cruel and wanton treatment of slaves, I would not be understood to say that they carried these principles into common practice. The contrary was almost universally the case.'

"'The regulations and colonial statutes respecting slavery seem to have been framed on the principles of humanity, and with attention to the genius of the Christian religion;' but the Dutch carried with them into their Eastern empire the Roman law regarding slavery in all its extent and rigour. 'A slave was considered as a real property, incapable of personal rights, from which consideration the ill-treatment of a master towards his slave was not so much estimated on the principle of personal injury, as that of a proprietor abusing his own property; and although a slave, under such a system, might obtain a portion of property for himself with the consent of his master, his possession was always precarious, and depended on the discretion of his proprietor (in the same manner as a *peculium adventitium* with the Romans), becoming only the unlimited property of the slave, if the master allowed him to keep it after his emancipation.'"

The Dutch colonial law, in spite of a certain unwieldiness, seems to have possessed many excellent points; but the system on which it was administered was "at once complicated and confused." The number of judges who formed a court was far too large, exceeding four. "There was no distinction known between the police and the judicial system of administration. At Batavia, however, there existed a Supreme Court of Judicature, and a Bench or Court of Aldermen, called the College of Schepmen; and at Sourabaya and Samarang inferior courts of justice had been established." "The only distinction which existed was that all the Company's servants should be amenable to the regular courts of justice, or to the Supreme Court at Batavia, while other persons of every description were under the jurisdiction of the Schepmen." This legal system, then, was applied to the Dutch colonists all over the island, and in some places to the natives and Chinese also.

"The Dutch legislated for the colonists, but took little interest in the system by which the judicial proceedings of their native subjects were guided, excepting in so far as their own advantage or security was concerned in them." "In the different Residencies were provincial courts, styled *landraads*, where the native form and law was left to take its course, with all its barbarities and tortures."

In the city of Batavia and its environs, natives and Chinese were tried by European judges, and were under European law in both criminal and civil cases. In the Jahatra and Priangen Regencies, where there were scarcely any foreign settlers, a court, the rule of which was European law, exercised jurisdiction over the natives. "In Bantam the criminal jurisdiction over the natives was left to the Sultan:" the Chinese were subject to European law. The Chinese were similarly placed in Cheribon; but "the natives were subject to a *landraad* (or local court), of which the Resident was president, and the Sultans members; and this court was, partly at least, directed by a *papáham*, or native code, compiled under the sanction of Government."

"In the eastern districts of the island the Javans seem always, in criminal matters, to have enjoyed their own laws, founded on ancient custom and the precepts of the Koran. Of these laws the Council of Batavia caused abstracts to be printed, for the guidance of the great *landraad* or High Court at *Samarang*, to which all the Javans in the European provinces, from Losári to Banyuwangi were amenable."

One more passage must be added to this description of the state of Java under the Dutch before the arrival of the British. It is a passage which speaks volumes.

"In answer," writes Raffles in the *History of Java* from which most of these extracts are quoted, "to what has been asserted concerning robberies, assassinations, and thefts, it may be stated, that during the residence of the English, an entire confidence was reposed in the people, and that confidence was never found misplaced. The English never used bars or bolts to their houses, never travelled with arms, and no instance occurred of their being ill-used. The Dutch, on the contrary, placed no confidence; all their windows were barred, and all their doors locked, to keep out the treacherous natives (as they called them), and they never moved five miles abroad without pistols and swords. What could be expected by a Government that derived a principal part of its revenue by the encouragement of vice, by the farms of gaming, cock-fighting, and opium shops? After the two former were abolished by the English, and the local government had done all in its power to discourage the latter, a visible amelioration took place in the morals of the lower ranks."

There was a lamentable falling off in the foreign trade of Java after the commencement of the war of the French Revolution; some of the best markets were almost entirely closed to it, and the intercourse with the mother-country was nearly destroyed. The total of exports to Holland and her Eastern possessions, from the year 1796–1806, amounted in value to only 7,097,963 Spanish dollars; the imports to 3,073,894 Spanish dollars; leaving a surplus of exports of 4,024,069 Spanish dollars. The Americans began to frequent the market of Batavia in 1798, and through them principally was the trade carried on till the conquest of the island by the British, except during the short interval of the peace of Amiens. No specie (with which Holland chiefly paid for her eastern commodities) was imported from the mother-country from 1759 downwards, except during 1802–3 and 1803–4, during which there was only the very inconsiderable sum of about half a million of rupees imported.

All these gigantic evils, widespread, deep-seated, and, with scarcely an exception, inherent in the Dutch colonial system itself, had culminated in a financial distress so pressing that, during the period immediately preceding the British occupation, forced loans had been exacted from private individuals to pay for military defences; more than four million of Rix dollars in a paper currency, which steadily decreased in value, had been thrown upon an exhausted market; the Government had been unable to pay even its lowest establishment; and, in the general wreck, the funds of the public charities themselves had been appropriated to the necessities of a sinking state. A calm consideration of all the facts that have been enumerated as to the condition of Java under Dutch rule will justify the conclusion that, for the interests of the inhabitants, the British expedition did not arrive a moment too soon.

CHAPTER V

THE CONQUEST OF JAVA

WHEN the route of the expedition had been decided on, the fleet, which numbered one hundred vessels, began on the 11th of June 1811 to leave Malacca. Twelve hundred sick were left behind at that port; but the transports, fifty-seven in number, still conveyed nearly 11,000 troops. The *Modeste*, with Lord Minto and Raffles on board, sailed a week later. She was accompanied by the brig *Minto*, under Captain Greigh's command, with Leyden for a passenger. The *Modeste*, being the fastest ship in the fleet, soon caught up the leading division. Lord Minto gives in his letters an amusing description of the prevalent timidity as to the route taken. "Commodore Broughton, who is," he wrote, "the most cautious navigator that ever wore a blue coat, was not satisfied to abide by Greigh's report, but ordered the *Modeste* to go ahead and reconnoitre the whole passage to the rendezvous, thinking, very properly, that I had better be drowned than he. As I was entirely of the same opinion, I accepted the service very thankfully. In reality I knew that George [his son, Captain the Honourable George Elliot] was much fitter to perform this duty than any other officer in the fleet, and I thought it would be amusing to myself." Lord Minto gives so admirable an account of the whole passage, that it may be inserted here:—

"H.M.S. *Modeste*, off Java; ended 3rd August 1811.

"The fleet having at length assembled at Malacca, it was despatched towards its destination in a number of small divisions, which sailed successively, each under charge of a frigate, and attended also by sloops of war or Company's cruisers.

"The *Modeste* was not attached to any division, and, being sure of overtaking the earliest and swiftest, we remained at anchor till the whole had departed. The fleet consisted of eighty-one sail of all descriptions, and it was despatched in many divisions, because we had several narrow straits and difficult passes before us, which must have occasioned confusion, and probably accident and loss, if so large a body of shipping had kept together. . . . The difficulty was this. As soon as what is called the south-east monsoon in the eastern seas sets in, the wind blows hard and pretty steadily from the east along the channel between the north of Java and the south of Borneo ; it blows to the north-west along the east coast of Sumatra, and between that coast and the Malay Peninsula ; it blows to the north between the west coast of Borneo and the Straits of Malacca. So that, starting from Malacca, the wind was directly contrary in every part of the course to the northern coast of Java. Besides this difficulty there is a current in the same direction as the wind throughout. To carry a great fleet of transports, not famous in general for working to windward, a long voyage directly against wind and current, did not appear promising. It was known, however, that with a little patience, a fleet can at that season make a passage down the Straits of Malacca by any one of the several passages which lead to the eastward. This is done by the help of squalls, which generally blow from the northward ; by occasional shifts of wind, and by alterations of tide or current, which afford a favourable start to the eastward. It was ascertained by investigation, inquiry, and actual survey and trial recently made for the present occasion, that after making the west coast of Borneo, land winds at night, and the sea breeze during part of the day, together with a slackening of the current, and even a favourable current during particular periods of the tide, will enable ships to make a passage along the coast to the southward without much delay ; and from the south-west point of Borneo, having the wind at east, you may stand at least as high as south to Java, and make that island as far to the east as Samarang—which is more than we desire. The plan was therefore settled on this foundation. The *Modeste* sailed from Malacca on 18th June. We soon passed a great part of the fleet, and left them in the Straits of Singapore, when we got into the open channel between those Straits and Borneo. . . . We cleared the Straits on 20th June at sunset, leaving a great part of the fleet at anchor behind us, and stood across towards Borneo. We made that island off Sambas, a little to the north of Pontiana. Here we came up with a division under the command of Captain Cole, which had sailed from Malacca some time before us, and which was preceded by another under Captain Edgell not yet in sight. We soon, however, came up with it, and had then the lead of all."

A proclamation, dated off Batavia, 4th August 1811, signed by Minto and countersigned by Raffles, was issued to the Dutch inhabitants, offering peace and protection to those who " pass cordially under the British dominion," and setting forth that—

" England has in every period, sometimes in concert with other Powers, sometimes single and alone, been the champion and defender of Europe, the hope of those whose fate was not yet consummated, the refuge and consolation of the fallen—that France has been with equal uniformity the common enemy of all nations. Between these two the option must be made, and on that question the extinction of their metropolis has left the colonies of Holland to their own free judgment. Their country has expired. If the sentiments which His Excellency has been desirous of ascribing to them should induce them to pass cordially under the British dominion, he offers friendship and protection during any contest which it may be necessary to maintain with those who would adhere to France."

A further proclamation was addressed to the native inhabitants, stating in the Malay and Javanese languages that "The English come as friends, and they expect to be received as such by every description of the native inhabitants, but as they have not entered the Eastern sea for purposes of ruin or destruction, but solely with the desire of securing to the Eastern nations the enjoyment of their ancient laws and institutions, and of protecting everyone from violence, oppression, and injustice, the inhabitants themselves must be aware that they cannot recommend themselves to such a Government by means of massacres and commotions. The English Government accordingly require that the native inhabitants remain for the present peaceable spectators of what is about to take place, and that they on no account act oppressively or take up arms against the French or Dutch, except when expressly called upon to do so by an English officer. All supplies will be paid for at full value, but you are not to supply the enemy, and you are also to impede the progress of the enemy's army from one part of the country to the other. The port of Batavia is open to native traders. All prows and vessels bringing provisions and merchandise will be kindly received and protected by the English ships of war."

The *Modeste* reached the coast of Java, opposite Batavia, on 29th July, and the remainder of the fleet began to come up twenty-four hours later. The whole passage of six weeks had been performed without the loss of a man or a ship. It banished the anxiety which had been almost overwhelming for the two men really responsible for the venture, and it was of happy augury for the success of the expedition. Raffles has described, in the autobiographical letter, his sensations as "the promised land" came in sight, and they are also revealed in the letter, previously cited, to his friend, the younger Ramsay.

The commander of the troops was General Sir Samuel Achmuty, between whom and Lord Minto there was a perfect agreement and understanding. In one of the latter's letters he says: "I have conceived the highest opinion of Sir Samuel Achmuty's talents, judgment, and, above all, *character*, from his correspondence. It is impossible that anything can disturb the harmony of this important service as far as he and I are concerned." Unlike some anticipations of the same nature, this was realised to the letter. On the 4th August the British expeditionary force was landed without opposition at Chillingching, a point on the coast ten or twelve miles east of Batavia, and it is said that Leyden, with equal enthusiasm and impetuosity, was the first man of the force to rush through the surf to the shore. Five days later, part of the army, under the command of Colonel Gillespie, occupied Batavia, which the Dutch evacuated without firing a shot; but on discovering the weakness of this detachment the enemy made a night attack, but were fortunately repulsed without any loss. The Dutch commander had concentrated all his available forces in the strong position of Cornelis, seven miles south of Batavia, on the line of hills. His advanced guard also held Weltevreeden, and General Janssens is affirmed to have felt and expressed great confidence in his ability to render a good account of the invaders.

The strength of the British force had originally been 5344 Europeans, 5777 natives, and 839 Lascars. Of these, 1200 were left, as stated, in the hospitals at Malacca, and during the six weeks' voyage 1500 more were added to the sick-list; so that the effective strength of the expedition at the moment of occupying Batavia was 9000 men. On the other hand, General Janssens had under him about 17,000 disciplined troops, many of his officers were Frenchmen who had seen service under Napoleon, and there was at least one complete battalion of French voltigeurs. The position of Cornelis had also been elaborately prepared, and strongly fortified with 280 guns, many of large calibre, disposed in the batteries and forts that crowned the heights above Weltevreeden; and it seemed to defy approach. This place had been carefully selected by Marshal Daendels for a stand, not merely on account of its natural advantages, but because it occupied a healthy site, and he knew that no European force could long preserve its health in the fetid air of Batavia. In imagination he saw the British force decimated by disease, and within a little time placed at the mercy of the defenders of the island. General Janssens shared these sanguine views, and intended to follow his predecessor's plan of campaign. He was destined to have an early awakening from those pleasant and confident anticipations.

The Franco-Dutch army held a strong advanced position at Weltevreeden, and there they were attacked in the afternoon of the second day after the occupation of Batavia by the British force. The struggle was short, sharp, and decisive. Notwithstanding their superior position, the enemy were driven out of their entrenchments with a loss in killed and wounded of 500 men, including several French officers; while the British force lost 17 killed and 73 wounded. The great importance of this preliminary success was, that it secured for the British troops a healthy position well above the miasma arising from the damp and unhealthy plains of Batavia. A lull of some days then followed, while the guns and mortars were brought up from the ships. During this interval several skirmishes took place. The most serious of these occurred on the 22nd August, when the British lost about 100 killed and wounded, but inflicted on their enemy a far heavier loss. Two days later the batteries were at last completed, and the artillery began a duel at a distance of not more than 800 yards. By the losses at Weltevreeden, desertions, and sickness, the force of General Janssens had now been reduced to 13,000 men, while the attacking army had rather less than 8000 men at the front.

In his official report Sir Samuel Achmuty describes the position at Cornelis in the following words:—"The enemy, greatly superior in numbers, was strongly entrenched in a position between the great river of Jacatra and the Sloken, an artificial watercourse, neither of which was fordable. This position was shut up by a deep trench, strongly palisaded. Seven redoubts and many batteries mounted with heavy cannon occupied the most commanding grounds within the lines. The fort of Cornelis was in the centre, and the whole of the works were defended by a numerous and well-organised artillery. The season was too far advanced, the heat too violent, and our number insufficient to admit of regular approaches. To carry the works by assault was the alternative, and on that I decided."

Just at this critical juncture a deserter came over and offered to lead a few troops by a bypath which would bring the men, without discovery, on the flank of the enemy's position on the Sloken; and the command of this column was intrusted to Colonel Gillespie, whose reputation for gallantry dated from the time of the Vellore Mutiny, and whose conduct of the earlier movements of the expeditionary force has been described. The troops selected for this task marched some hours before sunrise, and reached the enemy's lines unperceived. The supporting column, under Colonel Gibbs, lost its way, but the attack could not be deferred, as a collision with an outlying picket revealed the presence of the British troops. Gillespie at once gave the order to charge, and one redoubt was carried after another. In one of these, two gallant French officers, seeing defeat inevitable, fired the magazine; but when the attacks on the other sides became developed, the Franco-Dutch army abandoned their remaining positions and fled. Between five and six thousand men, including the regiment of voltigeurs, laid down their arms. The completeness of the victory arose from the vigour of the pursuit. Three hundred officers were among the prisoners, and General Janssens barely escaped a similar fate. He fled to Buitenzorg, thirty miles from the battlefield; but after a few hours' rest he was obliged to abandon that place on the approach of the English cavalry, and seek shelter in the eastern districts. The battle of Cornelis, won over superior numbers and an enemy occupying a strong and carefully prepared position, was among the most striking victories gained by an English army in the East. At least 4000 of the enemy were killed or wounded, while the total British loss was 500, of whom forty-eight were officers. No victory could have been more opportune, for it destroyed the hostile foreign army holding the island; and it crowned Lord Minto's adventurous policy with that prompt and early success which was necessary to establish its merit.

Two days after the battle of Cornelis an event happened that dimmed the satisfaction of military success. The enthusiasm of Leyden had done something towards sustaining the resolution of Lord Minto, and his marked literary skill had given an attractive aspect to schemes for the elevation of Malay character, and, it might even be, for the resuscitation of a Malay administration. When the army marched south from Batavia to attack the enemy's positions, he remained in the city—not inactive, but energetically engaged in the examination of official documents, and in the search for materials by means of which he might illustrate the system of government hitherto in force, and perhaps thus contribute to the simplification of the new government about to be established. His ardour allowed him no rest. The same spirit which impelled him to dash through the surf at Chillingching made him search the Dutch offices of Batavia with the closest care, so that none of their archives should escape him. The month was the hottest of the year: the fetid atmosphere of Batavia that Marshal Daendels had predicted would prove fatal to an English army, was at least fatal to one devoted seeker after knowledge. During his investigations he came upon a closed room, or "go-down," in one of the Dutch public offices—not the library, as has been stated. He forced open the door, and spent some time examining the papers on the shelves. He came out a stricken man, seized with that mysterious ague and fever for which doctors have discovered neither a name nor a cure, and which, not so many years later, attacked the illustrious Heber under very similar circumstances, and with an equally fatal result. Leyden entered the "go-down" on the 25th August with the noise of the cannonade of Cornelis in his ears; two days later he expired in the arms of his friend Raffles. Both Raffles and Lord Minto mourned his loss as that of a brother, and they laid him with their own hands in a grave in the Batavia cemetery, close to the very spot where, only a few years later, Oliva Raffles was to find her resting-place.

There is no doubt of the strong feeling of esteem and affection in which Raffles held his lost friend; and I think there is good reason to believe that, if Leyden had lived, the bond would have become a closer one through the marriage of Leyden with the last of Raffles's unmarried sisters. In a letter written in the following October to Mr. Marsden, Raffles said: "You will, I am sure, condole with me, as the friend of literature and virtue, in the loss I have lately sustained in the death of my dear friend, Dr. Leyden. He died at this place on the 27th of August, of a fever. We have lost in him a host of men. Had you known him, you would never have ceased to deplore his death. Eastern literature has lost in him its firmest support." This sentiment never grew cold in the bosom of Raffles. Five years later, in the introduction to his own *History of Java*, he wrote:—

"There was one (J. C. Leyden, who accompanied the expedition to Batavia in 1811, and expired in my arms a few days after the landing of the troops) dear to me in private friendship and esteem, who, had he lived, was of all men best calculated to have supplied those deficiencies which will be apparent in the very imperfect work now presented to the public. From his profound acquaintance with eastern languages and Indian history, from the unceasing activity of his great talents, his other prodigious acquirements, his extensive views, and his confident hope of illustrating national migrations from the scenes which he was approaching, much might have been expected; but just as he reached those shores on which he hoped to slake his ardent thirst for knowledge, he fell a victim to excessive exertion, deeply deplored by all, and by none more truly than myself."

In Lockhart's *Life of Scott* the reader will find the long and interesting letter which Scott wrote to his friend. That letter never reached the hands of him to whom it was addressed. It was returned to the writer after Leyden's death, and the care with which Sir Walter preserved it was one evidence of the strength of his affection for his old associate. He took the world into his confidence as to his feelings at the loss he, as well as literature, had suffered, and immortalised the name of Leyden in the well-known lines in his poem, *The Lord of the Isles*:—

> "Scenes sung by him who sings no more !
> His brief and bright career is o'er,
> And mute his tuneful strains ;
> Quenched is his lamp of varied lore,
> That loved the light of song to pour ;
> A distant and a deadly shore
> Has Leyden's cold remains !"

After the battle of Cornelis, General Janssens retired to Samarang, the next port on the northern coast of Java, eastward of Batavia. To a summons to surrender, and an appeal in the name of humanity to avert unnecessary bloodshed, he replied that he did not consider his means of defence exhausted, and that he could not, therefore, abandon the struggle. One Javanese chief had joined him with 1500 troops, and he may have anticipated that others would follow this example. There was, indeed, considerable risk of a national rising, for three-fourths of the island had been independent under the Dutch, and General Janssens hoped to recover, by a successful diplomacy that painted the English in the character of ruthless invaders, what he had lost in the field. For the success of such steps time was, however, necessary, and that was precisely what General Janssens could not be permitted to obtain. Sir Samuel Achmuty sailed with part of the army to attack Samarang. On the 10th of September that place was captured without loss, and on the 18th of the same month General Janssens made his formal surrender. The military success was rendered complete a little later by the occupation of the third great port of Sourabaya, and the capture of the formidable fort named Ludowyck at its entrance, on the strengthening of which Marshal Daendels had expended all his efforts and intelligence.

Before those operations were completed, Lord Minto had

issued his memorable proclamation on the government of Java. "An empire," he said in his despatch to the Court of Directors, "which for two centuries has contributed greatly to the power, prosperity, and grandeur of one of the principal and most respected States in Europe, has been thus wrested from the short usurpation of the French Government, added to the dominion of the British Crown, and converted from a seat of hostile machination and commercial competition into an augmentation of British power and prosperity." The proclamation, dated 11th September, reads as follows :—

"For the satisfaction of the inhabitants and people of Java, the following provisions are made public, in testimony of the sincere disposition of the British Government to promote their prosperity and welfare. The refusal of their late Government to treat for their interests, although disabled by the events of war from affording them any further protection, has rendered the consequent establishment of the British authority unconditional. But an English Government does not require the articles of a capitulation to impose those duties which are prompted by a sense of justice and a beneficent disposition. The people of Java are exhorted to consider their new connection with England as founded on principles of mutual advantage, and to be conducted in a spirit of kindness and affection.

"Providence has brought to them a protecting and benevolent Government. They will cheerfully perform the reciprocal duties of allegiance and attachment.

"1. His Majesty's subjects in Java will be entitled to the same general privileges as are enjoyed by the natural-born subjects of Great Britain in India, subject to such regulations as now exist, or may hereafter be provided, respecting residence in any of the Honourable Company's territories.

"2. They will have the same privilege and freedom of trade to, and with, all countries to the east of the Cape of Good Hope, and also with His Majesty's European dominions, as are possessed by natural-born subjects of Great Britain.

"3. Dutch gentlemen will be eligible to all offices of trust, and will enjoy the confidence of Government according to their respective characters, conduct, and talents, in common with British-born subjects.

"4. The vexatious system of monopoly, which is understood to have hitherto prevailed, in some instances to an oppressive and inconvenient extent, will be revised, and a more beneficial and politic principle of administration will be taken into consideration as soon, and to such extent, as full information on the subject can be obtained, as established usage and habit may admit, and as may be consistent with a due regard to the health and morals of the people.

"5. The Dutch laws will remain provisionally in force, under the modifications which will be hereinafter expressed, until the pleasure of the supreme authorities in England shall be known; and it is conceived that no material alteration therein is to be apprehended.

"The modifications to be now adopted are the following :—

"1. Neither torture nor mutilation shall make part of any sentence to be pronounced against criminals.

"2. When a British-born subject is convicted of any offence, no punishment shall be awarded against him more severe than would be inflicted by the laws of England for the same crime ; and, in case of doubt concerning the penalty by English law, reference shall be made to the Honourable the Recorder of Prince of Wales's Island, whose report shall be a sufficient warrant for awarding the penalty stated by him to be agreeable to the laws of England. No sentence against any British-born subject for any crime or misdemeanour shall be carried into execution until a report shall have been made to the Lieutenant-Governor.

"3. No sentence of death against any person whatever shall be carried into execution until report shall have been made to the Lieutenant-Governor.

"4. The Lieutenant-Governor will have the power of remitting, moderating, or confirming all penalties, excepting inconsiderable fines, short imprisonment, or slight corporal punishment.

"5. British-born subjects shall be amenable to the jurisdiction of the Dutch tribunals and to the Dutch laws, in all cases of civil complaint, or demands, whether they be plaintiffs or defendants.

"6. All British-born subjects shall be subject to the regulation of police, and to the jurisdiction of the magistrates charged with the execution thereof, and with the maintenance of peace, and with public tranquillity and security.

"7. All persons belonging to, or attached to, the army, who are by their condition subject to military law, shall, for the present, be tried for any crimes they may commit only by courts-martial, unless sent by the military authorities to civil courts.

"8. It being necessary in all countries that a power should exist of framing regulations in the nature of legislative provision adapted to change of circumstances, or to meet any emergency that may arise, and the great distance of the British authorities in Europe rendering it expedient that the said power should, for the present, reside in some accessible quarter, it is declared that the Lieutenant-Governor shall have full power and authority to pass such legislative regulations as, on deliberation and after due consultation and advice, may appear to him indispensably necessary, and that they shall have the full force of law. But the same shall be immediately reported to the Governor-General in Council in Bengal, together with the Lieutenant-Governor's reasons for passing the said regulations, and any representations that may have been submitted to him against the same ; and the regulations so passed will be confirmed or disallowed by the Governor-General in Council, with the shortest possible delay. The mode in which the Lieutenant-Governor shall be assisted with advice will hereafter be made known ; and such regulations will hereafter be made as may be thought most conducive to prompt, pure, and impartial administration of justice, civil and criminal.

"Regulations respecting the paper currency, as well as the relative value of coins circulating in Java, will be published in a separate paper of this date.

"The Government shall in the meanwhile, and until the pleasure of the supreme authorities in Great Britain shall be signified, be administered in the following manner :—All the powers of government shall be exercised by, and all acts and orders shall be done and issued in the name of His Excellency the Governor-General of India, the Right Honourable Lord Minto, during his residence in Java.

"His Excellency has been pleased to appoint the Honourable Thomas Raffles Lieutenant-Governor of Java, who will aid him in the execution of the said functions until his departure from the island. After the departure of the

Governor-General, the Honourable the Lieutenant-Governor will exercise in his own name and person the powers of government, and will be invested with all the authorities appertaining thereto in the fullest and amplest manner."

On the same day as this proclamation Lord Minto issued his commission to Mr. Stamford Raffles to act as Lieutenant-Governor of Java and its dependencies. In some way or other Lord Minto considered himself partly pledged to some other person for this appointment; but it is impossible to indicate who this was, beyond saying that it was no one connected with the Javan Expedition. The balance of probability points to Sir Robert Farquhar, whose early experience in the Malay Peninsula has been mentioned, and the Governor-General may have felt his hands freed by the fact that Farquhar had already been provided with a suitable post in the governorship of Mauritius. Whoever it was who had a prior promise of Java, and whatever the reasons were which led Lord Minto to ignore that promise, the supreme argument that directed the Governor-General's decision was, that he could not "conscientiously withhold it from the man who had won it." Raffles was raised to the high and responsible post of Lieutenant-Governor of this large and half-subjected island "as an acknowledgment of the services he had rendered, and in consideration of his peculiar fitness for the office." Raffles was at that moment only thirty years of age; yet every one who has followed the facts, and appreciated the manner in which he not only conceived the policy pursued in Java but executed many of the more important measures that contributed to and ensured its success, will allow that he thoroughly deserved his great reward. There was, in fact, no one else to compete with him, and the claims of Colonel Gillespie, who had taken so prominent and distinguished a part in the military operations, seemed sufficiently recognised by his selection to command the garrison left in the island, with a seat on the Council. Still there is no doubt that Lord Minto's commission, "requiring and commanding all persons belonging to His Majesty's and the Honourable East India Company's Civil, Military, and Marine Services, and all other persons whatsoever, resident on the said island or possessions, to take notice hereof and obey the said Thomas Stamford Raffles,

Esquire, as Lieutenant-Governor of the island of Java and its dependencies," did arouse some jealousy among those in the services who had been far outstripped in the race for official promotion by the young Secretary of the Penang Adminisration.

Lord Minto remained five weeks in Java after the issue of the proclamation establishing the new form of government; and with a view to simplifying the task of administration, and at the same time of propitiating colonial opinion, he nominated a few days before his departure a Council, of which Colonel Gillespie and two Dutch gentlemen, Messrs. H. W. Muntinghe and J. P. Cranssen, were to be the first members, for the purpose of assisting the Lieutenant-Governor in the difficult task of ruling the island.

Having completed all these measures, the Governor-General made his preparations for the return to India with Sir Samuel Achmuty and a large part of the expedition. On the 17th October 1811 Raffles gave a dinner and ball at "Ryswick," the official residence at Batavia, at which General Janssens and two Dutch generals, Lutzow and De Koch, were present. The description in the official correspondence states that the fireworks were spoilt by a heavy storm of rain. On the following day the foreign generals sailed for Europe, and in the evening Lord Minto again dined quietly with Raffles. On the 19th October Lord Minto left Batavia for Calcutta; but his interest in Java was by no means diminished, for almost the first thing he did on reaching his destination was to draft a long and exhaustive minute, dated 6th December, on the subject of its future administration.

The policy of the East India Company and the Home Government was not the same as that which Lord Minto, under the instigation of Raffles, and by the aid of a well-equipped and well-led Anglo-Indian force, had so successfully carried out. Lord Castlereagh's prohibition of all expeditions eastward has been mentioned, but, when Lord Minto received authority in 1810 to proceed to Java, he was empowered to accomplish something very different from what was done, and from what would even have been humane. The order, he said, in the minute referred to, "was to subdue the Dutch

Government, to destroy the fortifications, to distribute the ordnance, arms, and military stores, amongst the native chiefs and inhabitants, and then to retire from the country." Lord Minto did not obey that order in a single particular. The inevitable consequence of such a course "rendered the execution of that order absolutely, because morally, impossible." In establishing a British administration at all in Java, Lord Minto was obeying the dictates of a just and humane mind. He was even pursuing the course that common sense and a broad policy would have prescribed; but, none the less, he was disobeying the order of those by whose favour he was Governor-General.

Lord Minto's minute, which is far too long to quote in its entirety, endeavours to bring home to the minds of the authorities in London the anarchy that would inevitably have followed the execution of their orders.

"I have now to add to former impressions a personal and certain knowledge of the vehement and implacable animosity borne by the Javanese generally to the Dutch name, of the anxious and well-founded terror with which the European, and not less than them the Chinese, inhabitants contemplate any possible scenes of convulsion or disorder which might expose their property to the rapacious violence, and their lives to the barbarous and sanguinary hatred, of the native population."

For the permanent pacification of the island, Lord Minto lays emphasis on the necessity of establishing friendly relations with the Susuhunan, or Emperor of Java, resident at Solo, and the Sultan of Mataram who ruled at Jojocarta, and it will be seen how Raffles sought to give effect to these instructions. With regard to Raffles himself, the Governor-General again avowed a full confidence in his ability and intelligence. He had given "full explanations in personal conferences with that gentleman, who was perfectly prepared by previous communications and a perfect knowledge of my sentiments to fill up that sketch of the proposed plan." Notwithstanding the success of the expedition and the cogent arguments supporting the policy pursued, Lord Minto was still very doubtful as to what the Government and the Company would say and do. He warned Raffles of the risk of all their plans being upset; but he laid down one noble guiding principle for his conduct: "While we are in Java, let us do all the good we can"; and the sequel will show how well that exhortation was obeyed.

The overthrow of the Dutch power had by no means completed the subjugation of the whole of Java. More than two-fifths of the island had either lately defied the Dutch authority or never acknowledged it. In the Sunda division, embracing all the country to the west of the river Losari, the fertile and extensive district of Bantam (3428 square miles) was in a state of revolt; anarchy had prevailed there for years, and all thought of raising a revenue had been abandoned; while in the province of Cheribon (1334 square miles) "an audacious fanatic had, for a long period of time, raised the standard of rebellion," defying Dutch and native authority alike. Eastward of the Losari, in the region alone called Java by the natives, the Dutch Government had been limited to the narrow provinces lying along the northern coast, to those in the eastern peninsula, and to the island of Madura. The Susuhunan, or Emperor of Java, with his court at Suracarta or Solo, and the Sultan of Jojocarta, both reigning respectively over the extensive inland and southern districts of the Java division, kept up each a considerable military force, and had never allowed the Dutch to interfere in the revenues or the administration of their dominions. In the flourishing times of the Dutch Government the Governor-General at Batavia had exercised supreme control over many subordinate residencies and factories dotted about the whole Eastern Archipelago, including the Moluccas and a factory in Japan. The Moluccas were, however, at this time, left by Lord Minto under a separate government. Referring to the subject of outlying dependencies in a letter to the Court of Directors, dated Batavia, 27th of January 1816, Raffles says: "I was warranted by my instructions in resuming the influence and authority of this Government in the Eastern Seas." These instructions were no doubt embodied in the following passage from Lord Minto's minute last cited:—"You will pass orders respecting Madura, Macassar, Bali, and other islands."

The instructions left with the new Lieutenant-Governor were not merely to institute an improved civil administration and to establish justice on a firmer basis, but also to complete the conquest of Java by forming definite and, if possible, friendly relations with the leading native potentates, who had been either hostile or indifferent to the Dutch. Leaving the former subject for the next chapter, it will be better to conclude this with a brief account of the several military events which marked the period of the British administration.

Immediately after Lord Minto's departure Raffles despatched Residents to the native capitals; and he took especial pains in the endeavour to establish friendly and definite relations with the rulers of Jojocarta and of Palembang, a state on the eastern coast of Sumatra, but in dependent alliance with the Dutch power in Batavia. In November 1811 a Commission was sent to Palembang to take possession of the Dutch factory there, and to establish with its Sultan friendly relations under a more considerate convention. Such was the intention; and to give it a better chance of success Mr. Wardenaar, a Dutch gentleman who had been Member of the Supreme Council of Batavia, was appointed one of the Commissioners. For some reason that cannot be confidently explained, the Sultan adopted a hostile course, massacred the Dutch settlers, attempted to deal out the same treatment to the English officers, and openly defied the British power. In consequence of these acts Raffles took upon himself the responsibility of sending an expedition, under Colonel Gillespie, to bring the Sultan to a proper sense of his position.

Although Palembang is less than a week's favourable sailing from Batavia, contrary winds kept the expedition more than a month at sea. On the 19th of April 1812 it had made its way some distance up the river on which the chief town stands. The Sultan received them with a mixture of defiance and humility; but the batteries near the mouth of the river, with over 100 guns in position, were surrendered without resistance. The Sultan then fled from his capital, where serious disorders broke out. On hearing this news, Colonel Gillespie pressed on, with a mere handful of men, and seized the fort and palace, thus securing the strongest position and averting the massacre of the Chinese merchants. In consequence of his inhuman conduct the Sultan was deposed, and his brother, Sultan Ratoo, was installed in his place. The new ruler made the most satisfactory offers of alliance and friendship to the English, and ceded them the islands of Banca and Billiton in perpetuity. Raffles had already conceived the great idea of obtaining some capacious port for Britain in these seas, should the surrender of Java to the Dutch be carried out, and he had been told that the harbour of Klabbat, in Banca, was "the most secure in India, capable of every defence—the entrance to the harbour being between two rocks or promontories not half a pistol shot from each other—and a basin within with fine bottom and deep water, capable of containing, it is said, the navy of England." His representatives were instructed to make sure of this position; and now he had obtained it. Of Billiton, too, as a future naval station, he had also formed high expectations. How confident everyone felt that these annexations at least were to be permanent may be gathered from the last paragraph in Colonel Gillespie's report, showing how he had altered their nomenclature. "In establishing the British authority at Minto (previously called Minta by the natives), I declared the island of Banca to be named after H.R.H. the Duke of York, the capital town after the Right Hon. the Governor-General of all India, and the fort now building there after H.E. the Commander-in-Chief."

The Palembang trouble was speedily followed by a more serious one in the eastern districts of Java. In November 1811 Raffles had paid a first visit to Samarang, with the view of arranging matters with the great Javanese princes; and he returned in the belief that he had been successful. He had visited the Sultan of Jojocarta in his capital; and, while guaranteeing him his possessions, had received from him assurances of good conduct and a formal recognition of British sovereignty. The following striking description of this visit is taken from Lady Raffles's memoir:—"Mr. Raffles set out for Jojocarta accompanied by a part only of the 14th Regiment, a troop of the 22nd Light Dragoons, and the ordinary garrison of Bengal sepoys in the fort and at the

Residency House. This was all the force which at the moment he could command, and circumstances did not admit of delay. The service was one of imminent peril; the whole retinue was at one time in danger of being murdered. Mr. Raffles received the Sultan in the hall of audience. The Sultan was accompanied by several thousands of armed followers, who expressed in their behaviour an infuriated spirit of insolence, and several of his own suite actually unsheathed their creeses to indicate plainly that they only waited for the signal to perpetrate the work of destruction; had this been given, from the manner in which the English were surrounded, not a man could have escaped." The reader can easily conjure up in his own imagination this striking scene—the hall crowded with the retainers of this despot, the fierce and excitable countenances of the Malay warriors, ready at a sign to bury their murderous creeses and poisoned spears in the bodies of the few Europeans who had not merely come into their midst, but who claimed the right to give them the law; and in the centre of this disturbed and threatening scene the far from stalwart but energetic and impressive form of Raffles, calm, unmoved, stilling with eloquent Malayan phrases the storm, and convincing Sultan and vassals alike that in him they had a friend, perhaps, but certainly a master.

A few months later, however, further troubles ensued, and again Raffles hastened to Samarang to be close to the scene. At that moment the greater part of his available force was in Sumatra, and the result of that expedition was still unknown. The danger was far greater than had been conceived when Raffles left Batavia in May 1812. He found that the Sultan had succeeded in concluding an alliance with the Susuhunan of Solo, his hereditary enemy, and that there was a league established among the Javan princes for the expulsion of all the Europeans. They were emboldened to take these extreme steps by the knowledge that a large part of the British troops were absent from the island. Raffles came to the prompt conclusion that, great as was the peril, any delay in dealing with it would only make it greater. He therefore collected such force as he could, and was about to advance, when the fortunate arrival of Colonel Gillespie with, however, only a very small part of the troops from Palembang, strengthened his hands. Gillespie took charge of the military movements, and on 17th June the expedition, accompanied by the Lieutenant-Governor, arrived before the town of Jojocarta. Reluctant to shed blood at all times, and well aware that in this case sound policy demanded a peaceful solution, Raffles did everything in his power to effect an amicable arrangement with the Sultan; but his overtures were rejected with scorn. A solution had then to be found by force of arms; and the following is the official account sent by the Lieutenant-Governor to the Governor-General a few days later, namely, on 25th June:—

"Necessity having compelled me to resort to actual hostilities against Jojocarta, it affords me the highest satisfaction to communicate to your Lordship the successful and happy result of our operations. Having taken measures for concentrating the whole disposable force at Jojocarta, I proceeded in person, accompanied by Colonel Gillespie, as far as Klatten on the 16th, and to Jojocarta on the 17th inst.

"The Sultan refusing to comply with my summons, and several of our dragoons having been cut off in detail, decisive measures became necessary; and on the 18th, in the afternoon, we commenced a heavy cannonade from the fort on his Craton, or palace; it was immediately returned on his side, and although no further measure was taken by us during the whole of the 19th, no symptoms of concession were made by him. Our force was small, not exceeding 600 firelocks, and rather more than that number in dragoons, artillery, and sepoys. A part of our ammunition was cut off, and nothing remained for us but an assault, which was attempted and carried in less than three hours. On the morning of the 20th, at nine o'clock, the Craton was ours; the person of the Sultan, as well as that of the hereditary prince, secured, without plunder or harsh usage; and the country at our disposal.

"In order to estimate the services performed by the troops on this occasion, I should mention that the Craton was a regular fortified position about three miles in circumference, surrounded by a wide and deep ditch, with a wall forty-five feet high, defended by well-constructed bastions, and forming ramparts all round.

"The approach to the Craton being further secured by lower walls without the ditch on the opposite side of the road, and the gates protected by drawbridges after the European model, at the period of assault it was calculated that there could not be less than 11,000 armed men within the Craton, while large parties of one, two, three, and even four thousand occupied positions without the Craton, blocking up the main roads.

"Gillespie was himself. The assault was made by escalade; we soon got possession of the ramparts, and turned their own guns upon them. The hereditary prince took the first occasion to throw himself on our protection;

the Sultan was taken in his strongest hold ; and our plan throughout was most successful ; the loss on our side very inconsiderable, and comparatively nothing ; on the part of the enemy, dreadful.

"I regret to say that Gillespie himself was wounded in the left arm—a flesh wound, and although serious, not dangerous. Lieutenant Robinson, of the 78th, Lieutenants Paul and Maclean, of the 14th, were wounded, with no greater loss in non-commissioned officers and privates killed and wounded than about forty. Lieutenant Maclean is since dead. Our loss previous to the 25th was principally in the dragoons, eighteen men and horses being killed and wounded, Lieutenant Hall among the latter. Captain Young and Lieutenant Hunter were blown up and much burnt, but not dangerously.

"The steadiness with which the enemy received the attack, and the great military defences and resources within his power, have much enhanced the credit of our handful of troops.

"I may now congratulate your Lordship on the conquest of Java being substantially accomplished ; for although the great and valorous deeds which wrested the colony from the hands of a hostile European power placed the provinces on the sea-coast at our disposal, we never till this event could call ourselves masters of the more valuable provinces of the interior. Nay, our possessions at the sea-coast would always have been precarious, and had the military force been materially reduced much eventual danger was to have been apprehended. Java will long have reason to remember with gratitude the efforts of the 20th June.

"The hereditary prince has been raised to the throne, all the principal chieftains have submitted to his authority, and the country has every appearance of tranquillity. I passed from Jojocarta to this place (Samarang) in thirteen hours (about a hundred miles), and accounts from every quarter confirm my expectations that the arrangements I had made would prevent the possibility of commotion.

"The European power is for the first time paramount in Java. We are now able to dictate the terms of the future connection with the British Government and the native administration. A population of not less than a million has been wrested from the tyranny and oppression of an independent, ignorant, and cruel prince ; and a country yielding to none on earth in fertility and cultivation, affording a revenue of not less than a million of Spanish dollars in the year, placed at our disposal. The result at Jojocarta is decisive at Suracarta (Solo), and that court must necessarily fall under the same arrangement. The population and cultivation of the Emperor's dominions are not inferior to those of the Sultan's, and this statement alone will convey to your Lordship an idea of what has been obtained in the short space of five days.

"The Craton having fallen by assault, it was impossible to make any provision for Government to cover the expenses of the undertaking ; consequently the whole plunder became prize to the army. It is considerable, but it could not be in better hands ; they richly deserve what they got. I cannot speak too highly of the conduct of the army."

Lord Minto's complete approbation of these operations and arrangements was expressed in the following letter :—

"CALCUTTA, 15*th December* 1812.

"MY DEAR SIR,—I shall be impatient for the materials which are called for, because I am anxious to deliver without reserve or qualification the very high and favourable view I now have of that whole series of measures, beginning with the expedition to Palembang, and ending with the arrangement of the two Courts of Solo and Jojocarta, connected and combined with each other as those measures were. I consider the result of the latter proceeding as very glorious to your administration during the short period of which more will have been accomplished for the security of the European power, the tranquillity of the island, and the solid improvement of general prosperity and happiness, than several centuries have been able to perform, when the superiority of European power was exerted, unencumbered by the scruples of justice and good faith.

"Nothing can be more excellent than all your arrangements in the eastern districts of Java.

"With regard to Palembang and Banca, your latest reports have enabled us to approve, without reservation, the arrangement formed at Palembang, and the annexation of Banca to the territories of the East India Company, our minds being satisfied upon the two points of justice and expediency. The sovereignty of the Sultan of Palembang in Banca is placed beyond question, and leaves that dependence of Palembang indisputably subject, both to the laws of conquest in so just a war, and to the effect of cession from the authority under which it is now held.—Believe me, ever, my dear sir, most truly and affectionately yours, MINTO."

The firmness of this language as to the permanent acquisition of the island of Banca should be noted. Lord Minto had doubts as to the retention of Java; he had none as to his right to acquire in those seas territory which did not form part of the Dutch empire; and he fully believed that both the Company and the Government would gratefully ratify the acquisition of such places. Raffles more than shared the views and hopes of the Governor-General.

How rudely these views were to be falsified will be seen later on.

With a view to the suppression of piracy, it was deemed necessary to detach a force against Pangerong Anom, the chief of the piratical state of Sambas, on the west coast of Borneo. An expedition, consisting of a squadron of His Majesty's ships, and of a squadron of gunboats, sailed from Java in the month of October 1812, under the command of Captain Bowen. The attack on the batteries of Sambas, notwithstanding every exertion, was unsuccessful, and the squadron returned to Batavia. It was subsequently resolved to send an adequate land force to co-operate in the reduction of the place, which object was accomplished in the month of July 1813, by Lieutenant-Colonel Watson of H.M. 14th Regiment, with the loss of four officers wounded, eight men killed, and fifty-six wounded. A political agent had been sent to the several states on the coast of Borneo, for the purpose of inducing them, by means of amicable negotiation, to abandon the practice of piracy. Raffles declared that he had no view whatever to an increase of territorial possession in the arrangements to be adopted for the suppression of piracy. In consequence of the measures which had been taken, no pirate prows had made their appearance on the coast of Java, and the coasting trade had been perfectly safe. Two small posts had been established on two islands where the pirate prows usually put in for repairs and refitment.

With the exception of this, and some other minor operations against pirates, the little campaign in Jojocarta concluded all warlike operations in the island; and, with its effectual pacification, Raffles desired to reduce the garrison to smaller dimensions. He explained in the following despatch to the Court of Directors his intentions and his reasons for them; but, unfortunately, his colleague Gillespie, who had now attained the rank of Major-General, did not share these opinions, and wished the garrison, and especially the European part of it, to be maintained at its original strength. This was the most serious of many points of difference that arose between the Lieutenant-Governor and the Commander of the Forces in Java. Lord Minto, it may be observed, supported Raffles, and even went so far as to authorise him to carry out the measures he deemed best, without reference to Calcutta. The despatch mentioned reads as follows:—

"*January* 1, 1813.

"Some difference of opinion has latterly occurred between the Commander of the Forces and myself with regard to the military establishments on the island. These appear to have arisen from a desire on the part of the military commander to maintain as large a force, and to render that force as efficient as possible; while, on the other hand, the directions and injunctions which I had received from the Supreme Government obliged me to keep the same within defined limits. The force provisionally fixed for this island was intended and declared to be only for a defined and limited purpose—the maintenance of internal tranquillity, and security against any predatory attack on the part of the enemy. The Commander of the Forces, on the contrary, has been always in expectation of attack from Europe, and would prepare accordingly. The uncertainty with which any decision can be formed as to the future government of the colony has naturally induced His Majesty's officers to calculate upon Java becoming a King's colony, while the absence of all official information on the subject has weighed with me in maintaining unimpaired, as far as possible, the provisional arrangements made by Lord Minto with the view of Java becoming a permanent settlement of the Company.

"There are at present on the island three king's regiments, the 14th, 59th, and 78th, averaging about 800 men each; two troops of His Majesty's 22nd Dragoons; a detachment of the Royal Artillery from Ceylon; and two troops of Hussars, raised on the island but not yet attached to either the King's or the Company's army. The Sepoy battalions, of which there are five, are weak; but recruits to complete them to 800 men each are daily expected from Bengal, besides a corps of native cavalry raised expressly for the service of the island. These, with a detachment of the Bengal artillery, Madras pioneers, and the two colonial regiments of Amboyans and Javanese, compose the regular force which it falls on this Government to maintain, independent of a few police corps. I should not, however, omit to mention the Bengal European regiment, the headquarters of which are now on the island, with about 350 men, principally recruits, but rapidly improving in discipline.

"Were the question at once decided, I apprehend that the whole of the king's troops, with the exception of one, or perhaps two, regiments might be removed, and for the general service of the island their places might be much better supplied by natives of India. The European troops are here upon much heavier allowances than in India, and, on the whole, bear too heavy on the finances of the colony. The natives have a much greater dread of the Sepoy than of a European, and the saving would be immense. If possible, a Sepoy force should be maintained, even in the event of this island becoming a King's colony."

In concluding a chapter devoted to the military incidents connected with the British tenure of Java, the last few lines of that despatch may appropriately serve to introduce a dramatic incident, which the historians of Java have, in some unaccountable manner, ignored. Even Sir Stamford Raffles, who played the chief part in composing the trouble, has nothing to say about it in any of his published despatches; although no doubt his full narrative of the incident formed part of the voluminous and complete collection of Java papers, which were subsequently burnt, to his great injury and loss, on board the *Fame*. But as he recommended the employment of Sepoys, it would not be right to ignore an incident which showed that the lesson of Vellore had not been taken to heart, and that the pampered native soldiers, in their inner hearts, were ever ripe for mischief and revolt.

At the end of 1813 the volunteer battalion of native troops left at Solo began to show signs of discontent. The discipline seems to have been relaxed owing to the paucity of officers, and the men were under the belief that their detention in Java had been too protracted. At the same time, they had discovered in the monuments and writings of the Javanese many traces of a resemblance to primitive India, which made them jump to the conclusion that they were of the same race.

They thus established good relations with the Javanese of the old Imperial State; and, in a very little time, the Susuhunan heard of the promising conduct and friendly attitude of the native troops, and sent them gifts of money. No doubt his example was followed by his subjects, and the Sepoys of India passed a very agreeable time. This consideration swelled the sense of their own importance, and they already gave themselves out not merely as representatives of that native army which they alleged to be the main support of the Company's power, but also as themselves possessing the means to establish with their bayonets a new state in the island of Java. To the British authorities they alleged that they were badly treated, because detained too long in Java; to the Susuhunan they vowed their willingness to remain for ever as the support of his throne.

For a time the English authorities were in complete ignorance of these schemes. All they knew was that this battalion was not perfectly contented. They did not think of mutiny, much less of an attempt to subvert the British power for the sake of a native potentate. The Susuhunan was undoubtedly influenced by the confident representations of the Sepoys, and he established direct relations with them. The troops in his neighbourhood took his gifts; and in the expectation that the wealth of this ruler would satisfy the demands of all, wrote to their comrades, the two battalions at Weltevreeden and Surabaya, and endeavoured to enlist them in their plot. Without going so far as to say they met with complete acquiescence, it may be conjectured that the other regiments would not have held back had the light battalion mutinied as intended, and met with some success. There was, consequently, a very unsatisfactory feeling prevalent among the Indian troops in Java; and, to make the epidemic of treason complete, the corps of cavalry, specially recruited for service in the island, became infected with the virus.

The beginning of this movement is traceable to the end of 1813; but it was not until two years later that it began seriously to attract the attention of the English officers. In November 1815, Lieutenant Hart, the Assistant Resident at Solo, reported to his chief, Major Johnson, that an improper intercourse had for some time subsisted between the Susuhunan and the Sepoys on duty at Solo. Meetings had been held by men of the light battalion, and resolutions passed not to leave the island; for, by this time, it was known that Java was to be restored to the Dutch. Practical evidence was given of this by the fact that the Dutch colonists had resumed the wearing of the orange scarf; and the native princes were unaffectedly alarmed at the prospect of losing the new privileges they had acquired, and of possibly incurring penalties for their friendly relations with the English. The Susuhunan received the leaders of the Sepoys in the most secret part of his Craton; and it was reported that he bestowed "incredible quantities of gold, diamonds, and money" on them. A few weeks later, Jemadar Roshun Khan and others of the supposed ringleaders were arrested. In all, twenty of the Sepoys were remanded for trial. The difficulty of dealing with this matter was, at the same time, increased by a report from Colonel Barslem, commanding in the eastern districts of the island, to the effect that there was no disturbance at Court, and nothing but contentment and goodwill towards the British Government. That report, made to Raffles in person, induced him to suspend the severe measures that regard for military discipline alone would have instigated. The whole subject, however, had become so critical that he decided, on 1st January 1816, to proceed to the scene in person. But he had made up his mind to avoid anything like coercive measures, and to receive the excuses of the Susuhunan, so far as to do so would be consistent with the honour and character of the British Government.

On arriving at Samarang, Raffles found the place full of conflicting rumours. While some Sepoys had plotted to go over to the native powers, the mass of them seemed to believe that the British had sold them, with the island, to the Dutch. Immediately before his arrival Mattu Dhun Naik had been arrested as the chief conspirator, and on him correspondence had been found from Sepoys at Weltevreeden, of the following purport:—"You are the light battalion. If you mutiny or do anything first, we will join you." The "do anything" no doubt referred to the massacre of the English officers, which was to be the signal of revolt. The Chinese settlers were also to be murdered, and their property divided; while the Subahdar Dhokul Singh, as a Rajput of high caste, was to be proclaimed Governor. The evidence was conflicting as to how far the mass of the battalion was affected by the plots of a few dangerous men; and some at least remained true to their salt, for they sat up all night watching the movements of the disaffected.

The disaffection of the Sepoys and the proposition of their leaders had suggested far-reaching schemes to some restless spirits at Solo. The Emperor, a timid and dissipated man, had no wish for dangerous plots; but he allowed himself to be compromised by some of his more ambitious relatives. His brother, Pangerang Manco Boomee, conceived the idea of securing for his own son-in-law, Probogo, the government of Jojocarta, which in old days had been merely an appanage of the Emperor. By the aid of the native troops he felt confident of success; but he had to bring the matter before the Emperor, his brother, in order to secure the use of his name. The Emperor at first seems to have fallen in with his views, but when he learnt that the first act of the movement was to be the murder of the European officers, he expressed his horror and detestation of the treachery; and, what is more, he informed Major Johnson of the whole affair. The Prime Minister was also firmly attached to the British, and no doubt his representations had much to do with the Emperor's decision to follow a course of common sense and common humanity.

The first step taken by Raffles on reaching Samarang was to demand the surrender of Manco Boomee. The demand was complied with; and this personage was at once sent off to Batavia. The second was, on becoming satisfied of the Emperor's generally friendly disposition, to give him personal assurances, and to visit him in his palace. On the 9th January the interview took place. The Sultan was surrounded, as usual, by his numerous attendants and body-guard; Raffles was only accompanied by Major Johnson and two other officers. The public reception was followed by a private conference, when the Heir-Apparent and the Prime Minister were present. The course of that conference was summarised as follows in Raffles's despatch to Colonel Barslem, who was acting as head of the Government in his absence. Raffles began his address by saying that he had come to investigate the causes of certain relations between the Sepoys and the Court of Suracarta; but, as Manco Boomee had been given up, any indiscretion of the Susuhunan was forgiven. Raffles then went on to show how fully acquainted he was with the intrigue, whereupon the Sultan displayed symptoms of alarm. The Lieutenant-Governor hastened to relieve him, adding, as he writes, that "although all these circumstances had been reported to his prejudice, still that, with reference to the confidence placed in His Highness, it was almost impossible for me to believe them; that I had determined not to place entire confidence in reports which involved any question regarding his attachment; and that my object in thus informing him of the report to his prejudice was the more clearly to point out the consequences resulting from his having so far degraded his dignity as to put himself upon a level with inferior officers and private soldiers." Then came the practical point of the lecture, which was that the Empress, or Ratee, who had taken a sympathetic part in the intrigue, should be admonished; and that the Crown Prince should be allowed to assist his father in the government. To both of these demands the Sultan assented. Subsequent conversation revealed that the native prince was much alarmed at the prospect of the return of the Dutch, but that he wished for no change in the terms of the existing arrangements.

Being asked more definitely whether he wished the British to arrange anything special with the Dutch, and having received Raffles's assurance of his own personal friendship, the Susuhunan declared that he only wished to be always friends with the British, and that the existing arrangements should prove permanent. On the following day the Emperor visited Raffles in the British Residency, with a view to impressing the people; and, after Raffles left, the Emperor summoned all the officers and head men of his state to an interview in the Craton, and proclaimed that all was forgiven, and that henceforth he depended on them and the Prime Minister to prevent anything wrong from occurring. From Solo Raffles hastened to Jojocarta in order to pacify that district; and there, despite the suspicious movements of Pangerang Prang Wedono, he was able to settle the public mind without having recourse to force. In the meantime the Sepoys had been brought to a court-martial and sentenced to death; but Raffles, returning before the sentence had been carried out, read the proceedings of the court-martial, and finding its decision inconsistent with the policy decided upon on 1st January, before his departure eastward, summoned the Council; and, on their agreeing with him, caused the execution of the sentence to be suspended. The fact that the evacuation of Java was proceeding at the same moment led to some deviation from the strict course of discipline; and, although the evidence in the Batavia proceedings is not conclusive, it seems as if the guilty Sepoys finally escaped the extreme penalty which they so richly deserved. At least it is clear that no such penalty was carried out before Raffles departed from Java.

Raffles's own account of this expedition is contained in a subsequent letter home to the Secret Committee of the East India Company: "It affords me peculiar satisfaction to be enabled to assure your Honourable Committee that, notwithstanding the diminution which has been made in our force (on the urgent demands made some months ago for reinforcements to be sent to Bengal), this island, during the recent occurrences in the light battalion of Sepoys, has continued perfectly tranquil; and I have every reason to believe that the attachment of the Javanese to the present Government prevents any apprehension of their taking advantage of a moment which, under the circumstances, they might have been induced to lay hold of, and might possibly have found unusually favourable to such an object. Your Honourable Committee will perceive in the course of our proceedings that at the time when I proceeded to the eastern districts, the Court of Solo, apprehensive of hostile measures being adopted towards them, were collecting their best means of opposition; but the conciliatory line of policy which we have deemed it advisable and proper to adopt, especially under the present circumstances of the Colony, dissipated the alarm which was felt; and the reports of the Residents at both Courts agree in stating that the country has since been perfectly tranquil, and unattended with any extraordinary appearances of alarm or disquiet."

The manner in which he dealt with the difficulty raised by this disaffection among the troops, and through their plots with the native princes, who had been encouraged by the prospect of their military aid, furnishes striking evidence of his promptitude in meeting a danger, and of his personal courage and tact when acting alone. The military authorities wished to proceed to violent measures, and to make an example of several of the Javanese potentates. Had that course been adopted, there would have been a general rising and a long war. Raffles repelled the suggestion. Alone he went to the scene of threatening disaster, and by his boldness and moderation he calmed the situation. His wise and weighty words brought the Emperor round to a rational frame of mind; he played off the loyal against the disaffected; and, in a few days, he averted all risk of strife, and attached our allies to us by a firmer hold than before. Among his many achievements in Java not the least remarkable was his pacific settlement of this threatened mutiny and rebellion, an achievement which has been ignored in all previous accounts of his career.

CHAPTER VI

THE BRITISH ADMINISTRATION OF JAVA

WHEN Raffles, who had so largely contributed to the success of the measures for the establishment of British power in Java, was left alone to accomplish, single-handed, the more difficult task of justifying its conquest by the creation of a creditable administrative system, he took as his motto Lord Minto's observation, "While we are here, let us do all the good we can." It has now to be shown how thoroughly Raffles lived up to the level of a sentiment so entirely in harmony with his own; what a great and varied work he accomplished during his more than four years of government; and how he made that period, by the admission of the Dutch themselves, the brightest and most creditable era in the history of European colonisation in the island of Java. But, if the truth must be told, Raffles had larger views than his master. He would not let himself be trammelled by time or enforced conditions, and his enthusiasm bade him exclude the impossible. The only plausible criticism that has been passed on his measures is that they were too far-reaching, too much based on permanent considerations, and too independent of the fleeting views and interests of the moment. Raffles knew, and spared no effort to show, how valuable a possession Java was. But this did not accord with the views of those who wished it to be abandoned. He desired to break down once and for ever that barrier of Dutch selfishness and exclusiveness which had hindered British expansion eastwards, and which, to this hour, keeps some of the fairest and most favoured spots on the globe concealed from general knowledge, and confined in a state of unprogressive mediocrity. He saw that the opportunity had arrived; and, indifferent to the moves on the European chessboard, and the situation in India, he set himself with dogged determination to the task of showing that Java could be made as valuable a possession as any under the British crown; and that it might become the seat of an eastern empire extending throughout the Archipelago, and onwards to the ports of China and Japan, beside which even the India of the Moguls might seem a less attractive possession. As he was fearless of responsibility, he prosecuted his own measures without reference to the superior powers, because he knew that the delay caused by reference would make them useless and out of date, and was actuated by the conviction that the success and result of his proceedings would be their best and sufficient justification. With the exception of Lord Minto, none of those in power shared his views and hopes. The recollection of this simple fact will explain much that follows. But that Raffles had even a chance of carrying out his own policy, and of showing how successful it might prove, was due to the exceptionally full powers with which Lord Minto endowed him at the start. A perusal of the following passages from the order establishing the Lieutenant-Governorship of Java will show that Raffles was left in a position of indisputable superiority over critical or obstructive colleagues.

"If any difference of opinion should arise on any matter under deliberation, the opinion of the majority shall prevail, and the members of Council may record their sentiments on the consultations by a Minute bearing their signature. But if the Lieutenant-Governor should entertain a different opinion upon any question before Council from the majority, and should deem the matter of sufficient importance to enforce his own opinion, it shall be competent for him to do so, and the order passed by him shall have the full and valid effect of an order passed by the Lieutenant-Governor in Council.

"It is necessary, however, for this purpose that the Lieutenant-Governor should state on the consultations the grounds of his opinion on the question, and also his reasons for enforcing it contrary to the sentiments of the majority.

The proceedings of the Lieutenant-Governor in Council and the consultations of Council shall be kept with the greatest regularity ; and copies shall be transmitted by every favourable opportunity to Bengal and the Honourable Court of Directors.

"There shall be a Secret and Separate Department, in which affairs which the Lieutenant-Governor shall not think fit for communication to the members of Council will be transacted by the Lieutenant-Governor individually, and separately recorded.

"Of this description may be considered military movements and operations of importance in time of war or internal trouble. In these affairs the orders of the Lieutenant-Governor out of Council shall be valid, and of full force and effect."

One more fact should be borne in mind, and that was the entire absence of a regular establishment in Java. There was no body of civilians recruited by drafts from the mother-country, and inheriting from the past a traditional integrity, experience, and method. Untrained or half-trained men had to be put into offices in which they might do well, or might not, and for which their qualifications might suit or unfit them. That they actually did as well as the result proved, furnishes a testimonial to British character. There was even a dearth of copying clerks, and thus Raffles had to initiate the detailed procedure of every department, and to superintend its early working, and that often with very inadequate and inefficient assistance. He inspired self-respect and enthusiasm by the trust he reposed in others, and the trust in most cases met with a noble response.

The very first measure of the British administration in Java was put into effect before Lord Minto left the island. It was to continue the Dutch code, after stripping its application of the cruel and repulsive features of torture and excessive penalties which had been attached to it by the colonial administrators. There was consequently no change in the law under which the colonists and the islanders lived ; only it was provided that the cruelty and inhumanity which had become an excrescence on that law should cease. But, after Lord Minto left, Raffles went one step further, and introduced trial by jury; and the system, which in its essence was rather a mild than an entirely different interpretation of the Dutch law, worked so well that it was continued by the Dutch themselves after his time, and subsequently to the British evacuation of Java. No stronger or clearer tribute to its merit than this could be paid by the very authorities to whom, at a later period, Raffles's name became so hateful that they would not let him land on the shores of Java, even when he was in distress.

But the most serious and pressing matters that claimed attention came under the head of revenue rather than of the judicial branch of the administration. Lord Minto had said something on the subject in the following passage, bearing on the harsh and unwise system of taxing native produce:—

"Contingents of rice, and, indeed, of other productions, have been hitherto required of the cultivators by Government at an arbitrary rate. This also is a vicious system, to be abandoned as soon as possible. The system of contingents did not arise from the mere solicitude for the supply of the people, but was a measure alone of finance and control, to enable Government to derive a high revenue from a high price imposed on the consumer, and to keep the whole body of the people dependent on its pleasure for subsistence. I recommend a radical reform in this branch to the serious and early attention of Government. The principle of encouraging industry in the cultivation and improvement of land, by creating an interest in the effort and fruits of that industry, can be expected in Java only by a fundamental change of the whole system of landed property and tenure."

But the preliminary to all measures of reform, or modification of system, was the acquisition of sure and comprehensive information as to the relations which had subsisted in the island between the inhabitants and their Dutch rulers. No alteration could prove beneficial, unless it should be based on accurate knowledge; and so careful was Raffles in this matter that months—it would be more correct to say, the first two years—of his government were given up to the study of the situation, before the more important of his measures were put in force. If, on the one hand, this deliberation and delay prevented the revelation of all the merit of his proceedings within the brief period of his four and a half years' tenure of power, it, on the other, averted the commission of any of those mistakes which, in a strange country, and under such abnormal conditions as prevailed in Java, might only have been expected. Two Dutch gentlemen, Messrs. Muntinghe and Cranssen, had been appointed to act on the Lieutenant-Governor's Council; and each of these was requested in turn to preside over a commission composed of two Dutchmen under the superintendence of the principal English and Dutch secretaries, and appointed to collect from the various departments, and to register for the information of Government, all public records, plans, etc.; while the different heads of departments were required to give an account, on oath, of all documents in their charge. To assist the labours of this commission, Colonel Colin Mackenzie, of the Madras Engineers, was attached to it for the compilation of statistics on a scientific basis, and for the completion of surveys. Colonel Mackenzie was a highly distinguished officer, with whom Raffles maintained cordial relations. When he conducted the survey of Mysore, under Lord William Bentinck's orders, Leyden served with the commission as medical officer.

The first practical question to be settled was, how to procure a revenue with which to defray the cost of administration. The Dutch Government having monopolised the whole produce of the island,—less the barest cost of production left for the native labourers,—imposed no export duties; the commercial value of the article being a sufficient remuneration. But the British rulers at once radically altered this system, by claiming no monopoly of national labour, and by instituting a free trade in every article, except opium; to which the East India Company clung, as its last monopoly, until the year 1833, when the China trade was declared open. It was necessary, therefore, to give the Government its share in the trade by imposing a small export duty of three per cent. on sugar, indigo, arrack, and the other principal productions of the island. At the same time, the import duty was fixed at six per cent. In this manner a new revenue department was created in Java; and the development of its commerce, which became the prime object of Raffles's measures, gradually enriched the treasury of the State. But the foreign trade alone could furnish but a small part of the sum needed to support the administration and to defray the cost of a considerable army of occupation. Adequate revenue for such purposes could only be raised out of the soil itself; and in order to appreciate the special difficulties of the question, and the methods employed to overcome them, a glance must be taken at the then existing situation.

The following extract from Raffles's own *History of Java* sketches in outline the policy previously pursued by the Dutch:—

> "Thus ended, in the year 1758, a war which had lasted twelve years, in which the finest provinces of the island were laid waste, thousands slain on both sides, and the independence of the empire finally annihilated. The expenses incurred by the Dutch on account of the war, from the year 1746 until the peace in 1758, amounted to 4,286,006 florins; but, in the result, they acquired, if not the acknowledged sovereignty of the whole island, at least an effectual control over its future administration. . . . By the final settlement of the country [in 1758] the Dutch reserved to themselves the direct administration of all the provinces lying on the northern seacoast, from Cheribon to the eastern extremity of the island of Madura; but the inland and southern provinces, stretching from the highlands of Cheribon to Malang, were restored to the native princes. The terms on which the successors of these princes were permitted to exercise their sovereignty suffered no material alteration until the year 1808, when Marshal Daendels officially declared that the clauses of the existing treaties, by which those princes held their territory in fee from the Dutch, were void, and that, in future, he should consider them as independent princes, having no other relation to the European Government than such as must of necessity exist between a weaker and stronger state in the immediate neighbourhood of each other."

But the incidents of the last few years of Dutch rule had aggravated affairs, and had made it impossible to establish anything approaching to an equilibrium in the finances. The close blockade by the English fleet had practically killed the trade of the island. The system of the Dutch in their dealings with the natives had not merely stifled enterprise, but had led to a depopulation of the most important districts in the island. In Banyuwangi there were, in 1750, 80,000 people; in 1811, there were only 8000. This fertile district did not stand alone. In many others the natives simply fled before the advancing Dutch; and Raffles records that, in the more inaccessible regions, the Javanese might be found in the highest state of prosperity, virtue, and happiness. The exhaustion of the available resources of the island had been followed by the hypothecation of its future development. The Dutch authorities had no silver left in the Treasury. They had recourse to a paper currency, which speedily depreciated in value. Notwithstanding this, the difficulties in which he found himself placed, had induced Marshal Daendels to issue another million dollars of paper money; but he was only able to float this worthless paper by selling to some Chinamen three provinces, of which Probolingo was the most important, on condition that they bought up 50,000 dollars worth of this currency every six months. This issue became known as *Probolingo paper*; and to assist the Chinese in getting rid of it, the Dutch Governor issued a proclamation ordering every one to accept it as hard money. Notwithstanding the severe penalties threatened for disobedience, the paper never possessed a par value; and, at the time when the English landed in Java, it was quoted at a discount of 33 per cent. But the worst feature of these transactions was, that an extensive province, with 150,000 inhabitants, had been sold to a Chinese speculator, who had no regard for their interests, and thought only of wresting the last stiver from the wretched cultivators. The Javanese hated their Chinese taskmasters with a bitter hatred; but the Dutch found themselves no match for their almond-eyed colleagues. When the first instalment became due, the Chinese repaid the 50,000 dollars in *Probolingo paper*, and pointed to the Dutch proclamation compelling everyone to accept it in lieu of silver. While the Batavian Government failed to find any relief for its difficulties in these measures, Marshal Daendels appropriated for his own private use half the revenue of the celebrated Birds' Nest Rocks, which in good years produced a sum of £40,000 sterling.

The situation bristled with difficulties. The depreciated currency, bad in itself, was of still deeper significance as the symptom of the disorganised state of the island, which even the appropriation of the charitable funds had not alleviated. On the one hand, the Dutch had neglected the coffee plantations, and suppressed the cultivation of the grape because it threatened to compete with the similar industry of the Cape. On the other, they had sold present and prospective revenues to alien tax-gatherers; they had crushed internal traffic by onerous import duties between district and district; while the inhabitants were either humiliated and cowed under the cruel system of enforced labour, or had become refugees in those parts of the island which had not fallen under European sway. The English Governor had to redress these evils, without creating others. He had to improve the position of the Javanese races, without placing in their hands the power to end the European domination, whether represented by the Dutch or the English. He had to acquire the means of supporting a necessarily expensive government and garrison; and, above all, he had, in his own words, to utilise "the opportunity of bestowing on a whole nation the freedom which is everywhere the boast of British subjects."

The easier part of this task was accomplished by a few definite and well-judged measures. He abolished the enforced cultivation which had been the basis of the Dutch system; and he reduced the contingents of produce to the lowest possible dimensions, and even then restricted them to the one article of rice. He put an end to the practice of compulsory labour; and, although it was necessary to continue some form of compulsion, or at least of obligation, for the repair of the roads and the postal service, such obligation was deprived of its tyrannical features by the payment of a suitable and sufficient recompense. With regard to the cession of portions of territory to the Chinese speculators, the earliest opportunity was taken to buy out these aliens on fair terms, and to place the redeemed districts and their inhabitants on an equal footing with the rest of the island. In the case of Probolingo, the decision was taken only just in time; for, owing to the exactions of the Chinese proprietor, the whole population was on the point of making an exodus.

With regard to the dispensation of justice, Raffles revived the old village system; and, for the vast majority of disputes, the decisions of the duly elected village chief, aided by the village priest and elders, sufficed. When a settlement could not be effected by these local authorities, the matter might be referred to a higher tribunal composed of the British Resident, the Native Regent, the Chief Priest, and the Mahomedan Law Officer. Criminal cases wherein the islanders alone were involved, might be tried by this court; but the sentence could only be carried into effect after confirmation by the Lieutenant-Governor. The Resident's Court was held at different times and places within his jurisdiction, as necessity or convenience might dictate; and, by this simple method, justice was brought within the reach of every one. For capital charges the trial took place in a Circuit Court before a jury, composed of a foreman and four members; and the Circuit Judges, who were members of the old Dutch courts, made their tours at brief intervals, or whenever necessity rendered a visit desirable. This simple and sufficient judicial system produced the happiest results. Crime fell to a minimum point; the reports of the Residents and Judges were frequently the mere declaration that there was nothing to report; and, in one district with 250,000 people, producing an annual revenue of five lakhs of rupees, such a declaration was the rule rather than the exception. No doubt the tranquillity and obedience to the law thus secured was largely due to the measures taken to disarm the islanders by the calling in of guns and the enforcement of a licence system among those who retained them; while Europeans and the garrison were forbidden to carry arms in the streets. To these precautionary steps, and the general knowledge that justice was both easily obtained and also cheap and pure, must be attributed the extraordinary tranquillity of the island during the British administration.

The following passage is taken from a treatise drawn up in the office at Batavia under Raffles's supervision, if not chiefly by his own hand, and edited by Mr. Charles Assey. It was subsequently published in London in order to influence home opinion in Java, and it gives an interesting view of the islanders' character and mode of life as affected by the improved system Raffles had put in force:—

"It had been said that, 'When we consider the state of the natives of Java, their natural love of indolence, their blind and implicit obedience to the orders of their chiefs, we can hardly conceive them as feeling any repugnance to the feudatory system of the country.' But this is an extremely narrow view, and unjust to the character of this people. They are neither sunk in barbarism, nor worn out by effeminacy: they have been both mistaken and misrepresented; they are neither so indolent as to refuse to labour when they feel that the fruits of it are their own, nor so ignorant as to be indifferent to the comforts and luxuries of civilised society. The fixed principles of the human mind, as they have been traced in the different stages of civilisation elsewhere, are not peculiarly fettered in Java. If the Javanese appeared indolent, it is sufficient to remark, that, when their industry was exerted, they could never be secure that themselves, or their children, would inherit its fruits. If they have hitherto implicitly followed the orders of their chiefs, let it be noticed that they had no sensible knowledge of a higher authority, and had no access to any superior protection; and in proof that their character was more justly appreciated by those who thought more favourably of them, let us only advert to the fact that, since the cause of their habits has been removed, the effect has ceased; that the cultivation of the country is acknowledged to have increased and to be increasing, and that the inhabitants of the island have been capable and willing to engage in labours almost new to them, or to which they have for many years been unaccustomed. It is not just, therefore, to attribute either extreme indolence or apathy to their character.

"If proof of this position be required, it is only necessary to advert to the progress recently made in the culture of indigo and in shipbuilding. Within these last two years an indigo factory has been established in the Regency of Peccalongan. The gentleman who superintends it has stated, that the facilities of this manufacture considerably exceed those which he has found in Bengal; that the Javanese willingly enter into engagements to rent their lands to him, and to cultivate indigo on his account; and that, in consequence of the certainty of the seasons in this island, added to the comparative price of labour and the security derived from his being under no obligation to make advances of money to the cultivators, he will be enabled to produce indigo, equal in quality to Bengal indigo, at the rate of seventeen stivers per pound. In Bengal its average cost is understood to be one sicca-rupee per pound. Independently, therefore, of the certainty of irrigation, the want of which so often ruins the fairest prospect of indigo-planters in India, the article will thus be manufactured in Java at forty per cent. less than its cost in Bengal. When the readiness with which the Javanese have been found to engage themselves in this culture, and the extreme fertility of the soil, are considered, it will be acknowledged that the introduction of capital only is wanting to bring this branch of its produce to any extent that may be required.

"On the subject of shipbuilding I will only observe, that a vessel of between five and six hundred tons has lately been launched: others are in progress; and a ship of twelve hundred tons burthen is about to be put on the stocks in the eastern part of the island. The most valuable teak forests are situated there, and the convenience is afforded of floating down the teak-timber by means of the Solo River, near to the spot where the building yard may be constructed. Shipbuilding is increasing on this island, and will be the means of bringing capital to it at no distant period."

For administrative purposes the island was partly divided

into native regencies: and the Regents, after taking an oath of allegiance to the British sovereign, and of obedience to the Lieutenant-Governor, were intrusted with full authority to administer native affairs as under the Dutch régime, but subject to such alterations and additions as the new Government might decree The principal changes effected were the abolition of feudal service, and the withdrawal from the Regents of the collection of taxes. It was a matter of doubt and anxiety how far the new arrangements would work well; but while, on the one hand, the people were satisfied by the fixity of tenure and the regular remuneration for their labour which they obtained, the chiefs found not only no derogation to their rank in the new office intrusted to them, but, at the same time, a material recompense in the rental of lands attached to the office of Regent, and in the allowance of a commission on the net revenue collected. In this way their influence was enlisted in the task of raising the revenue to its highest attainable point. The great doubt attending the adoption of the new revenue system, involving a payment chiefly in money instead of in kind, was as to how far its restrictions on the authority of the native chiefs would affect their just rights and immunities, and thereby entail their hostility and opposition to the measure. Experience showed that the new duties, privileges, and authority of the Regents, round whom, by a natural process, the subordinate chiefs proceeded to group themselves, compensated them for any loss incurred in relinquishing the old system; and in only one case, which occurred in the first six months of the occupation, was the Executive under the necessity of asserting its right to remove these functionaries at pleasure. Behind the Regents, of course, stood the British Residents, of whom, excluding the dependencies, there were fifteen in the main island. But, perhaps, the real cause of the success of the new administrative measures was that the islanders were given a clear and considerable share, on the ryotwari system, in the produce of their own lands. Raffles himself clearly saw and pointed out that, while every regard should be paid to the rights of the chiefs, the only sure basis for British power was to make it necessary to the people's welfare.

The rice-lands had been appropriated, under the Dutch, to Chinese and other speculators; and, consequently, the chief product of the island produced no revenue. The monopoly of salt had also been sublet for an inadequate sum to another Chinese trader, and Raffles noted that these Chinese vampires were fast turning the peasants into slaves. After the lands had been carefully measured and valued, the new revenue system was introduced for the limited period of one year only in the district of Œloojamié, which Raffles found himself able to deliver from the hands of the Chinese controlling it; and when, in consequence of the dispute already described with the Susuhunan, the important district of Cadoe was taken under British control, the system was also introduced there on a larger scale. It was put in force about the same time in Bantam and Paccalongang, where the local troubles and the weakness of the prince had given the Government a favourable chance of promoting its own authority. So complete was the success of these measures, and the satisfaction they gave to rulers and ruled alike, that, two years after their first adoption, it was felt safe and politic to apply them to the whole island. But, even before the probationary period of twelve months was over, Raffles wrote to the Governor-General on their assured success. He said, "The change, in so for as it has been introduced, has been received with unequivocal pleasure and satisfaction; the people have already acquired a greater knowledge of the rights and privileges bestowed upon them than could, in so short a period of time, have possibly been expected; an ample provision has been made for the native chiefs in each district by allotments of land and attention to their family interests, and also by the establishment of an annual stipend—a measure which, by rendering them more immediately dependent on the Government, was calculated to secure their fidelity and attachment to it. They cannot but feel their situation materially benefited, since, instead of their former precarious condition, they now acquire a fixed and ample allowance, with all their former superiority of rank; and, although removed from any interference with the revenue of the country, they continue to be the chief officers of police in their respective districts, under the immediate authority of the European Resident, and will naturally be respected accordingly. The new system is in progress throughout the eastern districts, and I confidently anticipate that, within a very few months, I shall be able to submit ample evidence that it is equally productive to the public revenue, conducive to the prosperity and improvement of the colony, and grateful to the wishes and feelings of the inhabitants."

One of the first definite matters connected with the development of the natural resources of the island to which Raffles devoted himself, was the improvement of the coffee plantations, which had been much neglected under the Dutch. The Batavian and Preanger Regencies, which covered the greater part of the western end of the island, were reserved for the cultivation of coffee, just as, in a similar manner, the Blandong lands, in the centre of the island, had been retained for teak. The Government, with a view to encouraging its cultivation, in anticipation of the opening of the European and American markets to free competition, agreed to receive any surplus quantity at a fair and fixed price. Under the Dutch the output of coffee was limited to ten million pounds weight; this restriction was withdrawn; and, during the last two years and a half of the British rule, eleven million new coffee shrubs were planted. The estimate Raffles formed of the capacity of the coffee-fields was an annual output of fifty million pounds; and, before he left, this total seems to have been fully reached. With regard to the salt supply, Raffles took it completely under Government control. As a monopoly of the farmer to whom it had been assigned, its price had been irregular and exorbitant; in the hands of the Government the cost was kept down to a low sum, and the people were no longer victimised over an article so essential to their health. The exaction thus terminated had been felt the more bitterly because, in earlier times, the Dutch had not levied any heavy duties on rice or salt, seeking to propitiate native opinion by the cheapness of the prime articles of necessity. But the cost of the repressive measures adopted by Daendels and Janssens, added to a naturally bad financial position, had driven them to raise funds by this and every other device. Among the latter were the erection of bhandars, or toll-gates; and it was computed that the tolls levied at those places frequently raised the price of an article sent inland by seventy per cent. Their abolition was the crowning feat of what may be termed the measures designed for the amelioration of the daily lot of the islanders. These hitherto oppressed people now obtained legal protection, the unfettered right to follow, and enjoy the fruits of, their own industry, and the ability to procure all the necessities of their daily life without paying the excessive exactions of heartless monopolists or an embarrassed Government.

But, serious as was the position of the island at the commencement of the British occupation, on account both of the embarrassed state of the Government finances and of the depressed condition of industry and agriculture, the gravest problem with which the Lieutenant-Governor had to deal was undoubtedly the state of the currency. The *Probolingo paper* was far from being the only paper in circulation. The British authorities began by accepting responsibility for a sum of 7½ million rix-dollars; but, at the moment of their doing so, the value of this paper was 6½ rix-dollars to the Spanish dollar. Before the end of the first twelve months this paper, owing mainly to the necessity of paying the troops in silver, had further depreciated to 13 rix-dollars for one silver dollar, while there was no saying when or where the decline would stop. The fact that 36 lakhs of rupees had to be paid in silver annually to the troops was a constant drain; while the outbreak of the American War put an end to the prospect of exporting coffee, which might otherwise have relieved the situation. Under these circumstances every sagacious statesman would have agreed with Raffles's conclusion that it was "imperiously necessary to remove this paper currency from the market, and to replace it with such a circulating medium as could be supported in its credit, and rendered available for the public disbursements." After much deliberation it was resolved to recall the whole of the paper currency, partly by a sale of land, and partly by an issue of Treasury notes bearing 6 per cent. interest. The lands selected for sale were situated in the neighbourhood of the principal settlements, and the conditions of sale were framed so as to secure every necessary right of government.

Into the details of the sale it will be more convenient to enter when discussing the question in connection with the Gillespie charges; but here it may be observed that, by these measures, Government was relieved from the loss attendant on receiving payment of the revenues in a currency which, in a year, had suffered a depreciation of one hundred per cent. The first effect produced by the measures under consideration was that the depreciation ceased; and, before the period arrived for payment due for the lands purchased, the Batavia paper currency had nearly reached the rate acknowledged by the British Government. To facilitate the operation, the Lombard Bank—an institution of old standing—was re-established, and allowed to circulate notes on the value of security actually deposited. The bank was permitted to receive 9 per cent. for such advances, while it could afford, in consequence, a small interest on its notes; which thus passed freely into circulation. In this manner Raffles successfully grappled with a great currency difficulty. Looking further ahead, he predicted that, with the assurance of tranquillity, and the continuance of good government, trade would certainly revive; bullion would flow in; and it might become practicable to dispense with a paper currency altogether. In the memorial he drew up for the purpose of arousing official opinion in London to the importance of Java, he wrote as follows:—

"Already has the present Government recalled from circulation the 7,500,000 rix-dollars paper currency which were recognised at the period of the conquest. When it had reached the state of depreciation above described, a part of it was called in by sale of public lands, etc., to the amount of about 500,000 Spanish dollars, and the rest of it has since come into the general treasury in the ordinary receipt of the Government dues; it has since been declared out of circulation. Thus the generosity of the British Government has cleared off a debt under which the Dutch were weighed down in Java; and the total amount of Government securities, issued in lieu of that paper currency, has now been so far recalled and destroyed that it is estimated there is not more abroad than it is within the command of the Government to recall when necessary. It is not, however, to be supposed that this arrangement would accord with the wishes of Dutch colonists, or could be effected without their serious representation. The command of paper currency to any extent they might require, and which for many years has been within their reach, has produced an imaginary value of property that could only exist under such circumstances. Large properties were usually bought without the purchaser being able to pay for them. He was enabled to mortgage to the extent of two-thirds of the estimated value (and estimated in paper currency), and the mortgage was commonly transferred with the purchase; the rest could be borrowed; and thus many men are the nominal purchasers of large properties, who, in fact, have never paid for them, and can only look for the means of doing so in the facility of borrowing. These remarks are not, perhaps, very relevant to the subject, but they are useful in estimating the state of society and of property in Batavia and its neighbourhood, and will be a further proof of what has already been advanced, that the local interests of residents in Batavia can with difficulty be rendered compatible with the measures that are necessary to the general prosperity and improvement of the colony. Thus the restriction now placed on the loans of the Lombard Bank, and other measures of a similar nature adopted by the British Government to limit the issue of paper currency as much as possible, and the strict prohibition that now exists against the importation and traffic in slaves, cannot be expected to be very congenial with the views and wishes of the colonists in general; and it is natural that they should often be inclined to apprehend a political danger, where, in reality, the only danger is in the effect of prejudice. I am far from wishing to infer any want of liberality, and much less of humanity, among the class of land proprietors in Java. It comprehends many men of superior talent and amiable character; but where long established prejudices, and the ideas of personal interest, unite to oppose the abolition of slavery and feudal service, argument and reason are unable to convince; and although no one could, with justice or propriety, advise that their interests should be injured, it is difficult to persuade any one who looks through the former administration that the vital interests of the nation have not formerly been sacrificed to them, or that Java, if that system were continued, can ever become what it may be, and what it will be, if administered on more extended and generous principles."

In December 1812, General Gillespie gave his assent, as member of Council, to a limited sale of lands; and, on that occasion, he was aware that one of the principal purchasers was Mr. Muntinghe, the abler and more important of the two Dutch members of Council. It should also be stated that a sale of lands for the benefit of Government was one of the recognised modes in Java of replenishing the Exchequer. Sanctioned by usage, carried in its early stages into effect with the unanimous assent of the Council, and in its later with the approbation of the Dutch members, Raffles might reasonably assume that such a step would never be challenged, provided it accomplished the purpose that dictated its adoption. That it did accomplish that purpose is beyond the shadow of dispute. It restored the paper currency to its face value; it liquidated the floating responsibility of the British Government for the 7½ million rix-dollars; and it enabled those engaged in trade to conclude their transactions on a sound basis. But in spite of its necessity and its success, the very boldness of the measure, carried out without reference to the Supreme Government, seems to have somewhat startled Lord Minto, then on the point of resigning office; and the following letter, dated 22nd November 1813, breathes one word of caution:—

"On the financial operation of withdrawing the depreciated paper from circulation by a considerable sale of lands, the resolutions of this Government must be conveyed to you by my successor; but I am unwilling to withhold from you my individual sentiments on a measure of so much importance.

"I begin, therefore, by assenting without reservation to the absolute and exigent necessity which was the motive, and is the justification, of the proceeding. The revenues and all the demands of Government were paid in paper which could not be reissued; there was, therefore, a virtual suspension of receipt at the public treasury. To avoid this total loss, the paper must have been issued again, at the discount of the day, which would have discredited the currency still more, and would have involved an enormous and constantly recurring loss. This state of things left you no option but to withdraw the paper, to make room for some better medium of circulation; and the operation of the evil was too rapid to admit of delay.

"The only plan for the redemption of the paper which could be found, appears very clearly to have been precisely that to which you had recourse,—the sale of public property; and it must be deemed fortunate that this resource existed, and proved to be immediately available.

"I consider, therefore, your measure to have been an *able expedient* in a case of *great emergency*.

"At the same time, I conceive the *necessity* of a prompt remedy to form the essential, and, indeed, the indispensable, ground of the resolution that was taken; for I should not, I confess, have thought an extensive alienation of the public domains advisable in itself, under the particular circumstances of the colony at the time. First, it was too important a measure to be adopted during a provisional government, the duration of which is more than precarious. Secondly, it ought (and naturally would, without the pressure of immediate necessity) to have received the previous sanction of the Supreme Government. Thirdly, although my views, as you know, lead to the transfer of public territory to the management of individual industry, and the creation of a genuine landed interest, with all its immediate benefits and ameliorating tendencies, in the room of the deplorable system of vassalage and dependence under which land is now held in Java; yet I have felt that this change could not be brought about suddenly, partly from the very nature of all extensive changes, partly from the circumstances of the colony, which contains at present neither capital nor capitalists enough to afford a comparison between the value in the market, of land and money, either fair, or at all approaching to fair. I should have inclined, therefore, to small and partial sales of land, if alienation in perpetuity should have been thought advisable at all, proportioned in some degree to the disposable quantity of money in the hands of individuals. But the general course to be recommended I conceive to be short leases, followed by longer, and, ultimately, by perpetuities. I touch upon these points the more willingly, for the purpose of conveying to you a caution on the subject, founded on our knowledge of the sentiments which appear to be the most prevalent at home, but which you may not be apprised of.

"There is a great division of opinion on the question of permanent settlements, and the extension of that system to the newly acquired provinces under the Presidency of Bengal, which has, in a great degree, been carried into effect during my administration.

"The introduction of that system has been gradual in those provinces, but yet more sudden than is approved at home. But Java is in a state infinitely less favourable to perpetual alienations; and you may depend upon such measures, unsupported by particular exigency, being disapproved, and, indeed, disavowed and annulled by the authorities in England."

On the receipt of that letter, Raffles, unaware of the thunder-cloud that was about to burst on him, reconsidered the whole question of his policy in the matter of the currency; and, with the gratifying results of the policy shown every day, he had no hesitation in expressing the confident opinion that the line he had followed was the right one; that he had dealt with a difficult problem on correct principles; and that, if the same question were to arise again, he would deal with it in a similar manner. The following letter to Lord Minto, addressed to him in Europe, shows how confident Raffles felt in the security of his position on this question; and the accompanying Minute, which demonstrated his mastery of the subject, may be regarded as his weightiest exposition of the two most critical measures—the new land revenue system and the rehabilitation of the currency—associated with his rule in Java:—

"BUITENZORG, *13th February* 1814.

"Your Lordship is aware of the entire change of management which was contemplated by me some time previous to your quitting India; and, although no official notice has yet been taken of my Minute on the subject transmitted to the Supreme Government in July last, I have been able to collect a general opinion on the nature of the settlement you would most approve from the observations contained in your confidential letter of the 22nd November, in which you enter fully on the question of the sale of lands and the decided objections to perpetual settlement.

"I had already completed my arrangements for the land rental when that letter arrived; but, before I had put the finishing stroke to the judicial regulations and the general instructions to the collectors, the Fifth Report of the House of Commons fell into my hands; and you will be happy to hear that, on comparing what I had done and what I had in contemplation with what seemed most approved by the authorities in England, I found that I had exactly hit on a settlement which, while it was peculiarly applicable to Java, was considered the most advantageous one for India generally. The principles of the Ryotwar settlement had suggested themselves without my knowing that they had been adopted elsewhere; and, although I may not easily gain credit for the original design, the promoters and supporters of that settlement will no doubt find a strong argument in its favour from the circumstance of its having been so early and so easily adopted in a foreign and distant colony.

"The principles of the settlement which I have effected, as well as their application, are so fully stated in a Minute which I have recorded on the subject, that I cannot do better than forward it to you. In that Minute I have first attempted to prove the necessity and policy of the measure, which being established, an abstract statement of the settlement which has been effected is considered; and I have concluded by observing on the tenures of land and the principles of the detailed system of management which is in progress. May I request your Lordship's opinion on what has been done, and your suggestions on what ought to be attended to in future? Whether Java remains under my control or not, your sentiments on the subject will be most interesting to me. You will observe that I have throughout considered myself as the agent acting under your Lordship's instructions; and I can assure you that my ambition will be gratified by an assurance that I have not failed in acting up to your original design.

"I have said so much on the effects of the change, and they are so obvious on general principles, that I should but intrude on your time by enlarging upon them here. I cannot but look upon the accomplishment of this undertaking as the most conspicuous and important under my administration; and, in its success or otherwise, I was willing to stand or fall. I need not tell your Lordship that, while it was in agitation, I had many an uneasy hour; and I suffered no small share of mental anxiety and bodily fatigue while it was in progress; but, now that it has been happily accomplished, I am amply repaid for all. It was my lot personally to superintend the settlement in every district: the necessity of that personal superintendence obliged me to leave Batavia at three separate times, and during the last to be absent for three months from the capital; but my immediate presence in the different parts of the island could alone have concluded the settlement in so short a period; and it has had the advantage of rendering me intimately acquainted with everything. I have been able to judge for myself throughout; and, although I have not failed to avail myself of all the talent and experience I could find, I may safely say that I have in no case decided without a conviction brought home to my own mind that I was right.

"The arrangements for the interior of the country being completed, my next object will be to simplify and modify the unwieldy establishments of the towns, particularly those in Batavia.

"I have gone on as long as it was possible, from day to day, in the expectation of a change of Government; but I shall not feel myself satisfied in longer delaying those radical reforms so essential for the health and character of our Government. Much odium has already attached from the continuance of the Dutch institutions so long; and I owe it to my own character, and to your Lordship, to render my administration 'not only without fear, but without reproach.'

"Next to the internal administration of the Colony, I have to request your attention to the interests of the Eastern Islands generally. The kind caution which you sent me regarding our policy induced me to think very seriously on all I had done, and to weigh well the principles which I had laid down for my guidance. I became the more confirmed in the first view which I took on the subject.

"On the reception of the principles which I have in some cases adopted, and in others recommended, on the two great points of our home and foreign administration, must depend the character of my government; to you, my Lord, I submit them, in full confidence that they will be viewed with an indulgent eye.

"These great questions being submitted to your Lordship's judgment, I feel relieved from all the anxiety which attached previous to my putting them to paper. I consider them as now fairly before an impartial judge. I shall, unless otherwise directed by a superior authority, continue to be guided by the principles which I have laid down, and which have appeared to me, after the most deliberate consideration, to be just and right.

"I must now proceed to a point which I ought first to have adverted to. I allude to the firm support which I have invariably received from Major-General Nightingall. He is open and candid in his sentiments, regular and economical in all his public plans, particularly the military. I have reason to believe that he is now planning a general revision and reduction of the military establishment: he sees the necessity of it; and I am led to hope that the period is not far distant when all our financial difficulties will be removed. The expenses in the military department do not fall short of three lakhs of rupees in each month. This must be paid in silver; and silver is not to be obtained on any terms except by bills on Bengal, and these with difficulty.

"The great changes in Europe promise to create a demand for our Colonial produce, particularly the coffee; but it will be some time before that belonging to the Government or the produce under British administration will come into play. The larger quantity belonging to the capital must first be shipped off. The prize agents have at last sold the whole; but it will be a long time before tonnage can be obtained to carry it off: the coffee alone exceeds 150,000 piculs measures in pounds still in store. Silver is as scarce as ever, if not decreasing in quantity; the colonists are crying loudly for paper; but, as they would no sooner possess it than run it down to a discount, it cannot be issued; it will, therefore, be some time before Java is able to support an extensive foreign military establishment. . . . The intercourse with Japan has been opened, and we have received a very advantageous return in copper and camphor. I look forward to the possibility of establishing a permanent British interest in that quarter; but I will reserve this subject for another letter."

The concluding words of this letter will justify my interpolating here a side question of much interest, which subsequent events have rendered of greater rather than of less importance.

A striking illustration of the breadth of view which distinguished Raffles in his government of Java and in his attempt to found British predominance in the Archipelago, was afforded by his effort to establish a friendly and commercial intercourse with Japan. The reader will not see at once the connection that existed between the two islands, or appreciate the energy which, with his hands full at Batavia, urged him forth to cope with fresh difficulties at Nagasaki. A few words will explain the reasons and connecting relations which induced Raffles to make the effort to improve the position of his countrymen in the Far East.

By the middle of the seventeenth century the Dutch had expelled both the English and the Portuguese from Japan, as they had done from Java and the Malay Peninsula. They had recourse to the same exclusive policy: they represented their rivals, and the English in particular, as monsters of inhumanity; and their machinations in Japan undoubtedly led to that massacre of Christians in 1638, which put an end to the efforts of the Jesuits. The object for which they strove, and for the attainment of which they stifled their human feelings, was monopoly. They succeeded; but the monopoly thus obtained only secured, after all, the right to despatch two ships a year to Nagasaki. For a century and a half these two ships a year, passing between Batavia and Nagasaki, represented the only foreign trade of Japan: and the Dutch, satisfied with small results so long as no one else shared them, hugged themselves in the belief that they were undisputed masters of the situation. In addition to the value of their cargoes, these champions of freedom might include among their prizes the possession of the only factory and the only interpreters in the islands of Japan. The state of affairs was precisely like this when the British Government was set up at Batavia. Japan was the preserve of the Hollanders, and the memory of the old English factory at Firando had faded into obscurity.

Raffles had authority to establish the British power over the dependencies of Java. The Dutch factory in Japan was one of the number; and, when the season came for the departure of the two ships, he sent an order to the factor in charge to recognise British authority, and with it an English man of science, Dr. Ainslie, to report on the people and trade of Japan. As the more interesting part for us of the matter is the originality of the views expressed by Raffles on the subject of the Japanese, it will suffice to say here that the Dutch factor at Nagasaki refused to recognise the British, or to give up his stores. This defiance was of a formal character, and produced no decided results. It did not prevent the English Lieutenant-Governor from despatching the two ships a second year, or from utilising the services of the Dutch interpreters. In his resolution to push the trade at all hazards, and to break down for ever the barrier the Dutch had endeavoured to set up round that interesting country, he even fitted out on Government account a special commercial venture to Japan, and intrusted the control of its fortunes to a Dutchman named Wardaner, or, according to another spelling, Wardenaar. As a first attempt the expedition was sufficiently successful; but, commercially, it showed no great profit: and the Company was in no mood to patronise fresh ventures, unless they held forth the prospect of exceptional reward. Moreover, the decision to restore Java had then been formed; and, whatever might be effected in the way of tapping the trade of that island in the future, there was an end to all expectations of making Batavia the starting-point of our operations. At that moment, too, a wave of discouragement was passing over the British settlements in the Straits; and the most experienced European inhabitants declared that, as there was no hope of overthrowing the Dutch monopoly in those seas, the best policy was tamely to accept the situation.

How very different were Raffles's views may be seen from the following extracts. Soon after the establishment of the British Government in Java, Raffles had revived and re-animated the Batavian Society of Arts and Sciences, and the quotations given, "nearly as he had received the information from the verbal communications of Dr. Ainslie," constitute the more important passages on the subject of Japan in a presidential address Raffles delivered to the Society on 11th September 1815 :—

"Referring you, therefore, to the works of Kaempfer for an account of their history, institutions, and acquirements, as genuine data on which this interesting people may be appreciated, I need only offer a few notices on the character which they appeared to Dr. Ainslie to display, during a residence of four months, and as far as he had the opportunity of judging. They are represented to be a nervous, vigorous people, whose bodily and mental powers assimilate much nearer to those of Europe than what is attributed to Asiatics in general. Their features are masculine, and perfectly European, with the exception of the small lengthened Tartar eye, which almost universally prevails, and is the only feature of resemblance between them and the Chinese. The complexion is perfectly fair, and indeed blooming, the women of the higher classes being equally fair with Europeans, and having the bloom of health more generally prevalent among them than is usually found in Europe. For a people who have had very few, if any, external aids, the Japanese cannot but rank high in the scale of civilisation." . . . The Chinese "have been stationary at least as long as we have known them ; but the slightest impulse seems sufficient to give a determination to the Japanese character, which would progressively improve, until it attained the same height of civilisation with the European. Nothing, indeed, is so offensive to the feelings of a Japanese, as to be compared, in any one respect, with the Chinese. . . . The Japanese, with an apparent coldness like the stillness of the Spanish character, and derived nearly from the same causes—that system of espionage, and that principle of disunion, dictated by the principles of both Governments,—are represented to be eager of novelty, and warm in their attachments ; open to strangers ; and, bating the restrictions of their political institutions, a people who seem inclined to throw themselves into the hands of any nation of superior intelligence ; they have, at the same time, a great contempt and disregard of everything below their own standard of morals and habits, as instanced in the case of the Chinese."

In one of his earlier reports, prepared at Malacca for the information of Lord Minto, prior to the Java expedition, Raffles had called attention to the subject of Japan, and had stated that, "the only chance which we have for retaining the Japanese trade, is by gaining to our interest the present Dutch residents at Japan, and the Japanese corps of Dutch interpreters, at whatever price it may cost." It was on those lines he worked, and the result is recorded in the following letter to Lord Minto. The views he expresses are remarkable for their sagacity and foresight. They constitute perhaps the earliest appreciation of the Japanese by an

Englishman; while it is only in our own time that such views have become general:—

"Buitenzorg, *13th February* 1814.

"My Lord,—I now proceed to detail to you the result of our communication with Japan; in which, if we have not obtained complete success, we have at any rate opened the door for future intercourse; and, I trust, at no distant period, for the permanent establishment of the British interests in that quarter. Your Lordship will recollect the arrangement made for sending Dr. Ainslie, and the very little hope of success entertained by the Supreme Government. Had my views been confined to the continuance of the trade with Batavia on its former footing, that object would have been without difficulty accomplished; but I had considered the subject more extensively, and as it might affect our interests permanently. I was too well informed of the corruptions, and of the degraded state of the Dutch factory, to suppose for a moment that it would be either creditable or advantageous to carry on the trade on its former footing, or through Dutch agents. The information we have now obtained is conclusive on this point; and the very peculiar circumstances, in which we find ourselves placed, dictate the necessity and advantages of a more enlarged policy. . . . The trade heretofore carried on with Batavia forms no criterion by which the extent and value of the trade is to be judged, when a more liberal and upright policy is pursued. It was just as extensive as it suited the personal interest of the Resident to make it; but, on a different system, it may be contemplated that its importance will not fall short of that which is now attached to China. The restrictions which exist do not arise so much from the limitations and institutions of the Japanese, as from the nature and constitution of the Dutch factory; the degraded state of which would appear to have sunk the Dutch character very low in estimation. The Japanese are a highly polished people, considerably advanced in science, highly inquisitive and full of penetration.

"There seems no reason to doubt the estimate of the population (twenty-five millions); nor the high character given of the country, and of the people, by the early voyagers; and on the score of religion and its prejudices, on which so much has been industriously circulated by the Dutch, they are found to be simple and inoffensive. Perhaps, on further acquaintance, it may be found that the Dutch were not inactive agents in the dreadful massacre of the Catholics. The interpreters do not hesitate to throw out insinuations to that effect already. The ceremony of walking over the cross, and the degrading ceremonies to which the Dutch have represented themselves to be subject, are in a great measure fictitious; and, with the exception of the ceremony of obeisance by prostration to the emperor, unnecessary. The Dutch are only despised for the ceremonial which they perform to the inferior chiefs.

"A British factory once established, that of the Dutch would be superseded for ever; and all their misrepresentations and collusions would but serve to complete the destruction of their interests, and the detestation with which their character must be viewed, when compared with that of those who succeed them. The demand for woollens and hardware, the staple manufactures of Great Britain, would be unlimited. No prejudices are to be surmounted; the climate and habits of the people create a want which it would be our interest to supply; and the returns might either be made in those articles which we now receive from China, such as tea, silk, and cloths, or in copper, corn, or oil, the staples of Japan. In a word, Japan can furnish in return every article that is now obtained from China, of better quality, and at a lower price. The fact of the principal export from China to Japan being woollens speaks for itself; and the observations of Dr. Ainslie tend to prove that it would be an easy matter to supersede the ten Chinese junks now allowed to trade annually. Whether, therefore, we consider Japan separately, as affording an extensive field for the commercial capital of Great Britain, as affording a copious outlet for our staple manufactures, or, in a political view, as it may tend to the security of the China trade, it is most important. In Japan we should find all the advantages that could be derived from China without any of the humiliations, any of the uncertainties, any of the tricks, impositions, and difficulties, with which we are now hampered. As connected with the present China trade, would not a knowledge of our influence at Japan render the Chinese more humble? They look up to the Japanese as a most superior race of people, and the Japanese, in return, treat the highest Chinese with the greatest indignity. Or should any accident put a stop to the trade at Canton, either partially or *in toto*, would it not be of essential importance to be able to have recourse to Japan?

"In every point in which I can view the subject, it appears to me most important; and as the acquisition of the trade, and the permanent establishment of our interests, is almost within my grasp, I should consider it a dereliction of my public duty did I not strain every nerve to effect the accomplishment of an object in every way so inviting and so interesting. We are now no longer amused with the speculative dreams of what Japan is supposed to be: we have the evidence of a British agent to speak to every fact; and when his detailed Memoir is completed, in which he purposes taking an historical review of the trade and intercourse with Japan, I am confident it will be found that, in no instance, have we advanced what cannot be clearly proved. The question is of too much importance for your Lordship not to take a deep interest in it. I acknowledge that I am anxious to accomplish the task which I have undertaken, and I appeal with confidence, but with the utmost solicitude, to your Lordship to assist me, by urging a quick reply, and an immediate and particular attention to my requisitions.

"Java, my Lord, is yours, and every act of mine in its administration has been considered as springing from your parental direction; the British influence is now spreading into every quarter of the Archipelago; the civilisation of so large a portion of the human race will, I hope, emanate from the just and wise principles on which you established the British Empire in the Eastern Seas. Japan is yet unconnected with this conquest, and I have only to entreat that I may be empowered to act as your agent."

That letter never reached Lord Minto, whose death

occurred in June 1814, and Raffles's wish was doomed to disappointment. I have cited many beneficent acts to show that Raffles was a wise ruler, who based his proceedings on the broad principle that the prosperity of the people furnished the strength of the Government. But perhaps his most remarkable step, in its direct appeal to the heart, was his decision, on very slender authority, to abolish slavery throughout the Eastern Archipelago. In 1813 the British Legislature passed an act declaring the holding of slaves to be a felony; and remembering that the East India Company had given expression, on several occasions, to the pious opinion that slavery was abhorrent to it, and not to be tolerated within its dominion, Raffles concluded that he was free, and even enjoined, to take steps to remove the curse from his jurisdiction. He began by sending a mission to the native states, explaining that no importation of slaves would be permitted, and that all ships detected in the traffic would be seized. He saw that the total abolition of slavery would be attended with some difficulty, as much of the wealth of the chiefs consisted in slaves; but he felt sure that the prohibition, coupled with the simple regulation he put in force insisting on the registration of all slaves held at that moment, would eventually work out a complete remedy. After he had issued his decree, he was blamed by the Governor-General, Lord Moira, afterwards Marquis of Hastings, for taking this step on territory that was not definitely a possession of the Company, and that might have to be restored to the Dutch; but, in another despatch from the Court itself, he was absolutely censured for "disposing prematurely of property that might belong to the Company." As Lord Wellesley, in 1805, had proclaimed emancipation in India, it is a little difficult to follow the process of reasoning by which the East India Company put itself forward, at one moment as the champion of the rights of humanity, and at another as having the implied intention of treating human beings as chattels and saleable property. The official rebuff administered to Raffles, in a matter for which he was entitled to special credit, did not undo his good work. Before leaving Java he founded a society, entitled the Java Benevolent Society, for the special purpose of looking after the interests and ensuring the manumission of the slave classes; and it must be recorded to the credit of the Dutch that, after the restoration, they made no attempt to repeal Raffles's law forbidding slavery. The explanation of this creditable act appears to be due to the fact that, according to the Dutch Constitution, no colonial law—and Raffles's acts were as valid as those of any Dutch Governor of Batavia—could be repealed except by the Government in Europe. As the colonials were all in favour of slavery, the credit for its continued prohibition belongs to the home, rather than to the insular, authorities.

One may turn from these matters of State to one or two incidents of a more personal character, which will show that, in the midst of all his cares and the burdens of office, Raffles did not lose his interest in what were, in comparison, very ordinary affairs. He had deplored the insufficiency of Protestant religious effort in these regions; and, at his suggestion, his cousin, Dr. Raffles, had sent out two missionaries of his own persuasion to labour among the heathen in Java. The following letter from one of them, Mr. T. C. Supper, throws an interesting side-light on Raffles's life in Java; and is specially important as affording almost the last glimpse we have of Mrs. Olivia Raffles. It is addressed to Mr. Supper's patron, the Rev. Dr. Raffles, at Liverpool:—

"BATAVIA, *29th June* 1814.

"HIGHLY RESPECTED SIR,—On the 4th of June (the birthday of King George), in the morning, was a great *levée* at the Governor's house; many gentlemen came to congratulate the Governor and his lady; and on this occasion the Java Auxiliary Bible Society was erected, at which the Governor has been unanimously chosen to the chair, as also the Governess; and in this noble character his Excellency has been pleased to honour me with the important call to be a member of the Committee. In the evening was a ball and a grand supper at the Governor's house, to which we also were invited by the Governor himself. Mr. Ross said that it was the custom that all the gentlemen belonging to the Ministerial office may not refuse to come to such-like festivals, therefore we accepted the obliging invitation of his Excellency. But as I had to preach my first sermon on next day, I stopped only till nine o'clock in the evening, being excused by the Governor himself, upon my request, in a very kind manner, and he invited me to sup with him on Monday next. Mr. Ross and my brethren received also the same invitation, and we went to the said supper, when I had the honour to sit at table next to the Governor; and we conversed then much together concerning you and your respected parents, and I can assure you that he loves you all dearly; and though he is in a station more brilliant, according to the outward appearance, than that of the Prince Regent is, and he receives more honour than all the Royal Family together receive in England, yet he is very humble and kind, and no reasonable man can refuse him his entire confidence and profoundest esteem. It is true his Excellency, with all his kindness and wisdom, is also one of those great men who could not equally satisfy all men. While grateful men are completely satisfied with Governor Raffles, there are others who are discontented. But his Excellency has reason not to mind such ungrateful creatures, since the great Governor of the Universe cannot give them satisfaction.

. . . .

"On the 22nd of this month the Governor sent me a very obliging letter, in which he appointed me decisively to be stated minister of the D.C. at Batavia, with a salary of 200 Spanish mattes per month, and Mr. Brückner is appointed for Samarang, and Mr. Kam for Amboyna; both shall get also their salary from Government.

. . . .

"I remain, with gratitude and esteem, reverend sir, your humble servant,

"T. C. Supper."

That glimpse of Olivia Raffles, in the summer of 1814, being appointed, as "the Governess," to a seat on the Committee of the Java Auxiliary Bible Society, is the last view obtainable of the lady who, during the nine most important years of his life, had fulfilled for Raffles the parts of a loving wife and a true friend. For over three years she had dispensed the honours of Government House at "Ryswick," in Batavia, and at Buitenzorg, the country residence, thirty-five miles south of that place. That she played her part nobly is beyond dispute; but in November 1814, with that terrible suddenness which is the tragic element of human life in the tropics, Olivia Raffles was seized with a mortal illness, and was carried off almost before her husband realised the danger. There are no details to give of that closing scene. I have endeavoured to show who Olivia was, and to clear her name. All she was to Raffles himself can never be described. Her loss left him "a lone and stricken man." The monument he erected in the cemetery at Batavia, where she lies in close proximity to Leyden, with another in the garden of Buitenzorg, both of which are included among the illustrations of this volume, were but the feeble tributes of human love and a man's deep sense of loss. On the latter Raffles placed the following lines :—

"Oh Thou! whom ne'er my constant heart
One moment hath forgot,
Tho' fate severe hath made us part,
I'll still forget thee not."

The blow came at a moment of depression and even discomfiture, through Gillespie's charges; and when Raffles most needed consolation and support, he lost the tried and courageous friend who had shared and contributed to the rapidly won successes of his remarkable career. The death of Olivia Raffles did not stand alone among domestic afflictions, for about the same time he lost in quick succession the children she had borne him.

After this sad event Raffles was persuaded to seek a change of scene by making a tour in the island. He seized the opportunity to collect materials which were afterwards embodied in his *History of Java.* But his health did not improve, and so—

"It was thought advisable," writes Lady Raffles, "that he should leave Buitenzorg, and remove to Ciceroa, a more elevated situation. He took with him several of his staff, and a party of natives, whose good sense and intelligence had attracted his notice, and whom he had brought with him from the eastern part of the island. With these last he passed the greater part of every morning and evening in reading and translating, with the greatest rapidity and ease, the different legends with which they furnished him, particularly the 'Brata Yudha.' His translation of this singular and curious poem will be found in his *History of Java.* It was a work requiring considerable labour and time, but it was a common remark with him that if a man were fully and seriously determined on accomplishing any undertaking within human power at all, he would succeed by diligence and attention. At this time he rose early, and commenced business before breakfast; immediately after this he went through the official duties of the day; after which he devoted the remainder of the morning, till dinner-time, to the natives who were living with him. He dined at four o'clock, and took a walk for the sake of his health in the evening; and, until he retired to rest, he was occupied in reading, translating, and compiling. But his strength and health did not return, perhaps from his not being able to amuse his mind without over-exertion and too much application."

Let us turn from the view of this great and much-tried man, borne down by so severe and irreparable a shock, to see him in another light, recognising what was good in an alien creed, and the need for caution in attempting to substitute a truer and a higher faith.

The following letter is addressed to Dr. Raffles:—

Private.]

"BUITENZORG, *10th February* 1815.

"MY DEAR TOM,—That I may not incur the charge of neglect or unkindness, I am anxious to acknowledge and thank you for your frequent and very interesting communications—even before I am able to reply to them satisfactorily; this, therefore, must account for any conciseness at present.

"I have duly received your picture and the Hebrew Bible, for which I request you will accept my best thanks. The painter, or engraver, has by no means done you justice, and I cannot think this a true resemblance, particularly as the engraving in the last volume of the *Messiah* is quite of another stamp. That engraving I admire very much, and I would hope it were a true resemblance.

"I have read with much delight your edition of the *Messiah* of Klopstock, and I congratulate you, from my heart, on the success you have attained. Your sermon to the Missionary Society, which has lately found its way here, has pleased me much, and no one views with more interest than myself the rapid progress you are making.

"You ask me my opinion about missionaries in India, and if I had time at the present moment you should have it unreservedly: circumscribed, however, as my leisure is, I can only now say that I am a good deal more inclined than you are to let people go to heaven their own way. I foresee much mischief, much bitterness of heart and contention, by an inordinate desire after conversion. Religion and laws are so united in these countries that I don't see what good can arise by giving the people a new system of the one without also a new system of the other. The missionaries can only half do the business, and they leave the people in greater tribulation than they found them. My population on the island of Java alone, without including the dependent territory of the Archipelago, is somewhere about five millions. They are to a man Mahometans, but recently and very imperfectly converted. They still retain many of their ancient institutions (of Hindu origin), but these are gradually giving way to the Koran. Every village has its clergyman, and there may be upwards of three thousand spiritual teachers on the island. These not only assist in saving the soul, but protect the worldly property of the inhabitants by the application of the law. It is impossible to conceive better regulated communities than these villages, or a happier people than the Javanese, taking them generally; and I am ready to admit that it would go against my conscience to promote any plan which had not on its face the prospect of leaving them as well off as it found them. No attempt has yet been made to convert the Javanese to Christianity. Nor do I think any attempt likely to succeed under existing circumstances.

"Averse, however, as I may be to any partial measure, I am far from thinking that the condition of the people is not capable of improvement. I abhor and abominate the tenets of Mahometanism, and verily believe that it is the religion of all others most likely to enslave the minds and bodies of mankind; but I am Utopian enough to think that a new system altogether, founded on the principles of Christianity, and modified according to the temper of the people, would be far better than the naked revelation at once, which they would neither admire nor relish.

"If you will consent to leave the Javanese to their *own way* for the present, I will commute with you by recommending a vigorous conversion on Borneo, almost the largest island in the world, and thickly peopled by a race scarcely emerged from barbarism. Here you will invade no sacred institutions handed down from their forefathers. The way is clear. The people cannot be worse. You may make them better. At all events, it is worth the trial.

"That you may know my public sentiments on this point, I will extract a few passages from a paper which I delivered to Lord Minto on the invasion of the Dutch authority in these seas :—

"'The Malays, though accustomed to look up to the Arabs as their religious instructors, seldom hesitate to admit the superiority of both the Europeans and Chinese either to themselves or the Arabs in the arts of life and general science ; and it is certainly our interest to prevent the increase of the Arab influence among the Malay nations.

"'From similar considerations, as well as in conformity with instructions issued from the Fatherland, the Dutch nation appear to have pursued, as a principle of policy, the propagation of Christianity among the Eastern islands. The same plan had been previously followed by the Portuguese in their various Eastern possessions with great success, and there are now several small islands in the Malay Archipelago containing a large proportion of Christian population of the Catholic persuasion, as the islands of Sanzgir and Mindanawi. In many other islands the Protestant persuasion has made very considerable progress, and teachers, in the flourishing times of the Dutch, were dispersed over all the low chain of islands which extend from Bali and Tumbok to the great island of Timor. The islands in which the Christian faith has been most extensively diffused are the great island of Endé or Manggeras, the isles of Solor, Sabrang, and Ambrai, the island of Ternor, and the Moluccas. In many of these islands the natives, having no written character of their own, have been instructed in the Roman character, and taught to read Malay and other dialects in it. There have also been various formularies printed for their use, and translations have been made for the use of these Christians in some of their languages which have little or no affinity with the Malay. The propagation of Christianity among these islands is obviously liable to none of those objections which have been urged against it in our Indian possessions. A great proportion of the natives are still Pagans, under the influence of a wild and almost incorrigible superstition, the principles of which are not recorded in books, but are handed down like stories of ghosts, fairies, and witches, with all the uncertainty of tradition. Accordingly, in most instances, the people, though they stand in great awe of the priests as enchanters or dealers with invisible spirits, are very little attached to the superstition. Many of them are said to be very desirous of procuring instruction, and in some places they look up with a degree of veneration to the Moslems, as a people who have received something which they still want. Besides, the attachment of the Malays to the religion of Islam is by no means of that strength as to emancipate them from their old usages, nor to inspire them with that contempt and hatred for other religions as is found in many of the older Moslem kingdoms. On the advantages which must accrue from protecting Christianity in these Eastern islands, and by favouring its propagation, in preference to the doctrines of Islam, where it may be so easily propagated, it is unnecessary to enlarge in addressing your Lordship. Permit me, however, to allude to one remarkable fact which may serve to illustrate the necessity of attending to the subject as a matter of public importance. In our present settlements of Prince of Wales' Island and Malacca the impossibility of procuring servants for wages compels almost every person to have recourse to slaves, and a considerable quantity of these are Pagans, being chiefly Battas from the centre of Sumatra, Balimen from Bali, Dayaks from Borneo, besides natives of Timor and the more easterly islands. Of all these slaves which fall into the hands of the English, there is perhaps not a single one that becomes a Christian, but the whole of them become Moslems, and despise and hate their masters as infidels. Such is the woeful effect of our supineness and indifference, which, if it should extend to the East, would certainly not tend to the progress of general improvement among the Malays.'

"Such was my opinion before the Eastern islands fell under my sway, and my past experience has afforded me no grounds for altering it.

"I have had much pleasure in attending to your recommendations. The three clergymen who arrived here have been well provided for, and your friend Mr. Supper has been fixed at Batavia. He is a good, simple creature, rather silly, but amiable. He has unfortunately been in love, and as he made me his *confidant* I may perhaps have seen him on his weak side. He is doing very well, and seems much attached to you.

"Mr. Trout is not doing much, nor have I seen much of him. He has been very unwell, and I invited him to the country; but he got better and declined the invitation. He was rather distressed for money, and, on your recommendation, I countersigned his bills, and made myself answerable for the amount, by which he got them cashed.

"We had a very good man of your caste among us some time since, the Rev. Mr. Milne, who is attached to the mission in China. He is a liberal, well-informed, excellent man, and I cannot say too much in his favour. I gave him all the information and all the assistance he required while here, and he had an opportunity of seeing my Javanese subjects and of judging for himself. It is very likely he will say something about Java in his Reports to the Society, and though he did not find us *over* religious, I think he will report nothing very uncreditable to us. He is now in China, having touched at Malacca on his way, where he was kindly received by the chief authority on my recommendation. Such men as Mr. Milne must do good wherever they go, and are an honour to their country and to the cause they espouse. If he had remained longer among us, I verily believe it would have gone hard with some hardened sinners. As you are a Director of the Missionary Society, you may possibly have it in your power to promote Mr. Milne's views, and to serve him in the way he wishes to be served; and I am anxious you should do so. He has earned my public acknowledgments and praise, and at the same time gained my private friendship. Promote this man's views and interests. He is an honour to your society, and a jewel that cannot be too highly prized. Modest, unassuming, strictly kind and conciliating in everything he does, conviction is carried before the head inquires why.

"In one of your letters you express a wish to be furnished with some Indian manuscripts, as you have it in contemplation to apply yourself to Oriental literature; but you have not mentioned the language to which you mean first to apply—the Arabic, or the Sanscrit, or, perhaps, the Persian. I can comply with your wishes in either as soon as I know them, or in any other of the more modern languages of the continent of India or of the Eastern isles. Whenever I have a good opportunity of sending you a selection, I shall not fail in doing so; and, at all events, on my return to England, I shall be able to burthen the shelves of your library.

"In the meantime I would recommend you to read a Minute which I recorded, and which is now printing by Black & Parry, Company's Booksellers, Leadenhall Street, on the improved system of internal management which I have introduced into these Colonies. If you write to Black & Parry, or to Messrs. Boehm & Taylor, of Broad Street, they will send you a copy. The two regulations to which that Minute refers having been printed here, I enclose them herewith. I also forward to you the last volume of the *Transactions of the Batavian Literary Society*. We have established a Bible Society, and I have the honour to be President of it. Mr. Supper is the Secretary, but I cannot boast much either of the zeal of the members or the success of the institution.

"I am happy to hear such favourable accounts of your family. When you have the opportunity, I will thank you to remember me to them with kindness. —I remain, my dear Tom, yours affectionately, THOS. S. RAFFLES."

It will not be out of place to introduce here a reference to the scientific work accomplished by Raffles during his stay in Java. Not only did he personally examine into many subjects of interest in the physical world, and cultivate some of his most congenial studies in the botanical and zoological departments, but he encouraged and assisted others to devote all their energy and intellect to the same pursuits. Prominent among these was Dr. Thomas Horsfield, whose acquaintance Raffles had made on his first visit to Suracarta. From that time forward, both in Java and Sumatra, Dr. Horsfield served with Raffles in a scientific capacity, and, after the death of his chief, the doctor bore testimony to "the zeal, ardour, and liberality with which Sir Stamford both pursued and patronised science." In the reminiscences he provided on the subject, Dr. Horsfield called attention to "the affability and suavity of manner peculiar to Sir Stamford," his "perfect knowledge of the Malay language," and to the fact that "in all his measures his ruling object was general usefulness and the public good." The following letter, and the extracts from subsequent letters to the same naturalist, will show how Raffles stimulated and directed the efforts of his assistants and co-workers in the field of scientific investigation:—

"BUITENZORG, *June 18th*, 1814.

"TO DR. HORSFIELD.

"MY DEAR SIR,—I have to acknowledge the receipt of your letter of the 1st inst., and to offer an apology for not previously replying to your several interesting communications respecting Banca, which have been duly received: the late important events in Europe have come in upon us so thick and unexpectedly as almost to preclude the possibility of attending to other subjects.

"I request to assure you of my entire concurrence in the plan you propose of laying by for a time the completion of your Report on Banca, in order that you may be able to avail yourself of the favourable season to visit the southern districts of Java. A part of your Report on Banca, with the minerals which you forwarded to me at Samarang, has already been sent to Europe; but your later communications, with the drawings of the plants, still remain on my table. I had intended to forward them by one of the ships now under despatch; but the risk from American cruisers, and the change of affairs in Europe, have determined me to delay them until I can know your sentiments.

"The charts of Banca I forwarded by the *Isabella*, under charge of Captain Travers, with directions that they might be engraved at my own expense. Every preparation, therefore, for the printing of the paper will be made. In the despatches from the Court of Directors they simply acknowledge many of my letters;—this is the case with those forwarding your Reports.

"It is most probable, nay, almost certain, that a peace will soon take place; and it is clear, to my mind, that these colonies will, in such an event, revert to the Dutch. Under this impression I naturally look forward to the close of my administration in Java. Calculating upon such an event in the course of the next twelve or eighteen months, it has occurred to me that I can personally do more towards the establishment of the correspondence which you wish, and also in superintending the printing of your Banca work, than can be expected from friends at a distance. I am naturally deeply interested in the publication of your merits, and in obtaining for you a just and appropriate acknowledgment for your labours. And if such an event should happen as the restoration of this colony to the Dutch, I shall be still more interested in making known the attention which has been paid to science during the short period of the British dominion; at least I shall be anxious for it to be known that our pursuits in useful knowledge have kept pace with our other more ordinary pursuits. And it is not impossible that I may be tempted to give a short sketch of the political history and statistics of the Island myself, in which case I should have the opportunity of bringing your claims forward to public notice.

"I am inclined, therefore, to propose to you that, in our present uncertainty, the transmission of the further parts of your Report be delayed. A few months must decide the fate of Europe, and with it the fate of this colony. Should it remain to the English Government as a permanent possession, then they can be forwarded regularly as opportunities offer; otherwise, I propose to you to take charge of them myself, together with any other communication which may be prepared at the period of my leaving this colony. I request you will consider the opinion which I have given you regarding the possible and probable transfer of this colony as confidential: as yet I have no certain information, and my opinion arises from the natural inference to be drawn from the state of European politics at the present moment. I shall be happy to receive your further collections and to forward them by safe opportunities.—I remain, my dear sir, your attached friend, THOS. S. RAFFLES."

After this Raffles put Horsfield in communication with Sir Joseph Banks, President of the Royal Society, and, as Raffles said, the leader in England at that time in every branch of natural history. The following letter from Raffles is especially interesting in connection with the far-famed and mysterious edible birds' nests :—

"I have taken due care to comply with your wish respecting the books which you require from England. I am glad you have seen Gunung Prau ; some time since I had an intimation of the valuable ruins which you mention, and directed Mr. Cornelius to survey them and take drawings. At your leisure it would be useful if you would correct the map according to the information you received—the districts, or rather provinces, in the native parts of the island are very ill and irregularly defined in all the maps which I have seen. A sketch of the native provinces, with the principal places laid down as you have found them on your tour, would be interesting, as no actual survey has taken place, or is likely to take place, for many years. I hope, in describing the Karrang Bolong Rocks, you will favour us with some accounts of their inhabitants. Whatever naturalists may know on the subject, the public in general are very much divided in opinion regarding the process by which the edible nests are produced ; perhaps, indeed, you might prefer a separate paper on this subject. On what do the birds subsist, or is any peculiar food or nourishment required to produce the substance of which the nests are composed ? Is there any foundation in the opinion that certain scum produced by the surf of the sea is in request by them, or can the birds equally well build their nests inland, where they can have no immediate communication with the sea ? The process itself I apprehend to be something like honey-making. There is also said to be a difference between those of the cock and of the hen ; the former I apprehend to be resting-places made for convenience ; but, on the whole, I have to confess myself very ill-informed on the subject, although it is one of very general conversation and inquiry."

To the same correspondent he wrote later :—

"The natural history of the teak-tree, with an account of the different species growing on this island, is highly interesting in a public point of view, and would form a fair subject for a paper in the Transactions. The grain which the Javanese call Java-woot, and from which they pretend the name of Java for this island to have been derived, cannot be unknown to you ; I have it growing in my garden, and possess specimens of the flower and seed. The Javanese support the opinion that the seed of this plant was the principal article of food before rice was introduced ; and I feel some curiosity to ascertain if it be a grain peculiar to this island, or a grain already described and common to Western India. The grain has much the appearance of millet, and the ears are peculiarly rich and beautiful. You will oblige me by noticing the classical name, if already described ; and, if not, by classing it yourself, as it is a plant which seems unknown to Europeans at this end of the island."

In the same letter Raffles gives a graphic account of the ascent of a mountain, showing how he himself pursued science whenever the opportunity offered :—

"I was lately induced to ascend the Gunung Gidi, which I accomplished with some difficulty ; we found some parts extremely steep. At 12 o'clock (noon) the thermometer was at 55° Fahr., at six in the evening it fell to 47°, and soon to 46°, at which it continued until we retired to rest about nine. At daylight in the morning we found it at 45°; but the night was foggy and damp, and in clear weather I have no doubt the thermometer is some degrees lower. The barometer was out of order, and we did not take it; but calculating on the principle which has been adopted in the ascent of balloons, that 16 degrees difference of the thermometer gives a height of 3500 feet, we cannot estimate the Gidi at less than 7000 feet,—the difference in the thermometer being at least 32 degrees. The hill at Penang has been repeatedly measured, and the average results give 2750 feet; the difference in the thermometer averages 12 degrees, which, on the above principle, gives 2755. I shall endeavour to have the height of the Gidi ascertained from below; and, if you have not already ascertained the heights of the other principal hills, shall be happy to prosecute the inquiry throughout the island. I conclude you are aware that Mr. Heyland ascended Sindoro last year, and in the night observed the thermometer below freezing point. We had a most extensive prospect from the summit—Batavia roads, with the shipping so distinct that we could distinguish a ship from a brig on one side, and Wine Coops Bay still more distinct on the other; the islands all round were quite distinct, and we traced the sea beyond the southernmost point of Sumatra; the surf on the south coast was visible to the naked eye. To the eastward we included Indra Mayu point in the prospect, and Cheribon Hill rose high above the rest. I think we may say that we had nearly within our range all that part of the island which, by the former government, was *not* called *Java*."

Dr. Horsfield gives an interesting account of Raffles's archæological researches among the remarkable ruins in the island prior to the appearance of Mahomedanism:—

"In the month of May the Lieutenant-Governor reached the capital of Suracarta. He was accompanied by Lieutenant Watson, Lieutenant Baker, and several other military officers. Some particulars of this tour, which was truly characteristic of Sir Stamford's energy and perseverance, are preserved in a short diary kept by Lieutenant Watson. It may be interesting to preserve a specimen of this route: 'On the following day (after entering the dominions of the Emperor of Solo) we performed a long and arduous journey of nearly fifty miles through the forest of Dayu-luhur, a route which has never before been attempted by Europeans. On leaving Maganang the road entered at once into a thick forest of bamboos, which grow in clumps at some distance from each other, leaving the space between perfectly unoccupied with any kind of vegetation. At a considerable height the trees branch off and meet, giving a mutual support and forming a canopy so close and thick as almost to exclude the light at mid-day. Each clump forms with the adjacent ones on every side natural, lofty, Gothic arches, which, in the deep gloom that surrounds them, except from the partial light of torches, present as grand and awfully romantic a scene as can be well imagined.' In my return to the capital I prosecuted the same route which Sir Stamford afterwards followed, but he traversed in a few days a distance which occupied, at the rate of my usual progress, several weeks. This journey was in every point of view truly gratifying to Sir Stamford's mind. The scenery is in no part of Java more diversified or beautiful; part of the road winds through an extensive valley in which one of the largest rivers of the island flows to the southern ocean ; it then passes over the elevated ridges connected with the Gunung Prau ; subsequently enters the extensive plain of the Kedu, which is bounded on the north and south by two of the most majestic volcanic peaks of the island ; and finally leads between the Merapi and Merbabu to the extensive plain of Suracarta. This journey likewise afforded Sir Stamford an opportunity of examining in person those stupendous monumental remains of a hierarchy long since obsolete, which are promiscuously scattered through all parts of the island. In the dominions of the native princes they exist, however, in greater abundance, and possess a more important character. They consist of ruins of Hindu temples or pagodas, and of images, sculptures, and inscriptions; and the route which Sir Stamford pursued from Cheribon to the capital of Suracarta afforded a very convenient opportunity of inspecting those of Gunung Prau, Boro-budur, Brambanan, and Chandi-sewu. Many of these had previously been surveyed and delineated under his orders by proper officers ; but his personal examination was required to enable him to determine the accuracy of their plans and delineations, and to add those practical details which would give full authenticity to the descriptions. From the capital he subsequently proceeded to the grotesque antiquities at Suku, which possess a very peculiar character, and the existence of which had been communicated to the Resident at the Emperor's Court but a few weeks before the visit of the Lieutenant-Governor. On his further route to the eastward he also inspected the remains of Majapahit and the beautiful edifices of Singo Sari in the province of Malang. . . . Indeed, Sir Stamford has largely contributed to the gratification and instruction of the present generation by his labours in this department ; and it is but justice to allow that in this particular both his personal exertions and his general liberality have been very great."

The last of the extracts from his correspondence with Dr. Horsfield, shows in a favourable light the interest Raffles always took in promoting the worldly success of those who displayed merit :—

"The transfer of these colonies being now [25th November 1815] no longer doubtful, and there being fair grounds for expecting the arrival of the Dutch authorities in the spring of next year, I am desirous of making all my arrangements for the voyage home ; and I have requested Major Johnson to communicate to you the outline of my plans. Should you determine to attach yourself to me in proceeding to England, you may rest assured of the exertion of all the influence which I may possess in bringing forward to notice and reward those exertions and talents which only require to be known to be acknowledged."

The many and varied subjects which occupied the attention of Raffles during the period of his Lieutenant-Governorship, and which constituted the British administration of Java, have now been passed briefly in review ; but the most important of them all was undoubtedly the new system of land revenue, to which at present only brief reference has been made. That system, based unconsciously on the same principles as those which Sir Thomas Munro applied to the tenure and taxation of land in Madras, furnishes Raffles's claim to be considered a great administrator. His plan, owing to the shortness of the period of the British occupation of Java, had only a very short run of practical experience for the demonstration of its merits; but in less than two years his readjustment increased the revenue seven or eight times over. To cite the exact figures, he raised the land revenue in the Eastern districts from 818,128 rupees in 1808, under Marshal Daendels—the highest point attained by the Dutch—to 5,368,085 rupees in 1814, or six and a half times as much. This wonderful achievement was accomplished at the same time that the burdens on trade were lightened or removed. In the masterly and voluminous Minute of 11th February 1814, which sets forth in clear and expressive language the great land measure that had "for its object justice to individuals, the improvement of mankind, and the prosperity of the Government founded on the mutual advantage of the people," Raffles takes a survey of the situation in Java, and of the work he had done there. He shows that his settlement was a detailed one, "effected with each cultivator," that "leases were given in the Javanese language." Viewed in the light of these facts, surprise will not be felt when it is asserted that the new settlement was accepted "not only with readiness, but with gratitude." The merit of the land arrangement was enhanced because it was accompanied by the removal of heavy burdens on trade. The transit dues, which, as Mr. Crawfurd, one of Raffles's Residents, stated, averaged 47 per cent., were abolished; the port dues, which in the greater number of cases amounted to 46 per cent., were reduced to a level of 10 per cent.; and, when these fetters were removed, the trade that had been confined by them regained its elasticity, and reached a higher point than ever.

The Minute, which is unfortunately far too long to quote in its entirety, was printed in London, and circulated among a certain section of the official world. It is the apology and exposition of all Raffles did, or attempted to do, in respect of land administration during his term of authority; and the views set forth breathe a spirit of philanthropy as well as of sagacity. Much as he thought of the needs of his Government, he thought still more of the interests of the population. "I will not deny that my first view was directed to an amelioration of the condition of the inhabitants, and that I considered the improvement which it would afford to our finances rather as the justification than as affording the first impulse of the change." The force of that sentiment will appear clearer when it is contrasted with the views held by even so enlightened a Dutchman as Mr. Muntinghe, who laid down the principle, "Every colony does, or ought to, exist for the benefit of the mother-country." The following extract will show the exact rate of the land-tax imposed by Raffles as the sole impost of any kind either on agriculture or on the cultivators themselves:—"On mature consideration, and the best advice within my reach, I conceived that a fair equivalent for them [the old burdens], including the acknowledged Government share of the crop, the amount paid in personal taxes, and on the internal trade, and the value of forced services, might be found, one district with another, in establishing the Government share at about two-fifths of the rice crop, leaving the second crop and the fruit trees and gardens attached to the villages free from assessment, the cultivators free from personal taxes, and the inland trade unrestricted and untaxed. . . . When the land was of the first quality, a rent equal to one-half the produce in paddy was taken as the standard; when of the middling quality, a rent equal to two-fifths; and when of inferior quality, a rent equal to one-third of the produce."

In this Minute Raffles paid a full and generous tribute to the assistance rendered him by his English subordinates in the onerous task of carrying out "this entire change in the internal administration of the country." He wrote: "I should not, however, do justice to my own feelings or to the distinguished ability, zeal, integrity, and perseverance of the gentlemen who have assisted me in the introduction of this new system of management, did I not take this occasion to record my unreserved approbation of their conduct throughout, and my personal acknowledgments to them individually for the willing share which they have taken in carrying my plans into effect. On so early a connection with this island, without a regular establishment, it might naturally have been expected that instruments would not have been found to effect so important a change; but the greater the doubt in this respect, the greater the honour, the credit, and the claim of those who have come forward. I might challenge a better exhibition of the British character to be afforded. Placed in situations which, but a few years ago, were considered only as affording a fortune to the individual, in many instances where it was out of the power of the strongest Government to restrict, and so uncertain in their tenure that every blast that blew was expected to bring the news of a change which would remove them from the island, they have, without an exception, felt the honour and character of the British nation prompt them above every selfish consideration, and in the short space of six months enabled me to effect a revolution which two centuries of the Dutch administration could scarcely dream of."

The following extracts from the Journal of his friend and aide-de-camp, Captain Travers, give such a faithful and graphic view of Raffles's mode of life during this period, that they cannot be omitted:—

"The native courts of Jojocarta and Suracarta became troublesome soon after the establishment of the British power in Java, and Mr. Raffles determined on visiting them for the purpose of satisfying himself as to the merits of the complaints then made, and to inquire into the abuses which were known to exist. The distance was considerable, but his own personal convenience he never considered. The rapidity with which he travelled exceeded anything ever known on the island before. The average rate was more than twelve miles per hour. Unfortunately he was but badly recompensed for the exertion, as the arrangements he then made, and the tranquillity he established, were but of short duration, as a reference to the records of Government will show.

"At the time these operations were carrying on [at Palembang, in the spring of 1812], Mr. Raffles was availing himself of every opportunity of gaining local knowledge. The native chiefs were constant guests at his table, and there was not a moment of his time which he did not contrive to devote to some useful purpose. The only recreation he ever indulged in, and that was absolutely necessary for the preservation of his health, was an evening drive, and occasionally a ride in the morning. He was not, however, at this time an early riser, owing to his often writing till a very late hour at night. He was moderate at table, but so full of life and spirits, that on public occasions he would often sit much longer than agreed with him. In general, the hour for dinner was four o'clock, which enabled the party to take a drive in the evening; but on all public days, and when the party was large, dinner was at seven o'clock. At Samarang the society, of course, was small in comparison with Batavia, but on public occasions sixty and eighty were often assembled at the Government House, and at balls from one hundred and fifty to one hundred and eighty. Mr. Raffles never retired early, always remained till after supper, was affable, animated, agreeable, and attentive to all, and never seemed fatigued, although perhaps at his desk all morning, and on the following day would be at business at ten o'clock. In conducting the detail of government, and giving his orders to those immediately connected with his own office, his manner was most pleasing—mild, yet firm; he quickly formed his decision, and gave his orders with a clearness and perspicuity which was most satisfactory to everyone connected with him; he was ever courteous and kind, easy of access at all times, exacting but little from his staff, who were most devotedly attached to him. The generosity of his disposition, and the liberality of his sentiments, were most conspicuous, and universally acknowledged. As a public servant, no man could apply himself with more zeal and attention to the arduous duties of his office. He never allowed himself the least relaxation, and was ever alert in the discharge of the important trust committed to him; and it is astonishing how long his health continued good under such great exertions both of mind and body. Whilst remaining at Samarang, a fleet arrived at Batavia from England, bound to China, and at the same time a vessel was reported ready to sail from thence to Batavia, which determined Mr. Raffles on proceeding there without delay, to receive the despatches: on which occasion, Mr. Assey, Secretary to Government, and myself, accompanied him. We embarked on board a small vessel, the *Hamston*, and had a very quick passage of only seventy-two hours, during which time he drew up the report on the capture of Jojocarta,—entering into a full and clear account of the circumstances which rendered this measure absolutely necessary for the preservation of peace on the Island. We landed at seven o'clock in the evening, when a grand public ball was given at Weltevreeden, to celebrate the anniversary of the Prince Regent's birthday. At this entertainment Mr. Raffles, to the astonishment of all present, attended, as it was supposed he was at Samarang. He was the life and spirit of the entertainment. Not less than three hundred persons were assembled; and, indeed, on all similar occasions, which were always duly celebrated under Mr. Raffles' government, he contributed greatly to promote and encourage the gaiety and amusement of the party. After remaining a short time, he returned overland to Samarang, where he was most actively employed in completing the arrangements attendant on the capture of Jojocarta, which, of course, brought an accession of territory to the Government, and which called for local knowledge and personal observation, to render profitable and advantageous. After obtaining all the information within his reach, Mr. Raffles and his family returned to Buitenzorg, at the close of 1812, where, of course, some arrears of public business awaited his arrival, and to which he devoted the most zealous assiduity. . . . At the time Major-General Sir Miles Nightingall arrived to take command of the troops in Java, Mr. Raffles was busily engaged in his favourite plan, and making suitable arrangements for the introduction of an improved system of internal management, and the establishment of a land-rental on the island, a measure which has given to his administration a lustre and widely-spread fame, which never can be forgotten. The measure is so fully explained, the necessity for its adoption so clearly pointed out in the public records of Government, that I shall confine myself to the private circumstances connected with its introduction. When first this measure was proposed, it met, if not with opposition, with at least such a cold and cautious approval from the members of Council, some of whom spoke from long experience, and a supposed knowledge of the native character, as would have damped the ardour of a less zealous mind than Mr. Raffles possessed; and indeed it was the opinion of almost every Dutchman with whom he conversed, that such a system would never succeed, and that the attempt to introduce it would be attended with very bad consequences. But Mr. Raffles had formed a very different opinion, founded upon the soundest principles of reasoning, and with a philanthropy peculiar to his character, he made himself perfectly acquainted with the reception which such a change of system would experience generally throughout the island; and the result justified the opinion he then gave. It was in 1813 Mr. Raffles first acquainted the Council of his intention to amend the system of land-revenue on the island, and the Minute which he then recorded clearly and distinctly develops the just and liberal, as well as very able and enlightened, view which he then took of the subject. In obtaining the necessary information to enable him to frame such a system as, whilst it abolished the vicious practice hitherto pursued on the island, would strengthen the resources of the Government, and, by doing away with feudal servitude, encourage industry in the cultivation and improvement of the land, the greatest exertions were required on Mr. Raffles's part, and he devoted himself with his accustomed enthusiasm to the task; night and day he worked at it. To satisfy himself upon all local points, to obtain personal intercourse and become acquainted with the character of the native chiefs connected with, or in any way effected by this new system, Mr. Raffles deemed it advisable to proceed to the eastern parts of the island, where he remained a considerable time, and visited every place, often undergoing the greatest personal exertions and fatigue, which few accompanying him were able to encounter; indeed, several were sufferers from the very long journeys he made, riding sometimes sixty and seventy miles in one day, a fatigue which very few constitutions are equal to in an Eastern climate. To give effect to the measure he was aware that his personal presence would afford an influence and energy not otherwise to be obtained, whilst all delay for official reference would be avoided. He therefore did not return to Batavia till he had the satisfaction of seeing the complete success of this measure, which gave to his administration the credit of abolishing the most vicious and barbarous system, and of introducing one which gave to a most deserving and industrious population a freedom which had been hitherto most cruelly withheld from them.

"Mr. Raffles returned to Batavia in good health and high spirits, naturally elated with the complete success of all his plans; and, finding in General Nightingall a cordial supporter, I consider that at this period he felt more enjoyment than at any other during his administration in Java. The most friendly intercourse subsisted between the Governor's and General Nightingall's families; they were constantly together; and to the purest feelings of friendship and attachment which General Nightingall felt towards Mr. Raffles, he seemed to add the highest opinion and admiration of the shining talents and abilities which he found him to possess. At Buitenzorg the house was constantly filled with visitors, and I well remember at the time when Mr. Raffles was drawing up the Minute of Council which he recorded on the 11th of February 1814, we had a large party at breakfast, dinner, and supper, from which he never absented himself, but, on the contrary, was always one of the most animated at table, and yet contrived to find time sufficient to write that Minute, which in itself would establish him to be a man of considerable ability and acquirement; and this was written and composed so quickly, that he required three clerks to keep up and copy what he wrote, so that, in fact, this Minute was written with the greatest possible haste; Mr. Raffles's object being to have a copy made and sent home by a vessel then under despatch in the roads at Batavia, and this he accomplished. But Mr. Raffles's quickness at composition was remarkable. He wrote a very fine, clear, legible hand; and I have often seen him write a letter at the same time that he was dictating to two assistants."

The recording of this Minute on the 11th of February 1814, represents the supreme moment of Raffles's success and power in the island of Java. He had accomplished a great work; the results had demonstrated its complete and rapid success: and he had the unusual satisfaction of being able to set forth in his own language both the causes and the consequences of his administrative actions. As he said in his covering letter to Lord Minto, already quoted, his administration aimed at being "not only without fear, but without reproach."

Eleven days after he had recorded this Minute, he experienced a rude awakening by the receipt from Calcutta of the despatch from the Supreme Government of the 14th of January 1814, enclosing Gillespie's charges. Those charges were of a grave nature; and Raffles, confident in the integrity of his intentions, as well as in the success of his public measures, felt this aspersion of his public character and private honour most acutely. The covering despatch, couched in language very different from that employed by Lord Minto, and laying down, even before his explantion had been asked for, that he had done things which ought not to have been done, except after reference to the Governor-General, showed Raffles how the times had altered, and that there had arisen in the land another Pharaoh "which knew not Joseph." Lord Moira, afterwards the first Marquis of Hastings, was not Lord Minto. Lord Minto was a civilian, not ill-disposed towards soldiers, as soldiers, but indisposed to find in the military profession the best administrators of a civil government. Lord Moira was a soldier, brought up in a narrow school, prejudiced in favour of the military profession, and, it must also be added, disinclined to encourage original merit. Raffles had made a reputation in an entirely independent capacity, which placed him on a level with, and almost in a state of separation from, the Governor-General of Bengal. That was not a position which Lord Moira would help to perpetuate. The Lieutenant-Governor of Java was as much his subordinate as the Resident at Lucknow or Delhi; and he expected the occupant of the Government House at Batavia to take his orders and the form of his policy from Calcutta, and not to give it an independent and distinct form of his own. At Lord Minto's earnest solicitation, Lord Moira had promised to look after Raffles, as a deserving servant of the Company, and to ratify his succession to the reserved post at Bencoolen; but this was not the same thing as promising the continuance of Lord Minto's policy in Java, which had been merely to give Raffles a free hand. When General Gillespie arrived in Calcutta, at the end of 1813, he found the ground ready for his masked attack on the character and position of the colleague whom he had just left under the pretension of reconciliation. The consideration of that attack will form the substance of the ensuing chapter; but the following extract from the journal of Captain Travers will give the reader an eye-witness's view of the way in which Raffles received this unexpected assault:—

"Immediately after recording the Minute herein alluded to, despatches were received from Bengal, communicating to Mr. Raffles the unlooked-for and very unexpected intelligence of Major-General Gillespie having presented to the Supreme Government a list of charges against his administration in Java. These charges were of a most grave and serious nature; but Mr. Raffles met them like an innocent man. On the first perusal of them his plan of reply was formed; and he answered every charge in the most clear, full, and satisfactory manner, as will be seen on reference to the book printed at Batavia, containing these charges and reply. But it is well worthy of remark that when Mr. Raffles had finished his answer to the charges, he handed the whole to General Nightingall to peruse, who, having gone through them, declared that although (as he declared on his first assuming the command of the forces in the island) it was his fixed intention to have avoided all interference with past occurrences, and to have kept clear of any differences which had taken place previous to his arrival; yet, after a careful perusal of the documents which had been laid before him, and with a full and firm conviction on his mind of the entire innocence of

Mr. Raffles of all and every charge brought forward by Major-General Gillespie, he could no longer remain a quiet spectator, and therefore in the handsomest, because altogether unsolicited, manner, he came forward to offer Mr. Raffles all the support and assistance in his power to give. Nothing could be more gratifying to Mr. Raffles's feelings on such an occasion than to have the support of an officer of General Nighingall's respectable character, obtained solely by a confidence in the rectitude and purity of the conduct he adopted since the commencement of his administration, every act of which was known to and most carefully examined by General Nightingall previous to his making this kind and friendly offer ; and, indeed, it will only require a momentary look at the charges to feel convinced of their unfounded nature. At the time when these charges were received, and their reception was a surprise to every person, the Government House at Buitenzorg was quite filled with strangers. A large party, composed of Dutch and English, had been invited to witness the performance of a play which was got up chiefly by the members of the Governor's staff. During this anxious time, when Mr. Raffles had so much upon his mind, not a visitor could perceive the slightest alteration in his manner ; he was the same cheerful, animated person they had always found him ; at dinner, and in the evening, he appeared perfectly disengaged, and only seemed anxious how best to promote and encourage the amusement, and to contribute to the happiness and enjoyment of all around him. When the clear and satisfactory reply was drawn out, repelling every charge brought against Mr. Raffles, a proposition was made in Council, and was recommended by General Nightingall, that confidential friends should be sent in charge of copies of these despatches to Bengal and to England, to meet the *ex parte* statements which were known to be in circulation in both places. Mr. Assey, then Secretary to Government, was selected to proceed to Bengal ; and as a vessel was then under despatch for England, it was deemed advisable to send me in charge of those despatches, together with a copy of the charges, and the reply sent to the Supreme Government. Before the vessel reached England the fate of Java had been decided ; its restoration to the Dutch had been agreed upon, and consequently Java and its dependencies ceased to be of any interest to Great Britain."

The closing acts of Lord Minto as Governor-General showed how deep was his faith in Raffles's integrity and ability, and how anxious he was to make the interests of his able lieutenant safe in every eventuality. Very soon after his return from Java, Lord Minto saw that there was small chance of the annexation of that island by the Company; and although hope in the other alternative of its becoming a King's colony remained longer, that hope too was eventually dispelled. In the contingency of the evacuation of Java, the official status of Raffles became very inferior, and almost uncertain. Having ruled a great dependency with extraordinarily full powers, he would have reason to esteem himself fortunate if he were allowed to resume a humble and subordinate position at Penang. Lord Minto not merely realised the injustice of such treatment for one who had toiled so well but he took steps in good time to avert it, by securing for Raffles an honourable place of retreat at Bencoolen, or Fort Marlborough, in the island of Sumatra. The following letters from Lord Minto will show how the appointment was made; and they furnish a testimonial to the forethought and warm heart of that statesman:—

"*February 22nd*, 1813.

"I have already written to you concerning the operations of this event (the arrival of General Maitland) upon your situation ; and I need not repeat my former communication on a subject which is, however, deeply and sensibly interesting to my wishes and feelings.

"But I have to acquaint you with an honourable retreat, if your present office should pass into other hands. Mr. Parker has been compelled by ill-health to quit Bencoolen. If any obstacle should arise to the views which I suppose you might entertain on Java, in the event of a change of Government, or if you should prefer the Residency of Fort Marlborough to any other situation that might be open for you in the East, my resolution is to appoint you to succeed Mr. Parker. It must not be forgotten, at the same time, that the orders of the Court of Directors are to place a civil servant of the Bengal establishment in that office. That circumstance will not prevent me from appointing you, because I flatter myself the claims which made so strong an impression on me will be admitted by others ; and I am unwilling to doubt the Court's confirmation of the measure, and the many weighty and forcible considerations which certainly recommend it. If there should be any hesitation on the subject, I should feel some reliance on the early exertion I shall have an opportunity of making in person at home, my departure from hence being fixed for next January. . . . Pray let me know your wishes on the subject of your appointment to Bencoolen as soon as possible. But I shall take care to make the office accessible to you by an actual appointment, subject to your own option, as soon as I know with certainty that the present Government of Java is to be changed. You have had, and will still have, many competitors here, and some of the very *highest* rank, merit, and pretensions in India ; but so far as the power of this Government can avail, you may consider the affair as decided."

In a second letter Lord Minto wrote:—

"CALCUTTA, *May 10th*, 1813.

'Although nothing is certain, I should think, on the whole, that Lord Moira will arrive in Bengal in July, or say, by the 1st of August. This expectation occasions a great embarrassment and anxiety about you ; for the final decision concerning Java may not be known in the country during my government, and there will consequently be a difficulty in appointing you to Bencoolen, if that should be the case ; for I presume you would not wish to renounce Java definitively until the necessity of doing so should be positively ascertained. What I can do at present is to keep Bencoolen open. If I should learn, while I am in office, that you are certainly to be relieved at an early period, I shall make your appointment to Fort Marlborough, and send it to you at Batavia, that you may go at once from Java to your own station. All that can be said is that I shall be watchful for your interest, and shall omit nothing that depends on me to accomplish what I think due to your merits and services, as well as to evince the esteem and affection which I have sincere pleasure in professing towards you."

And again :—

"*June 22nd*, 1813.

"I cannot safely wait longer for authentic accounts of the resolution taken in England concerning Java ; and I have, therefore, adopted the measure of at once appointing you formally to Fort Marlborough ; to take effect on your being relieved from your present office or resigning it ; the allowances to commence from the time of your departure from Java. . . . I learnt with great pleasure that you have determined to accept the Residency of Fort Marlborough. When I first made this proposition I was not aware that I might soon lose the power of making the appointment. I have since felt considerable uneasiness lest I should be overtaken by an event which cannot be distant, and disabled from accomplishing an object which I have so much at heart."

Lord Minto's farewell letter to his friend and able colleague shows the exceptional strength of his regard for Stamford Raffles :—

"CALCUTTA, *November* 1813.

"In taking leave of my public relation with you, as I must in this letter, I am at a loss how to proceed. On the one hand, there are so many points, or rather extensive subjects, on which a free communication of my sentiments is due to you, that every hour which remains of my residence in India would be too few to acquit myself of that debt, in a manner entirely satisfactory to myself or you. On the other hand, the last, or, I may say more properly, the posthumous duties of my station in India, added to the preparations for my departure, and the very interesting offices of society and friendship which belong to the occasion, leave only moments, when days would be wanted, for the demands still outstanding against me. You will therefore not impute to me want of interest in the matter I have now before me, if I aim at conciseness and brevity in a greater degree than I am accustomed to do. . . . You will accept, therefore, what I am now able to offer, as only the friendly suggestions of the deep and lively interest I can never cease to take in all that concerns your public trust, and your personal reputation and welfare. . . . I have had an early communication with Lord Moira concerning your appointment to Bencoolen ; and I have the happiness to say that he acquiesced entirely in the arrangement that was made, and specifically in the propriety of your continuing to administer the government of Java, until the future destiny of that island should be fixed by the Government at home."

This communication, if not absolutely the last Raffles received from Lord Minto, may be regarded as practically concluding their intercourse; for, although Raffles addressed several important letters to his patron in Europe, the early death of Lord Minto deprived him of his most powerful ally and supporter. The loss came just at the moment when Raffles most wanted an advocate in London; for, if Lord Minto could not have altered the policy decided on with regard to Java, he would certainly have vindicated the character of his friend, and thus compelled the softening of the language in which the charges made against him were couched. But very soon after his return to England, and before the nature of the Gillespie charges was known at home, Lord Minto died. In an address to the Batavian Society, as well as in several other published documents, Raffles paid his tribute of gratitude and sorrow to the memory of his departed chief. The following extract from that address will show how profound was the grief caused by the late Governor-General's premature death:—

"A series of domestic afflictions, alas! but too well known to you all, have followed in such quick succession to the melancholy event which it has long been my duty to communicate, that until the present hour I have felt myself in every way unequal to the trying task of publicly announcing to you the death of our noble and enlightened patron, the late Earl of Minto; an event so unlooked for, and so painfully calamitous in its immediate effects, that, to use the energetic language of Mr. Muntinghe, it '*obliged us*,' as it were, '*to close our lips before the Almighty*.' For how difficult was it to be reconciled to our wishes, and to our natural conceptions of right and wrong, that a man of such public and private worth should have been lost to his country, and snatched away from the embraces of his friends and family, at the very moment he was to receive the only reward which, in this world, could recompense his past labours—a calm and placid recollection of the arduous, but successful career he had run! How difficult was it to be reconciled to our ideas of remunerative justice, that the man who had so successfully served his country, should only live to see his triumphs completed, but not be allowed to enjoy them; that he should not even have been allowed to live the necessary space of time to make the extent of his services known, and to describe the nature of the conquests he had made! . . . If not so strong and intense in their feeling, yet of the same nature and more extensive in their operation, were the ties which attached him to this colony—to the whole community of Java, and especially to our Society. A tender and parental care for the island of Java was publicly avowed on different occasions: the proofs of it were received; the European community was saved and preserved by his humanity, and on his responsibility; for the native administration principles were laid down, on which the whole of the present structure has been raised; and in every instance a wish was evinced of improving the successes of war, as much in favour of the conquered as of the conqueror. It would not be proper, on this occasion, to enter into particulars; but who does not gratefully recollect the general tenor of his Lordship's conduct and demeanour while on Java? administering aid and assistance with his own hands to the maimed and wounded of his enemies; setting, in the midst of his successes, an example of moderation and simplicity of manner even to the vanquished—proceeding often in public without any other signs of greatness and distinction than what the whole community, singly and jointly, were eager to show him; never missing an opportunity of doing even a temporary good; and conciliating, by these means, the minds of the public to such a degree that enemies were rendered friends, and that the names of conqueror and subduer were lost in those of protector and liberator."

The Congress of Vienna, in 1814, provided for the restoration to their original owners of conquests taken directly from France; and, on the 13th of August in that year, Lord Castlereagh signed a Convention with the Dutch representative binding Great Britain to hand over to Holland all the possessions she held in the Eastern isles on the 1st of January 1803. The signature of that Convention committed us to a definite course; and, although it was not the most advantageous, it may be admitted that the balance of necessity, if not of argument, was in its favour. The receipt of the news as to this irrevocable decision was delayed in reaching Java; and it was so quickly followed by the intelligence of Napoleon's return from Elba and the reopening of the European struggle, that Raffles, and many others, thought that, after all, the restoration of the island might, in the interests of Java itself, be avoided. The Ministers in London, however, recked nothing of the interests of Java; their hands were tied by the necessity they were under of conforming their own measures to the principle on which the map of Europe was to be rearranged. Raffles, in his courageous desire to uphold the local view, ran counter to the policy of the Government; and might have brought censure on himself through his pertinacity. But, on this occasion, the decision was so irrevocably made that nothing could alter it. Still, the final efforts made by Raffles with that aim in view deserve to be recorded; and the following memorial to the Court is one of them:—

"To the HONOURABLE THE COURT OF DIRECTORS OF THE EAST INDIA COMPANY, LONDON.

"I request respectfully to advert to the principal questions commented upon by your Honourable Court, and to point out the proof that all the circumstances of the case could not then have been before you. These questions are the propriety or otherwise of retaining a political influence in the Eastern Archipelago, the introduction of the present system of land revenue, the proceedings which have taken place at Palembang, and especially the financial embarrassments which have accrued from the possession of Java by the British Government.

"On the first question I have only to refer to my Minute connected with this subject to prove that the arrangements contemplated were in accordance with the views of the late Earl of Minto, and had for their object the due preservation of what may be termed the police of the Eastern Seas, and the consequent security of commerce with Java itself, united with the maritime and commercial interests of Great Britain and the Honourable Company. When the island of Java and its immediate dependencies first became subject to the Crown of Great Britain, it was the intention of the late Governor-General to allow the Moluccas to revert to their former connection with, and dependence on, the superior authority of Batavia; in which would be vested the same control in the Eastern Archipelago which had existed in the flourishing times of the Dutch Government of these colonies. The measure was not carried into effect, but still I was warranted by my instructions in resuming the influence and authority of this Government in the Eastern Seas, and the despatches of the Supreme Government at the period of the attack made upon the piratical State of Sambas will show that so far the connections established by me in the Eastern States were sanctioned by the approval of the Governor-General in Council. On the arrival of the Earl of Moira, when a different view of this question seems to have been taken by the Supreme Government, I was directed to confine the jurisdiction of the Colonial Government to the island of Java and its immediate dependencies. The order was obeyed; but it is in my power to state that many injurious consequences may result from it to the present weight and dignity of the British Government in those seas, and to any influence or commercial connection which it might be thought desirable to continue or to establish in them hereafter.

"With regard to the amended system of land revenue which I have introduced in this island, I undertake to prove from the public records, that so far from having been hastily digested and introduced, as your Honourable Court would appear to have been informed, it was originally designed by the late Earl of Minto previously to his quitting Java; that it was deliberately considered for two years before it was introduced; and its practicability and justice formed a principal object of inquiry in a competent Commission, at the head of which Lieutenant-Colonel Colin Mackenzie, of your Madras establishment, was for a considerable time employed; and, further, that it was carried into effect gradually, with attention to the rights and to the interests of the native chiefs and to the acknowledged benefit and amelioration of the native population; that, in short, so far from having subverted the just rights and authority of numerous individuals, or alienated the minds of any class of the people from the British Government, it has placed the rights of all classes on a foundation which they never before possessed; and, in the acknowledged tranquillity of the country, increase of industry, improvement of revenue, and known attachment of the Javanese to the existing system, prove that it has been equally beneficial to the interests of Government, and conclusively improving to the industry and happiness of the extensive population of this island. That these are facts, the now flourishing state of public industry in Java, the peace that universally prevails among its inhabitants, and the diminution of crime among them, with the improvement that is felt, and will in a separate despatch be shown to exist, in our finances, give abundant proof. I appeal with confidence to the public records in proof of this assertion.

"I am further most anxious to offer to your consideration some data relative to the financial state of this colony, not only as they support and evince the accuracy of my original expectations and estimate of its value and importance, but as they clearly show that, although the early possession of this colony was embarrassing to the finances of the British Government, time only was required to prove it a source of power and wealth to whatever nation may possess it. The early administration of this colony was unavoidably and necessarily expensive, its revenues were concealed or wasted, its former Government was in a state of bankruptcy; but it is no longer difficult to show, by the unerring evidence of figures, the rapid and great improvement which has been effected in its revenues and resources, or to trace the springs from which that improvement has flowed. This subject, however, on account of the details necessary to be entered into, is reserved for a separate despatch, which I hope to accompany by statements drawn up to the latest date of my administration.

"Conscious in my own mind that my constant study has been to promote, to the best of my abilities, the interest and honour of my country, and to render the establishment of a British administration in these colonies a memorable era among them in the amelioration and improvement of this population, I have the honour to be, with the highest respect, honourable sirs, your most obedient and faithful, humble servant, T. S. RAFFLES.

"BATAVIA, *27th January* 1816."

But the most eloquent and impassioned plea he put before his countrymen for the retention of Java was contained in the peroration to his pamphlet on the condition of that island, "As it was, as it is, as it will be." He was fighting a lost battle; but it is impossible not to admire the courage of his convictions, and the resourcefulness of his reasoning:—

"Shall such a nation as the Javanese, such an extensive population as are within the control and influence of the Government of this colony, be again abandoned to the feudal bondage and humiliation under which they have groaned? Shall Great Britain, to whose lasting honour it is on record that slavery has been discouraged or abolished in every country where her dominion or influence extended, permit the population of Bali, of Celebes, and of the isles adjacent, to be again made the subject of traffic in Java? Shall she not rather embrace the moment, when the triumph of her arms has opened the way to a new empire in these seas, to stretch a protecting hand over the Eastern Archipelago, and establish the amelioration and prosperity of its inhabitants, by placing them under her own government and protection?

"Let us look round the numerous islands dependent on, or connected with, Java, and view it as the centre of an Eastern insular empire, from the Straits of Malacca to the kingdom of Japan and to New Holland. We shall find that they have a mutual interest and dependency on each other, and, on the whole, repay with ample profit the cares and beneficence of the European power.

"Java is by nature formed to be the centre of such an empire. Having a population numerous and of the character already described, it now furnishes a revenue beyond its own charges. Its superabundant produce supplies the neighbouring islands with rice, salt, and other articles of necessity; in return Banca furnishes its tin, Palembang its pepper and rattans, and Borneo its gold dust. The situation of Java also points it out as the emporium from whence the spices should be circulated; for it has been found by experience that they incur considerable damage during a voyage to Europe, unless repacked and picked after having quitted their native atmosphere. The returning vessels would convey the supplies necessary for the consumption of these islands, and thus economy and convenience unite in recommending the natural course of this branch of Oriental commerce. Moreover, it must be observed that the Moluccas, if not held by the same European power which possesses Java, would require a defensive military establishment, equally expensive and destructive in those unhealthy islands.

"Thus the local produce of Java, added to the returns of its dependencies, secures a profitable commercial intercourse both with India and with Europe. The Banca tin and edible birds' nests have a sure and certain market in China; the teak timber and rice also have been found to answer well. In return may be had the teas of China and other articles that are purchased for the Europe market with bullion, or by a losing barter for European manufactures; and with Japan the trade is acknowledged to be even more beneficial.

"I am not competent to say to what extent this trade may be carried; but thus much may be asserted, on the authority of what has passed since the establishment of the British Government, that the re-establishment of the British flag in Japan is not only not impracticable, but has been principally prevented by the intrigue and misrepresentation of the power already there, who wished not the introduction of another European power, however friendly. Those who have been engaged in the commercial adventures undertaken from Java during the last three years have reported that the Japanese are inclined to receive British visitors; that, though they have been induced to imbibe a prejudice unfavourable to the British name, they study its language, and are aware of its character; and that, although the jealous spirit of their Government would render a free or general trade impossible, they have not the decided aversion which has been attributed to them, and would be glad to extend the commercial intercourse mutually, much beyond what has of late been carried forward. Copper, camphor, and lackered-ware are the principal exports from Japan to Java, in return for European manufactures (especially woollens and hardware), India piece goods, and a small quantity of the produce of these islands; but there seems great reason to think that the importations of Japan might be very considerably extended, and besides the articles hitherto brought in return, tea may be obtained, in quality equal to that of China, and a variety of drugs which are in demand in Europe. The population of Japan exceeds thirty millions. Their character is declared to be frank, honest, and high-minded; the very reverse, in short, to that of the Chinese; and the climate of their country brings many of the European manufactures into general use, whenever they can be procured. To draw further inferences from these circumstances would be a repetition of what has already been advanced. But it would not be practicable on the present occasion to go through a complete review of the commercial facilities of this colony, and to enter into a narrative of its commerce with Europe and India, or the mutual benefit that would result in a few years by establishing a constant intercourse between it and New Holland on one side, and Ceylon on the other. The conveniences of its local situation in the trade between Europe and China, the consumption of many manufactures of India in this colony, its powerful rivalship of India in many of those products which form exports from thence to Europe, and the general economy and advantage of rendering it a half-way house and depôt in the commerce between Europe and the countries east of the Malay Peninsula, would form subjects of consideration too important and too extensive to be at present entered upon. That they do exist, however, will probably be admitted without much discussion, and it may be sufficient on the present occasion to express an opinion that the more they are examined the more will they, in all probability, be found to strengthen the argument which has been adduced in this sketch.

"Nor is it of slight importance, that experience has now proved the climate of Java to be fully as congenial to the constitution of Europeans as that of most parts of India. Since the first effects resulting from the change of habit and diet after a long voyage, and an arduous though short campaign, had ceased, and a greater knowledge of the country had led to the establishment of cantonments inland, it has been shown by the military returns, that the European troops are more healthy in this island than on the continent of India. His Majesty's 59th Regiment of Foot proceeded to Bengal a few months ago, about a thousand strong, and had not more than fifty men sick. His Majesty's 78th Regiment, now on the island, are equally healthy; and so well are the Sepoys become satisfied and comfortable in Java, that it is notorious many petitions were made among them to remain, when, lately, one of the battalions returned to India.

"If it could be certain that the newly established sovereignty of the Netherlands would for ever remain in ties of amity and defensive alliance with Great Britain; if it were sure that the British nation would obtain for ever the just reward of her sacrifices and of her generosity, by being admitted to an equal share of the commerce of these seas; it might be less a matter of importance, whether the administration of Java and its dependencies reverted to its former possessors or not; but such is the uncertainty of political events, that even family alliance is but a feeble barrier against political expedience; and admitting even that Great Britain could be satisfied with giving back her conquest, on condition of obtaining for herself a future share in this commerce, and securing to the numerous population who now look up to her for protection, a promise that the freedom which has been given to them shall be continued, it is impossible to calculate on a certainty of the future. The distance from Europe, the difficulty, not to say impossibility, of obtaining redress of injury from such a distance, and the local opposition of interest, backed by all the prejudices of long-established feelings on this subject, would effectually prevent it. And shall the page of history be forgotten? Shall the experience of past times, when Great Britain had factories and colonies in these seas, be lost?

"Let Great Britain, then, consolidate her Eastern Empire by retaining the command of the Eastern Archipelago. It is not necessary that she should exclude other nations from a participation in its commerce; but let the British flag continue to wave in the colonies, where it has now for the first time been pre-eminent; and let the numerous population, who, I will affirm it without danger of its being disproved, will deeply regret the day when they are returned to their former masters, and who have in many instances expressed their fears and apprehensions that it should be so, be secured under a government, where the feudal rights and bondage, which are in the mouths of the European colonists in Java, cannot be put in practice. Even security of the present British Empire in the East recommends, though it may not demand, such an arrangement; for had the projects of Buonaparte been equalled by his means, had a few years of peace been allowed him to throw in the force for whom the barracks and supplies were ready, not only would it have been extremely difficult to have conquered this island, or to have prevented the extending monoply of its government, but its fertility and productiveness in much of the produce of British India, and its superior facility of connection with China, would, after a few years of peaceable possession and administration, have rendered it a troublesome rival to our Eastern possessions. Change but the name, and the same situation of things may again occur. Besides, this colony connot be to Holland what it may be to Great Britain. Its prosperity and its benefit to the mother-country depend chiefly on a steady perseverance in the principles of extensive and liberal commerce, and on an amelioration of the state of the native population; but the present commercial poverty of the Dutch nation would prevent her being able to undertake the former, and the local interests and prejudices, resulting from a vitiated habit of centuries, would continue effectually to oppress the latter, whatever might be the intentions of the authorities in Europe."

In spite of these efforts, the restoration of Java was soon seen to be inevitable; and, although Raffles wrote to one of his intimate friends that he should "leave Java with a heavy heart," he hoped that his work there would not be ignored; and that he would himself come home "with some little honour and credit." No doubt the last two years of his stay in the island were filled with anxiety, in consequence of Gillespie's charges, and the delay of the Bengal authorities in publishing their decision upon them. When, as will be shown in the next chapter, they passed a decision which left the honour of Raffles cleared from the aspersions of his assailants, and consequently secured for him his succession to the reserved post at Bencoolen, the Government had already, on the 5th of May 1815, come to the conclusion, on other grounds and for financial considerations, as it was said, to replace Raffles as Lieutenant-Governor by another official. Mr. Fendall was appointed to the post, and his chief task was to be the transfer of the island to the Dutch authorities. On the 5th of March 1816, the Dutch officer, Captain Nahuys, arrived with the tidings that in a few weeks the new Dutch Governor-General, with a force of 3500 European troops, would reach Batavia. On the 11th of March, a few days after the arrival of Captain Nahuys, Raffles received the despatch ordering him to give over his charge to Mr. Fendall. When the new official arrived, Raffles, who had been so alarmingly reduced in health that he had been obliged to leave Buitenzorg for another house in the higher altitude of Ciceroa, started from Buitenzorg at 3 a.m., and hastened to "Ryswick" in Batavia, for the purpose of meeting the new Lieutenant-Governor and of handing over his charge to him with suitable honours. When Mr. Fendall arrived, Raffles introduced him to the leading officials and residents; begged his attention to the interests of the people who had relied on British justice and protection; and recommended to his consideration those who had served under the English Government. Mr. Fendall met him in a proper spirit. He looked over the file of Government business, and expressed his approbation of everything that had been done; while he took into his service the whole of Raffles's staff. It was not the most appropriate ending for the most creditable and successful Government Java has ever known; but Mr. Fendall's tact and gentleness softened down its worst features. He continued in the course laid down by his predecessor during the few months he remained in power, until, on the 16th of August, he handed over to the Dutch the island of Java and its dependencies, with the exception of Banca and Banjarmassin.

At first Raffles had intended to proceed direct to Bencoolen; but the state of his health was such that the doctors gave him imperative orders to return to Europe as the only means of saving his life. His health was temporarily shattered by severe illness due to his excessive exertions in his administration, to the anxiety and disappointment caused by the attack on his proceedings, and to the grief arising from keenly felt and irreparable domestic losses. Under this heavy combination of depressing circumstances and adverse fortune, Raffles would have broken down, if he had not been supported by a dauntless spirit, and by the profound conviction that indisputable facts would eventually obtain for him complete exoneration from blame and the applause of his countrymen.

But even before he left Java, he was to receive some encouraging assurance that his work had been appreciated by those most intimately acquainted with it. As soon as it was realised that his departure was imminent and inevitable, the leading European and native residents subscribed for a handsome service of plate, which was presented to him after his arrival in England. The accompanying address bore 214 signatures, of which 170 were Dutch. Addresses were presented him by the judges of the courts, the magistrates, and the chief Dutch citizens. To emphasise the hold he had acquired over his Dutch colleagues, it may be mentioned that his last days in Java were passed in the house of one colleague, Mr. Cranssen at Jacatra, and that his other colleague, Mr. Muntinghe, was the most prominent in drafting and delivering the farewell addresses. The members of the Batavian Society of Arts and Sciences, which he had revived and raised to a higher point of activity than it had ever possessed under the Dutch, subscribed for a bust of their patron and president as an ornament to their hall; and from the highest to the lowest in the island, there was a general movement of regret and regard towards one who was evidently not appreciated, as he deserved to be, by his own Government. The princes of the island expressed their grief in terms of Oriental hyperbole. The Susuhunan, or Emperor, addressed him as "his grandfather"; and declared that he would never forget, and should ever be grateful for, the good Raffles had wrought for Java and the Javanese. Similar letters of regret were received from the Sultan of Jojocarta and other native potentates. There is no reason for questioning the sincerity and depth of this sentiment. The late Colonel Sir Henry Yule, whose critical acumen has never been questioned, and who was not free from prejudice in the case of Sir Stamford Raffles, admits as much in his lecture on Java, and contributes one telling anecdote to substantiate the assumption:

"That it (the restoration of Java) was regretted by the

people of Java at the time, I believe there is no real doubt. The old Dutch Government had been mean and oppressive; Daendels had been ferociously oppressive. The sweeping changes introduced by Raffles, if all were not wise, were all conceived in a spirit of liberality and justice; they were such as touched all and left no room for that indifference to change of rulers which is said to characterise Asiatic peasantry. I heard a parable on the subject related by one of the few who remember those days. Fendall, the Lieutenant-Governor who succeeded Raffles, asked an old Javanese chief whether the people liked the notion of getting back their old Dutch masters. 'Certainly!' said the chief with irony, 'can't you fancy a young and beautiful widow, who has been joined to a harsh and withered old man, but has lost him and is wedded to a liberal and gallant young bridegroom—can't you fancy how she will rejoice when she finds the old man returned to life again and come to claim her?'"

"The deep interest," writes Lady Raffles, "which Mr. Raffles took in the happiness of the Javanese, induced him to exert every faculty of his mind to instruct and improve them; and this was to him comparatively easy, even in the pressure of all the more direct and ordinary business of his station. He was gifted with a power of such rapid decision, his discrimination was so clear, and his arrangements so immediate and perfect, that he was able to effect more business, of every kind, than any single person of those around him could have thought possible. It is stated by some of those who were in the habit of observing him at this time, that they have seen him write upwards of twenty sheets of minutes, orders, etc. etc, without any correction or even alteration being necessary. He required three clerks to copy and keep up with what he wrote, and he frequently dictated to two persons whilst engaged in writing letters himself."

Raffles took his passage home in the *Ganges*, a fine vessel then lying in the Batavia roads, and the *Ganges* was to weigh anchor on March 25, 1816. He was accompanied to England by a little party of devoted friends: Captains Travers and Garnham, who had been his aides-de-camp in Java; Sir Thomas Sevestre, his medical attendant; and last, but not least, "his faithful servant Lewis, a native of Malacca, who had lived with him many years"; while a gentleman well known to them all, who had made a large fortune in Java during the British occupation, and a Javanese chief, much attached to Raffles, Raden-Rana-Dipura, also went with them. The scene on the morning of his departure from the land he had laboured in and loved so fervently, was a touching and grateful one. The sunny weather, the glancing water, and a fair wind, smiled and sighed regretfully to bid the voyager farewell. "The roads of Batavia," writes Lady Raffles, "were filled with boats, crowded with people of various nations, all anxious to pay the last tribute of respect within their power to one for whom they entertained the most lively affection. On reaching the vessel, he found the decks filled with offerings of every description — fruits, flowers, poultry,—whatever they thought would promote his comfort on the voyage. It is impossible to describe the scene which took place when the order was given to weigh anchor; the people felt that they had lost the greatest friend whom Java ever possessed."

As "old Burrows," who was one of them, told Abdulla's translator, Raffles undoubtedly possessed the power of attaching his subordinates deeply to him; and of all the testimonies that his efforts had not been thrown away, or left unappreciated, none touched Raffles so nearly as the address of the members of his personal staff, which was not shown him until they had been several days out at sea, when Captain Travers laid it before him, under circumstances thus described in that gentleman's journal :—

"Our voyage commenced under the most favourable circumstances; the weather was mild, the wind fair. On the third day after leaving Batavia roads, being intrusted with the address to Mr. Raffles from his own immediate staff, to present to him after our getting out to sea, I waited upon him in his cabin with it; and the scene which ensued was the most distressing I had ever witnessed. After perusing it, he became so completely overcome as to be unable to utter a word; but the moment he began to recover a little, he took up his pen, and whilst the feeling and impression was fresh, he wrote the beautiful and affectionately-expressed reply, which was afterwards printed by his friends, and is attached to the addresses and replies presented on the occasion of his leaving Java. The presentation of this address was altogether unexpected on Mr. Raffles' part; and as it was meant to convey to him the sentiments of cordial and heartfelt esteem and affection of those who had the best opportunity of judging of the spotless integrity and amiable qualities which shed a lustre over his private life, as well as the purity and uprightness of his public conduct, it was but natural to suppose that such a testimonial must have been most gratifying at such a moment, and he certainly prized it very highly."

The following is the text of the address, signed by the gentlemen who had composed His Excellency's staff, and who had been employed in stations more particularly connected with his person:—

"DEAR SIR,—Among the varied and distinguished proofs of regard and veneration which you have received from all classes and descriptions of people in this island, on your approaching departure, we hope you will accept from us a more silent, but not less cordial, assurance of the regret we feel at losing you; of the grateful and pleasing remembrance we shall ever entertain towards you; of the respect and affection, in short, which can cease only with our existence. We have now, dear sir, known you long; and though some of us have not had the happiness till of late years, we all equally feel that it is impossible to know you without acquiring that cordial and heartfelt attachment which binds us to you, as it were, through life, and renders us as interested in your happiness and prosperity, as we can be in our own.

"Whatever may be our future destination, and however it may be our chance to be scattered, when we return to our different fixed situations in life, we can never forget the time we have passed in Java. The public sentiment has expressed what is due there to the energies and value of your administration, which the more it is examined the more it will be admired. It belongs rather to us to express what we have witnessed and felt—to bear testimony to the spotless integrity and amiable qualities which shed a mild lustre over your private life. These we acknowledge with gratitude, and these are imprinted in our hearts too strongly to be ever erased.

"You will not receive these expressions of our regard until you have left us; and when, perhaps, it will be long ere we meet again.

"Accept them then, dear sir, as the genuine feelings of our hearts; and allow us to request your acceptance of a small token of our remembrance, in the shape of a piece of plate, which we have requested our mutual friends, Captain Travers and Garnham, to purchase and deliver to you in England. It bears no great value among the more splendid tokens which you have received of the public esteem; but it may serve to remind you of those who are, with the sincerest regard and attachment, dear sir, your faithful friends and servants,

"C. ASSEY, THOMAS M'QUOID, R. C. GARNHAM, THOS. O. TRAVERS, J. DALGAIRNS, C. METHVEN, T. SEVESTRE, J. ECKFORD, THOMAS WATSON, H. G. JOURDAN, W. COTES.

"To the Hon. T. S. RAFFLES, Esq., etc. etc.
"BATAVIA, *March* 24, 1816."

Raffles's noble reply contains an impassioned tribute to Mrs. Olivia Raffles, and for that reason finds no place in the Memoir of Lady Raffles. It reads as follows:—

"On board the *Ganges*, off Anjin, *March 30th*, 1816.

"MY DEAR AND VALUED FRIENDS,—This last and unexpected proof of your attachment and esteem is too much for me; it is more than, in the shattered state of my existence, I can bear without an emotion, which renders it impossible for me to reconcile my feelings with the ordinary course of consideration. You have struck chords which vibrate too powerfully—which agitate me too much to admit of any attempt to express to you what my feelings are on the occasion of your address.

"You have been with me in the days of happiness and joy—in the hours that were beguiled away under the enchanting spell of one, of whom the recollection awakens feelings which I cannot suppress. You have supported and comforted me under the affliction of her loss—you have witnessed the severe hand of Providence, in depriving me of those whom I held most dear, snatched from us and the world, ere we could look around us! You have seen and felt what the envious and disappointed have done to supplant me in the public opinion, and to shake the credit of my public, and the value of my private, character; and now that I bend before a storm, which it is neither in my power to avert nor control, you come forward to say, that, as children of one family, you will hold to me through life. What must be my emotions I leave to the feelings which dictated your address to decide, for, in truth, I cannot express my own. I accept your gift, and will hold it as a sacred PUSAKA, dear to me from many a bitter, and yet many a pleasing recollection. I dare not say more, but in the same spirit, my dear and estimable friends, in which you have often seen me brave the adversities of this life, let me turn from the sad remembrance of my sorrows to the bright and cheering prospects that are now before you. Let me congratulate those of you whom I leave behind, on the protecting and fostering care under which you are now placed—a consideration and delicacy towards me personally, unexampled as it was unexpected, may have first induced the wish, but it is to your own endowments, your own virtues, your own amiable dispositions alone that you are chiefly indebted for that decision in your favour, which has induced my noble-minded and honourable successor to continue you about his person, in the same relation as you stood towards mine. In very truth, I cannot answer your appeal to my heart—it has struck too deep; but the wound, though painful, is not without an agreeable sensation. You have opened a spring that will for ever flow in the purest kindness and affection towards you.

"May the day be not distant when, after a fair and honourable career of public life, we may meet again in that happy land to which eventually all our views are turned. Then, when we reflect upon the duties we have performed for our country, and upon the many happy days we have passed in Java, may it be my pride to say that, while at the head of the Government, I directed my country's cause in the track of honour and integrity, I had the support and advice of men as able and honourable; that, while as the head of a great family, it was my fortunate lot to dispense liberty and rights among millions; as the simple head of a domestic circle, it was my still greater good fortune to endear to me men whom it is honourable to call friends—men whose honour and integrity are beyond reproach, whose hearts beat with the genuine warmth of human nature, and whose private virtues and personal qualifications are acknowledged by all.

"Let this last mark of your attention—let your kind present, which I value beyond the wealth of Golconda (for it is the gift of pure friendship), be as a seal to the bond of union between us, and let us ever meet as sincere and attached friends.

"May every blessing attend you, and may you long continue to be distinguished as the brightest ornaments of the profession to which you belong.

(Signed) "T. S. RAFFLES.

"To CHARLES ASSEY, Esq., THOMAS M'QUOID, Esq.,
Captain GARNHAM, Captain TRAVERS, etc. etc."

Such general and unqualified demonstrations of respect, affection, and regret cannot be obtained from any people under false pretences. The reality of the benefits Raffles conferred on the inhabitants of Java is no more to be questioned than the sincerity of the motives which inspired his policy; but the reflections naturally suggested by his four and a half years' government of the island may be reserved until the separate episode of Gillespie's charges has been passed in review in the next chapter.

CHAPTER VII

GILLESPIE'S CHARGES

General Robert Rollo Gillespie, whose name figured prominently in connection with the military operations resulting in the conquest of Java, was a brave soldier. The possession of mere courage, which in the ordinary acceptation of the term is the attribute of most soldiers, and, perhaps, even of the majority of human beings, does not, however, confer any exemption from the ordinary obligations men owe to each other, and especially to those who may be associated with them in any public enterprise. A libeller is not less the traducer of his neighbour's name because he has obtained the Victoria Cross; and the soldier who endeavours to blacken the character of his civilian colleague, because the greater fame of the latter has overshadowed his own military exploits, cannot claim immunity from the penalty of his sinister attack. It was his own reputation which Robert Rollo Gillespie permanently injured when he was impelled by envy and petty spite to bring false and refuted charges against the public and private character of Stamford Raffles. Gillespie had not profited by his own experience; for the earlier part of his military career had been dimmed by false charges made against himself, which it had taken years to refute, and which ought to have rendered him more careful before casting aspersions on another.

At the time of the Vellore Mutiny in 1806, Gillespie's name had been brought forward as the officer who had been drawn up by a rope over the wall, and who had then encouraged the handful of Englishmen to hold out until the dragoons could arrive. During the invasion of Java, as the leader of the advanced division, he had specially distinguished himself at Cornelis. In the expedition to Palembang, and again in the assault on Jojocarta, he had shown much enterprise and spirit. As the reward of the earlier of these services, he was left in command of the garrison, with a seat on the Council. But the capacity he exhibited in the field did not characterise his advice at the Council Board; and the most careful examination of the Council meetings at Batavia or Buitenzorg has shown that ill-health or disinclination soon made his attendance infrequent. It was only after his disputes with Raffles which marked the year 1813 that his appearance in Council became regular, and then with the definite object of opposing and thwarting the Lieutenant-Governor. One cause of future difference, indeed, revealed itself during the first few months of the occupation; and that was Gillespie's failure to appreciate the fact that economy was the most imperative policy in Java. He made several appointments on the staff and in the medical departments of the army; and Raffles, not deeming them necessary, had refused to accept, and, indeed, annulled them. On another occasion, too, after the successful assault on the Craton at Jojocarta, in June 1812, the troops, with Gillespie's acquiescence, had divided the plunder of a captured town without any reference to Raffles; and the latter had promptly protested against this disregard of his authority. Gillespie, however, admitted the error, and exculpated himself on the ground that he had been severely wounded on the occasion, and thus was incapable of exercising a proper control. These minor differences probably had no serious consequences; but they must be noticed. They did not, at all events, affect the warmth of the language in which Raffles in his public proclamations always thanked General Gillespie for the courage and celerity that characterised his operations in the field.

A more serious question came on for discussion, when Raffles, in his anxious desire to diminish the expenditure, proposed that the European part of the garrison should be reduced, and that the military establishment should be placed on a more economical footing. Gillespie entertained very different views, and fought the question hard; but even then Raffles, although he had been intrusted with it, refused to exercise his power to overrule the views of his colleagues in any extreme necessity and to act independently of them. He would not have hesitated to employ that power against any other colleague; but, in the case of Gillespie he refrained, and referred the matter to Calcutta, from which place orders were received for the return of two English regiments. Lord Minto had no hesitation in saying that Raffles was in the right; and, as a way out of the difficulty, for the relations between the two men were now hopelessly strained, he arranged for Gillespie to be transferred to a command on the Bengal Establishment. On the 15th of October 1813 Gillespie left Java; and Raffles, who, after much controversy, had gone through a formal reconciliation with him, issued a farewell order, in which he stated: "In common with every one interested in the colony, I must ever feel the highest sense of the important share you had in the conquest. . . . The name of Gillespie will stand allied to that of Java."

The following letter from Lord Minto will show exactly how Gillespie's removal from Java was brought about:—

"CALCUTTA, 22*nd May* 1813.

"Sir George Nugent proposed appointing General Nightingall to take the command in Java, and place General Gillespie on the staff in Bengal. This plan combined so many advantages, that I instantly conveyed to the Commander-in-Chief my hearty, and, I must add, *joyful* concurrence in every part of the proposition. The first benefit, afforded by this measure, will be to relieve your Government from obstacles which it has become next to impossible to surmount, and yourself from personal vexation, very difficult to live under. On the other hand, a good retreat, or rather an honourable and advantageous station, is prepared for Gillespie, whose military character and services I shall always admire and venerate; and I shall always rejoice in the opportunity of testifying those sentiments, by contributing, as far as my power goes, to confer upon him those honours and advantages to which, notwithstanding his civil defects, he is so eminently entitled as a soldier. Another desirable consequence of this exchange, I hope, may be the superseding the necessity of investigating and pronouncing upon his political conduct in Java.

"I shall now say a word of General Nightingall; of his military qualifications I am not able to speak, of my own knowledge, but he has seen a good deal of service, and has, I understand, served with distinction. This I can say, however, that he is a man of honour, and a gentleman in the highest degree; his manners, in all respects, as amiable as I really believe his conduct to be."

Such differences between Raffles and Gillespie as have been already mentioned related to military matters, with which, perhaps, Gillespie thought the other had no right to interfere; and when they resulted in even an honourable removal from Java, there is no doubt that his resentment was kindled. So long as Lord Minto was in power, Gillespie knew that it would be useless to attack Raffles; but Lord Minto's term of office was on the eve of closing when Gillespie reached Bengal; and Lord Moira, a man of other views and prejudices, indifferent to Raffles and Java, and ignorant of both, took up the reins of authority within a few weeks of Gillespie's arrival at Calcutta. Raffles, favoured by fortune in his public career up to this crisis, was now first to feel her inconstancy; for nothing could have been more ill-timed for him than that his sworn enemy Gillespie should reach Calcutta at a moment when a new Governor-General had just come out. The misfortune was the greater when it is recollected that Lord Moira was a man impregnated with the hereditary prejudices of his class, as well as with those of his military profession. He would forgive much to a man of family and a soldier; but Raffles was described to him as an upstart and an adventurer, who owed his rise to his own complaisance and to Lord Minto's excessive favour. When the charge was made, with much plausibility, that the Lieutenant-Governor was also venal, Lord Moira's mind was poisoned against him, and he allowed himself to form conclusions in anticipation of the evidence. The departure of Gillespie from Java had seemed to lighten Raffles's load; it was, as events turned out, a calamity: for it gave his formidable antagonist the opportunity, which under any other circumstances could not have presented itself, of exercising his malevolence.

But if the real cause of Gillespie's dislike of Raffles was that the Commander of the Forces in Java had been overruled in professional matters, the ground selected for attack was the civil administration, and especially the sale of lands which Raffles had ordered as the means of taking up the depreciated paper. In all those matters Raffles's influence had finally prevailed over the objections and opposition of Gillespie. The decision to have recourse to that plan was taken in November 1812, when Raffles and Mr. Muntinghe were the only Members of Council present, Gillespie being away on one of his frequent periods of absence through ill-health. The papers and the record of the Council meeting were, however, sent to the latter for perusal, and for the expression of his opinion; and he replied with a Minute, dated the 5th of December 1812, stating that in his opinion "a measure of such magnitude" should not have been decided on "without a previous reference to the Supreme Government." The most serious argument in this Minute is that the uncertainty as to whether Java was to be retained by the Company or converted into a King's colony, rendered it inadvisable to make a permanent disposal of lands. Let it be at once admitted that General Gillespie was fully entitled to hold and to express that opinion; and that the opinion itself was based on what might be called the commonplace view of the situation in the island. It was safe, in no way committing its author, and ineffectual. Eighteen days later Gillespie consented so far to modify it that, on the reduction by Raffles of the quantity of land put up for sale, he recorded a fresh Minute, to the effect that "no other expedient of less magnitude, or future consequence to the state of the colony, to meet the exigency being available, he would not withhold his acquiescence in a limited sale, nor will he be inclined to object to the extent now proposed by the Board." General Gillespie was, consequently, an assenting party to that sale of lands which he afterwards proceeded to criticise and condemn. It should also be noted, at this stage, that Gillespie refused to accede to the proposition that the Sepoys should be paid in paper money, and he also persistently ignored the fact that the peremptory orders of the Supreme Government forbade any drawing of bills on Bengal.

The calm consideration of these public matters was rendered difficult, if not impossible, by the importation into the question of personal grievances, on the ground of which the Commanding Officer attempted to fasten upon the Lieutenant-Governor a charge of indelicacy and discourtesy. Ill-health had obliged General Gillespie to take up his residence at Chipanas, a place in the mountains where there were mineral springs. He acquired there a house and a coffee plantation, for which he declined to pay any taxes. He employed Javanese as cultivators and labourers on the estate, as well as in building a new house; he refused to pay, or, at least, did not before his departure pay, them any wages; although the order that all work should be properly recompensed formed one of the first principles of the new Government. The form may have been veiled, and the extent of its application was limited; but the principle of General Gillespie's conduct was the same as the *corvée* system of Marshal Daendels. The Regent reported this state of affairs to the Resident, who, in turn, passed the complaint on to the Lieutenant-Governor; but Raffles, before taking any steps to vindicate the reputation of the Government thus injured by one of its chief members, sent a Dutch gentleman to report privately to him on the state of affairs at Chipanas; and it was only when he found that there was no doubt as to the facts that he brought the transgression before the notice of its perpetrator. This is the matter on which General Gillespie complains that Raffles treated him with indelicacy, and detracted from the dignity and authority of the Commander of the Forces. On that personal point the judgment passed by Mr. Archibald Seton, as member of the Governor-General's Council, may be here quoted. In this matter "the action of Mr. Raffles was marked by justice, moderation, and an unusual degree of politeness." Notwithstanding these several public and private matters of dispute, Raffles and Gillespie went through a formal reconciliation on the eve of the latter's departure; and the Lieutenant-Governor had no reason to anticipate that General Gillespie was about to make, behind his back, an attack which he had not dared to commence on the spot.

On the 25th of December 1813, General Gillespie's charges were first brought before the Governor-General's Council. The subject was divided by the Council into seventeen heads of inquiry into the conduct of the Lieutenant-Governor of Java; and its consideration was postponed until the next week's meeting, in order that General Gillespie might give more specific information on these articles. On the 1st of January 1814, General Gillespie attended, and gave in written and verbal replies ; in the course of which he referred to Mr. C. G. Blagrave, late Secretary at Batavia, as one of his authorities. Mr. Blagrave's hostility to Raffles, by whom he had been removed from his post in Java, was notorious, and his evidence in such a matter would have been received by an impartial tribunal with scepticism. Still he was summoned to give it, and to attend the Council on the 15th of January. All these proceedings were conducted in the Secret Department; and everyone was enjoined to observe the greatest secrecy in the matter. On the day named, Mr. Blagrave's reply was read, and a despatch of that date was drafted to Raffles enclosing the proceedings of these meetings of Council, and the full statement of the charges made by General Gillespie in the first place, and supported by Mr. C. G. Blagrave in the second. The Secretary to Government was directed to state that " the object of his Lordship in Council in referring the documents to you is to obtain from you the fullest explanations respecting the transaction to which they relate, and to afford to you the most ample means of justifying your own conduct in those instances in which it may at all appear to be impeached by the facts stated, or the opinions expressed, by Major-General Gillespie or Mr. Blagrave." The despatch also contained this paragraph : " There is, however, one article which, above all others, requires explanation, which is the purchase stated to have been made by you, either singly or jointly with other persons, of some of the Government lands. You will consequently feel the propriety of stating distinctly whether you had any share in these purchases ; and, if so, the grounds on which you conceived that such a measure could be reconciled to the faithful discharge of the high official state held by you on the island of Java." This was the thunderbolt that unexpectedly fell on Raffles's head at the very moment that he felt most secure and successful. He had just sent off his famous Minute on the land question to London and Calcutta, in a despatch which he felt sure would redound to his own honour ; and in the midst of gaiety, at the pinnacle of his own confidence and self-satisfaction, when thoughts only of the broadest policy and national advantage filled his mind, he received an indictment which placed a false construction on his acts, and charged him with the basest betrayal of his trust. He received the despatch on the 24th of February 1814, and he at once sat down and penned this indignant denial :—

"I have this day had the honour to receive your despatch of the 15th ult., and having carefully perused the proceedings of the Supreme Government containing the charges which Major-General Gillespie has endeavoured to fasten on my administration and character, I lose not a moment in requesting you to convey to His Excellency the Right Honourable the Governor-General in Council an unqualified assurance that I feel perfectly competent of my ability to prove to his Lordship's satisfaction that the greater part of the circumstances stated by Major-General Gillespie and Mr. Blagrave are utterly devoid of foundation ; that the remainder can be easily accounted for ; and that the insinuations which have been made by both parties will be found to be in no way borne out by the simple facts of the case."

The preparation not so much of his reply, but of the proofs from the official files, occupied three weeks, and his defence is contained in a despatch of one hundred and twenty-one paragraphs, with his specific replies to the seventeen charges,—his replies alone covering one hundred and ten closely printed pages. It is obviously impossible to transfer to these pages the full text of such evidence. The papers were printed and circulated by Raffles himself, and admit of easy reference. One strong piece of evidence as to the confidence he felt in his own innocence was the manner in which he begged for publicity, and circulated in every quarter the text of the accusation and the text of his defence. He scorned the hollow and deceptive seclusion of the Secret and Separate Department of the Government of India. The following private letter to his friend, William Brown Ramsay, will give the reader an idea of his inner thoughts at that supremely critical moment :—

"BUITENZORG, *March 21st*, 1814.

"While you are quietly gliding on in the smooth and sunny stream of private life, it is my lot to be tossed on boisterous billows, and to be annoyed with all the clouds and evils which ensue from party spirit.

"Without family pretensions, fortune, or powerful friends, it has been my lot to obtain the high station which I now fill; and I have not been without my due proportion of envy in consequence.

"After this, you will not be surprised at what follows. You are aware of the differences which occurred between me and Major-General Gillespie, and that he, in consequence, applied to be relieved from the military command. Arriving in Bengal after Lord Minto had left it, he found the new Governor-General unacquainted with all that had previously passed, and succeeded, to a certain extent, in impressing him favourably in his behalf. He was committed, in the course of some of our differences, by assertions which he had made; and finding that he had succeeded in directing the current of public opinion a good deal against me, he has brought regular charges against both my administration and character. The whole are, I thank God, easily to be repelled; and the closer the investigation, the purer my conduct will appear. Lord Minto is fully aware of the violent faction which has taken up arms against me, and will defend me in England. In India I have possession, and a clear character to maintain it; let Satan do his worst. . . . My enemies have said much, and written much; but, in the end, truth and honesty must prevail."

The Seventeen Heads of Inquiry were, in their order, as follows:—

First.—The expediency of the sale of the Government lands.

Second.—Whether the sale was, generally speaking, made in the mode most conducive to the interests of Government?

Third.—Whether the Lieutenant-Governor and Mr. M'Quoid and another Commissioner became joint-owners of any of the coffee plantations; and, if so, to what extent?

Fourth.—Whether any of the plantations were disposed of by private sale to individuals; and, if so, on adequate and proper terms, or otherwise?

Fifth.—Whether an offer was made, through the late secretary to Government, for one of the coffee plantations, of 5000 dollars more than was actually paid by the Lieutenant-Governor and the persons united with him in purchasing the plantation?

Sixth.—The violation of the regulations of the island and of the principles of policy by the union in the person of Mr. M'Quoid of the office of Landrost and Resident of several Regencies.

Seventh.—The compatibility of the offices mentioned in the preceding article with the character recently acquired by Mr. M'Quoid of joint-proprietor of extensive tracts of land to which the influence of the above-mentioned office extended.

Eighth.—The other offices supposed to be held by Mr. M'Quoid, and their compatibility with each other.

Ninth.—The propriety of the alteration made in the rate of profit which the holders of the coffee lands themselves enjoy; the former rate being a quarter, the present three-quarters.

Tenth.—The rate at which the coffee lands were purchased by the Lieutenant-Governor and his co-operators, with reference, on the one hand, to the intrinsic value of the lands, and, on the other, to the prices paid by other individuals.

Eleventh.—The discouragement or prohibition of coffee plantations in other parts of the island, with the supposed view of enhancing the value of those acquired at the public sales, especially by the Lieutenant-Governor and his co-partners.

Twelfth.—The policy of the measures adopted with respect to the Treasury Notes and Lombard Bank.

Thirteenth.—The expediency and propriety of the stoppage of issue of paper money from the Orphan Chamber, especially at the period when such stoppage is stated to have taken place.

Fourteenth.—The policy and justice of the restrictions established on the authority of the native chiefs (see Proclamation).

Fifteenth.—The expediency and propriety of the pledge made to receive on the part of Government any surplus quantity of coffee at a nameable and fixed rate, when a higher price for it cannot be obtained in the market.

Sixteenth.—The conditions on which Mr. M'Quoid is reported to have obtained the contract for birds' nests, and the propriety of such contract.

Seventeenth.—The construction of military works and application of military stores by the Lieutenant-Governor without the concurrence of his Council, and the object of such works.

It is impossible and unnecessary to enter into a discussion of all these points; but it may be noted that Raffles demolished some of them with a breath. Such were the twelfth and thirteenth heads, wherein General Gillespie's inferences were "entirely erroneous from his being unacquainted with the real nature of the paper currency in question." In this case the simple facts were exactly the opposite of what was alleged. The ninth, eleventh, and fifteenth heads were also based on an erroneous reading of the facts. The military arrangements arraigned in section seventeen were alleged by General Gillespie to have been taken on the part of Raffles with the view of enhancing the value of his own property. Raffles had no difficulty whatever in showing that this could not be the case, because the works, directed against pirates, were in a completely opposite quarter of the island from the estate purchased by him and others, and separated from it by an impassable tract of country. The spirit of the attack on Raffles's official position and private character is clearly revealed by the recklessness of the more easily refuted charges.

Without entering upon the policy of the sale of lands as the only available means of taking up the depreciated paper currency, which was sufficiently described in the last chapter, and which Lord Minto termed "an able expedient in a case of great emergency," the charges assailing the personal honour of Raffles were those included in the second, third, fourth, and fifth heads, and also in the sixteenth. Of these the most vital were the third and fifth. On the principle that the greater absorbs the less, it is to these points that I shall devote most space, placing before the reader the supporting evidence of General Gillespie and Mr. Blagrave, together with the defence and explanation of Raffles.

General Gillespie stated in his charge on the third head: "I have reason to believe that the Lieutenant-Governor, Mr. M'Quoid, and another Commissioner, became joint-owners of a part of the coffee plantation in the Regencies. To what extent I cannot precisely answer, though, if I am correctly informed, the purchase was very considerable." Mr. Blagrave supplemented and supported this statement with the following assertion:—"I was not present at the sale of the Government lands but was informed by Mr. M'Quoid that Mr. Raffles and himself had purchased estates in the Regencies. I understand from the same authority that the Lieutenant-Governor, Mr. Engelhard, and M. de Wilde were joint-purchasers of some other lots, also in the Regencies. It was, indeed, generally talked of and believed that such was the case. The sale of the lands in the Batavia Regencies was never recorded on the public proceedings of the Government while I held the office of secretary at Java; I therefore cannot state the names of the particular estates in which the Lieutenant-Governor became interested."

On the fifth head General Gillespie knew nothing but he said: "I was informed by Mr. C. Blagrave that an offer was made by letter, which came before him, from M. de Frize [Vriese] for one of the estates in the Regencies, and that he understood the sum to be 5000 dollars more than the estimated value by the Commissioners." On this head it will be noticed that Mr. Blagrave is the sole accuser, and his charge reads as follows:—"A letter came into my possession from a M. de Vriese, assistant to the Resident at Buitenzorg, dated, I believe, in December 1812, offering a sum of money (to the best of my recollection, 45,000 Spanish dollars) for one of the lots in the Regencies, which letter I forwarded to the Lieutenant-Governor for his instructions, together with one of a similar nature from Mr. de Wilde. As the tenders for the purchase of the Government lands were to be made through the private secretary to the Lieutenant-Governor, I concluded that these letters would be replied to through that channel; subsequently, however, to the day of sale (in the month of February) I was sent, by order of the Lieutenant-Governor, on a commission to Tjanjore with the Civil Commissioner (Mr. Hope), accompanied by Mr. M'Quoid. M. de Vriese, who resides at Tjanjore, joined us at the Regent's house, where we had met for the purposes of the Commission, and, entering into a conversation with Mr. M'Quoid respecting the sale of the Government lands, expressed himself much disappointed and dissatisfied at the treatment he had experienced. M. de Vriese observed that he understood Mr. de Wilde had been accommodated with the estate he had offered for, while he (M. de Vriese), though he had tendered 5000 dollars more for the lot he required than the amount of the estimate by the Commissioners for the sale of the land, had not even received a reply to his application. I am not aware of the sum actually paid for this by the Lieutenant-Governor and the persons who were associated or supposed to be united with him in the purchase."

The unprejudiced reader will have no hesitation in forming the opinion that when one member of an administration prefers a grave indictment against another member, and especially against his chief, he ought to have a surer foundation for his statements than "I believe," "to the best of my recollection," and "I am not aware"—in the case of essential details. Were so great a latitude granted in the drafting of accusations, every disappointed and dismissed subordinate, such as Mr. Blagrave was, would take his revenge in assailing the character of his superior.

The sixteenth head was amplified by General Gillespie as follows:—"A mountain was discovered in the Regencies to possess a portion of birds' nests, which was advertised for sale for seven (7) years—as I have understood there was no competition, from the ignorance of persons who might have been inclined to bid—and it was accordingly purchased by Mr. M'Quoid for 12 hundred dollars per annum for seven years. It has been reported to me that the mountain is worth from 40 to 60 thousand dollars annually, and is within the control of Mr. M'Quoid, as General Resident over the Regencies." On this point Mr. Blagrave added nothing.

The charges against Raffles, therefore, amounted to this: he had become a purchaser of Government lands; he had caused to be rejected a tender for a higher sum than that at which one particular lot had been knocked down to him and others; and he had rewarded his assistant and co-partner, Mr. M'Quoid, for his co-operation in these matters with several appointments, and with the lease, at an unduly small sum, of a mountain containing the edible birds' nests.

If substantiated, these charges were sufficient to have disqualified Raffles from holding any administrative office, and to have permanently destroyed his reputation. But even before the answers to them were called for and received, an impartial and considerate Governor-General would have compelled the accusers to frame their charges in a more definite and positive form, and to recognise that they had incurred a serious responsibility and the risk of that penalty which sooner or later devolves on all fabricators of false charges.

Raffles had already explained his part in the purchase of Government lands, in a Minute, dated the 18th of February 1814, or a week before the text of the Gillespie charges reached his hands. There was, consequently, no necessity for him to make a defence on this head, because he had already explained everything relating to it. Four lots of land were registered in the office of the magistrates with the name of the Lieutenant-Governor included among the proprietors, and the circumstances under which the purchase was made, together with the reasons that induced Raffles to intervene personally in the matter, are set forth in the Minute mentioned. The information in the earlier document is, consequently, much more valuable than that given in any formal defence against a specific and serious charge.

With regard to the imperative necessity of the sale, Raffles shows that, as the paper had depreciated more in the last month—prior to November 1812—than in the preceding twelve, the six months' delay for the purpose of reference to the Supreme Government "might have increased the difficulties of the local government a hundredfold." It was also undoubtedly a difficulty that should be dealt with out of local resources; and the only local resources were the public lands. The Dutch, whose laws were continued during our occupation, had always recognised a sale of such lands as legitimate; and, in the first year's budget of the British Administration, a sale of public lands had actually figured among the assets, and had been passed by the Supreme Government without comment. As to the necessity and legitimacy of a sale of lands, and as to the impossibility of reference, if the sale was to accomplish its intended object, there cannot be a difference of opinion. The reasons which induced Raffles to participate personally in the purchase of lands had better be given in his own words:

"A few days previous to the intended sale, Mr. Engelhard, formerly Governor of Java, and a gentleman of the highest rank and most considerable influence in this island, addressed me a letter, of which the enclosed is a translation, and waited upon me personally to know my sentiments; on which I informed him that my former observations were made in the general nature of the conversation, and that I never had any serious idea on the subject. He became, however, exceedingly pressing, and, on the next day, submitted to me the annexed papers, showing what the estates, if purchased, might be safely bought for, the other, what he conceived they might be worth upon a speculation. Although I felt disinclined to participate in any purchase, and did not possess the funds required to meet the proposal of Mr. Engelhard, I hesitated within myself whether, after his pressing invitation, and the rumours which had been industriously spread abroad regarding the possibility and even legality of the sale, it would be prudent for me to reject them. I had heard some days before from Mr. Timmerman Thyssen, a merchant of considerable respectability, and strongly attached to the British Government, that the reports were likely to injure the sale; and party spirit then rose so high that such surmises were readily caught at; on consideration, therefore, I thought that my acceding to the proposal of Mr. Engelhard would at once remove all doubts in his mind. This was essential, because, if he had withdrawn from his avowed intention of purchasing, the suspicions and doubts that must have arisen in the minds of others would undoubtedly have been injurious to the public interest, as well as to the credit of Government. The lands which he proposed to purchase were those adjoining to his estate at Buitenzorg. They were a convenient acquisition to the Governor, inasmuch as they would afford Europe vegetables, and enable him to establish a herd of cattle, and obtain the convenience attached to a farm, of which the Government House at Buitenzorg had been deprived by the sale of the lands in its immediate neighbourhood by Marshal Daendels. I did not possess the funds required to participate in the sale, but Mr. Robinson assisted me with what money might be necessary, and the share which I had in the purchase was, in fact, rather in name than in reality; it was agreed that not less than one-half should stand in my name, as a smaller participation would not look well in the situation I held;

but that half should be divided between us. On the sale taking place, the lots were sold for something short of 60,000 Spanish dollars, being far above the price first contemplated by Mr. Engelhard; and this high amount was bid by him in the confidence of my finding the funds for half the purchase; but that he would do so was only known to Mr. Engelhard and the gentlemen interested. . . . It being subsequently found necessary that a person accustomed to the Javanese should be appointed to reside upon the estate to administer it, Mr. de Wilde was selected; and, that he might have an interest in its good management, became a partner to the extent of one-sixth; and, to complete the funds requisite for the purchase, Mr. M'Quoid took one-sixth, but did not bid at the sale. Thus the four lots became the property of four persons, as situated in the list of purchasers. Such is the concise and plain statement of my personal concern in the recent sale of lands."

Let us consider the situation as it presented itself at that moment on public grounds to the Lieutenant-Governor. It was a critical moment. To buy or not to buy, that was the question. Not to buy was to render extremely improbable that improvement of the financial situation which the sale of lands was designed to effect. For purchasers, unsupported by the participation of Mr. Engelhard, would have held off, feeling no confidence in the stability of any purchases made; while Engelhard's participation was contingent upon that of the Lieutenant-Governor himself. But for Raffles to buy was to expose himself to the risk of terrible misrepresentation; yet he never hesitated an instant when he saw that it was the only mode of attaining success in the task of extricating the Government from its difficulty. On the general proposition that the responsible head of a Government should not become the purchaser of Government property there will be general agreement; on the special case concerning Raffles, who will venture not to say that it was the exception needed to prove the rule?

Some premonitory rumour seems to have reached Raffles that his participation in the purchase was being challenged and misrepresented; and, although he had gone in for it " more on public than on private grounds"; and, although he did not "think it was wrong to purchase public property at a public sale," he requested his co-partners, "as a favour," to take over his share at the price he paid for it. When the whole transaction was thus concluded, Raffles found himself a not inconsiderable loser; but at the moment of the receipt of the charges in Java, he was no longer a holder of any share in any estate whatever. His formal reply on this point had, therefore, in the main, to be a mere reiteration of the statements set forth in the despatch of the 18th of February 1814.

Leaving aside for the moment the point whether the member of a Government had, under the special circumstances prevailing in Java, the right to buy any property, it is important to note that Raffles next proceeds to demolish the statement that a tender higher by 5000 dollars was not taken into notice. He shows that the tender was considered and rejected as inadequate, and that, whereas it amounted to 6923 silver dollars, the lot was actually purchased by him and his partners for 36,500 silver dollars. Mr. de Vriese, the person alleged by Mr. Blagrave to have made this higher tender, sent in an *affidavit*, dated the 5th of March 1814, completely refuting the statement of the discharged secretary, and substantiating the accuracy of the just-cited record of the only sale in which Raffles was either directly or indirectly interested. I give the full text of this important document:—

"To the question you have put to me concerning the sum I offered for a spot of land in the Regency of Tjanjore, which was sold with other lands in January 1813, and if I could recollect having held a conversation with you (Mr. M'Quoid), in the presence of Mr. Blagrave, concerning these lands, about a month after the public sale, on which occasion I remarked that, although my offer was 5000 Spanish dollars more than the valuation of the Commission appointed to carry into effect the sale of the lands, my speculation to purchase this lot was unsuccessful, I declare, and I am ready to confirm it with an oath, that I offered 45,000 rix-dollars paper money, or about 7000 Spanish dollars silver, for a lot of land called Goenong Parang, known under No. 7, which sum appeared to me sufficient, because the land was too distant for the sale and transport of its produce to other places. I recollect perfectly well that you (M'Quoid) were at Tjipanas with Mr. Blagrave, but I declare that I never made a remark on the failure of my attempt to purchase the said land. I must add that I could not be deceived in this respect, however, as I was present at the sale. I had it in my power to have bid what I thought fit, but the lot having sold for 30,500 Spanish dollars, that sum exceeded my calculations. Further, I declare that I never heard of any valuation of the lands in the Regency of Tjanjore being made by the Commissioners."

This sworn statement completely disposed of the story as to the rejected higher tender, and proved that Raffles and his friends paid five times what Mr. Vriese had offered. Whoever else suffered, it is sufficiently clear, therefore, that the Government was not defrauded. With regard to the Birds' Nest Rock described under head sixteen, Raffles had no difficulty in showing that it was a very trifling matter, and that 1250 dollars was a fair rent, because, in the first year, the total sale of birds' nests did not reach that sum, while General Gillespie's assertion of its being worth from fifty to sixty thousand dollars a year was a pure fiction. Among minor charges, General Gillespie alleged that the new silver coin contained an undue proportion of alloy. Raffles smashed up this allegation by showing that he had recommended a nearer approximation to the Calcutta sicca-rupee, but had been overruled by General Gillespie and Mr. Cranssen. If any one was to blame on this point, it was not Raffles, but Gillespie himself. In face of such extraordinary indifference to facts, and such an exposure of ignorance as to what really took place, doubt is natural as to whether General Gillespie may not have been mentally somewhat overstrained.

No one who goes through the voluminous evidence carefully can arrive at any other conclusion than that the charges in all their details were grossly and wilfully exaggerated and misstated by General Gillespie and Mr. Blagrave; and, as General Gillespie had gone through a formal reconciliation with Raffles,—Lord Minto's son, Captain the Honourable G. Elliot, acting as mediator,—there is no room to doubt that a deep-rooted and vindictive malice was at the bottom of the attack. The charges were also clearly and candidly refuted, not merely by Raffles, but also by Mr. Muntinghe, the Dutch member of Council, for whose Minute in support of Raffles I would, if possible, make room. A question, which is one that different people will decide in different ways, of course remains open—Was Raffles, the Lieutenant-Governor of Java, justified in becoming a purchaser of lands put up for sale by the Government of which he was the head? There is no doubt that his participation encouraged the sale, and brought in buyers; there is no doubt, also, that his motives were pure, and that he concealed nothing; and it is incontestable that, far from making any money, he was actually out of pocket when the transaction was concluded. But he would have been more prudent if he had allowed his original doubts to control his judgment, and had thus abstained from participation in the purchase of any public property. If General Gillespie had protested at the time,—for he was present at the actual sale,—and had, there and then, insisted on a reference to the Supreme Government on the simple point, as to whether a member of the Government ought to purchase Government property, he would have discharged his duty; no one could have criticised his action, and the question would have been decided once and for all. But he did nothing of the kind; he was silent when he should have spoken out; and, when malice prompted him to utter charges behind the back of the man he assailed, and to whom his latest attitude had been one of feigned friendship, he would have studied his honour better if he had remained silent still.

Neither Gillespie nor Blagrave spared Raffles's feelings. On the flimsiest arguments they attacked and misrepresented every act of his administration. They would have rejoiced if their secretly delivered assault had hurled him from his pride of place, and ruined his reputation. There is no reason for showing tenderness to their memories. Gillespie was a fiery-tempered and impetuous soldier, who, if he had made charges in hot blood, would have been granted an easy sentence, on the ground that he spoke without thinking, and that his thoughts were the hasty impressions of the moment. But his attack on Raffles was not of this unpremeditated character. It was not a case of virtuous indignation at the conduct of a colleague as being unworthy of a British official. The carefully planned attack, furtively delivered when Raffles was far away, and possibly without a friend at court, delivered, too, when the possibility of a reconciliation had lulled his enemy into the belief that all disputes were over, and that the hatchet was buried between them, savoured rather of the Italian brigand than of the English officer. In the case of Gillespie, the originating cause of the attack may have been apprehension lest Raffles should take steps to expose all his proceedings on the island; in that of Blagrave, it was open resentment at the loss of an official appointment.

General Gillespie's high-handed and unwarrantable proceedings at Chipanas in taking forced labour for his own purposes, have been mentioned; and the helpless natives were on the point of resorting to the only remedy within their power, —which was a general exodus,—when the intervention of the Lieutenant-Governor put an end to the tyranny. But a far more serious indictment of the General could be framed on the charges of "his forcibly demanding a virgin from the orphan school at Samarang," and of his having participated in a case of abduction from the house of a Mr. Sluyter at Batavia. These cases were not the only instances of the kind; and Major Robison, for some time Resident at Palembang, preferred a serious accusation against General Gillespie's moral proceedings and character during the expedition to that place. General Gillespie did everything in his power to suppress discussion, and to prevent inquiry into these matters; and Raffles, out of regard for the dignity of the head of the army, "did not deem it consistent with delicacy to push the inquiry further than he, the party most concerned, deemed it proper to urge." Had these points been referred to the Supreme Government, there can be no hesitation in saying that, despite his reputation for courage, Gillespie would probably have been removed from his command in Java.

Mr. Blagrave's conduct in the post of Secretary to the Batavia Government had been so reprehensible that it entailed his dismissal. His post in the Company's service was on the establishment of the Moluccas; but, as he passed through Batavia, Raffles, having no one eligible for the post, appointed him Acting-Secretary. A brief experience showed that "he was wholly incapable of performing the duties of the office, and, in short, neither his general talents nor his personal habits were such as to enable" Raffles to make him a confidential secretary. He became involved as a co-partner in the purchase of a ship; and it was clearly proved that, while he received the sum of money at which he transferred his property in it, he omitted to pay the original owner the amount agreed upon. At first Raffles agreed to overlook this transaction, on the understanding that Mr. Blagrave was to get rid of the speculation; but, as his incompetence became more evident in the post of Secretary, and, as his opposition to the Lieutenant-Governor became marked and outspoken, Raffles gave him orders to vacate the secretaryship, and to proceed to Amboyna to take up his definite appointment. At first Mr. Blagrave consented; but, in a few days, he changed his mind, and defied Raffles to remove him without reference to the Supreme Government. This defiance was equally futile and absurd. It entailed his summary dismissal, and the immediate appointment of a successor. To crown his acts, he then left Java without notice; and, instead of proceeding to the Moluccas, took his passage to Calcutta. At that moment he was in debt to the Company in the sum of nearly 7000 silver dollars. Such were the two men who allied themselves together at Calcutta for the overthrow of Raffles. Their accusations were marked by malevolence, but the reckless manner in which they set them forth contributed to their own refutation and discomfiture.

When Raffles had drawn up his detailed and exhaustive replies to the charges, it was suggested by Sir Miles Nightingall, Gillespie's successor in the military command, that trusty friends should be sent in charge of them to London as well as to Calcutta. Captain Travers was accordingly despatched to England; and Mr. Charles Assey, Secretary to the Batavia Government, was deputed to Calcutta, where his long and extensive knowledge of the work of the secretarial department at Batavia would prove, it was hoped, useful in clearing up any uncertainty. Mr. Assey was a most capable man, and his public writings on the position of the rival States of England and Holland in the Eastern Archipelago are, even to this day, worth perusal. His ship was unfortunately delayed on its voyage, so that Raffles's answers did not reach Calcutta until the autumn; by which time Gillespie was dead, having met a soldier's fate at the attack on Kalunga during the Nepaulese War. The Supreme Government showed an extraordinary reluctance to grapple with the question; which was an additional injustice and injury to Raffles, over whose head the charges hung in suspense. In London, also, Captain Travers found such an aversion to discuss any matter relating to Java, that "despatches from that place were not even opened in Leadenhall Street."

At last, in May 1815, when the final decision to evacuate Java had been taken under the Treaty of Vienna and Lord Castlereagh's Convention, the Governor-General's Council took up the matter. Mr. N. B. Edmonstone wrote an exhaustive and admirable Minute of two hundred and eighty paragraphs, vindicating the character of Raffles's administration, and exonerating him from the heavy accusations of Gillespie and Blagrave. It is impossible even to summarise that Minute, but it is easy of reference in the India Office Record Department. Mr. Edmonstone's conclusion on the personal charge reads as follows:—"Of the integrity of his conduct, of the purity of the motives which regulated his proceedings, of his zealous and laborious exertions in the prosecution of measures which, whatever may be our judgment of them, appeared to him conducive to the interests of the public service, I entertain an entire conviction."

If such was the opinion of one member of the Council, that of another, Mr. Archibald Seton, was equally emphatic and favourable. It was expressed in the Minute he recorded on the 18th of June 1815, in which he associated himself with his colleague's opinions. After speaking of the land settlement as "a delicate, important, and complicated question," and bearing testimony to the high character of Mr. M'Quoid, represented by the assailants as Raffles's tool throughout all these transactions, Mr. Seton went on as follows:—"Upon the whole, I think it is to be regretted that a charge of so foul a nature, and which so deeply involves the public and private character of the Lieutenant-Governor, should have been brought forward in consequence of impressions which, as far as I am able to judge, must have originated in misinformation. . . . There are no grounds for imputing to Mr. Raffles any improper motive, or for supposing that in the course of his efforts he personally derived any advantage." With the following further quotation my extracts from Mr. Seton's Minute must end:—

"It will be evident from what has been stated, that, in all his public measures, Mr. Raffles appears to me to have been actuated by the purest motives, by an ardent zeal for the prosperity of the colony confided to his charge, and by an honourable and conscientious desire to contribute to the attainment of that object. . . . That Mr. Raffles has not succeeded in his endeavours may, I think, be attributed to the exhausted state in which he found the island, to the annihilation of its export trade, to a want of specie, and, under the great disadvantage of these difficulties, to the fatal necessity of engaging in early and expensive wars with the Sultans of Palembang and Jojocarta. . . . In so far, therefore, as the circumstance of Mr. Raffles's becoming a purchaser either affects his moral character or influenced the results of the sale, I am bound in justice to declare, on the grounds above stated, that in my opinion, while his conduct was pure and correct, it evidently tended to promote the interests of Government."

Lord Moira's own Minute was not issued till the 17th of October 1815. It was far from being a document sympathetic to Raffles; but no attempt was made by the Governor-General to answer the weighty reasoning and powerful exposition of facts put forward by Messrs. Edmonstone and Seton; on the crucial point, however, viz. the right Raffles possessed to the Bencoolen appointment, Lord Moira decided in favour of Raffles. But it was not until the year 1818 that the Governor-General came fully round to Raffles's side, and rendered him tardy justice. The passage giving the practical conclusions of his Minute reads as follows:—

"With reference to that part of the Honourable Court's instructions which relates to the appointment of Mr. Raffles to the Residency of Fort Marlborough, the Governor-General in Council observes that nothing has appeared in the course of the deliberations respecting Mr. Raffles's conduct to authorise an opinion affecting his moral character, and although he has not succeeded in administering the extensive and important duties of the Government of Java with that degree of efficiency which is indispensable to secure the advantages held out by Mr. Raffles himself from the possession of the colony, yet there does not appear to be reason to apprehend that Mr. Raffles is not competent to acquit himself with due benefit to his employers in the less complicated duties of the Residency at Bencoolen. The Governor-General in Council accordingly considers himself bound in justice to leave unshaken the reserved appointment of Mr. Raffles to the situation of Resident at Fort Marlborough, of which Mr. Raffles is to take possession as soon as another person shall be selected for the Government of Java."

The language of the Governor-General's Minute naturally hurt Raffles's feelings, although the final decision certainly cleared his official character, and expressly confirmed the reversion to Bencoolen, provided for him by the thoughtfulness of Lord Minto. He had already, it will be remembered, communicated all the papers to the Court in London, and his well-proved friend, Captain Travers, had given there verbal explanations. On receiving the decision of the Supreme Government in India, Raffles addressed a long letter to the Court, of which I need only give the two following paragraphs. In it he announced his intention of memorialising the Court for a more complete and unstinted acquittal. The letter was written from Batavia on the 1st of January 1816:—

"Although the Supreme Government have in these proceedings been pleased to observe that 'nothing has appeared in the course of the deliberations respecting my conduct to authorise an opinion affecting my moral character,' and have further declared that 'they found themselves bound in justice to leave unshaken my reserved appointment to the situation of Fort Marlborough,' a determination which appears by the orders of your Honourable Court to be considered by you as the proof or test of my having explained my conduct to the satisfaction of the Right Honourable the Governor-General in Council . . . with respect to the Memorial, which I have stated it to be my intention to present to your Honourable Court, I request to observe that, had the above been the only points at issue, had the questions affecting my personal integrity and honour been fully and candidly decided upon, I would not thus have claimed your protection; but, conscious in my own mind that my constant study has been to promote, to the best of my abilities, the interests and honour of my country, and to render the establishment of a British administration in these colonies a memorable era among them in the amelioration and improvement of their population, I would have bowed with deference to the judgment of a superior authority; for this memorial, however, will be reserved that more circumstantial and detailed review of the proceedings which the present Governor-General has adopted towards me personally, and which will form the main ground of my appeal to your Honourable Court."

The final decision of the Court was not given until the 13th of February 1817, but then it was given in the frankest and fullest manner, without reservation or qualification, as recorded in the Public Letter, of which the following is the full text:—

"We have received your letter in this department, of the 8th December 1815, in which you draw our attention to your proceedings relative to the charges which were preferred by the late Major-General Gillespie and Mr. Blagrave against Mr. Raffles, late Lieutenant-Governor of Java, and communicated the judgment you have formed and recorded, as the result of a deliberate investigation of those charges. After a scrupulous examination of all the documents, both accusatory and exculpatory, connected with this important subject, and an attentive perusal of the Minutes of the Governor-General, and of the other members composing the Council, when it was under consideration, we think it due to Mr. Raffles, to the interests of our service, and to the cause of truth, explicitly to declare our decided conviction, that the charges, in as far as they went to impeach the moral character of that gentleman, have not only not been made good, but that they have been disproved, to an extent which is seldom practicable in a case of defence.

"It is not our intention now to discuss the expediency of the leading measures of the administration of Java, while Mr. Raffles presided over the government of the Island. The policy of these measures is not only separable from the motives which dictated them; but there are cogent reasons why they should be kept altogether distinct and separate on the present occasion. Before pronouncing upon the financial operations of that Government, we are desirous of fuller information and further time to deliberate on their tendency and effects, as well as on the circumstances under which they were adopted.

"Were their unreasonableness, improvidence, and inefficiency clearly established, this would only indicate error or defect of judgment, or, at most, incompetence in Mr. Raffles for the high and, in many respects, exceedingly difficult, situation which he filled.

"But the purity, as well as the propriety, of many of his acts, as Lieutenant-Governor, having been arraigned, accusations having been lodged against him, which if substantiated must have proved fatal to his character, and highly injurious, if not ruinous to his future prospects in life, his conduct having been subjected to a regular and solemn investigation, and this investigation having demonstrated to our minds the utter groundlessness of the charges exhibited against him, in so far as they affected his honour, we think that he is entitled to all the advantage of this opinion, and of an early and public expression of it.

" Mr. Edmondstone, in his elaborate and able Minute, has taken so comprehensive and just a view of all the acts which constituted the grounds of imputation against the personal character of Mr. Raffles, that it is quite unnecessary for us to enter into a detailed scrutiny of the matters, either of charge or refutation. On most, if not all, of the points at issue, we concur with Mr. Edmonstone, both in his reasonings and conclusions; and whatever judgment may be ultimately passed on the various measures of the late Government of Java, which underwent review in the course of the investigation into the conduct of its head, we are satisfied, not merely that they stand exempt from any sordid or selfish taint, but that they sprung from motives perfectly correct and laudable.

" If we notice the circumstance of Mr. Raffles having been a purchaser of lands at the public sales on the island, it is for the purpose, not so much of animadverting, after all that has passed, on the indiscretion of the act (for it was unquestionably very indiscreet), as of expressing our firm persuasion that he has stated without equivocation or reserve the reasons which induced him to engage in these transactions, and that they do not at all derogate from those principles of integrity by which we believe his public conduct to have been uniformly governed."

The making of the charges was a serious, and might well have been a fatal, blow to the credit and reputation Raffles had gained by the administration of Java. Their successful repulse, the admission gradually extracted from authorities in India and England—none of them too well disposed towards Raffles, and all agreed in thinking he attached an excessive importance to Java—that he was wronged thereby was a triumph of a quite unique description, and one which almost made the accusation an advantage. At least they enabled Raffles to give a far more detailed account of his own work than would have been possible if he had not had to vindicate himself. It is sometimes said that the work Raffles performed in Java was not of a very durable nature; "he pulled down much," it is said, "but he constructed little." The eminent critic, Colonel Sir Henry Yule, who used that phrase, was of a notoriously exacting nature; but wonder may at least be expressed as to what more he expected Raffles to accomplish to his four and a half years' administration. What are the facts that justify a more favourable conclusion? Raffles will be, and is, remembered in Java for three things. The first was the clearing off of the obligations in paper currency, the legacy of Dutch incompetence and indifference to the cardinal points of right and wrong. The second was the improved system of land revenue that made the Government's income dependent on the people's prosperity. The third was the softening of the old code of justice, the abolition of torture, and the institution of trial by jury. Were these small deeds? The abolition of slavery, the increase of the revenue to seven times the highest total previously reached by the Dutch, and the spreading of a feeling of confidence among the native chiefs—all have a right to be termed great achievements. Perhaps the strongest evidence of their merit is that Raffles's measures were accepted by the Dutch after the restoration, and continued by them. They form part of that new Dutch government of Java, which, in one of his last letters to Lord Minto, Raffles thus describes: "If I were to believe that the Javanese were ever again to be ruled on the former principles of government, I should, indeed, quit Java with a heavy heart; but a brighter prospect is, I hope, before them. Holland is not only re-established, but I hope renovated; her princes have been educated in the best of all *schools* —adversity: and I will hope the people of Java will be as happy, if not happier, under the Dutch, than under the English." If something of this hope was realised, it was due to the fact that Dutch colonial authorities showed the wisdom to borrow and to carry on the reforms, improvements, and higher tone introduced by Raffles himself. The credit he deserves for introducing them, and for all else he did, was much enhanced by the circumstances under which he accomplished them. "I have been forced to act in every measure of importance on my own responsibility, not from the superior authorities being ignorant of the real interests of the colony, but from a hesitation on their part to involve themselves with the Government which might be finally fixed"; so he wrote to Sir Hugh Inglis, the Chairman of the Company. But he was also interfered with at critical junctures, and his position was undermined and weakened by charges that ought never to have been encouraged by the Government of India. Arraigned and suspected by those who should have supported him, Raffles never swerved from his course, or faltered in his work, and by that work he will stand in the estimation of his fellow-men, and in the light of history.

CHAPTER VIII

RETURN TO ENGLAND

THE ship in which Raffles first sailed to the East was, it will be remembered, named the *Ganges*; and, by a singular coincidence, it was in a vessel of the same name that he made his first voyage back to England. The incidents of the passage homeward are preserved in the journal kept by Captain Travers, already more than once quoted. Travers, after a journey to London in defence of his chief, had returned to Batavia and resumed his duties on the personal staff of the Lieutenant-Governor. He was now to prove himself the principal support of one almost unfitted by ill-health to face the trials of a long period at sea. Raffles had described himself in one of his last letters from Java as "a lonely man, like one that has long since been dead, to whom activity and the cares of public responsibility are now almost necessary for existence"; and he went on to say, "I want leisure to recover from the effects of that weight of responsibility which has almost weighed me down, yet I am high and proud in my own integrity."

It was, therefore, in a state of physical collapse that Raffles embarked on the *Ganges*, and more than once during the first weeks of the voyage it seemed probable that he would not survive to reach land. Anxiety on the point was not finally dispelled until the ship had rounded the Cape, when every day witnessed an improvement in his health, and the gradual recovery of his naturally good spirits. The loyalty and devotion of men like Travers, Charles Assey, and Horsfield, furnished some consolation and counterpoise for the defection and the sinister attacks of Gillespie and Blagrave. The only incident of sufficient interest to deserve notice on the home voyage was the stoppage at St. Helena, and the interview that followed there with Napoleon. Raffles himself left no written record of the scene, or his impressions, and the following brief summary from the journal of Captain Travers may suffice as an account of the event. The reader will recollect that Napoleon had then been less than twelve months on the island, and that the short period since the cessation of the contest had not allowed of any abatement in the bitter and angry feelings towards Frenchmen engendered by over twenty years of war.

The precautions taken for the safe custody of the great and dreaded prisoner were such that not even a British ship was allowed to enter the harbour. On approaching the island the *Ganges* was brought to by a signal from the guard-ship, and officers came on board to inquire as to the ship's requirements, and to state that no one could be permitted to land. Captain Travers succeeded in sending off a letter to the Admiral's secretary, stating that Mr. Raffles, late Lieutenant-Governor of Java, was on board, and asking that an exception might be made in his favour. While this communication was in transit, the party on the *Ganges* gave loud expression to their disappointment; but Raffles, with more command of himself, endeavoured to reconcile his companions to their fate, and in place of looking from the deck at a spot which could not be reached, and the sight of which would only tend to excite their chagrin and annoyance, he suggested that they should all retire to their cabins, and commit to paper their feelings at the moment, which would at least amuse them during their detention. However, the sense of disappointment was soon relieved; for the Admiral, Sir George Cockburn, sent special permission to land, while the Governor, Sir Hudson Lowe, accompanied that courtesy with an invitation to dinner. Permission to visit Napoleon was then requested; and that also was granted. The following is almost a verbatim extract from Captain Travers's journal:—

"Our first object was to see Marshal Bertrand, whom we found in a miserably poor habitation, together with his charming Countess. The Marshal received us with the easy air of a well-bred gentlemen, and the Countess with great affability and good humour, contrasting her present abode with that which she lately occupied in France. The Marshal seemed to feel anxious that we should not be disappointed in the object of our visit, but expressed some fears, in consequence of his royal master having signified his intention not to receive any visitors for some days; he, however, kindly offered us letters to Count Las Casas. With this letter we proceeded to Longwood, and were most kindly and politely received by Count Las Casas, with whom we enjoyed some very agreeable conversation. . . . Mr. Raffles received a note from Count Las Casas, saying that the Emperor would see us, and we accordingly returned to Longwood; where, before being introduced, we found this once great man in earnest conversation with Countess Bertrand, who was walking with him in the garden; General Gourgaud preceded, Marshal Bertrand, Count Las Casas, Captain Poniatowsky, and a page followed, all uncovered. On our arrival being announced, we were quickly informed that the Emperor would receive us in the garden; and Count Las Casas added, that although it had been the Emperor's intention not to see any person for some days, yet on being told that it was Mr. Raffles, late Governor of Java, who wished the interview, he immediately consented to see us.

"On our approaching, Napoleon turned quickly round to receive us, and taking off his hat, put it under his arm. His reception was not only not dignified or graceful, but absolutely vulgar and authoritative. He put a series of questions to Mr. Raffles in such quick succession as to render it impossible to reply to one before another was put. His first request was to have Mr. Raffles' name pronounced distinctly. He then asked him in what country he was born? how long he had been in India? whether he had accompanied the expedition against the island of Java? who commanded? and on being told, Sir Samuel Achmuty, he seemed to recollect his name, and made some observations to Las Casas respecting him. He was particular in asking the extent of force, and the regiments employed, and then inquired if Mr. Raffles delivered up the island to the Dutch, or was relieved by another governor. He appeared to be acquainted with the value and importance of the island, but put some strange questions to Mr. Raffles, such as how the King of Java conducted himself. On Mr. Raffles explaining, he seemed most attentive, and then asked whether the spice plantations at Amboyna were doing well, and whether the Spice Islands were to be also restored to the Dutch. He then asked the name of the ship in which we were going home, with what cargo laden, and which was best, Bourbon or Java coffee; all these questions were put with great rapidity, and before replied to, he turned round to Captain Garnham and myself, asked our names, and what service we had seen; whether we were ever wounded, or were ever taken prisoners; how long we had been in India, and several other similar questions. He then again addressed himself to Mr. Raffles, and seemed interested with his remarks on Java. He conversed with Sir Thomas Sevestre, and put similar questions to him with those he had put to Garnham and myself. On his making a slight inclination of the head, we prepared to take our leave, and on our making our bow we parted, Napoleon continuing his walk, and we returning to the house. During the whole time of our interview, as Napoleon remained uncovered, common politeness obliged us to keep our hats in our hands: and at no time was it found necessary to give him any title, either of general or emperor. Las Casas returned with us to the house, where a cold collation was prepared. He was most polite and attentive, and seemed much pleased with Mr. Raffles, with whom he conversed most freely. Of Napoleon he spoke in terms of the highest possible praise, and seemed to lament most bitterly his present situation."

The rest of the voyage to England was uneventful; and the nearer the ship approached northern latitudes, the more did Raffles's health improve and his spirits rise. He was the life of the party, laying himself out to provide entertainment for his companions. On the 6th of July his thirty-fifth birthday was celebrated on board ship by a dinner, to which Captain Nesh, who was sailing in company, was invited by Captain Falconer of the *Ganges*. Travers writes: "We drank toasts in bumpers, and made speeches without number, and concluded the day as we had commenced it, with rejoicings; not a little increased, perhaps, by the prospect before us of so soon touching the blessed shores of Old England once again, from which we had been so long absent."

Raffles sent on a letter to his friend, W. B. Ramsay, notifying his approach; and the following extracts will show the spirit in which he approached England:—

"To be plain, I must tell you, my dear friend, that after suffering severely from an illness brought on in consequence of great anxiety and personal fatigue, I embarked on the 25th March last from Batavia, and am now looking out for the English coast. My party consists of three gentlemen and my family, among whom I have to reckon your friend Travers, who, if not too lazy to write, ought to tell you a great deal more about the matter; for myself, although I am considerably recovered, I yet remain wretchedly thin and sallow, with a jaundiced eye and shapeless leg. Yet, I thank God, my spirit is high and untamed, and the meeting of friends will, I hope, soon restore me to my usual health. I return to you, however, a poor solitary wretch; and the rocks of Albion, which under other circumstances would have met my eyes with joy and gladness, will not now present themselves without reflections which I cannot dwell upon." . . .

In the same letter to his old friend and companion, Raffles refers to the Gillespie affair; and, after stating that "the whole course of proceedings adopted towards me by the

Governor-General has been such that it was impossible for me to rest satisfied with this tardy and incomplete judgment," he expressed his confidence in obtaining full justice from the Court, because " I have a cause that will carry conviction."

On the 11th of July the *Ganges* reached Falmouth, where Raffles and his party landed in one of the shore boats that came out to meet the two Indiamen. Captain Falconer, the commander of the vessel, in evidence of his respect, fired the salute to which Raffles's rank as a Governor entitled him ; and the example was followed by Captain Nesh in the companion ship, the *Auspicious*. Both ships, although with native crews, gave three hearty cheers. Under these encouraging expressions of respect and goodwill, Raffles landed in England, having been absent a little more than eleven years. After passing the Custom-House formalities, the party proceeded to the inn, "where," Captain Travers writes, " we ordered the best dinner procurable at the place, to be got ready as quickly as possible, and passed a most joyous agreeable evening." From Falmouth they went to Truro, near which place Raffles inspected a copper-mine, and, from what he saw, expressed his belief in the superiority of the Japanese copper. On the 16th of July Raffles reached London, and reported himself at the India House the following morning.

Within a week of his arrival Raffles had taken the house, 23 Berners Street, which he occupied during the term of his residence in London, and there, as soon as they could be conveyed from the *Ganges* after her arrival in the London Docks, he collected the rare articles, furniture, and curiosities, he had brought back from Java. The meagre details of his life in England during the next fifteen months alone, provided by Lady Raffles in her Memoir, can fortunately be amplified from his voluminous correspondence with his cousin, Dr. Thomas Raffles, as well as by some reminiscences drawn up by that gentleman at a later period for family reference ; from both of which sources selections are now published for the first time.

Raffles returned to England as a man of recognised distinction and public character ; but the ingenuous simplicity of his disposition is shown in the following little incident, which occurred during the first few days after his arrival. I give the description in the words of Dr. Raffles, from whose reminiscences it is taken :—

"One of his first visits was to his aunt, for they were very fond of each other. He left his equipage, which was a splendid one,—and private carriages with rich liveries were not so common then as they are now, and were indeed a great rarity in the quiet corner of London in which my father lived,—and, walking the length of Princes Street, knocked at old No. 14, and on the opening of the door went at once into the sort of parlour-kitchen where my mother was, busied as usual about her household affairs. 'I knew well,' he said, 'where at this time of the day I should find you,' and taking his accustomed seat in an old arm-chair by the fire-side, where he had often sat, made her at once, by his affectionate and playful manner, quite unconscious of the elevation to which he had attained since he had last sat there. 'Aunt,' he said, 'you know I used to tell you, when a boy, that I should be a duke before I die.' 'Ah,' she replied, 'and I used to say that it would be "Duke of *Puddle Dock*,"' which was a proverb in London at that day, referring to a wretched locality in Wapping, and with which aspiring lads, who had great notions of the greatness they should hereafter attain, were twitted. But he had actually attained to far more than a dukedom, having had Oriental kings and regents under him."

He also visited his uncle, John Raffles, near Birmingham; and his cousin, from whom I have just quoted, came up to see him in London, thus reviving the affectionate relations of earlier days, and causing a frequent and confidential correspondence, which thenceforward continued for the remaining ten years of Raffles's life.

In a letter to his wife, dated July 31st, 1816, Dr. Raffles gives an interesting little glimpse of his cousin :—

"He did not know me, nor did I for a moment recognise him. . . . He had lost nothing of himself but his colour and his flesh. . . . He intends to publish an account of Java, and is very busy in getting maps, etc., prepared for the work. He has very extensive collections of Javanese literature of his own collecting. I am amazed at his industry. In one day he wrote two hundred letters with his own hand, and dictated to two secretaries besides." [Those who were with him in Java had seen him write more than twenty sheets of minutes, orders, etc., which needed no subsequent correction; while he required three clerks to copy and keep up with what he wrote.]

And on the 2nd of August Dr. Raffles wrote again:—

"My cousin has an unbounded flow of spirits; I fear too much for his strength. . . . Such was the devotion of the native inhabitants [of Java] to him, . . . that they declared they were willing to give to the Dutch whatever they enjoyed from the island before its conquest by the English, if they would but resign it. . . . They declared that they would express their sentiments to the King of England, and the native powers were coming down in a body to address my cousin on the subject, and entreat him to stay amongst them; but this he prevented by the quickness of his departure, for it was only determined that he should come to England a few days before he sailed.

"He has brought over Eastern curiosities and treasures to the amount of thirty tons weight, in upwards of two hundred immense packages. He has some presents for the Prince Regent."

On the 5th of August he writes:—

"Yesterday I preached in the evening at Paddington. My cousin and his party were there."

Raffles's respect for conscientious scruples, although they hindered his cousin's worldly advancement, is illustrated by the following conversation, recorded in Dr. Raffles's reminiscences:—

"The first time we were together and alone was in the carriage. He was going to the India House, and I accompanied him. So soon as we had left the door he turned to me and said, 'Well, Tom, you are a parson, and I hear great things of you; and nothing would gratify me more than to be instrumental in promoting your advancement, and my position is such that I should have anything in reason that I might choose to ask. But I can do nothing for you; you are not of our Church.' I thanked him for the expression of his desire to serve me, but said I wanted nothing. 'Well,' he said, 'it may be so; but tell me why you are not of our Church.' I answered that I supposed he did not want a long argument upon the subject. 'No,' he replied, 'but give me one or two of your strong reasons.' 'Well,' I said, 'I will ask you one question, could you declare your hearty assent and consent (*ex animo*) to *all and everything* contained in the Book of Common Prayer?' 'Why,' he said, 'I never read the Book of Common Prayer through; but, apart from that, I will say that I could give my assent and consent to all and everything contained in no book whatever—except one—that is the Bible! That book is perfect: there is nothing false or erroneous in that; but all other books are the productions of fallible men, and must partake more or less of the fallibility of their authors.' 'Then,' said I, 'you could not be a clergyman in the Established Church of England!' 'And if that is required,' he replied, 'I shall never ask you another question on the subject. I honour you and respect your conscience;' and he kept his word."

After his cousin's return to Liverpool, Raffles was ordered by his doctor to proceed to Cheltenham and take the waters; but he was soon recalled to town by business. During this visit to Cheltenham he seems to have made the acquaintance of the lady who became his second wife, Miss Sophia Hull.

In another letter Raffles gives a brief account of a visit he had paid to Birmingham, mentioned a few lines back:—

"As you might have expected, we were received [at Hayley] with the greatest hospitality and affection by my Uncle John and family. He is exactly what he was—with the advantage of being a better Christian; and, as for my aunt, I think she is, if possible, a more extraordinary character than ever. I could fill a volume with the account of our discussions on almost every subject; but you must be content with knowing that we were most highly amused and gratified. It was impossible to leave Bewdley at the time I had fixed, and therefore I spent two days with Caroline [his cousin] instead of one. I like Harmer very much, and think Caroline much improved."

Very soon after his arrival in England Raffles, as we have seen, took up seriously his long-contemplated project of writing the *History of Java*. He had brought home with him the original text of the Javanese national poem, the *Brata Yudha* or "Holy War," of which he had made a literal translation. His cousin was a man of some poetical capacity, and had published a small volume of poetry. It occurred to Raffles that he might render some of the *Brata Yudha* into metre, after the example of Macpherson's *Ossian*, and he accordingly invited and obtained Dr. Raffles's co-operation. Several of the passages, as rendered by Dr Raffles, appear in the account of the *Brata Yudha* provided in the *History of Java*.

In October 1816, the last of Raffles's sisters, Harriett, who had gone out to Penang in 1809, married Mr. Browne, a gentleman holding a post in one of the offices at Somerset House. A month later Raffles had completed his arrangement for publishing his History through Messrs. Black & Parry, publishers to the India House, and the predecessors of the long well-known firm of W. H. Allen & Co. The book did not come out until the following April, when it was very flatteringly received by the public and the reviewers,—the two quarterlies honouring it with a special notice. The progress of the book was hampered by several attacks of illness, during one of which its author was nearly killed by an overdose of mercury. The following letter mentions an important fact, viz. Raffles's second marriage. The lady of his choice was Sophia, daughter of T. W. Hull, Esq., of County Down, Ireland, who had been for some time resident at Cheltenham. Raffles's account of the event is given in his own words written to Dr. Raffles :—

"HENLEY-UPON-THAMES, *23rd February* 1817.

"MY DEAR COUSIN,—You will, I doubt not, approve of the change I have made in my condition in again taking to myself a wife ; and when I apprise you that neither rank, fortune, nor beauty have had weight on the occasion, I think I may fairly anticipate your approval of my selection. The Lady, whose name is Sophia, is turned of thirty ; she is devotedly attached to me, and possesses every qualification of the heart and mind calculated to render me happy. More, I need not say. If you are anxious to know more of her, and will not wait till the period when I hope to make you personally acquainted, you or your Mary may open the correspondence with two lines, which she will be most happy to receive and acknowledge.

"I shall return towards the vicinity of London to-morrow, and letters to Berners Street will always reach me in a few hours. . . . My ulterior movements are not yet finally determined upon. I have received from the Public Authorities in this country the most full and satisfactory conclusion to the affair of Gillespie's charges. When I return to town I will send you a copy of the paragraphs. They end with leaving Sumatra open to me, and, as there seems an inclination to extend my political authority there, I think it almost certain that I shall go out in the course of the year. . . . Believe me, most affectionately yours,

"THOS. S. RAFFLES."

In explanation of the reference in this letter to the Public Authorities, it should be stated that the Court of Directors "in consideration of the zeal and talents displayed during the period he filled the office of Lieutenant-Governor of Java, conferred upon him the title of Lieutenant-Governor of Bencoolen, as a peculiar mark of the favourable sentiments which the Court entertained of his merits and services."

Raffles's reputation, as a man of science and the late ruler of an important colonial possession, brought him into contact with the most fashionable as well as the most famous men of the day. His relations with the Duke and Duchess of Somerset—the latter a sister of the Duke of Hamilton,—the Earl and Countess Harcourt, and, above all, with Prince Leopold and the Princess Charlotte, were of a specially cordial and durable nature. That he was able to win his way into the most exclusive set of the British Court speaks well for his culture and manners, for his friends were among the most discriminating and exacting personages then to be found in the highest circles during the regency. Raffles visited them in their country homes: Maiden Bradley, Nuneham, and Claremont had open doors for him. His correspondence with the Duchess of Somerset went on to the end of his life, and will be frequently quoted; while his relations with Prince Leopold and his wife, the Princess Charlotte,—the future Queen of this Empire, as it was hoped by an admiring nation,—promised to open to him the highest offices of the State. There is no doubt that it was his intimacy with the royal personages at Claremont which provided the warrant for Dr. Raffles's statement that his cousin's name was mentioned as a possible future Governor-General of India. An incident will show the reader how great that intimacy was. After the publication, in May 1817, of his *History of Java*, which was dedicated, by permission, to the Prince Regent, Raffles attended the next levée, when the Regent availed himself of the occasion to express, in the most public and handsome manner, his approbation of the work, and of Raffles's public acts of administration of which it was the record. On Raffles's approach the Prince ordered the whole progress of the levée to be suspended.

"His attendants formed a circle round him, and in the presence of them all the Regent said he was happy to embrace that opportunity of thanking him for the entertainment and information he had derived from the perusal of the greater part of the volumes, and also of expressing the high sense he entertained of the eminent services he had rendered to his country by his conduct in the government of Java. What the Prince said occupied nearly twenty minutes. He then conferred upon him the honour of knighthood."

I extract from Dr. Raffles's reminiscences some interesting incidents of his relations with several members of the Royal Family:—

"He told me that the Queen (Charlotte) heard so much of the curious and precious things which he had brought from India, and especially of the furniture,—tables, chairs, etc., which he had presented to the Princess Charlotte, made of the Kiabooka wood of India, which adorned the dining and drawing-rooms at Claremont,—that she expressed the intention of coming to see him: the fact is, she also wanted to obtain some portion for herself. 'Of course,' he said, 'I could not allow the Queen of England to come to me;' but he sent word to her Majesty, by Lady Harcourt (through whom the Queen's message had been conveyed to him), that he would do himself the honour of waiting upon her Majesty, at any time and place she might please to appoint. To this arrangement her Majesty assented, and named *St. Leonard's*, the seat of the Countess Harcourt, who was one of the Ladies-in-waiting, and one of her Majesty's personal friends, as the place of the interview. Lord and Lady Harcourt were also personal and, indeed, intimate friends of Sir Stamford. Of course he was there in good time, and he told me that, while waiting for the Queen, he talked with Lady Harcourt about me. 'And what,' said I, 'could you say about me?'—'O,' he said, 'I told her that you were a Dissenting minister,—that I had been to visit you at Liverpool,—that I had heard you preach twice, long sermons, without a book.'—'Ah,' said Lady Harcourt, 'but you must not tell the Queen that, *for she hates Dissenters!*' At length her Majesty arrived, and after the formalities of introduction, etc., it was proposed that they should take a walk in the park. But we had not gone far when her Majesty said, 'I hear wonderful things of the treasures you have brought from India, and everybody is in raptures with the beautiful tables, etc., which you have given to the Princess Charlotte.'—'Of course,' said he, 'I was obliged to say that I should be greatly honoured if her Majesty would accept a specimen of the wood for her residence at Frogmore.' The offer was graciously accepted; and he told me that he ordered a pair of tables, which were being made for Sir Joseph Banks, to be sent immediately to Frogmore. The next thing was an invitation, or rather a *command*, from the Queen, to spend an evening with her at Frogmore. There he met Lord Amherst, who was just on the point of sailing as Governor-General of India; the Queen introduced them to each other, and he passed the evening very pleasantly in conversation with Lord Amherst on matters connected with India.

"Sir Stamford was very intimate (if such an expression may be used in relation to the intercourse of persons of such exalted rank with others) with the lamented Princess Charlotte and Prince (now King) Leopold. He was often their guest at Claremont. I have a letter from him dated there. The Regent, her father, was most tenacious on the subject of the honour and deference due to her as heir-presumptive to the throne; and yet he was meanly jealous of her, and no one whom she honoured with her friendship ever received special favour from him. Hence the mere *knighthood* which he received at his hands, when all expected, as all agreed it was richly deserved, a *baronetage*. The honour of knighthood could not be very highly esteemed by him [Sir Stamford], when he had in his own establishment a man of equal rank, as his body physician, Sir Thomas Sevestre. In his case, at anyrate, he did more honour to the title than it conferred on him. He told me a curious fix in which on one occasion he was placed between these illustrious personages, and the judicious way in which he got out of it. The Princess invited him to dine at Claremont on a certain day. Immediately after his acceptance of that invitation came the *commands* of the Regent to dine with him at Carlton House on the same day. Here was a difficulty ; and the course he took to extricate himself was this. He wrote to Sir Benjamin Bloomfield to know whether it was His Royal Highness's pleasure that an invitation from the Princess Charlotte should be considered as a command. In reply, Sir Benjamin informed him that it was the Regent's pleasure that, as heir-presumptive to the throne, an invitation from Her Royal Highness should be considered in the light of a command. He then wrote to Sir Benjamin saying that he had the commands of Her Royal Highness the Princess Charlotte to dine with her at Claremont on the day in question, and could not therefore have the honour of dining on that day with His Royal Highness the Prince Regent.

"The Princess Charlotte and Prince Leopold had a great regard for him. He told me of a proof of it which was given to him the last time he was at Claremont. The Prince said to him, 'Sir Stamford, the Princess and myself are much indebted to you for the many expressions you have given to us of your regard. Allow me to put this ring upon your finger as a token of our united regard'—thus presenting him with a diamond ring worth £400 ; and the Princess, looking over her shoulder at him, added—'And sometimes wear that for my sake.' I believe he mourned the loss of that ring more than any other of the many precious things that perished in the burning of the *Fame*. But the loss of the amiable Princess herself, so soon after this parting interview, touched him most tenderly, for he had a sincere regard for her, beyond any consideration of rank, or wealth, or honour, to which he might have attained, had both their lives been prolonged. There was no doubt entertained at the time, that if he had survived he would have been Governor-General of India ; while she would have been but too much delighted to have raised him to the peerage in that capacity. No one more thoroughly despised the knighthood which her father had conferred upon him than she did,—a feeling in which the Prince fully participated. He told me that the tone and manner of Prince Leopold was quite ludicrous, when, on his first visit after he had been dubbed, he turned to the Princess and said, 'Why, Charlotte, they have made him a knight ! !' Sir Stamford's eldest son was called Leopold ; and a beautiful letter from the Prince to him on his birth he was bringing home with him for my collection of autographs. But that also perished in the *Fame*. What treasures has the ocean swallowed up ! "

Raffles could not have obtained a higher testimonial than the esteem and regard which Prince Leopold of Saxe-Coburg bestowed upon him. That prince, one of the most accomplished men of his time, and justly ranked among the ablest rulers of his age in Europe when he mounted the throne of Belgium,—a country which owes so much in European estimation to his wisdom and that of his son and successor,—was a discriminating judge of men, slow to give his confidence, and preserving his dignity and delicate position among the circles of English society, ever prejudiced against anything foreign, by a reserve and restraint which restricted the number of those admitted to his intimacy. But on Raffles, this prince—to judge by the test of time—imposed no period of probation. He read his character at a glance, and admitted him to the inner circle of his friends. It speaks much for the natural grace of Raffles's manners, that they should have proved as effective in opening the doors of Claremont and the barriers of Prince Leopold's confidence as they had been in propitiating Malay students and Javanese princes. Nor is there any doubt that the Princess Charlotte, "England's hope," of whom the nation then expected as much as Queen Victoria has realised, extended to Raffles the same feelings of esteem as those entertained for him by her husband. The premature death of that gifted princess cast a cloud over English life, and part of the shadow fell with a special darkness on the career of Raffles. With the death of his wife, Prince Leopold ceased for many years to exercise any influence in English public life; and thus Raffles lost the support and regard of the two members of the Royal Family who best appreciated his capacity and character, and whose good opinion it was then the highest honour for any one to possess.

There is one interview I should like to describe, that between Raffles and the aged Warren Hastings, a statesman with whom he had many points of similarity; but the materials are wanting. I can only give his letter to Dr. Fisher, Bishop of Salisbury, arranging the interview, and even the date is unfortunately missing from it:—

"Mr. Raffles presents his compliments to the Bishop of Salisbury, and can assure his Lordship that nothing will afford him more pleasure than the honour of being personally known to Mr. Hastings, and the opportunity of evincing his respect and veneration for a character so truly great. The Duke and Duchess of Somerset intend honouring Mr. Raffles with a visit at three o'clock on

Monday next. Perhaps that time may be convenient; if not, any more early hour on that day, Tuesday or Wednesday, that Mr. Hastings will name, will be perfectly convenient to Mr. Raffles.

"Mr. Raffles will esteem himself honoured in the company of Mrs. Fisher and the ladies.

"BERNERS STREET, 23,
"*Friday.*"

In connection with Sir Stamford's knighthood it will not be without interest to state that the following arms were granted to him, and are duly recorded at the Herald's office:—

Raffles (granted to Sir Thomas Stamford Raffles, Lieutenant-Governor of Java, and subsequently of Fort Marlborough in Sumatra).—Erminois an eagle with two heads displayed gules, charged on the breast with an Eastern crown or, a chief vert, thereon pendent from a chain two oval medallions in pale, the one bearing Arabic characters, and the other a dagger in fesse, blade wavy, point towards the dexter in relief gold. Crest—Out of an Eastern crown or, a griffin's head purp. beaked and gorged with a collar gemel gold. Motto—*Auspicium melioris aevi.* These armorial bearings appear on the front cover of this volume. At the same time Sir Stamford's portrait was painted by Mr. George Francis Joseph, A.R.A., and, after long remaining in the possession of his sister, Mrs. Flint, and his nephew, the Rev. W. C. Raffles Flint, it was presented by the latter, in 1859, to the National Portrait Gallery, where it occupies a prominent position. The frontispiece to this volume is a photogravure from this portrait.

In the spring of 1817 Sir Stamford Raffles decided to make a tour on the Continent; and, as his sister, Mrs. Flint, was to be of the party, he proposed to his cousin to join him. The following letter contains the invitation, which was eventually accepted:—

"CLAREMONT, *27th April* 1817.

"REV. THOMAS RAFFLES.

"MY DEAR COUSIN,—My plan is to visit Paris and Brussels, and to see all besides that I can in the space of six weeks or two months, the limit which I am obliged to fix for my continental tour; and I have every reason to hope that I shall be able to set out upon it between the 10th and 15th of next month. In this expectation we have declined all engagements after the 10th, in order to have a few quiet days to ourselves before we set off.

"Now, my dear cousin, if you can possibly manage to be of our party I can promise that you will find it a pleasant and interesting trip, and I am sure I need not say how happy it will make us to have you as a *compagnon de voyage*. Indeed, so much has my head run upon such an arrangement, that we are fully calculating upon it, and our disappointment will be great indeed if you cannot manage to join. On your account, and to ensure your company, I shall not mind a handful of days. Let me know what you can do ; and do, I conjure you, go if you can.

"My eventual plans are to proceed to India about August ; but a few weeks' delay will be of no importance, as my departure entirely depends upon my own convenience and pleasure. Mrs. Raffles and Mary Anne will accompany me on the Continent, and are equally anxious with myself to know how far it is possible for you to go with us.

"After exerting all my energies to compress my book into one volume, I have been forced to make two of it. The next week will, however, complete the second volume ; and the work will be well out before the 10th, the day announced for my leaving London, etc. etc. THOS. S. RAFFLES.

"I am here to dine with Prince Leopold and the Princess Charlotte, and seize a few moments of spare time, which I never have at home, to scrawl these few lines."

Dr. Raffles accepted the invitation, and a very pleasant tour resulted, which was considerably extended beyond the original plan. Switzerland, Savoy, and the Rhine were visited as well as France and Belgium ; while the whole journey lasted six weeks. Dr. Raffles published his own letters written during the tour, and thus became the historian of this continental trip, one of the first taken after the Great Peace. The work, which had considerable merit, attracted much attention, and went through five editions in England, while it was reprinted and widely read in America. It was also constantly used as a guide-book. The book was dedicated by the author to Sir Stamford. Raffles himself was very much struck by the agricultural resources of France and the happiness of her people. The following extracts from a letter to the Duchess of Somerset, dated Brussels, July 14th, 1817, will show how he went to the root of things :—

"When I see every man cultivating his own field, I cannot but think him happier far than when he is cultivating the field of another ; even if he labours more, that labour is still lighter which is his pride and pleasure, than that which is his burden and sorrow. . . . Upon the whole, I cannot but think that, notwithstanding agriculture as a science may be almost unknown in France, and that France as a nation has been greatly impoverished both in men and money, there is a foundation in the present state of her land and peasantry to support a much greater nation than France ever yet was."

The truth of this did not become a commonplace until after 1871.

At the end of the journey Raffles paid a visit to the King of the Netherlands, and made intercessions in favour of his former Dutch colleagues, as well as of the princes of Java. He was the more successful because the Dutch authorities had already reported on the merits of his administration; but he observed in a letter to Mr. Marsden, written from Berners Street, on the 27th of July 1817, that, although "the King himself, and his leading minister seem to mean well, they have too great a hankering after profit, and *immediate* profit, for any liberal system to thrive under them." After the return from the Continent, Raffles visited his cousin at Liverpool; and then, with his wife, paid a brief visit to Ireland. After a final visit to his friends, the Duke of Somerset and Sir Hugh Inglis, in September 1817, Raffles made his arrangements to leave England for Sumatra, to take up there his reserved appointment as Lieutenant-Governor of Fort Marlborough.

The *Lady Raffles*, a new Indiaman, named after Raffles's wife, in which he had taken his passage, sailed from Falmouth on the 15th of November 1817, and reached Bencoolen after a tedious passage on the following 20th of March. A farewell message to Dr. Raffles, on the eve of his departure from Portsmouth, reads as follows:—

"My dear Cousin,—Only one word from the *Lady Raffles*, under weigh at Spithead with a fair breeze, and all on board. Heaven bless you and yours! We are all well, and unite in love and affection to you. T. S. Raffles."

"Lady Raffles," wrote Sir Stamford to Mr. William Marsden from Bencoolen on the 7th of April 1818, "presented me with a beautiful little girl when to the southward of the Cape. At the suggestion of the Radin [the Javanese chief who had accompanied him to England], my daughter has received the name of Tunjong Segára (the Lily of the Sea), in addition to those of Charlotte Sophia."

As there have been many references to Dr. Thomas Raffles in this chapter, this will be a suitable place to introduce the following personal particulars about this distinguished Congregational minister. A memoir of his career was written and published by his eldest son, Thomas Stamford Raffles, Police-Magistrate of Liverpool from 1860 to 1891. The following account is taken from Picton's *Memorials of Liverpool*:—

"The Reverend Thomas (afterwards Dr.) Raffles, who for nearly half a century maintained a position [at Great George Street Chapel] of popularity as a preacher and respect as a public man which very few have enjoyed. In 1861 he resigned his charge, and on August 18, 1863, he entered into his rest, and was interred at the Necropolis on the 24th. Such a funeral has rarely been witnessed in the town of Liverpool. The shops along the line of procession were closed, the bells of the churches rang muffled peals; the mayor and magistrates and principal inhabitants joined in the procession, which was lined along the route by 50,000 persons. . . .

"Returning up the hill to Mason Street, the last house but one at the southern end, on the west side, was long the residence of the Rev. T. Raffles, LL.D., who has been mentioned in a previous chapter. The house was roomy and convenient, with a large garden behind, raised up on a high terrace, considerably above the level of the street. Many of the most eminent public men, both of England and America, have here, at one time or another, been the doctor's guests. His company was much sought after. His genial flow of conversation, full of anecdote and fun; his inimitable dramatic power in telling a story, set off by his portly presence and the silver tones of his voice; his extensive collection of autographs and relics, many of them unique, which he delighted to exhibit, and to bring out their points to the best advantage, rendered a visit to Mason Street something to be stored up in the mind for future pleasant reminiscence."

CHAPTER IX

SUMATRA

WHEN Raffles reached the settlement of Bencoolen and landed amidst the dreary swamps that line the river, the scene, however uninviting, was, for a naturalist from Java, the entrance to a wonderland of fresh delights. Clothed with forests, which, for the size and loveliness of their trees and the rare colouring of the flowers that brighten their wildernesses, can scarcely find a rival even in those Eastern seas, Sumatra is the home of an animal kingdom, sometimes, as in the case of the Siamang ape, unique, and again and again exhibiting distinct local characteristics. It is indeed a little continent of clearly modelled form; and it stands, with its vast area of 170,744 square miles, its length of 1047 miles, and an extreme breadth of 230 miles, like a gigantic rampart reared by Nature to shelter the end of the Malay Peninsula and the Straits of Malacca from the great sea beyond. A range of mountains runs from its northern to its southern end, broken for the most part into three or four lines of heights, and bearing in its earth-tossed declivities lake after lake whose waters, resting in silenced craters, are perhaps prophetic of the destiny of not less than sixteen still active volcanoes. This long "Chain Mountain" of Sumatra, averaging from 1500 to 6000 feet in height, draws throughout its whole course towards the open sea: while, to the northward, the Golden Mountain lifts its sunlit head 6879 feet into the air; and not far south of the equator, Indrapura, overtopping every other summit in the island, and its crest wreathed ever and again in ragged clouds of smoke and dust, attains an altitude of fully 11,800 feet. On its eastern side the island presents a gradual slope; the central chain passing and dwindling, in the north, through ever-lessening offshoots to the coast-line, but in the broader, southern part reaching it through alluvial plains, whose long, winding rivers, with deltas often interlinked, permit of navigation far into the interior. On their other side, the mountains fall with abrupt and angry petulance towards the sea-level; where the Indian Ocean, broken by a rank of smaller islands, sobs and thunders down the western coast. The district of Bencoolen is a long and narrow strip of territory, running to a considerable distance northward from the most southerly point of the whole island.

As a mark of their confidence the East India Company had raised the rank Raffles was to hold at Bencoolen from that of a Resident to that of a Lieutenant-Governor. At the same time, it must be noted that they were sending him to the most backward and the least promising of all their Eastern possessions. In the seventeenth century the Settlement of Bencoolen, situated on a river of the same name and protected by Fort Marlborough, had been one of the most cherished of English stations. On the west coast of Sumatra our traders had long hoped to find a compensation for expulsion from Java, and the East India Company had given freely of its treasures and resources to realise the prospect. For one hundred and fifty years the East India Company expended there £100,000 a year; and the annual return in a few tons of pepper was altogether inadequate. This prolonged outlay, leading to constantly recurrent fits of disappointment, had made the Court impatient in all matters relating to Bencoolen. The feeling with which they regarded Penang in 1808 applied in an intensified form to the west coast of Sumatra in 1818; and Raffles was sent to a place thoroughly discredited, where only radical reforms and an immediate outlay could produce any change, while measures of the kind had no chance of acceptance or sanction in Leadenhall Street. Raffles himself fully realised the well-nigh hopeless position of Bencoolen; and although he threw himself with energy and promptitude into the task of raising its fortunes, his main thought, it will be seen, was to create a new interest and to found a new centre of power in the midst of the Eastern Archipelago. Almost his first letter contains these words: "From what I have seen of Sumatra, I would not give one Java for a thousand such islands."

Raffles reached Bencoolen on the 22th of March 1818, and the following letter, adressed to Mr. William Marsden, shows in what a deplorable state it was at that moment:—

"BENCOOLEN, *April* 7, 1818.

"MY DEAR SIR,—I have only time to advise you of our safe arrival here. We had a very tedious passage of more than four months, exclusive of our detention at Falmouth. . . . This is without exception the most wretched place I ever beheld. I cannot convey to you an adequate idea of the state of ruin and dilapidation which surrounds me. What with natural impediments, bad government, and the awful visitations of Providence which we have recently experienced in repeated earthquakes, we have scarcely a dwelling in which to lay our heads, or wherewithal to satisfy the cravings of nature. The roads are impassable; the highways in the town overrun with rank grass; the Government House a den of ravenous dogs and polecats. The natives say that Bencoolen is now a *tána mati* (dead land). In truth, I could never have conceived anything half so bad. We will try and make it better; and if I am well supported from home, the west coast may yet be turned to account. You must, however, be prepared for the abolition of slavery; the emancipation of the country people from the forced cultivation of pepper; the discontinuance of the gaming and cock-fighting farms; and a thousand other practices equally disgraceful and repugnant to the British character and Government. A complete and thorough reform is indispensable, and reductions must be made throughout."

The reforms suggested in this letter touched very closely the existing modes of raising the Company's revenue; for the most prolific sources of profit were "the gaming and cock-fighting farms," which were publicly patronised by Government. There was also a small body of African slaves, the property of the Company; and the prevailing opinion was that they were better off in slavery than they would be as freed men. It was also generally maintained that the Malay character was so hopelessly vile and degraded that there was no possibility of elevating it, and that, consequently, any reforms would be both useless and unwise. These views were entirely opposed to everything Raffles had thought or done. The reforms he had instituted in Java were to be attempted in Bencoolen, where, it seemed to him, the British reputation demanded that slavery should cease, discreditable practices be discouraged, and labour be both emancipated from its fetters and made free in its efforts and reward. Raffles saw this ; and he did not lose a day in making a start with the needed administrative changes. He said " the forced services and forced deliveries at inadequate rates must be abolished. The labourer must be allowed to cultivate pepper, or not, at pleasure ; and such radical changes made throughout as will enable the people to distinguish the political influence of the British Government from the commercial speculations of the Company and their agents." His very first acts were the emancipation of the slaves and the closing of all gaming-houses. For these humanitarian, and, if the character of the Government was to be at all considered, these inevitable measures, he received a censure to the effect that he had showed precipitation in dealing with the Company's property. The censure was the more marked, because he had obtained possession of the island of Pulo Nias, on the west coast of Sumatra, immediately north of the Equator, with the special object of suppressing the slave traffic.

On the 19th of January 1821, he gave Mr. Marsden a bright little picture of this promising attempt to suppress the slave trade :—

"I have much satisfaction in reporting that the chiefs of Pulo Nias have ceded the sovereignty of that island to the Company. Our principal station is at Tello Dalum, near the southern extremity, and in a fine harbour, affording good and safe shelter and accommodation for ships of any size, at all seasons of the year. The extent of population and cultivation, and the general state of civilisation, have far exceeded my most sanguine expectations. The population is certainly not less than 230,000 souls. Not a vestige of primeval forest is to be found on the island ; the whole has disappeared before the force of industry ; the whole island is a sheet of the richest cultivation that can be imagined, and the interior surpasses in beauty and fertility the richest parts of continental India, if not of Java.

"The people, and in particular the Chiefs, are active and intelligent, rich and powerful, and, as far as we can judge of their character, are the very reverse of those we find on this coast. They have cheerfully entered into our views for abolishing the slave trade ; and the people, and the country in general, promise much."

His next measures were to invite the native Princes to follow his example and to assist his efforts ; while he propitiated their goodwill, by withdrawing several obnoxious regulations passed after the murder of a former Resident, Mr Parr, and by allowing them to carry their creeses within the bounds of Fort Marlborough.

But if the affairs of Bencoolen occupied much of his attention, the contest with the Dutch for pre-eminence—it would be more correct to say for equality—in the Eastern seas soon absorbed his mind.

In connection with this subject the Court of Directors had given him special instructions:—

"It is highly desirable that the Court of Directors should receive early and constant information of the proceedings of the Dutch and other European nations, as well as of the Americans, in the Eastern Archipelago. The Court, therefore, desire that you will direct your attention to the object of regularly obtaining such information, and that you will transmit the same to them by every convenient opportunity, accompanied by such observations as may occur to you, whether of a political or commercial nature. You will furnish the Supreme Government with copies of these communications. In the event of any such communications appearing to you to be of a nature to require secrecy, you will address your letter to the Secret Committee."

The following extracts from his letters will show how Raffles took up and renewed the struggle he had previously sustained in relation to Java:—

"*April* 14, 1818.

"Prepared as I was for the jealousy and assumption of the Dutch Commissioners in the East, I have found myself surprised by the unreserved avowal they have made of their principles, their steady determination to lower the British character in the eyes of the natives, and the measures they have already adopted towards the annihilation of our commerce, and of our intercourse with the native traders throughout the Malayan Archipelago. Not satisfied with shutting the Eastern ports against our shipping, and prohibiting the natives from commercial intercourse with the English, they have despatched Commissioners to every spot in the Archipelago where it is probable we might attempt to form settlements, or where the independence of the native chiefs afford anything like a free port to our shipping. Thus not only the Lampong country has been resumed, but also Pontiana and the minor ports of Borneo, and even Bali, where European flag was never before hoisted, are now considered by them subject to their authority, and measures taken for their subjugation. A Commissioner also long since sailed from Batavia for Palembang, to organise, as it is said, all that part of Sumatra ; and every native prow and vessel is now required to hoist a Dutch flag, and to take out a Dutch pass from Batavia for one of the ports thus placed under their influence ; so that whatever trade may still be carried on by the English with the native ports of the Archipelago, must already be in violation of the Dutch regulations, and at the risk of seizure by their cruisers, who have not hesitated repeatedly to fire into English ships. The commanders of the country ships look to me to protect their interests, and even to support the dignity of the British flag ; and it is to be hoped some immediate notice will be taken by our Government of these proceedings."

The obvious facts of the situation proved that the Dutch possessed a vastly superior position over the English in these seas. As Raffles wrote in the same letter :—

"The Dutch possess the only passes through which ships must sail into this Archipelago—the Straits of Sunda and of Malacca ; and the British have not now an inch of ground to stand upon between the Cape of Good Hope and China ; nor a single friendly port at which they can water or obtain refreshment."

These views had been set forth at far greater length, and in an extremely able manner in a paper entitled "Our Interests in the Eastern Archipelago," which Raffles, shortly before leaving England, drew up for George Canning's information. I give the substance of this remarkable paper, because it throws light on Raffles's policy, and is quite prophetic with regard to a then undreamt-of French empire in Indo-China :—

"By far the largest and most valuable share of this commerce is, in a great measure, at the disposal of the power in possession of Java, Banca, and the Moluccas, and the other Colonies and establishments surrendered to the Dutch ; it constitutes perhaps two-thirds of the whole. Of the next, a considerable portion, perhaps a sixth of the whole, is at the disposal of chiefs who have at some time or other bound themselves by treaty to admit none but the Dutch to the benefit of it. The present validity of most of these treaties, however, may be well contested by the British Government. The remaining sixth of the whole commerce is unquestionably open to competition. I shall therefore call it the independent trade.

"The foreign trade of the Archipelago has, from the earliest period, been carried at certain emporia, whither the produce of the islands is brought by Chinese, Arab, and native traders. Acheen, Malacca, and Bantam were the principal emporia when Europeans first visited the East. The Dutch, in their more prosperous times, forced most of the trade to Batavia, which thus became the principal emporium of the islands; but the unhealthiness of the place and the impolicy of the Dutch had so lowered this port in the estimation of the native traders, that in the year 1790 a large portion of it was removed to the native port of Rhio; and the English, having opened friendly communications with the different chiefs of the other islands of the Archipelago, traded to their ports direct. From the occupation of Malacca by the British troops in 1795, the English may be considered to have enjoyed nearly all the northern trade of the Archipelago; and, by their clandestine trade with Batavia and the Moluccas, to have obtained at least an equal share of the limited trade then attempted to be carried on by the Dutch. As the trade of the Dutch still further declined, that of the English increased, until, on the conquest of Java in 1811, the whole fell into their hands.

"The disposition of the Dutch to deprive us of all share in the independent trade is to be inferred from their unremitted exertions in former times to prevent our obtaining it, and from their present unequivocal language and conduct. In the zenith of their power they had brought most of the native princes under their subjection; and, where they did not acquire territorial rights, generally obtained grants of an exclusive trade, requiring all native vessels to carry their pass and flag, and restricting them from entering except at ports where the Dutch had establishments. At their instigation it was that the natives cut off our early settlements; and there is little doubt that many of our vessels which have been burnt in the roads of Batavia and elsewhere were set fire to by their orders. Their commercial ambition and their animosity against British trade, was never greater than at this moment. They are deeply impressed with the recollection of their ancient maritime and commercial grandeur, and would favour any other nation, especially the Americans, to our prejudice.

"Of the disposition of the mother-country, the actual contemplation of a prohibitory duty on British shipping trading to their colonies in the Archipelago is some evidence; and various incidents which took place at the moment of transferring the colony are sufficient to prove the assuming spirit of the Colonial Government. . . . The Dutch Commissioners have positively refused to guarantee or acknowledge any of the treaties entered into by the British Government on Java, or any of those relations of comparative independence on the part of the natives which the British Government had sanctioned; indeed, for them to have behaved well to the British seems now to be punished as a crime.

"Supposing, however, the disposition of the Dutch to be more favourable to us than it appears, would prudence allow us to depend upon its continuance for the possession of a commerce which, I hope to show, we have the means of securing to ourselves by a better tenure than their good pleasure? . . .

"To these means what can we oppose? To their system of taking possession of unoccupied ports, and of making treaties of monopoly with the natives, we can oppose the same system. There are yet, at least there were when the last accounts came away, ports of which we may take possession before them, and princes at liberty to make treaties with us in favour of our commerce. To their intimidation of the natives we may oppose a Court of Protection. To their imposition of heavy duties on our regular trade with the Dutch colonies, no resistance can be made in the islands; but, to the effect of such a measure, we can oppose the facility of obtaining our goods free of duty. To the vexatious and violent measures which may be directed against our independent commerce, we may oppose a British authority at hand charged with the special duty of seeing justice done. . . . To the last means of exclusion, viz. that of degrading us in the eyes of the natives, we may oppose, in the first instance, a strict regard to the engagements which we have already made with them, either expressly or by implication; and, afterwards, early information and prompt notice of the calumnies that may be propagated against us, of the arrogant pretensions that may be set up, and of all other insults that may be offered to us, by the Dutch.

"I shall now proceed to point out the specific measures, by which, it appears to me, that we may best avail ourselves of those means of defence. These are—first, a distinct declaration to the Dutch Government in Europe and Asia, and perhaps to the native princes of the Eastern islands, that we will consider the Dutch Government bound to fulfil those engagements which we have, either directly or by implication, contracted with the native powers during the last twenty-three years, and especially during the British government of Java. We consider ourselves bound and entitled to insist on their doing so. That having accepted the benefit of those Acts which are favourable to them, they cannot reject the burden of those which they may deem otherwise. No provision was made in our agreements with the native princes for the contingency of the Colonies reverting to Holland. The language which we held out to them was that of a Government competent to made agreements in perpetuity. Without such a language, we never could have done what we have done for the Eastern islands.

"The British Government considered the native princes as independent sovereigns, and treated with them accordingly. The Dutch have refused to guarantee our treaties, and appear to consider those faithful allies to [the] British nation as mere vassals, who are now subjected to their vengeance and rapacity.

"Of little use, however, would be the recognition on the part of the Dutch of our engagements with the natives, unless we were at hand to watch over the fulfilment of them: and this leads me to the second measure which I propose for the protection of our commerce in the Eastern Archipelago against the power of the Dutch to exclude us from it, viz. our taking immediate possession of a port in the Eastern Archipelago, the best adapted for communication with the native princes; for a general knowledge of what is going on at sea, and on shore, throughout the Archipelago; for the resort of the independent trade, and the trade with our allies; for the protection of our commerce and all our interests, and more especially for an *entrepôt* for our merchandise.

"The only two stations which we possess in the neighbourhood of the Archipelago, viz. Bencoolen and Prince of Wales['s] Island, are far too remote from the scene to answer any of these purposes. The former is on the western coast of Sumatra, out of the reach of the native trade of the Archipelago, and independent of this disadvantage, from the nature of the coast, and the occasional violence of the sea and surf, not to be approached by the native craft without great danger of loss. The latter is situated considerably to the northward of Malacca, and, though to be approached with safety by native vessels, is so distant from the principal native ports of the Archipelago, that, under the uncertainty of the passage up the Straits, but few native vessels are induced to go there; for the small portion of the trade it has hitherto enjoyed, it was chiefly indebted to the temporary possession of Malacca, where heavy duties were imposed in order to force the trade up. . . .

"The station which I would recommend, if attainable, is the island of Banca. Till its late surrender, it had been exclusively British. The Dutch flag had never been hoisted there. The population had accumulated under the British alone to the amount of at least 10,000 souls. The tin mines, the most valuable and productive in the world, afforded a large surplus revenue. Considerable sums had been expended on it. It possesses a noble harbour, good roadstead, and lies in the direct passage between the Straits of Sunda and Malacca.

"Could this island be purchased out of the very heavy sum of money due by the Dutch Government to the East India Company in balance of the accounts of Java, it would very soon pay the cost.

"Next to Banca the island of Bintang, at the extremity of the Malay Peninsula, appears to be possessed of the largest share of those advantages which should be sought on such a station. The Dutch had formerly a factory on this island at Rhio, which was destroyed in 1795. Ever since then it has been under the independent sovereignty of the Sultan of Lingen, from whom it is probable that either the island itself, or permission to establish a factory upon it, might be obtained on terms similar to those on which we hold Prince of Wales['s] Island. It possesses one of the best harbours in the Eastern seas, a considerable population (not less than 10,000 souls), and is perhaps more favourably situated for a general commercial *entrepôt* than Banca. It is now the general resort of pirates and smugglers, and the circumstance of its being the principal station of the Arab and Bugis traders on the western side of the Archipelago, is a proof of the facilities which it possesses for trade. It would be a commercial station for communication with the China ships passing either through the Straits of Sunda or Malacca, completely outflank Malacca, and intercept its trade in the same manner as Malacca has already intercepted that of Prince of Wales['s] Island. The advantages which this station possesses for becoming a general emporium of the Eastern trade are well depicted in a secret report made by the Governor of Malacca to the Dutch Commissioners-General in 1793, and from which the following are extracts:—

"'There could be no port in these seas more dangerously situated to undermine our trade than Bintang. All vessels coming from China, Cambodia, Siam, Patani, and Trangano, from which places several vessels come annually to Malacca, must pass in sight of that island, which forms the southern side of the Strait of Sincapore at its opening from the China seas. It lies also in the track of the vessels in which the people of Borneo and Celebes come here for the purpose of trade. It is also conveniently situated for the natives of Banca to smuggle tin instead of delivering it to their prince. In consequence of many of these places producing tin and pepper, this produce was brought to Rhio, the principal port of Bintang; and we could not prevent it, because the chiefs are not bound by any treaties to furnish these articles to the Dutch exclusively. The high price obtained by the merchants for tin and pepper at Rhio, compared to that given by the Company, induced them to take these articles to Rhio, and even encouraged the smugglers. Rhio thus became the principal mart or emporium of these articles, which attracted the English and other foreign merchants, as well as natives, to the place. The trade of the Chinese increased also by rapid degrees, as well as that of the Portuguese of Macao, who are obliged to pass this island, and who touch at it very often.'

"Should difficulties occur in the attainment of this station, the western coast of Borneo has also many recommendations, particularly the immediate vicinity of Sambas and Pontiana, inland of which are the principal gold-mines now worked on Borneo, and a Chinese population of not less than 100,000 souls. Off this part of the coast of Borneo there is a small island affording between itself and the main island a very good harbour, which has been surveyed.

"As the object of the British Government is not extension of territory, and as it would depend for the maintenance of its relations with the native States rather upon the respect with which the national character is received by those States, and an adequate naval force, than on a military power—a military force merely sufficient for the respectability of the flag and the security of the station, is all that would be required. Indeed, it would be desirable to demonstrate to the native States, as well as to the Dutch, that the object of such an establishment is not dominion. It is not likely that a force exceeding five hundred men would, under any circumstances, be required, or that the expense would be greater than what has been incurred at Malacca and Padang (a Dutch dependency on the west coast, now transferred) for the last twenty years. No new expense or increase of establishment is therefore to be calculated upon, as this measure may, in fact, be considered a simple transfer of those establishments.

"Both Prince of Wales['s] Island and Bencoolen have long been losing establishments, the former to the amount of £80,000 a year, and the latter of £50,000 a year, and, now that Malacca and Padang are restored to the Dutch, must prove still more so, as those dependencies were by far the most valuable trading ports of those two settlements. By an eventual reduction of these establishments to a scale which will admit of their paying their own expenses, and connecting them with such a station as I have proposed within the Archipelago, they might mutually assist each other and become a source of wealth and power. The question seems now to be whether the East India Company are content to maintain these two losing establishments in the Eastern seas by continuing the present system, or whether they will, by a small outlay and the acquisition of a third station within the Archipelago, attempt the only feasible means in their power of removing the incumbrance.

"I have confined my view of the dangers to which our trade in the Eastern islands is exposed, to the most imminent of them only; but there are others which, if not absolutely alarming, are still not to be neglected, and against which the same measures which I have recommended are calculated to afford a security.

"The commercial ambition and activity of America, Russia, and France are daily increasing. What is to prevent them from taking possession of those advantages which the Dutch and English, in the extent of their Asiatic dominion, seem to have overlooked?

"Is not Russia extending her influence on all sides? Has not France, in renouncing the Mauritius and all right of erecting forts on the continent of India, acquired a fresh motive for making establishments in the Eastern seas? What could be a more convenient stepping-stone to Siam and Cochin China, with which she has been always so desirous of establishing an intercourse? The Americans have already a considerable trade with the Eastern islands, and are favourably looked upon. Would any of these nations be desirable neighbours?

"Another collateral advantage of an establishment such as I have been recommending, consists in the means it would afford of protecting our commerce against pirates, whose haunts we should be better able to learn, and whose purposes to counteract; another is in the wholesome restraint it would impose upon the conduct of our own countrymen trading in the Archipelago. Our duty to other nations, and to the cause of justice, no less than a regard for our national character, requires that the peaceable natives of the islands should not be kept at the mercy of every mercantile adventurer of our own nation. The inducements and facilities to rapine are too numerous in that quarter to be overlooked.

"Another collateral advantage is in the means we should acquire of maintaining those measures the British Government [has] taken, not altogether without success, for the abolition of the slave-trade in the Archipelago, and in fostering the growth of industry and civilisation among the tribes which have so long been detained in barbarism by that odious commerce.

"Should the attention of the British Government be directed to the importance of civilising Borneo, or of a trade with Japan; should the independent principles now prevalent in South America extend to the Philippine Islands, and an opportunity be offered of instituting advantageous communication with them; such an establishment as I propose would afford important facilities, and, in the meantime, it would enable us to collect such information as might direct our judgment on all these points.

"Having thus endeavoured to show the extent and nature of the trade of the Eastern islands; for what share of it we may still be candidates; to what dangers and difficulties our endeavours to obtain that share are at present subject; by what means those dangers and difficulties may be opposed; and what collateral advantages we might hope to derive from the adoption of those means; I shall now point out the urgency of the moment, the necessity of doing speedily whatever is to be done.

"If we much longer postpone demanding that the engagements which we contracted as Governors of Java and its dependencies shall be fulfilled by the Dutch, and that the relations with the native princes, whether of alliance or independence, which we have recognised while we ruled in those seas, shall be maintained by our successors, our silence will be construed into an abandonment of our right to speak, we shall strengthen what appears to be the best objection that can at present be made to such a claim, viz. that it comes too late, that the Dutch have already pledged themselves to the contrary and cannot retract, especially at our suggestion, without disgrace.

"Again, the impression of British generosity in surrendering the Dutch colonies at all is rapidly subsiding, as is also, among the native chiefs, the impression of our power; and it is clear that, with respect to taking possession of a vacant port, or making a treaty for privileges with an independent chief, the prize is to the swiftest.

"But there is also a particular circumstance which requires our immediate vigilance. An extensive marine is fitting out at Batavia, ostensibly for the suppression of piracy. Unless we go hand in hand in maintaining the general security of the Eastern Seas, and show ourselves immediately as a party interested, so as to share the influence which the display of this armament is calculated to produce on the minds of the native chiefs, it will easily be made the means of resuming that absolute sovereignty over the Archipelago which is the avowed object of the Dutch policy, and which is so highly important to our honour and interest to prevent."

The policy unfolded in this State Paper, which has now

been placed before the public, and is preserved among Lord Bexley's (Nicholas Vansittart) papers in the British Museum, was that on the accomplishment of which Raffles had set his heart. It would have secured all our national requirements, without encroaching on the fair domain of the Dutch; and it justifies what Mr. Charles Assey wrote in his remarkable treatise on *The Trade to China and the Indian Archipelago*, published in 1819, that "it is a tribute justly due to the judgment and foresight of Sir Stamford Raffles to add that, if *his* views and wishes had been carried into execution, a chain of establishments, wholly unconnected with the conquest of Java, and independent of the provisional possession of that island, would have been formed along the track of the China Sea, and would have obtained without difficulty every one of those national objects of which it may with truth be said that the longer they are delayed the greater will be found the necessity of securing them."

If the general question between the Dutch and the English, as represented by Raffles, was a wide one, it was on a comparatively small and definite point that the rupture came. Raffles wished to uphold the sanctity of all the treaties he had signed with the native chiefs of the Archipelago during our tenure of Java; but the case of Palembang seemed to offer a specially favourable instance on which to make a stand. There we had deposed a bloodthirsty tyrant, who had murdered Dutchmen, and installed a more liberal-minded Sultan, who had ceded to us in perpetuity the isles of Banca and Billiton. No European flag had ever been hoisted there when the Union Jack was unfurled by Raffles in 1812. Were these possessions to be pronounced lost because the Congress of Vienna had decreed a restoration of territory, and because Lord Castlereagh had given up Java? The Dutch had never owned them; and it is clear that, in his contentions, Raffles was morally, and by the law of nations, in the right. Unfortunately the question was not understood in England; and, for a time, it was convenient for Ministers to think that Raffles had set his heart on forcing a quarrel with the Dutch, and not that he was endeavouring to uphold national rights without the necessity or the excuse for any quarrel at all.

The Ministry at home wanted to maintain cordial relations with the Netherlands, and was even then considering the exchange of territory that took place a few years later. In the midst of these discussions came the tidings that Raffles had taken a high tone with the Dutch, that he had drawn up a public protest against their proceedings, and that he had even published it.

The point at issue was a simple one. Banca, ceded to us by the Sultan of Palembang, had been ceded by us in turn to the Dutch; but Billiton had not been given up, and Raffles wished to retain it. But above all he wished to preserve Palembang as a "free port." To succeed in this meant a long and sustained struggle with the Dutch for power and influence. With such views it can be imagined how indignant Raffles felt; and how necessary he deemed it to take decided action, when he learnt that the Dutch had sent an expedition to Palembang, deposed the Sultan we had installed, and actually reinstated the prince who was the murderer of their own countrymen. His former colleague in Java, Mr Muntinghe, had been intrusted with these operations, against which Raffles at once made a formal protest. Not content with such an ineffectual mode of procedure, he sent Captain Francis Salmond with a small force across the island from Bencoolen to Palembang. The journey was accomplished in twelve days, and is noticeable as the first effected by any European from one coast to the other. The mission proved a failure, owing to the high-handed and unscrupulous conduct of our rivals. The Sultan dependent on us could only write to Raffles, "I have nothing to send my friend but tears, which never cease to flow." The British officer and his escort were made prisoners, and sent, on board a Dutch man-of-war, to Batavia. It was then that Raffles drafted his Protest, which was published in full in the *Annual Register* for the year 1819; and there is no doubt from what has been stated, and also from the account given of the same events by Mr. Kielstra in the Dutch *De Gids*, translated by Mr. G. G. Batten, that the Government ought to have supported him in that Protest. Instead, however, of affording him support, George Canning was so angry at the publication of the Protest that he wished to recall Sir Stamford from Bencoolen; and Mr. Assey states that it was only on further reflection that the Prime Minister allowed the decision to be left in the hands of the Government at Calcutta. Thus Raffles was once more blamed, when he ought to have been praised and supported; but time brought him, in this as in other matters, some compensation. Five years later George Canning wrote him the following letter, the original of which is in the possession of the Rev. R. B. Raffles:—

"GLOUCESTER LODGE, *Octr.* 11, 1824.

"DEAR SIR,—Far from thinking that the Letter, which you have done me the honour to write to me, requires any apology, I assure you that I am greatly pleased and gratified to learn that the Treaty with the Netherland Govt. respecting our Interests in the Eastern Seas, appears to you to be just in its principles, and satisfactory in its terms.

"There could not be a more competent judgment than yours on such a subject, or one which I should have been more desirous of having in favour of our mode of dealing with it.

"I cannot deny that your extreme activity in stirring difficult questions, and the freedom with which you committed your Government, without their knowledge or authority to measures which might have brought a war upon them, unprepared, did at one time oblige me to speak my mind to you in Instructions of no very mild reprehension.

"But I was not the less anxious to retain those fruits of your policy which appeared to me really worth preserving, and I have long forgotten every particular of your conduct in the Eastern Seas, except the zeal and ability by which it was distinguished.—I have the honour to be, dear sir, your obed. and faithful ser. GEO. CANNING.

"SIR S. RAFFLES."

Curbed and censured by his Government in the endeavour directly to oppose Dutch encroachment, which even took such a form as stopping the postal service between Bencoolen and Batavia, Raffles, as it will be pleasant to show in the next chapter, effectually accomplished his own ends, and secured the position of his country, by the foundation of Singapore. But the conclusion of the Palembang incident led him to write: "I have long given over politics, and, as for the Dutch, I have derived much more satisfaction from the brutes of the forest."

A brief review may now be taken of his residence at Bencoolen; and, so far as is possible, this may be done by reproducing his own correspondence. The condition of the Sumatran population was extremely degraded, and the relations between them and the European settlers were far from cordial. Even the chiefs and the higher classes were kept at arm's length. Sir Stamford at once adopted a different course. He opened his doors; he abolished the bodyguard to which he was entitled; and he went freely among the people. It was, however, mainly to education and missionary effort that he looked for improvement, as the following letters to his cousin, Dr. Raffles, show:—

"At Sea, *9th November* 1819,
"Within three days' sail of Calcutta.

"MY DEAR COUSIN,—As I know the warm interest you feel in our plans of improvement, I lose no time in inclosing under a separate cover a copy of the first proceedings which have been printed of our Bible Society, and a still more interesting account of our Schools. The latter forms but a part of a more general and extensive plan I have set on foot for the spread of knowledge and the growth of moral principles throughout the Archipelago. Much of [my] time has latterly been devoted to these objects, and if I am able to carry my plan for the establishment of a Native College at Singapore, the system will be complete. If you refer to the map and the commanding position of Singapore, situated at the extremity of the Malay Peninsula, you will at once see what a field is opened for our operations. It is very probable that I shall print a few copies of a Paper which I have drawn up on this subject, in which case I shall not fail to send you a copy.

"The Baptist Mission establishment, of which Mr. Ryland is secretary, have lately written to me on the subject of sending out missionaries. My answer is encouraging, and I have accompanied it by some general observations on the plan of conversion. We have already one young man and a small printing press, but we require active zeal, and I shall find enough to do for all you can send out; but let them make haste. Years roll on very fast. Two years have now elapsed since I left England, and in five or six more I hope to be thinking of returning. There is no political objection whatever to missionaries in this part of the East, and so far from obstructing, they may be expected to hasten and assist the plans which are already in operation.

"If the object of my present voyage is accomplished to my satisfaction, I shall look to a much more extensive influence in the further East than I have yet enjoyed; and, although the Dutch come like mildew upon the fairest hopes of the field, it will still be left sufficiently extensive and interesting to occupy the full devotion of my time and thoughts. My immediate influence will be felt over not less than thirty millions, while indirectly and eventually it may include ten times that amount! It is unnecessary to say more, etc. etc.—Devotedly and affectionately yours, T. S. RAFFLES."

The very next day he returned to the subject in a second letter to the same correspondent:—

"Off the Sandheads, Bengal,
"*10th November* 1819.

"MY DEAR COUSIN,—If I had possessed half the enthusiasm and poetry which is in your soul, I should not have been thus long without sending you a companion for your excellent sermon in defence of missionary exertions. That production has always appeared to me unrivalled in its kind, and to do you more credit than any of your other publications, however highly I appreciate them all. In attempting to vie with such a bright and brilliant effusion, the attempt is, perhaps, rather audacious; but, as you have in point of subject the acknowledged vantage ground, you must make allowance for deficiency in this respect. I am no parson, and, as you well know, not given to preaching, but yet I may do some good in breaking up the ground and preparing the soil for ready and advantageous culture. You take all Asia within your grasp. I only claim indulgence for one half—the portion which is least known, but not the least populous. I advocate the cause of thirty millions immediately, and of three hundred millions eventually, and think this sufficient. To be serious, I wish to bespeak your good offices and the exertion of all your energies in support of an institution I am about to form for generally educating the higher class of natives. The enclosed paper will place you in full possession of my views, plans, and anticipations in this respect, and I shall not detain you here by a repetition of them.

"I have written to Mr. Wilberforce on the subject, and am anxious that he should take us under the parental wing of the African Institution. I promise glorious results; and all I ask is support and encouragement, not so much for myself, but to aid and foster a proper spirit in those who must practically assist, and on whom the immediate superintendence and labour must fall when I am over the seas and far away. All improvements of this nature must be slow and gradual, and we should look a good way forward. The short time that I may remain in India will only serve to set the machine in motion; and how uncertain after all is life! Unless some permanent support is found in England, an accident to me might destroy all my brightest anticipations. I know you will commend my endeavours, and I calculate upon your seconding them.

"I also enclose you the first proceedings of our School Committee at Bencoolen, by which you will perceive that we are not idle with regard to the lower orders. This Committee do not take so extensive a view of the state of society, the real character of the people, and the circumstances in which they have been placed, as the Report of another Committee has done, of which I have sent a copy to Mr. Wilberforce. I would recommend your obtaining a perusal of the latter; and should you visit London, that you see Mr. Auber at the India

House, who will give you every information regarding my political and personal plans and prospects. I would wish you indeed to be at all times in communication with him. I am now on my way to Calcutta, in the hopes of forwarding all my plans ; and, if I am successful, you shall soon hear further from me, etc. etc., T. S. RAFFLES."

With the following third letter to Dr. Raffles this part of the subject may be dismissed. It may, however, be noted that his sanguine hopes with regard to these particular missionaries were not realised, and that he expressed the opinion that he could himself have made as much progress in a year as they would do in a century :—

"BENCOOLEN, *17th July* 1820.

"MY DEAR COUSIN,—I have now before me your letter of the 18th December, delivered to me by Messrs. Burton and Evans, who arrived here early in last month, and are both likely to do well for themselves and the good cause in which they are embarked. I like them much, and they seem disposed to meet all my wishes. If anything, they are rather above than below the standard I would have fixed ; and I am fearful they are hardly prepared for the difficulties and privations of missionary life in such a barbarous country as this. They do not, however, appear to want zeal. They are scholars and gentlemen, and their wives are well calculated to aid their endeavours. Mr. Evans and his wife remain at Bencoolen, where they purpose opening a school on the 15th of next month. I have assisted them by placing the children of our Free School under their superintendence and advancing them funds to commence the undertaking. Mr. Burton proposes fixing himself at Tappanooly or Nuttal, in the northern part of Sumatra, with a view to the conversion of the Battas and people of Pulo Nias. The field for his exertions is new and interesting, and I hope he will have energy and courage enough to explore it. The world knows so little of these people, and their habits and customs are so peculiar, that all the information he collects will be useful. You are, of course, aware that they are cannibals. The population of the Batta country does not fall short of a million, and throughout the country it is the invariable law, not only that prisoners taken in war should be eaten, but that capital punishment should also be inflicted by *eating the prisoner alive* for the five great crimes. You may rely on the fact, and that *eating alive* is as common with them as hanging in England. I have lately passed some part of my time in this part of the country, and can vouch for the correctness of what I state. The island of Nias lies off the coast of Sumatra, nearly opposite Nuttal, and contains a population of above a hundred thousand souls. They have no religion whatever, and I am convinced that an active government and zealous missionary may do wonders among them.

"Of our progress at Bencoolen I can now speak with more confidence than when I last wrote to you. The native school has fully answered my expectation, and upwards of seventy children distinguished themselves at the last annual examination. I am now extending the plan, so as to include a school of industry, in which the children will be instructed in the useful arts. The arrival of the missionaries is most fortunate, and I hope they will in time complete what we have so successfully begun. The progress, however, must necessarily be slow.

"I have lately made a very long stride towards the general civilisation of the country, by the establishment of a property in the land, and the introduction of order and regulation, on the principles of a fixed and steady government. You would, I am sure, be gratified with the details, had I time to send them, but my health has not been very good for some weeks, and I dare not write much. Hereafter you shall have all the particulars, and it is not improbable some of them will find their way to the press. My attention is chiefly directed to agriculture, and I am endeavouring to improve the grain produce of the country. This is the basis of all national prosperity; and in countries like Sumatra, constitutes and comprises all that is important. We have an Agricultural Society, of which I am President, in which we discuss without restraint or reserve all questions concerning the produce of the land and the condition of Society. The latter is most peculiar, and not to be explained in few words. You have probably read Bowditch's *Mission to Ashantee.* I think I could give you a picture as striking, novel, and interesting, but this must be reserved for a future period. . . . I sent you a few gods by the *Borneo*, but this is a heathenish country, and we neither have gods of one kind or other,—neither true gods or false gods, neither invisible or visible ones, neither gods of brass or gods of stone. The people of Nias have a few wooden gods, but they are hardly worth sending.

"I have now three children—two boys and a girl—and finer children were never seen. They are in high health and spirits, and show every intelligence and disposition which the fond parents could desire. Mrs. Flint, with her boy, is with us, so is Lady Raffles's brother; and our family circle is, in consequence, pretty large."

Social intercourse seemed to Sir Stamford Raffles one of the means best calculated to attract native sympathy to his person and government. For that reason he was hospitable and easy of access to all. But he also determined to go into the interior, and to visit parts of the island that had never been seen by any of his predecessors, nor even by any European. The old assumption was that a range of impassable mountains traversed the island from north to south. Raffles exposed the baselessness of this statement by several journeys; during which he visited the Hill of Mists, the Sacred Mountain, and the capital of the ancient kingdom of Menangkabu, which was interesting to him from his Malay studies. He discovered, with regard to the country, that it was far richer than any one had conceived; that agriculture was nearly as advanced as in Java; and that, in soil and climate, the interior of Sumatra was in no way inferior to the sister island. He also discovered what a very simple and charming people the Malays of Sumatra are. Lady Raffles provides a very graphic description of these tours, in some of which she accompanied her husband; and the following extract from her Memoir, relating to a journey in 1818 through the Southern Residencies to Passumah, will give the reader a very clear idea of the subject, while it contains at least one incident which reflects equal credit on Raffles and the race over whom he was appointed to govern:—

"The pleasure of this journey was great to Sir Stamford, as it opened to him a field of future usefulness. He saw that it was not only the barren coast which he had to improve, but a country rich in all the bounties of nature, and a people ready and willing to profit by his influence and advice. One old chief, on taking leave, actually fell on his neck and wept; and soon after walked the whole way from Tanjungalum, the most distant place visited, to see him again at Bencoolen. Such simple, uncivilised people are soon won by kindness; they are, like children, easy to lead, hard to drive. It was Sir Stamford's extreme simplicity of mind and manners that rendered him so peculiarly attractive to them, as they are always ready to be kind and attentive, provided they meet with encouragement and sympathy, thus affording a proof that the heart is the best teacher of true politeness. The editor, on reaching Merambung, lay down under the shade of a tree, being much fatigued with walking; the rest of the party dispersed in various directions to make the necessary arrangements, and seek for shelter, when a Malay girl approached with great grace of manners, and, on being asked if she wanted anything, replied, 'No, but seeing you were quite alone, I thought you might like to have a little *bichara* (talk), and so I am come to offer you some *siri* (betel), and sit beside you.' And no courtier could have discussed trifling general subjects in a better manner, or have better refrained from asking questions which were interesting to herself only; her object was to entertain a stranger, which she did with the greatest degree of refinement and politeness."

With regard to Menangkabu, the parent, or at least the imperial, state of the Malayan race, Raffles wrote much. In that district was found the gold which in early days was exported to Malacca, and had made that port famous; there stood the most celebrated Mount Ophir, of which the brother peak was on the mainland; there also the earliest specimens of the Kawi character, which Raffles was fortunate enough to light upon almost by haphazard, were to be traced. Of the capital, Pageruyung, nothing remains except "the large flat stone on which the Sultan used to sit on days of public ceremony."

Perhaps the most interesting of all his discoveries during

any of these tours was that of the gigantic flower, called by the natives Petiman Sikinlili, or Devil's betel-box. The credit of its discovery must be shared between Stamford Raffles and his medical assistant and naturalist, Dr. Joseph Arnold; and when a new name had to be given to it, none was thought more appropriate than the combination of the names of its two discoverers. This vegetable Titan became known, therefore, as *Rafflesia-Arnoldi.* Raffles wrote the following description of it:—

"It is perhaps the largest and most magnificent flower in the world, and is so distinct from every other flower, that I know not to what I can compare it; its dimensions will astonish you. It measured across from the extremity of the petals rather more than a yard, the nectarium was nine inches wide, and as deep; estimated to contain a gallon and a half of water, and the weight of the whole flower fifteen pounds. This gigantic flower is parasite on the lower stems and roots of the Cissus Angustifolia of Bosc. It appears at first in the form of a small round knob, which gradually increases in size. The flower-bud is invested by numerous membranaceous sheaths, which surround it in successive layers, and expand as the bud enlarges, until at length they form a cup round its base. . . . The inside of the cup is of an intense purple, and more or less densely yellow, with soft flexible spines of the same colour; towards the mouth it is marked with numerous depressed spots of the purest white, contrasting strongly with the purple of the surrounding substance, which is considerably elevated on the lower side. The petals are of a brick-red, with numerous pustular spots of a lighter colour. The whole substance of the flower is not less than half an inch thick, and of a firm fleshy consistence."

We have now reached a melancholy period in Raffles's life; and it commenced, to a certain extent, with the discovery of that flower. Raffles's description of it is given in a letter to the Duchess of Somerset, dated the 11th of July 1818. On the 26th of that month Dr. Joseph Arnold died at Padang, after a few days' fever, which originated in the hardships of that inland journey. Dr. Arnold was an able and enthusiastic naturalist. He had served during the Corunna expedition, of which he gave a vivid description in a diary; and also in the Mediterranean, during the later years of the European struggle. In 1815 he performed a remarkable journey from New South Wales to Java; and in 1817 he was recommended to Raffles by Sir Joseph Banks. He belonged to a family of hereditary merchant-adventurers long resident at Lowestoft and Beccles. One of his ancestors, Thomas Arnold, had been chief-constable of the former place in 1574; another bearer of the same name died as captain in the Royal Navy in 1773; and a third had served under Lord Anson, when he circumnavigated the globe. Of Dr. Joseph Arnold, Raffles wrote: "He had endeared himself to Lady Raffles and myself by his most amiable disposition and unassuming manners; he formed part of our family, and I regret his loss as that of a sincere friend. To the best disposition he added a most cultivated mind; and, in a public point of view, his loss will be severely felt."

But far worse blows were to follow. In a number of letters to his mother, written during the year 1818, Raffles reveals his love of children, and his special affection for his own. His daughter with the poetic Javan name of Tunjong Segára was also named Charlotte, after the Princess Charlotte and the Duchess of Somerset, and she is described in one of these letters as being "as lovely and beautiful as an angel"; his elder son, Leopold, called after Prince Leopold, is declared to be "forward for his age and already quite companionable"; and the younger son, Stamford Marsden, was "doing wonderfully well, and will not fall short of the others." Here is another tender reference to his children in a letter to the Duchess of Somerset: "My dear little Charlotte is, of all creatures, the most angelic I ever beheld. She has those inborn graces which, as she expands, must attract the admiration of everyone; but she has a soft heart, and is so full of mildness and gentleness, that I fear she will have many trials to go through in this unfeeling world. Her brother Leopold, however, will take her part, for he has the spirit of a lion, and is absolutely beautiful; but I will not tire you with any more family matters." Yet one more extract from this correspondence will complete this picture of domestic happiness. "Charlotte and Leopold manage to talk two or three languages, and are a great source of satisfaction to us." In a letter, written after the death of the Princess Charlotte in 1817, to Colonel Addenbrooke, late equerry to that Princess, Raffles said:—

"Your account of our amiable and invaluable Prince has given me the greatest satisfaction. He has indeed had his trials; my heart overflows when I think of him and of his sufferings; and though far removed and separated from the passing scene, be assured I listen with no common interest to all that is said of and about him.

"I have told you that Lady Raffles has presented me with a son and a daughter; from the circumstance of the latter having been born on the voyage, the Javans, who are a poetic people, wished her to be named Tunjong Segára, meaning Lotos of the Sea; and a more appropriate name for purity or innocence could not have been conceived. I gratified their wish, but at the same time my own, by prefixing a more Christian and a more consecrated name, 'Charlotte.' My son has been christened Leopold; and thus will Leopold and Charlotte be commemorated in my domestic circle as names ever dear and ever respected; and that of my daughter, while associated with the emblem of purity, handed down in remembrance of one whose virtues will never be forgotten."

Such was the happy circle into which the dread visitant forced his way in the year 1821, desolating the hearth and blighting the hopes thus recorded.

From Bencoolen, on the 29th of January 1822, Sir Stamford wrote to Dr. Raffles as follows:—

"For the last six months I have been so completely unnerved that I have scarcely written to any of my friends at home. We had hardly recovered the loss of Sophia's eldest brother, when poor Auber was carried off after a few days' illness. A week after this we lost our eldest boy, Leopold, and, on the 4th of this month, Marsden, our only remaining boy, followed him to the grave. This has not been all, on the 14th we lost Charlotte, our eldest girl, and are now nearly childless!!

"To these severe and trying afflictions I have to add the loss of nearly all our best and tried friends in this country, and that both Sophia and myself have suffered most seriously from long and alarming illnesses. From the latter we are now fortunately somewhat recovered; but our hearts are nearly broken, and our spirits sunk, I fear not to rise again,—at least in this country.

"In order to save, if possible, our only child, Ella, an infant, we propose sending her to England immediately. This will be another trial for Sophia; but I have great confidence in her strength of mind; and if her constitution does but stand, I shall persevere for a year or two more. You will, however, be glad to hear we are now looking homeward. These events, and the injury my constitution has suffered, have brought us to the determination of leaving India at all events early in 1824, and I have written home for a successor accordingly. So that, at all events, I must go then. We never were very covetous of affluence, and riches are now of less value to us than ever. Under existing circumstances, I prefer an honourable retirement to a longer perseverance, to the complete ruin of our health and future comfort. This is a very hasty scrawl: but it may serve to account for my not writing more at length, and to give you the assurance that in all our afflictions we do not forget you. God's will be done; and we must be satisfied. Indeed, we ought to be grateful for what is left, etc., T. S. R."

The following extracts from two further letters complete the sad story; but with regard to his daughter, Ella Sophia, sent home in charge of Nurse Grimes, it may be interesting to state that she was the only one of all Sir Stamford's children who grew up, and that she herself died before she was twenty, in the year 1841, at St. Leonards-on-Sea.

On the 17th of April 1822 he again writes to Dr. Raffles from Bencoolen:—

"We now pass our time in great retirement. I have lately completed a very comfortable country house, and much of my time is taken up in agricultural pursuits. I am by far the most active farmer in the country, and, as President of the Agricultural Society, not only take precedence at the board, but in the field. I have a dozen ploughs constantly going; and, before I quit the estate, I hope it will realise a revenue of two or three thousand a year, besides feeding its population. It is an experiment: but it will encourage others, and, as it is a property which belongs to the Company, no one can accuse me of interested views in the efforts I am making. It is possible that in England I may look with interest to the returns in money which my oats and barley may afford, but here I am quite satisfied with seeing and collecting the produce of my industry and exertions, keeping my mind and hands clear and clean from any pecuniary consideration whatever. I am cultivating and improving for the mere love of the thing, and the desire of employing my time advantageously for others.

"Our sugar at last proceeds very well, but the disappointment in the mills, etc., has been great indeed. Probably it may occasion a total loss of expected advantages, not less than £2000. It was only a few weeks ago that I received the letters from Messrs. Littledale. We then immediately set to work to construct a mill here as well as we could, and it has now commenced to work at the rate of half a ton a day. The sugar is excellent, and I have no doubt the rum will be of equally good quality. This is the first of my mechanical operations, for which I take to myself no little credit, considering our want of assistance and experience. We took our model from the *Encyclopedia*, etc.,

"T. S. RAFFLES."

In the Straits of Banca, on the 1st of October 1822, he again writes to Dr. Raffles :—

"Our correspondence has latterly flagged, though I hardly know why, except it be that we may neither of us have had heart or spirit enough to enter on the sad subjects which have most absorbed our attention. You will, I think, be glad to hear that we have quitted Bencoolen for a season, for, though I still adhere to its being, on the whole, as healthy as other parts of the East, the melancholy events which have accumulated in our own family must produce a contrary impression on all who look to us with interest and affection. Death, as if he seemed determined to glut himself to the last, snatched from us two days before we sailed another member of our family, my invaluable and highly-respected friend, Dr. Jack. He had supplied the place of Dr. Arnold ; and all my future views in life were intimately blended with plans and projects which we had formed. He was to accompany me to England, and has left a blank which will not be easily or speedily filled up. I am now on my passage to Singapore, accompanied by Sophia and her younger brother ; and my plan is to remain there about six months, with the view of arranging and modelling something like a constitution for the place, and transferring its future management to a successor. Should God spare our lives, we then look to return to Bencoolen for the purpose of winding up ; and then, about the end of the year, if it is not too presumptuous to look forward so far after what has passed, we contemplate the prospect of revisiting old England. At all events, no views of ambition, no chances of pecuniary advantage, will weigh with us beyond that period ; and, considering the precarious state of our health and the many ties at home, it seems in the natural course of things that we should then take this step.

"From Bencoolen I sent you the second volume of our *Malayan Transactions*, which I think you will find much more interesting than the first. I doubt whether we shall get another out during my stay in India. Our schools, etc., do not go on so prosperously as I could have wished, and I am by no means satisfied with the conduct or zeal of our Baptist missionaries, who have disappointed me not a little. On this subject, however, I may communicate to you more fully hereafter ; and, as I have allowed them an opportunity to retrieve their character during my absence, I am unwilling to go into the question at present. From my friend, Mr. Milne, and the London Missionary Society's agents, I expect a more satisfactory result ; and I am still sanguine in my hope that Singapore will stand foremost in effecting the grand object of Christian civilisation and improvement."

To the loss of Dr. Jack in 1822 was added, in 1823, that of Captain Francis Salmond, brother of Colonel Salmond, of the India Board, and of whom Raffles wrote : "My dear and valued friend Salmond is no more. This last blow has been almost too much for us ; for Salmond was as dear and intimate with us as our family. I have just opened his will, and find he has nominated me as his sole executor in the following words :—'I appoint my *only* friend, Sir Stamford

Raffles, to be my executor; and I pray to God he will take charge of my estate and children.' The loss of poor Salmond is quite a deathblow to the settlement. How is it that all we love and esteem, all those whose principles we admire, and in whom we can place confidence, are thus carried off, while the vile and worthless remain?" Four years before those lines were penned Salmond had written, in a letter to his sisters, "Our Governor is a good friend of mine, and his lady a most pleasant woman. The rest of our settlement only so so."

It was without regret, and, indeed, with a lively sense of gratification, that Sir Stamford Raffles made his preparations to leave Sumatra; but the following letter shows that his interest in its condition remained unabated to the last; although the attempt to stir up the East India Company to pay any heed to the requirements of this settlement was like flogging a dead horse. They were sick of the west coast, and wished to get rid of it,—a wish soon to be gratified. Raffles had done his best in Sumatra, as he had done in Java, but his efforts were all in vain. His project of introducing English colonists gradually to the number of twenty or thirty thousand was scouted, but he could at least declare of Bencoolen itself, that, before he left, it "no longer exhibited the melancholy and forlorn aspect in which I found it." The following letter to Dr. Raffles is dated from Bencoolen, on the 15th of November 1823:—

"This circumstance [the birth of another daughter had been followed by Lady Raffles's illness from fever], added to the state of my own health, which does not improve, makes me extremely anxious to quit a place where we can look back with so little satisfaction, or forward with so little confidence. We hope to obtain a conveyance in the course of a month or two, or, at all events, to get away in the course of February or March, so as to be with you about July.

"I have already informed you that I resigned the charge of Singapore, and of all questions with the Dutch, in June last, as preparatory to my winding up on this coast, and proceeding to Europe. I enclose you a printed copy of the address presented to me on the occasion by the merchants of the place, with my reply, which will show you the sort of policy which I wish to support at that settlement. I have heard nothing more of the question with the Dutch, but I doubt not that it will be agitated on my arrival in England. I rely more on the support of the mercantile community than upon any liberal views of the Ministry, by whom I have been opposed as much throughout as by the Dutch.

"Of this place I have nothing at present very particular to communicate, or that will not as conveniently be left for personal intercourse; but it will be satisfactory to you to know that we are doing wonders with our schools, and that our Bible Society is not inactive. The two missionaries whom we have here, Messrs. Robinson and Ward, are very zealous, and Reports are now framing to be laid before the general meeting on the 1st of January, which will, I hope, prove that we have not been inactive, and that the results are as great as we could rationally have expected in so short a time.

"I entreat you, however, not to make use of my authority, on this or other subjects, in the *Investigator*, except with my previous consent, as the folks in this country are very apt to take advantage of any unguarded expression. The only point of political interest that may be worth your noticing is the following, to which you can easily give publicity by saying that accounts from Sumatra have been received to such and such effect.

"Considerable interest has lately been excited by the progress in Sumatra of the Mahometan sect usually termed the Padries, or more correctly, the Putehs or Whites, in opposition to the Etams or Blacks; by which latter term they designate all who do not embrace their doctrines.

"It was to the ravages of these people that I alluded in my account of the journey to Menangkabu, as having repeatedly pillaged and burnt the capital of that celebrated seat of Malay empire; and it is with them that the Dutch, since their occupation of Padang, have been involved in a desperate and relentless war, neither party giving quarter, and prices being set upon the heads of the principal chiefs.

"The first notice of this powerful sect, which had its origin near Mount Ophir, was about ten years ago; but it has been during the last three, and principally since the occupation of Padang by the Dutch, that it has become formidable, and occasioned alarm for the safety of the European settlements on the west coast of Sumatra.

"The policy of the British Government has hitherto been that of neutrality, considering that the question related principally to peculiar doctrines of Mahometanism, in which the natives might be best left to themselves; but the success of the Padries during the last year, in which they have overrun nearly the whole of the rich and populous countries of the interior, has at length called for measures of decision even on the part of the British authority. A considerable force was detached from Bengal in September last direct to Nuttal; and measures are in progress for the adoption of offensive measures, should negociation fail. The tenets of the Padries require that all Mahometans shall refrain from the use of opium, from cock-fighting, and other Malayan vices; that they should wear a peculiar dress, and submit to ecclesiastical authority. The Malays who form the population of the coast districts are averse to this change, as altering their habits and departing from their ancient customs; and the European Governments are actually employed in protecting them against the improvement which would necessarily follow from their adoption of the tenets of the Padries. . . . The resources of these people seem considerable, and their engagements with the Dutch have taught them to know their own strength. Their power in the interior of Sumatra may now be considered as completely established; and various speculations are formed as to the result.

"We thus see one of the finest islands in the world, on which we have had establishments for upwards of a century without once venturing to improve the condition of the people, or to send one Christian missionary among them, giving way before the desolating influence of the false Prophet of Mecca, and becoming rapidly a strong Mahometan resting-ground, with our eyes open and with scarcely one effort made by ourselves to oppose them by a purer faith. The missionaries we have lately employed in Sumatra are too few in number to do much: that they will do good, as far as their influence reaches, there can be no doubt; but that influence will long be limited to our own immediate stations, unless we encrease their numbers. Instead of three missionaries we ought to have three hundred; and the object of these three hundred should, in the first place, be to initiate three thousand of the natives to act as missionaries in the interior. There are yet hundreds of thousands, perhaps millions, in Sumatra who, at this moment, possess no religion at all. Among these we may include the Battas. The Padries are now on their very borders, with the Koran in one hand and the sword in the other; and the only missionary we have is an isolated individual, residing under the protection of the British factory at Tappanooly, but who has not the means of penetrating into the interior. This individual, however (Mr. Burton), has translated part of the Scriptures into the Batta language, and his success in this respect is highly praiseworthy to his application and character: but alone he can do little beyond the influence of our own factory, which does not extend one mile inland."

In Java, Raffles had been all for the tenants, and had adopted the ryotwari system; but in Sumatra he saw that the same course would not do, and supported feudalism. At least this showed breadth of mind, and the following extract from a letter dated Bencoolen the 22nd of July 1820, bears on the subject:—

"I have assumed a new character among them, that of Lord Paramount; the chiefs are my barons bold, and the people their vassals. Under this constitution, and by the establishment of a right of property in the soil, I am enabled to do wonders, and if time is only given to persevere in the same course for a few years, I think I shall be able to lay the foundation of a new order of things on a basis that shall not easily be shaken. My attention is at present principally directed to agriculture: an Agricultural Society has been established, of which I am President, in which we discuss, without reserve, all questions which relate to the produce of the soil and the people who cultivate it. Agriculture is everywhere the only solid basis of national prosperity, and in countries like Sumatra it constitutes and comprises nearly all that is valuable and interesting."

While Raffles was pleading for time to enable his measures to bear fruit, and was hoping to raise Sumatra from its slough of misery and depression, by making it a field of British colonisation, the East India Company was only thinking of how to be quickly and finally relieved of its possession.

I may conclude this chapter with the significant and dramatic passage of arms between Raffles and the Baron Van der Capellen, the Dutch Governor of the Indies at Batavia. In June 1823, Raffles, accompanied by his wife, arrived in Batavia Roads, on board the ship *Hero*. He had decided not to land himself, but he requested permission from the baron for his wife to land, as she was "in a very delicate state of health, and suffered much at sea." Van der Capellen addressed him a letter in very bad French, stating that "Raffles's visit could only be extremely disagreeable to him," but conceding a grudging permission for Lady Raffles to land "during a few days." Raffles said in a letter to a friend, "Had Bonaparte returned to life, and anchored in the Downs, it would not have excited greater agitation in England than my arrival has done here. Here fear and apprehension are everything; and to these all courtesy, principle, and interest give way." The late Sir Henry Yule, by no means an enthusiastic admirer of Raffles, said: "The correspondence that passed is very amusing, and Raffles's reply to the letter of the Dutch baron, whose apprehensions had made him forget his good manners, is an inimitable example of the application of the lash with unexceptionable politeness but with stinging severity on every line. Sir Stamford did not land, but for the week that the ship lay in Batavia Roads the people were not to be restrained, and all ranks flocked to visit their lost British Governor."

The following is the text of the letter to which Sir Henry Yule alludes:—

"To His Excellency Baron VAN DER CAPELLEN.

"SIR,—Your Excellency's letter was delivered to me during the night.

"I am sorry that what was intended merely as a mark of respect, should have given rise to the extreme surprise which you express. I felt it right to inform your Excellency of my being in the roads of Batavia, and I stated the circumstance which had led to it.

"You would appear to have been misinformed, in supposing that it was my intention or my desire to land or court a personal interview. My landing in Java, while under your Excellency's government, could only have been attended with painful feelings, public as well as private, and there certainly has been nothing in the conduct of your Excellency which could have rendered me particularly desirous of personal communication or acquaintance.

"I caused it to be publicly known before I embarked, that I neither intended nor wished to land ; and under these circumstances I trust you will admit, that the proscription you have thought proper to issue might, in common courtesy, have been delayed, until a solicitation on my part might have called for it. Your Excellency also appears to have been misinformed, when you state that I might or should have avoided touching at Batavia, knowing how disagreeable it would be to you. I can assure you it was a matter of absolute necessity, in every way against my wishes and feelings ; though I must say, I never for a moment supposed it would have given rise to any apprehensions or unpleasant feelings on your part. You have, sir, thought proper to refer to political differences, and to the complaints which you have thought proper to make against my proceedings, which you considered to be directed against the interests of your Sovereign ; on which it is necessary for me to call to your recollection, that I have at least had similar grounds of complaining of some of the proceedings of your government, and that the very acts on my part, which you call into question, arose solely from a conviction, that such proceedings on your Excellency's part were directed against the interests of my country. The decision, as to whose views on the subject have been most correct, remains with higher authorities ; and while I cheerfully give your Excellency the credit of having acted as you deemed best for the interests of your country, I hope you will judge equally charitably of the motives which may have dictated my conduct.

"I have thought the above explanation due as well to your Excellency as myself, as I should have presumed you to have been as incapable of offering a personal incivility, as I am of receiving one without noticing it as it deserves.

"I did not, sir, consider it necessary to request your permission for Lady Raffles to land, as I could not suppose it to be so in the present state of civilised society, but I have now respectfully to request that, as she is in delicate health, your Excellency will ensure her a safe passport to the ship whenever she may be desirous of re-embarking.—I have the honour to be, etc.,

"T. S. Raffles."

CHAPTER X

THE FOUNDING OF SINGAPORE

In order to appreciate the full merit and value of the service Sir Stamford Raffles rendered to his country in founding the colony and city of Singapore, it is necessary to take into consideration the chief incidents of the long rivalry with the Dutch to which the acquisition of that island placed for Great Britain a victorious conclusion. The triumph was the more signal because it was achieved at a time when it seemed least likely of attainment; for, as Raffles wrote in one of his letters, "the Dutch had hardly left us an inch of ground to stand upon." At such a juncture it was scarcely to be hoped that we should obtain possession of a place which, from its superior natural advantages, would entirely overshadow and supersede all the Dutch colonies and ports in the Eastern Archipelago. The history of the complete transaction about to be recorded will show that the whole credit is due to Raffles, in a greater and more unlimited sense than has been thought, and that he secured the prize in the teeth of the opposition, disparagement, and censure of the Supreme Government at Calcutta, and of the Secret Committee of the East India Company at home. The story will corroborate Gordon's memorable saying, that —England was never made by her politicians, but by her adventurers; and the name of Raffles will stand in history as one of those far-sighted and adventurous sons, side by side with the names of Warren Hastings and the other builders of our Eastern Empire.

In the sixteenth century the Dutch, aided by subsidies and other support from England, did something for the cause of liberty in Europe. Having achieved their own independence, they have done everything in their power, during three centuries, to keep every race brought into contact with them under a yoke of servitude; they have systematically pursued the policy of excluding others from every mart and island that has come within their sphere of authority; while their highest object was always to secure a monopoly for themselves. What was true in Japan and Java in the seventeenth century, and throughout the Eastern Archipelago during the eighteenth century, has been not less evident in the Transvaal. Domesticity is a Dutch virtue; in colonial affairs it was exhibited in the refusal to allow any stranger to cross the threshold. Those who opposed Alva and the Inquisition on the Scheldt, were themselves the tyrants and the torturers at Surat, Batavia, and Nagasaki. The massacre of Amboyna in 1624, with the impaling of the English prisoners, stands on a par with the Black Hole tragedy in Bengal, but it was perpetrated by one race of Europeans upon another, similar in creed as well as in colour, to whom, moreover, the perpetrators then stood recently indebted for loyal comradeship on the field of Zutphen. The massacre of the Christians in Japan, the expulsion of Jesuit influence, the closing of the English factory at Firando,—all due to Dutch intrigue and incentive,—were occurrences that did not redound to the credit of the most enterprising European nation in the Far East. They were traders; but the sweetness of trade, in their opinion, consisted more in excluding others from having a share in the profit than in the magnitude of the profit itself. If, from a general survey, we pass to details, the impression left is still more striking. What Dutch rule signified in Java has been shown. The state of the island was revealed in depopulation, discontent, and a bankrupt exchequer. The inhabitants were ruled by a code of laws which sanctioned torture, and inflicted capital punishment for trivial offences. Among the blackest pages of European colonisation are those recording the work of the Dutch in the Eastern Archipelago. A patriotic Dutchman would wish to have the whole record obliterated.

The Castlereagh Convention of 1814 provided for the restoration to the Dutch of all the possessions they had held on the 1st of January 1803. When they resumed possession of Java, they regained the colony in a vastly improved condition, and with a much increased revenue. These greater resources, due to British energy and ability, were perverted to the purpose of extending Dutch and restricting British influence. When the British Government, out of its excessive generosity, ignored Billiton, ceded Banca, refused to support Raffles in his protests about Palembang on one side of Sumatra, and Padang on the other, and generally allowed the Dutch to think that Great Britain did not care one jot for the whole of the Archipelago, the opportunity was afforded for our historic rivals to extend their possessions and influence around the southern points of the Malay Peninsula. Raffles alone saw clearly their purpose and their policy; but, unfortunately, his own Government had been led to adopt the view that he was set on involving it with the Dutch, and that his judgment was not to be trusted in any matters at issue with them. A prolongation of this period of indifference would inevitably have given the Dutch complete command of the Straits of Malacca, and would have left us no spot of territory to secure for our own necessities and requirements. Fortunately Raffles grasped the full significance of the situation before it was too late; and the improvement that took place in his relations with the Governor-General, the Earl of Moira, now raised to the Marquisate of Hastings, provided him with an opening, which he promptly seized.

The Marquis of Hastings had not been very cordial, or even fair, in his exculpation of Raffles on Gillespie's charges; but increased knowledge of the Java administration, and possibly Mr. Fendall's favourable opinion of Raffles's work had modified his views of the latter's ability, and in 1818 Lord Hastings was ready at least to admit that Raffles was an able administrator. Raffles wrote to the Governor-General advising him of his safe arrival at Bencoolen, and asking permission to visit Calcutta for the purpose of bringing the position of Sumatra and of affairs in the Archipelago under the immediate attention of Government. He had much gratification in receiving the following reply:—

"*July 6th*, 1818.

"SIR,—I have the honour to acknowledge your letter, and to offer my congratulations on your safe arrival.

"It was painful to me, that I had, in the course of my public duty, to express an opinion unfavourable to certain of your measures in Java. The disapprobation, as you would perceive, affected their prudence alone; on the other hand, no person can have felt more strongly than I did your anxious and unwearied exertions for ameliorating the condition of the native inhabitants under your sway. The procedure was no less recommended by wisdom than by benevolence; and the results have been highly creditable to the British Government. I request you to consider yourself at liberty to carry into execution your wish of visiting Bengal, whensoever your convenience and the state of affairs in the Island may afford an eligible opportunity. The means of rendering the settlement at Bencoolen more advantageous to the Honourable Company than it now appears to be, are certainly more likely to be struck out in oral discussion.—I am, etc.,

"HASTINGS."

Raffles, with opportunities, that could not be recovered, slipping through his fingers every day, was prompt to take advantage of the Governor-General's permission to visit him at Calcutta.

"Sir Stamford," writes Lady Raffles, "embarked in a very small vessel, which had no better accommodation than one small cabin, with only a port-hole to admit air, where centipedes and scorpions roved about without interruption; but personal convenience was never considered by him if it interfered with duty, and no better opportunity was likely to occur. The vessel lost a mast in the Bay of Bengal, and, owing to a drunken pilot, was literally upset in the middle of the night upon a dangerous bank at the mouth of the river Hooghly, where Sir Stamford was obliged to remain until boats were sent from Calcutta to take him out of the vessel."

He arrived early in October 1818; and he at once placed two matters before Lord Hastings as being of pressing importance. One was the situation in Sumatra itself, and the other was the encroachment of the Dutch, and the imperative necessity thereby created for Great Britain to secure some post south of Malacca and ensuring the passage through the Straits. On the former point he was unsuccessful. Lord Hastings decided to concede to the Dutch their pretensions in Sumatra: and it is sufficiently clear that he was induced to take this step in deference, partly to instructions from home, and partly because he was already favouring the exchange of territory subsequently effected in 1824–26 by the surrender of Bencoolen for Malacca. But, on the latter point, Raffles brought Lord Hastings round to his way of thinking; and the Governor-General at last realised that, for the preservation of the national interest, it was obligatory for the Government of India to strike a prompt and decisive blow in the very quarter where the Dutch had been carrying all before them. At that stage Raffles wrote the following letter to his friend Mr. Marsden:—

"CALCUTTA, *October* 16, 1818.

"To WILLIAM MARSDEN, Esq.

"MY DEAR SIR,—You will be happy to hear that I have made my peace with the Marquess of Hastings, and that his Lordship has at last acknowledged my exertions in Java in flattering terms. This was one object of my visit to Calcutta, and on it depended, in a great measure, the success of the others. I am now struggling hard to interest the Supreme Government in the Eastern islands; and the measures taken by me at Palembang, etc., will, I doubt not, lead to the advantage of some defined line of policy being laid down for the future. With regard to the Dutch proceedings at Palembang, of which I hope you are, ere this, fully apprised, Lord Hastings has unequivocally declared, that his mind is made up as to the moral turpitude of the transaction, and that he considers this but as one of a course of measures directed in hostility to the British interests and name in the Eastern Seas. My despatches are now under consideration, and it is uncertain what may be the immediate result. There is but one opinion in regard to the manner in which our interests have been sacrificed by the transfer of Java, etc., and it is clear that the Government at home will be called upon from hence to interfere for the security of our trade; but in the meantime, and pending the reference to Europe, I fear that nothing decisive will be done. Lord Hastings is, I know, inclined to recommend our exchanging Bencoolen for Malacca, and to make the equator the limit. . . . They [the Government at Calcutta] possess no information which can assist the decision in Europe; what they forward will be obtained from me; and I am not aware of any advantage which will arise from delaying a decision till their references arrive. Every day, every hour, that the Dutch are left to themselves, their influence increases, and our difficulties will be proportionally increased."

The result of this visit to Calcutta was, therefore, the establishment of something like friendly relations between

Raffles and the Governor-General. The written documents will show what those relations exactly were: but Raffles believed them to be more completely and perfectly cordial than they proved to be in reality. In the inner mind of Lord Hastings a doubt of his associate in the enterprise seems to have survived; and even if there had been no such doubt, the angry and disparaging despatches of the Secret Committee at home, a committee bitterly hostile to Raffles,—whose friends on the Board had all their influence tasked to prevent its procuring his final recall,—would still have produced some uncertainty in the Governor-General's mode of dealing with his subordinate of Bencoolen. Still, while Raffles had made up his mind that he could rely on Lord Hastings—whose last words were, "Sir Stamford, you may depend upon me,"—and quoted freely his confidential *verbal* instructions from the Supreme Authority in India, the Governor-General does not seem to have decided in his own mind anything more than that something had to be done in the Straits, and that Raffles was the only man available to attempt it. He did not give Raffles his entire confidence; and consequently he would, as will be seen, have backed out of the business altogether at the first check, only his emissary was too prompt and too strong for him. When Raffles left the Hooghly to discover a post south of Malacca, the die was cast. He knew the hostility and vacillation of his superiors, and it would have been folly to have allowed them the chance of undoing their own deeds.

On the 14th of November 1818, Raffles wrote from Calcutta to Mr. Marsden:—

> "I have now to inform you that it is determined to keep the command of the Straits of Malacca, by forming establishments at Acheen and Rhio, and that I leave Calcutta in a fortnight, as the agent to effect this important object. Acheen I conceive to be completely within our power, but the Dutch may be beforehand with us at Rhio."

And again, from the same place, he wrote to the Duchess of Somerset, on the 26th of November 1818:—

"I have at last succeeded in making the authorities in Bengal sensible of their supineness in allowing the Dutch to exclude us from the Eastern seas; but I fear it is now too late to retrieve what we have lost. I have full powers to do all we can; and if anything is to be done, I think I need not assure your Grace that it shall be done—and quickly done."

As the precise nature of the Instructions given to Raffles by Lord Hastings are most important, and have never been published, I give the full text of the official documents preserved in the Political Department of the India Office:—

"To the Honourable Sir THOMAS STAMFORD RAFFLES, etc. etc.

"HONOURABLE SIR,—In pursuance of the intention signified in my letter of the 10th of October, addressed to you and Captain Coombs, I have now the honour to communicate to you the instructions of the Governor-General in Council for the regulation of your proceedings in the execution of the separate duties which it is his Lordship's purpose to confide to your management, after the conclusion of the negotiations of Acheen.

"2. The proceedings of the Dutch Authorities in the Eastern seas, as represented to this Government by your despatches, and those of the Governor in Council of Prince of Wales's Island, leave no room to doubt that it is their policy, by possessing themselves of all the most commanding stations in that quarter, to extend their supremacy over the whole Archipelago. The success of this project would have the effect of completely excluding our shipping from the trade with the Eastern islands, except on the terms which the Dutch Authorities might impose, and would give them the entire command of the only channels for the direct trade between China and Europe, which, under circumstances easily supposeable, without contemplating actual hostilities, would greatly impede the prosecution of that valuable commerce.

"3. Under these impressions it appears to the Governor-General in Council to be an object of essential importance to our political and commercial interests, to secure the free passage of the Straits of Malacca, the only channel left to us since the restitution of Java and the other Dutch possessions. It is chiefly with this view that the proposed arrangement at Acheen has been determined on without further reference to the authorities at home; but the most material point to attain, and that which will indeed constitute the only effectual means of accomplishing the object of securing a free passage, is the establishment of a Station beyond Malacca, such as may command the southern entrance of those Straits.

"4. The Port of Rhio appears, from all the information before the Governor-General in Council, to possess the greatest advantages for this purpose. Its position, just beyond the entrance of the Straits, exactly in the track of shipping passing in or out of them, enables it effectually to command both the Straits of Malacca and of Sincapore. The harbour is capacious and well adapted for the safety and supply of shipping. The Dutch possess no right, and have as yet stated no pretension to interfere with the independence of this state, which is generally acknowledged. The disposition of the native authorities to cultivate an intimate connection with us, which has probably been strengthened by their apprehension of the designs of the Dutch, may be inferred from the alacrity with which they entered into the engagement, lately proposed to them by Major Farquhar, under the authority of the Government of Prince of Wales's Island, while that engagement offers the most favourable opening for improving and confirming our connection with the Government of the country.

"5. The arrangements formed by Major Farquhar might indeed suffice for all our purposes, which are purely commercial, and quite unconnected with any views of political power or extension of territory, if there were any security for their permanency against the possible designs of the Dutch. But although those engagements provide for the freedom and security of our commercial interests, they do not go to the exclusion of the political ascendency of the Dutch, which, if once established, would speedily be followed by the annihilation of the independence of the Native Government, and consequently of our commercial privileges. The recent proceedings of the Netherlandish authorities at Pontiana, as exhibited in Major Farquhar's report, form a strong ground for apprehension that they will not hesitate to employ their preponderant naval and military power, for the destruction of the independence of any of the Malay states, where they may wish to establish a control, and that no intercourse would be permitted between the states thus falling under their power and British subjects, excepting on the terms they might think fit to impose.

"6. The maintenance of our existing engagements, therefore, with the Chief of Rhio and other states in that quarter, as well as the more general objects adverted to in this despatch, seem to point out the necessity of supporting the arrangements made with those states, by measures of a different character from what under other circumstances would have been necessary.

"7. Of these, as already observed, the improvement of our connection with Rhio and the establishment, if practicable, with the consent of the Native Government of a British Post there, are the most likely to answer the object we have in view, without involving us in any discussions with the Netherlandish Power.

"8. In the event, therefore, of the Dutch not having preoccupied Rhio, and its being practicable to obtain the footing required by means of negotiations with the native chief, it is the desire of the Governor-General in Council that measures should be immediately taken for permanently establishing the British interests at that port, and His Lordship is pleased to confide the negotiations and arrangements directed to this object to your judgment and discretion.

"9. It is expressly to be understood, and it will be incumbent on you always to keep in mind, that the object in fixing upon a Post of this nature is not the extension of any territorial influence, but strictly limited to the occupation of an advantageous position for the protection of our commerce.

"10. Your familiarity with the nature and objects of the measures in contemplation, and your intimate acquaintance with the character of the people, render it superfluous to furnish you with any specific instructions regarding the mode of opening and conducting the negotiation.

"11. The precise nature of the arrangement to be concluded is also left to your judgment, governed by the general principles already stated. His Lordship in Council is assured that you will omit no effort to accomplish the object in view, in the manner most desirable for the security of our interests, and most satisfactory to the native authority. The long experience and peculiar qualifications of Major Farquhar, the late resident at Malacca, and his late employment at Rhio and Lingen, eminently fit him for the command of the Post which it is desirable to establish, and the local superintendence of our interests and affairs. Major Farquhar will accordingly be instructed to accompany you to Rhio, and, in the event of your concluding a satisfactory arrangement with the native authority, you will leave that officer at Rhio, under such instructions as circumstances may dictate, and consider yourself at liberty to proceed to Bencoolen, where your presence will be required. Whatever troops and stores may be necessary in the first instance, are to be furnished by the Governor in Council of Prince of Wales's Island, who will receive the instructions of the Governor-General in Council on the subject.

"12. In the arrangements contemplated by the Governor-General in Council, for the security of our interests in the Eastern Seas, and of which those now directed at Acheen and Rhio form the most important that can be effected under the authority of this Government, pending the references made to Europe, it is the intention and desire of his lordship to consider Acheen, and all interests within the Straits of Malacca, under the immediate superintendence of the Government of Penang, and to place our relations with Rhio and Lingen, and the general management of our interests beyond the Straits of Malacca, under your immediate control as Lieutenant-Governor of Bencoolen. A communication to this effect has been made to the Government of Prince of Wales's Island, from whom you will receive the most cordial assistance and support in the execution of the measures confided to you.

"13. An application has been made to His Excellency, the Naval Commander-in-Chief, that a frigate may be appointed to proceed to Prince of Wales's Island for the purpose of conveying you to Rhio and eventually to Bencoolen, and arrangements are in progress for permanently stationing two of the Company's cruisers to the eastward. One of these will be available for the service of the Post to be established at Rhio, but to provide against any delay in its arrival, or in that of the frigate at Prince of Wales's Island, and to enable you to dismiss the surveying vessels as already directed, you are apprised that measures have been taken for engaging and equipping a vessel in this port, which will be at your disposal for the service of the present mission, and eventually for your conveyance to Fort Marlborough.

"14. Copies of the Treaties concluded by Major Farquhar with the Chiefs of Rhio, Lingen, and Siack, and of his despatch to the Government of Prince of Wales's Island, are enclosed for your information. Siack being within the Straits, the further arrangements with that state will fall within the province of the Government of Prince of Wales's Island, but it is proper you should be apprised of our relations with it. Lingen is closely connected with Rhio, and you will, of course, follow up the Treaty concluded by Major Farquhar with the former, by such measures as may be requisite for supporting our interests there, conformably with the principles explained in this despatch. It will probably not be requisite to form any establishment at Lingen, but this is a point which must be determined by further information and observation on the spot. A very limited establishment, at all events, will be sufficient.

"15. The allowances received by Major Farquhar, as Resident at Malacca, will constitute a proper scale of remuneration for the duties which it is now proposed to assign to him. You will fix provisionally, and subject to the confirmation of the Governor-General in Council, the other salaries and establishments that may be requisite for giving effect to the several measures now contemplated, and you will be sensible of the importance of attending to economy in all the arrangements now conditionally authorised.

"16. You will receive from the Persian Secretary, credentials to the Chiefs from the Governor-General, of which English drafts are herewith transmitted. You are already provided with suitable presents.

"17. These instructions are framed under an impression that the Dutch have not formed any establishment at Rhio. In the event of their having done so at the period of your arrival, you will, of course, abstain from all negotiation and collision, and observe the same line as is pointed out in the event of such an occurrence at Acheen.

"18. A copy of the letter addressed to the Government of Prince of Wales's Island by the Governor-General in Council on the subject of this despatch, is enclosed for your information, and you will communicate immediately with Colonel Bannerman on all points connected with the present service.—I have the honour to be, etc. etc. (Signed) J. ADAM,

"*Chief Secretary to Government.*

"FORT-WILLIAM,
"The 28*th November* 1818."

These instructions were supplemented a week later in the following further despatch:—

"To the Honourable Sir THOMAS STAMFORD RAFFLES, etc. etc.

"HONOURABLE SIR,—Since the Instructions contained in my letter of the 28th ultimo were presented, it has occurred to the Governor-General in Council, that in the event of the previous occupation of Rhio by the Dutch, or other circumstances preventing the accomplishment of our views at that port and at Lingen, it might be expedient to endeavour to establish a connection with the Sultan of Johor on the same footing as is now contemplated with Rhio and Lingen.

"2. The position of Johor renders it nearly, or perhaps entirely, as convenient a post for our purpose as Rhio; but the imperfect information possessed by the Government, both of the local circumstances of the town and harbour and the condition and relations of the State of Johor, induce the Governor-General in Council to prefer a connection with the Chief of Rhio, and his immediate superior, the Rajah of Lingen, if it be practicable. For the same reason it will be incumbent on us, even if we find ourselves excluded from the latter, to act with caution and circumspection before we enter into any engagements with a State of which we know so little as Johor.

"3. It will be necessary therefore, in any event, to make a previous inquiry with a view to obtain correct information on the following points:—

"1st. The local capabilities of Johor for a British port, such as we are desirous of establishing at the mouth of the Straits of Malacca; the extent and capacity of the harbour, means of supply, and other points of this nature.

"2nd. The actual political condition and relations of the State of Johor, the degree of independent authority exercised by the Chief—his power of maintaining any engagements which he may contract, his relations with other States, especially the Dutch settlement at Malacca, and the Government of Siam. There is some reason to think that the Dutch will claim authority over the State of Johor by virtue of some old engagements, and, though it is possible the pretension might be successfully combated, it will not be consistent with the policy or present views of the Governor-General in Council to raise a question of this sort with the Netherlandish Authorities. You are aware also of the considerations which make the Governor-General in Council reluctant to engage in any measures that would bring us into collision with the Government of Siam.

"4. In the event of our views at Rhio and Lingen being unattainable, and of the information you may procure concerning Johor being entirely satisfactory on the points above adverted to, you will be pleased to open a negotiation with the Chief of Johor, and carry into effect at that place an arrangement similar to the one at present contemplated at Rhio.

"5. In the contemplation of your having recourse to this measure, a letter has been addressed to the Chief of Johor by the Governor-General, and amended credentials comprehending that State have been prepared. You will receive both those documents from the Persian Secretary, and will make use of them according to your discretion in the case, and under the reservations stated in this letter.—I have the honour to be, etc. etc.,

(Signed) "J. ADAM,
"*Chief Secretary to Government.*

"COUNCIL CHAMBER,
5th December 1818."

What, therefore, Raffles was instructed to do, in consequence of the Dutch attempt to extend their supremacy over the whole Archipelago was this:—He was to secure "the establishment of a station beyond Malacca, such as may command the southern entrance of those Straits" (*i.e.* of Malacca). The Port of Rhio was mentioned as the most likely place; and, with unjustifiable confidence, it was alleged that the Dutch had no rights or pretensions there. The new post, "with the general management of our interests beyond the Straits of Malacca," was to be placed under the control of Raffles as Lieutenant-Governor of Bencoolen. The supplementary instructions are of the greater importance, because they applied to the actual situation with which Raffles had to deal. If the Dutch had already occupied Rhio, he was to endeavour to establish a connection with the Sultan of Johore; and if the information obtained proved entirely satisfactory as to the capabilities of its port, he was to conclude with that prince the desired and necessary arrangement.

Such were Raffles's instructions. What was passing through his own mind may be gathered from the following letter to Mr. Marsden, written immediately after his departure from Calcutta. It is a very significant document, because it contains his first specific reference to Singapore, and showed that he had already thought that this old capital and mart, the Lion City of the Malays, might be revived as a British station:—

"*Nearchus*, off the Sandheads,
"*December* 12, 1818.

"To Mr. MARSDEN.

"MY DEAR SIR,—We are now on our way to the eastward, in the hope of doing something, but I much fear the Dutch have hardly left us an inch of ground to stand upon. My attention is principally turned to Johore, and you must not be surprised if my next letter to you is dated from the site of the ancient city of Singapura.—Yours, etc.,

"T. S. RAFFLES."

His fear that the Dutch had not left him an inch of ground seemed to be verified when, on arriving at Prince of Wales's Island, he learnt that they had occupied Rhio. He wrote mournfully, "By neglecting to occupy the place we lost Rhio"; but this loss strengthened his conviction that Singapore offered the only spot which would enable us to counteract the Dutch efforts. In a despatch, dated 1st January 1819, to Colonel Bannerman, that is to say, within the first twenty-four hours after his arrival at Penang, Raffles described the object of his mission as being—"To make a stand in some Post eastward of Malacca, where the Dutch may not have preoccupied, and where, in support of our arrangements, we may maintain the British flag flying, pending the reference which must necessarily be made to higher authorities." Further on, in the same letter, occurs this memorable passage: "The island of Singapore, or the Districts of Old Johore, appear to me to possess peculiar and great advantages in this respect."

It seemed for a brief space as if further delay must ensue: for Raffles's instructions were to proceed first to Acheen; and after some days he sent Major Farquhar eastwards on an errand to Rhio. That officer was on the point of leaving for Europe, and was only induced by Raffles's efforts to defer his intention. In consequence of the objections raised by the

Governor of Prince of Wales's Island to the course the Governor-General had decided on in Acheen, Raffles consented, at Colonel Bannerman's pressing request, to defer that part of his mission, pending a reference to Calcutta. Colonel Bannerman's "earnest entreaty" to Raffles was dated 18th January, and the latter's reply was given the same day. On the 19th Raffles sailed south, with the object of catching up Major Farquhar. That officer strongly recommended the Carimon islands in the Straits of Malacca, and Raffles, with a personal predilection for the Singapura associated with Malay history, and with instructions to negotiate at Johore, had still a sufficiently open mind to induce him to yield to Major Farquhar's request to go out of his way and examine the advantages of a possible station on that group. Raffles did more than this, for he sent Captain Ross to survey it. His report was unfavourable; and an interesting private letter from someone on Ross's ship, describes "Carimon as a perfect jungle, and not calculated for a settlement." After Raffles left Penang, he met Farquhar returning from Rhio, and together they proceeded to Carimon. The proposal to occupy it had been put forward by Farquhar in October 1818, and the Penang authorities had described it as fantastic and injudicious. The Supreme Government had pronounced its advantages very inferior to those of Rhio, and, after inspection, both Raffles and Farquhar agreed that it would not meet the requirements of the case. Before Raffles proceeded to Carimon, the site of the new station had been practically settled in his own mind, for, in addition to the letter of 1st January and the earlier note to Mr. Marsden, already quoted, he wrote the following letter to Mr. Adam, the Secretary to the Supreme Government, under date 16th January 1819, almost a fortnight before the occupation of the island of Singapore. It exists among the Political Records of the Government of India:—

"The island of Sincapore, independently of the straits and harbour of Johore, which it both forms and commands, has, on its southern shores, and by means of the several smaller islands which lie off it, excellent anchorage and smaller harbours, and seems in every respect most peculiarly adapted for our object. Its position in the straits of Singapore is far more convenient and commanding than even Rhio, for our China trade passing down the straits of Malacca, and every native vessel that sails through the Straits of Rhio must pass in sight of it.

"The town of Johore is, in the main, at some distance up the river, the banks of which are said to be low; but, on the score of salubrity, there does not seem to be any objection to a station at Sincapore, or on the opposite shore towards Point Romanea, or on any of the smaller islands which lie off this part of the coast. The larger harbour of Johore is declared by professional men whom I have consulted, and by every Eastern trader of experience to whom I have been able to refer, to be capacious and easily defensible, and, the British flag once hoisted, there would be no want of supplies to meet the immediate necessities of our establishment."

This official despatch, which amplifies the views set forth in the letter of 1st of January, and the reference in the letter to Mr. Marsden, already quoted, are the written comments made by Raffles on the subject of Singapore *before* its occupation; but Lady Raffles states in her memoir that "even before he left England [in 1817] Sir Stamford contemplated this, to him, classical spot as a place favourably situated to become a British station." In one of his own letters, to be hereafter quoted, Raffles states that his knowledge of Singapore was derived from his own Malay studies. As Singapore was a dependency of the Sultan of Johore, the evidence seems tolerably conclusive that it was Raffles himself who prompted the enlargement of his instructions by the permission, if Rhio was occupied, to negotiate with that potentate. Such an assumption is strengthened by the fact that Raffles, on leaving Calcutta, and while still off the Sandheads, sent orders to Bencoolen for the relieved troops from that place to return to Bengal by the Straits of Sunda, so that he might fall in with them on his journey south of Malacca, and, in case of necessity, avail himself of their services. This arrangement was another proof of his forethought; but, as it turned out, his instructions did not reach Bencoolen until March, by which time the fate of Singapore had been settled. Raffles was called to account for this step of his in moving troops; but, in the pressure of other matters, and owing to the point not arising until after it had been decided to retain Singapore, the measure was condoned. But we cannot overlook its significance as showing his determination to succeed in the task of establishing a post commanding the straits.

Having, at the earnest request of Major William Farquhar, the same officer who had protested against the demolition of Malacca, and who had worked with Raffles in the collection of information at that place in 1811 for the Java expedition, gone out of his way to inspect Carimon, Raffles sailed onwards for Johore. His little squadron consisted of four vessels in all, and they cast anchor on the 28th of January, off the island of St. John's. The natives came out in boats, and, to Raffles's inquiry whether there were any Dutch, a negative answer was promptly given. The next morning Raffles landed on the main island of Singapore, near the present Esplanade, and on this spot he hoisted the Union Jack on the morning of the 29th of January 1819. On the following day he concluded a preliminary arrangement with the Sultan of Johore and the Tumung'gung of Singapore; and on the 5th of February a definite treaty was signed by Raffles and the two chiefs named, by which, in return for an annual payment of 5000 dollars to the former, and 3000 dollars to the latter, those princes ceded the settlement of Singapore to the English, and pledged themselves to grant "no treaty or settlement to any power, European or American."

The date of the occupation and founding of Singapore has been variously given. In Lady Raffles's Memoir the day is erroneously, and perhaps through a slip of the pen, recorded as the 29th of February 1819—an impossible date. So usually careful a writer as Sir Henry Yule put it in his Glossary as the 23rd of February; but when the Rev. R. B. Raffles wrote pointing out that the date must be the 29th of January, Yule admitted the mistake, and, without controversy, accepted the emendation. In connection with the statue to his cousin at Singapore, unveiled in 1887, Mr.

Raffles also wrote to the Governor on this question ; and, in a volume of the Straits Branch of the Royal Asiatic Society, entitled *Notes and Queries No.* 4, issued with No. 17 of the Journal, his letter setting right this important point is duly recorded. I may add that in the records of the Political Department at the India Office, the correct date is given, viz. the 29th of January 1819.

In a lengthy despatch, dated 13th February 1819, to Mr. Adam, Secretary to Government, Raffles wrote : " I have now the satisfaction to report, for the information of the Most Noble the Governor-General in Council, that those objects have been fully and substantially accomplished, and that a British Station commanding the southern entrance of the Straits of Malacca, and combining extraordinary local advantages with a peculiarly admirable geographical position, has been established at Singapore, the ancient capital of the King of Johore, on terms and conditions which I trust will meet the approbation and confirmation of his Lordship in Council." Raffles then proceeded to state that, in the first place, he went, at Major Farquhar's request, to Carimon, but " the position on the whole was not sufficiently inviting. I accordingly proceeded to Singapore, where I found a harbour I believe unrivalled in these seas, either with reference to its extent or to the shelter and safety which it affords." On arriving at St. John's, the natives assured him that the Dutch authority was unknown, and that Rhio possessed no authority over Johore. Raffles concludes by expressing his confidence that the Dutch could prefer no valid claim to Singapore.

From a very early period of his residence in the East, Raffles had been on the lookout for a harbour which would provide safe and ample accommodation for a large fleet ; and it is only reasonable to suppose that his mind was directed to this object by the naval preparations for the expedition in 1811, and by conversations with Captain Greigh. He thought at one time that he had discovered the desired object in Banca, where there was a natural harbour which would hold the English navy, and later on in the neighbouring island of Billiton. His last discovery in 1818, before leaving Bencoolen for Calcutta, was the harbour of Caloombyan in

Samangca Bay, in the Straits of Sunda. The one uppermost thought of all those years was the discovery of a harbour and naval station, such as would place England in a position of equality with the Dutch in the Eastern Archipelago. It was his dominant idea; and when he surveyed the wide roadstead of Singapore, peacefully sheltered by the isles and yet on the high road to the Far East, he saw at a glance that he had at last attained his heart's desire. It was at such a moment that he poured out his innermost thoughts to his friends in what might truly be called a pæan of victory. On the 22nd of February 1819 he wrote from Penang to the Duchess of Somerset:—

"I have also to communicate to you a political event of great import, namely, the accomplishment of the great object which I have always had in view, by forming a permanent British establishment in the Malayan Archipelago, by which the progress of the Dutch supremacy may be checked, and our interests, political and commercial, secured. It has been my good fortune to establish this station in a position combining every possible advantage, geographical and local; and if I only meet with ordinary support from the higher powers, I shall effectually check the plans of the Dutch. . . .

"I must, however, tell you where you are to look for it on the map. Follow me from Calcutta, within the Nicobar and Andaman Islands, to Prince of Wales's Island, then accompany me down the Straits of Malacca, past the town of Malacca, and round the south-western point of the Peninsula. You will then enter what are called the Straits of Singapore, and in Marsden's map of Sumatra you will observe an island to the north of these straits called Singapura; this is the spot, the site of the ancient maritime capital of the Malays, and within the walls of these fortifications, raised not less than six centuries ago, on which I have planted the British flag, where, I trust, it will long triumphantly wave."

In a letter, written from Singapore on the 10th of June 1819, to Colonel Addenbrooke, late Equerry to Her Royal Highness Princess Charlotte, Raffles obviously intends to acquaint Prince Leopold, through the Colonel, with his success in the Eastern seas:—

"I shall say nothing of the importance which I attach to the permanence of the position I have taken up at Singapore; it is a child of my own. But for my Malay studies I should hardly have known that such a place existed: not only the European, but the Indian world was also ignorant of it. . . . I am sure you will wish me success; and I will therefore only add, that if my plans are confirmed at home, it is my intention to make this my principal residence, and to devote the remaining years of my stay in the East to the advancement of a colony which, in every way in which it can be viewed, bids fair to be one of the most important, and at the same time one of the least expensive and troublesome, which we possess. Our object is not territory, but trade; a great commercial emporium, and a *fulcrum*, whence we may extend our influence politically as circumstances may hereafter require. By taking immediate possession, we put a *negative* to the Dutch claim of exclusion, and at the same time revive the drooping confidence of our allies and friends. One free port in these seas must eventually destroy the spell of Dutch monopoly; and what *Malta* is in the West, that may *Singapore* become in the East."

It was, perhaps, to his friend, Charles Assey, that he wrote with the fullest detail, both because that gentleman's knowledge of the Straits was very extensive, and because Mr. Assey's views closely coincided with his own. The extract from Sir Stamford's letter is included in the covering letter from Mr. Assey to Dr. Raffles:—

"BECCLES, SUFFOLK, *August 9th*, 1819.

"MY DEAR SIR,—Having very lately received from Sir Stamford Raffles some intimation of his proceedings on the mission upon which he was sent in November last, I do myself the pleasure of communicating them to you.

"Upon his arrival at Penang he found the Government at that place wholly indisposed towards his plans, and of opinion that it was useless to make any attempt in the Straits of Malacca, in consequence of the ascendency which the Dutch had obtained—in short, I am sorry to find that he is at issue with the Governor of Penang on this subject, and their respective Minutes will no doubt have come before the Higher Authorities: however, he persevered, and has been successful, having formed an Establishment at Singaporra, in the Straits of Sincapore. He says:—

"'You will be happy to hear that the Station of Singapore

contains every advantage, geographical and local, that we can desire—an excellent harbour, which I was the first to discover; capital facilities for defence to shipping if necessary; and the port in the direct track of the China trade. We have a flag at St. John's [St. John's Island, where the quarantine station has been placed], and every ship passing through the Straits must go within half a mile of it—in short, you have only to ask any India captain his opinion of the importance of this station, even without the harbour which has been discovered. Mynheer will probably enter into a paper war on the subject; but we may, I think, combat their arguments without any difficulty. They had established themselves at Rhio, and by virtue of a treaty, which they had forced the Raja of that place to sign, they assume a right of excluding us from all the islands and declaring the people their vassals. The legitimate successor to the empire of Johor is with us, and, on the ruins of the ancient capital, has signed a treaty with us which places Sincapore and the neighbouring islands under our protection. We do not meddle with the Dutch at Rhio.'

"I am entirely out of the way of learning what effect the receipt of these despatches has had, but I was informed that Ministers were, about ten days ago, in consultation with regard to the interests of this country in the Indian islands; and it is to be hoped that the actual arrival of this moment, when the encroachments of the Dutch have very nearly come to the point of shutting out our trade from every port between Penang and the Moluccas, will induce Ministers to adopt a decided policy: it is due to the population of these countries that they should not be thus abandoned; the peculiarity of their situation, the want of those prejudices which fetter the Hindoo tribes, and the disposition they have shown to receive the customs and the religion of Europe, ought to prevent their being left in the state of vassalage and of darkness in which the Dutch dominion will retain them; but, unless the public voice declare against it, I fear that the welfare of millions in that part of the world will weigh but little in the scale against the convenience and policy of European Continental objects. Would it be possible to interest the commercial world also, and to unite in a general feeling towards the Eastern Archipelago? I cannot help thinking that some of the members of Administration are aware of the importance of the moment, and that Mr. Canning would be disposed to listen to the suggestion of his Liverpool friends on this subject. But these, my dear sir, are perhaps only flights of imagination, which are owing to the perfect conviction I feel of the national importance of the object.—I remain your very faithful servant,

"C. Assey."

What Raffles thought about and anticipated from the occupation of Singapore may be brought to a conclusion with the two following interesting letters, one to Mr. Marsden, and the other to his cousin, Dr. Raffles :—

"SINGAPORE, *January* 31*st*, 1819.

"TO MR. MARSDEN.

"MY DEAR SIR,—Here I am at Singapore, true to my word, and in the enjoyment of all the pleasure which a footing on such classic ground must inspire. The lines of the old city, and of its defences, are still to be traced, and within its ramparts the British Union waves unmolested. . . . It is only now left for me to solicit your support in behalf of my more recent attempt to extend the British influence. Most certainly the Dutch never had a factory in the island of Singapore ; and it does not appear to me that their recent arrangements with a subordinate authority at Rhio can or ought to interfere with our permanent establishment here. I have, however, a violent opposition to surmount on the part of the Government of Penang. . . .

"This place possesses an excellent harbour, and everything that can be desired for a British port in the island of St. John's, which forms the south-western point of the harbour. We have commanded [probably a misreading for "here command"] an intercourse with all the ships passing through the Straits of Singapore. We are within a week's sail of China, close to Siam, and in the very seat of the Malayan Empire. This, therefore, will probably be my last attempt. If I am deserted now, I must fain return to Bencoolen, and become philosopher. . . . I expect to conclude all my arrangements at this place in the course of a few days, and then to return to Penang, where I have left Lady Raffles, and my anxiety to get there, on her account, is very great. From Penang my course will probably bend towards Acheen, where I have to establish the British influence on a permanent footing ; from thence I shall proceed to Bencoolen. . . . If I keep Singapore I shall be quite satisfied ; and in a few years our influence over the Archipelago, as far as concerns our commerce, will be fully established."

The letter to Dr. Raffles is dated from Bencoolen, July 17th, 1820, when the fate of Singapore was still far from certain :—

. . . .

"My settlement of Singapore continues to thrive most wonderfully. It is all and everything I could wish, and if no untimely fate awaits it, promises to become the emporium and the pride of the East. I learn with much regret the prejudice and malignity by which I am attacked at home for the desperate struggle I have maintained against the Dutch. Instead of being supported by my own Government, I find them deserting me and giving way in every instance to the unscrupulous and enormous pretensions of the Dutch. All, however, is safe so far ; and, if matters are only allowed to remain as they are, all will go well. The great blow has been struck ; and though I may personally suffer in the scuffle, the nation must be benefited. I should not be surprised were the

Ministers to recall me ; though I should on many accounts regret it at the present moment.

"Were the value of Singapore properly appreciated, I am confident that all England would be in its favour. It positively takes nothing from the Dutch, and is to us everything. It gives us the command of China and Japan, with Siam and Cambodia, Cochin China, etc.—to say nothing of the Islands themselves. What you observe regarding the introduction of British cottons through this port to China is a most important question. The affair is perfectly practicable, and nothing more easy. I had framed a plan, and am still bent upon the object ; but, until I know from England how I am to be supported in what I have so far done, it would be premature to suggest any speculation. Confirm Singapore and establish my authority in the Archipelago on the principle I have suggested, and it will not be long before there is abundant demand for this description of our manufactures at least. Upwards of 10,000 tons of raw cotton are annually sent to China from our territories in India. Why should we send our raw produce to encourage the industry of a foreign nation at the expense of our own manufactures ? If India cannot manufacture sufficiently cheap, England can ; and it is idle to talk of the cheapness of our goods unless we can bring them into fair competition. I see no reason why China may not be in a great measure clothed from England. No people study cheapness so much ; and, if we can undersell them, we have only to find the way of introducing the article. The monopoly of the East India Company in England, and of the Hong merchants in China, precludes the idea of anything like fair competition in our own ships, or at the Port of Canton. Not but the East India Company can, and perhaps will, assist as far as in them lies ; but their ships are too expensive ; the articles would also pass through the Hong merchants before they reached the general trader and consumer ; and their intermediate profits would form another barrier.

"At Singapore, however, every object may be obtained. Let the Commercial interests for the present drop every idea of a direct trade to China, and let them concentrate their influence in supporting Singapore, and they will do ten times better. As a free port it is as much to them as the possession of Macao ; and it is here that their voyages should finish,—the Chinese themselves coming to Singapore and purchasing. They have the means of importing into the different ports of Canton without the restraints and peculations of the Hong merchants. Many of the Chinese Viceroys are themselves engaged clandestinely in external trade, and Singapore may, as a free port, thus become the connecting link and grand *entrepôt* between Europe, Asia, and China. It is, in fact, fast becoming so. Vessels come from China to Singapore in five days.

"All will however depend on its remaining under good government, and the port being regulated on the principles I have laid down. What these are you may learn from Mr. Auber [Deputy-Secretary] at the India House, who is fully apprised of all my views and plans."

It will be proper to give the text of the proclamation notifying the occupation of Singapore. After one week's negotiation with the Sultan, Raffles was able to issue the following :—

" PROCLAMATION.

" A Treaty having been this day concluded between the British Government and the native authorities, and a British Establishment having been in consequence founded at Singapore, the Honourable Sir T. S. Raffles, Lieutenant-Governor of Bencoolen and its dependencies, Agent to the Governor-General, is pleased to certify the appointment by the Supreme Government of Major William Farquhar of the Madras Engineers to be Resident, and to command the troops at Singapore and its dependencies, and all persons are hereby directed to obey Major Farquhar accordingly. It is further notified that the Residency of Singapore has been placed under the Government of Fort Marlborough, and is to be considered a dependency thereof; of which all persons concerned are desired to take notice.

" Dated at Singapore this 6th day of February 1819."

In accordance with his instructions, Raffles thus appointed Major William Farquhar first Resident of Singapore, under his authority as Lieutenant-Governor of Bencoolen, and under conditions that may be more specifically described in connection with Farquhar's later proceedings. Having thus initiated the undertaking, Raffles sailed northwards to Penang, there to take up the other half of his commission in relation to the Acheen affair. He expected trouble from the Dutch; but when he left Penang about the 15th of February, he had no idea how bitter the opposition from the British authorities at that place was to prove. Sixty-five years later the *Singapore Free Press* of the 4th of October 1884, in commenting on Sir Stamford Raffles's proclamation and the accompanying letter of instructions to Major Farquhar, wrote: " It is impossible to read the letter, which is too long to print here, without remarking the great foresight and high-minded policy of the writer. It contained instructions of a political nature which after events proved to have been almost prophetic."

When Malacca came into our hands in 1826, some very curious native documents, with Dutch translations of them, throwing light on Raffles's movements, were found among the archives of the Governor. In February 1819, Tuan Raja Tumung'gung wrote to the Governor of Malacca describing the arrival of Raffles and Major Farquhar, and stating that the latter had gone to Rhio, while Raffles remained at Singapore, landing his men and his stores and announcing his intention of remaining there. He also goes on to say that Tunku Long, a native rajah, arrived from Rhio, and that Raffles thereupon acknowledged him as Sultan of Johore, under the style of Sultan Hussein. Sultan Hussein wrote to the Sultan of Rhio explaining his flight, and apologising for having allowed himself to be proclaimed Sultan, but none the less retaining the position and dignity in which the English authorities had installed him. At the same time, he and his associate, the Bandahara of Pahang, addressed these explanatory letters to the chief at Rhio and the Dutch governor, with the view of securing their own retreat if the Dutch should prove more than a match for the English. There was nothing strange in such feelings and subterfuges, considering the influence and reputation of the Dutch; but the following letter from Major Farquhar will show the exact value of these communications. Farquhar having heard, after Raffles's departure, of the Dutch protest, wrote to Colonel Bannerman, Governor of Prince of Wales's Island, as follows:—

"HONBLE. SIR,—Having obtained what I conceive to be authentic information that the Governor of Malacca has addressed a letter to you intimating that the British Establishment recently formed at Singapore has been effected in a forcible manner without the previous consent of the Local Authorities of the country, and having at the same time ascertained that this information has been grounded on a letter from hence by his Highness the Tumung'gung to Mr. Adrian Kock of Malacca, I beg leave herewith to transmit an explanatory document, signed by Tunkoo Long, Sultan of Johore, and the Tumung'gung of Singapore, which will no doubt remove every doubt which may have arisen in your mind relative to the proceedings which have taken place.

"I must also take the liberty to request that in the event of the erroneous statement the Honble. Mr. Timmerman Thyssen is said to have transmitted having been received and subsequently forwarded on to the Supreme Government, you will have the goodness to transmit a copy of the present despatch for the information of the Most Noble the Governor-General by the first opportunity.—I have the honour to be, etc. etc.,

WM. FARQUHAR, *Resident.*"

"SINGAPORE, 1*st March* 1819."

" ENCLOSURE.

"This is to make known to all whom it may concern, that our friend Major William Farquhar, British Resident of the Settlement of Singapore, has called upon me to declare whether or not any letter or letters have been written by me to the Governor of Malacca, or to any person under his authority, or to the Rajah Mooda of Rhio, intimating that the factory which the English have recently established here was forcibly formed entirely against my will ; I hereby freely acknowledge that I did write a letter to Mr. Adrian Kock of Malacca, and one to the Rajah Mooda of Rhio, to the above effect, but my motive for so writing arose solely from the apprehension of bringing on me the vengeance of the Dutch at some future period.

"But I here call God and His Prophet to witness that the English established themselves at Singapore with my free will and consent ; and that from the arrival of the Honourable Sir Thomas Stamford Raffles no troops or effects were landed, or anything executed but with the free accord of myself and of the Sultan of Johore. In token of the truth whereof we have hereunto affixed our respective Seals."

"At Singapore this 1st day of March 1819.

"A true translation.

"WM. FARQUHAR, *Resident, etc.*"

Major Farquhar's information was correct. The Governor of Malacca had protested against the British occupation of Singapore on the 10th of February 1819, on the ground that the Dutch had signed à Treaty, on the 26th of November 1818, with the Sultans of Johore, Pahang, Rhio, Lingen, and dependencies, by which they had obtained an exclusive right to found a station. There was nothing extraordinary about this Dutch protest. It was a document Raffles fully expected as a commencement for the inevitable paper war he foresaw, and had prophesied in his letters. What made it extraordinary, what almost produced the very dangers and collision the Governor alleged it to be his desire to avoid, was the unparalleled action of Colonel Bannerman, the English Governor of Prince of Wales's Island. On receiving this protest from the Dutch Governor, he forwarded it to Calcutta, with a supporting Minute of his own ! This was bad enough ; but, when a mere rumour reached him that the Dutch were fitting out an expedition at Batavia, he sent the following pusillanimous letter to the Dutch Governor of Malacca. England has reason to be proud of the many great men who have contributed to her fame ; but there have been others who have done what they could to mar the achievements of their wiser and bolder countrymen. Among the latter must be ranked Colonel J. A. Bannerman.

"To the Honourable J. S. TIMMERMAN THYSSEN, Esq.,
"Governor of Malacca.

"HONBLE. SIR, — Information having reached me that the Netherlanders' Government of Java are, it is strongly believed, preparing to send up a force with orders to seize the English detachment posted at Singapore under the command of Major Farquhar, I conceive it is a duty I owe to you, as much as to myself, to apprise you immediately that the whole subject respecting the occupation of that island was referred by me to the Most Noble the Governor-General on the 17th ultimo, and that his Lordship's reply may be expected before the expiration of twenty or thirty days from this date.

"Pending this reference therefore, motives of humanity I hope you will allow, as well as the undoubted duty of preserving undisturbed the very friendly relations subsisting between our respective countries, call upon us to adopt ourselves and to recommend to the Netherlands Government of Java the same moderation and goodwill as have hitherto attended the transactions between your Government and mine. With this view I have a right to expect that you will join your best endeavours with mine in deprecating any such violent measure on the part of the Java Government as would lead to a cruel effusion of blood and excite a collision between Great Britain and Holland.

"I am the more induced to make this appeal to you as Sir Stamford Raffles is not under the control of this Government, and I am really unacquainted with the nature of the reply he may have returned to your communication of the Treaty existing between your Government and the Kingdom of Rhio, etc.—I have the honour to remain, etc. etc., J. A. BANNERMAN.

"P. W. ISLAND, *17th March* 1819.

"*P.S.*—I have the honour to add that Sir Stamford Raffles is now absent from this settlement."

The extraordinary baseness of this despatch sent to a quasi-hostile Power, was rendered the more glaring by the fact that Colonel Bannerman was already in possession of Major Farquhar's urgent request for reinforcements to enable him to hold the post of Singapore against the attack then threatening from Batavia. Colonel Bannerman turned a deaf ear to that request, until he received a sharp warning, as will be shown, from Bengal. The following is the text of Major Farquhar's appeal:—

"To the Honourable J. A BANNERMAN, Esq.,
"Governor in Council, Prince of Wales's Island.

"HONBLE. SIR, — I consider it an indispensable part of my duty to transmit for your information by an express prow the enclosed copy of a letter which I have just received from Captain D. Ross, commanding the Honourable Company's ship *Discovery*, containing intelligence of a very extraordinary and important tendency. As you are fully acquainted with the strength of the party at present doing duty here, I feel assured that you will adopt such measures as you conceive the nature of Captain Ross's report and the urgency of the present case may demand. In the meantime I have only to say that everything here shall be held in readiness, as far as our means will admit, to resist any hostile attack on the part of the Batavian Government. We are at present much in need of a supply of money, and have no means of procuring any here.—I have the honour to be, etc. etc., W. FARQUHAR.

"SINGAPORE, *6th March* 1819.

"*P.S.*—Permit me to request that the despatch-boat may be sent back without loss of time."

"ENCLOSURE.

"To Major W. FARQUHAR.

"DEAR SIR,—On my way down the Straits I called at Malacca, and think it but right that you should be acquainted with my having learned from undoubted authority that the Governor of Malacca, about eight days ago, sent off a despatch to Batavia, recommending very strongly that a force should be sent up to seize the party now at Singapore, and urging the facility with which such a measure may be accomplished when they are not to receive reinforcements immediately. My authority is very good, and, had I not determined on calling here, I was about to take up a prow to convey the above information to you. It would appear to be from some information which the Governor received by a Malay ship from Penang, which induced his immediately sending off to Batavia.—I remain, etc., D. ROSS.

"*6th March* 1819."

Notwithstanding that application, Bannerman refused to send any aid; and, in the following despatch, reminded Farquhar that the resident at Singapore had in his own hands the means to remove his party from the threatened position. With the prevalence of such a spirit among the representatives of Great Britain in the Eastern Archipelago, surprise will cease to be felt at the fact that the Dutch had maintained their exclusive system so well and so long. The following is Colonel Bannerman's letter to Major Farquhar:—

"To Major W. FARQUHAR.

"SIR,—I have the honour to acknowledge the receipt this day of your letter of the 6th instant.

"The intelligence you have thought it your duty to communicate to me, although very important, you must have been well aware could excite no surprise in my mind, in as much as you were personally and distinctly apprised by me before you quitted this island, that you were proceeding in an undertaking which was in violation of the orders of the Supreme Government, and which would expose you to a hostile attack from the Netherlanders.

"I have now, therefore, to enclose for your information copies of two important Letters lately received from the Supreme Government on the subject of the Dutch occupation of Rhio, and a copy of the correspondence which passed between Sir Stamford Raffles and myself after his arrival from Singapoor.

"Although it is not the province of this Government to furnish you with any instructions, yet a perusal of the enclosed documents may serve to guide your judgment, how far you will be justified in shedding blood in the maintenance of your post, and particularly after the communication made to the Netherlanders by the Chiefs of Johore and Singapoor, which will certainly induce them to consider every resistance on your part as adding violence to injustice.

"The Honourable Company's cruiser *Nearchus* and hired brig *Ganges* will afford you ample means for removing your party from Singapoor in the event of such a measure becoming, in your judgment, proper and necessary; but I have distinctly to acquaint you that you must not expect any reinforcements from this Government until a reply is received from the Governor-General in Council, as it is the decided conviction of this Government that any force from this island could not oppose the overpowering armament at the disposal of the Batavian Government, and would only widen the breach which the late proceedings at Singapoor have made between the British and Netherlandish Authorities.

"Another European officer, however, and a further supply of cash, equal to the payment of your detachment for two months, shall be forwarded by the very first opportunity.

"I have also to acquaint you that your letter conveying the recantation of the Chiefs of Johore and Singapoor, as well as your present letter, shall be transmitted to the Supreme Government immediately.

"In conclusion, I must beg particularly to apprise you that after the receipt of the present information respecting the views of the Governor-General and the sentiments of this Government, you will not be justified in the measure of shedding blood by pleading hereafter that your honour as a soldier compelled you to make resistance. As a soldier, I must unequivocally declare to you that your personal honour is in no degree implicated in the present occasion to render the shedding of blood necessary.—I have the honour to be, etc. etc.,

"J. A. BANNERMAN.

"P. W. ISLAND, 16*th March* 1819."

The opposition of the Penang Governor to the whole project of founding a new station south of Malacca went back to November 1818, when Major Farquhar was intent on occupying the Carimon group; and it became intensified on learning that Raffles, whose name signified in those seas implacable hostility to the Dutch, had been appointed by Lord Hastings to discover such a station, and, when discovered, to hold it within his Government. However much

Bannerman must be blamed, he at least saw clearly enough that the Station in the Straits would supersede Penang; and, reading his duty in a local light, he fought hard to preserve his own government from extinction. What is more, he very nearly succeeded in his purpose; and no one has ever realised, or perhaps known, how nearly the occupation of Singapore fell through or ran the risk of early repudiation. In his first despatch to the Supreme Government, after the arrival of Raffles at Penang on the 1st of January, Bannerman declared that the Dutch would never allow the step to be taken; that their rights over Rhio were indisputable; and that the whole idea was only another of "Sir Stamford Raffles's aberrations." This despatch, coupled with the fact that the Dutch had occupied Rhio, made a great impression on Lord Hastings, for, on the 20th of February 1819, he wrote as follows to Colonel Bannerman:—"Sir Thomas Raffles was not justified in sending Major Farquhar eastward after the Dutch protested; and, if the Post has not yet been obtained, he is to desist from any further attempt to establish one." The Governor-General's despatch, which, as will have been seen, was written in the absence of correct and definite information, also contains threats against Sir Thomas Raffles, should he have provoked a collision with the Dutch. Fortunately the question of the Post had been settled three weeks before that despatch was penned; but it may be pointed out that, while the vacillation of Lord Hastings deprives him of much of the share he has been allowed in the establishment of Singapore, his irritation was due to the hostile reflections made on Raffles's policy by the Secret Committee of the Court of Directors. The state of feeling in London is very clearly revealed in the following letter from Mr. Charles Assey, who, writing to Dr. Raffles from 57 Berners Street, London, on the 3rd of May [1819], makes the following interesting statement:—

"We have been under considerable apprehension lately. Ministers were most excessively angry at the publication of his, Sir Stamford's, recent Protests and Proceedings with the Dutch Authorities, especially those in the Cabinet, who have had the credit of concluding the arrangements under which the restitution of Java was to be effected, and they were earnest in requiring his removal from Bencoolen. The fortunate arrival of intelligence, however, from Calcutta of his reception by my Lord Hastings, and his subsequent mission to Rhio under the immediate direction and orders of the Governor-General in Council, enabled his friends to interpose with greater effect, and I am happy in being able to communicate to you that the original expression of the sentiments of the authorities here is much softened, and we confidently trust that nothing will happen to his prejudice at Bencoolen, because it is left to the Government in India to determine the necessity of any change. In the meantime Sir Stamford has been apprised of the feeling of Ministers towards him, and when he is thus convinced that he cannot expect the support which he had anticipated, it is to be hoped that he will remain quiet. He is undoubtedly right in principle, and the day will come when the national advantage of his propositions and the value of his active exertions will be acknowledged; but at present expediency seems to be more the order of the day,—and the secrets of European politics are opposed to him."

While the strength of the confidence Lord Hastings felt in the policy and person of his colleague was shaken by the communications he received from home, Colonel Bannerman was raised to the seventh heaven of delight and of reliance upon his own superior knowledge and good sense by the implied censure of Raffles in the despatch from Lord Hastings of the 20th of February 1819. It was at this moment of supreme self-satisfaction that he drew up the following Minute, in which he would have sealed the fate of "the Post Sir S. Raffles had so injudiciously chosen." The Minute is a delightful sample of unctuous and short-sighted self-righteousness, but let its quotation be justified as pilloring a typical advocate of the Little England school, and the veritable Thersites of the Singapore exploit:—

"*14th of March* 1819.

"THE GOVERNOR.

"I have the honour to present to the Board a letter from Major Farquhar, dated 1st instant, conveying intelligence of a very extraordinary communication which the Chiefs of Johore and Singapoor appear to have spontaneously and clandestinely made to the Rajah Mooda of Rhio, and to Mr. Adrian Kock, the Senior Member of the Dutch Council at Malacca.

"Although the circumstance mentioned in Major Farquhar's letter had not previously come to our knowledge, yet I conceive we are bound to forward these documents by the very first opportunity to the Governor-General.

"It is, however, very unfortunate that Major Farquhar's present communication, instead of removing the mischievous impressions which the secret correspondence of the Chiefs may have excited, will, on the contrary, only serve to strengthen them materially in the minds of the Hollanders, and nowhere more so than in Europe, where the inference will undoubtedly be, that whilst the secret letters of these Native Chiefs were spontaneous and untutored, their recantation forwarded by Major Farquhar was written under the control of that officer.

"There is one fact, however, deducible from this correspondence, and which I must notice, as it substantiates the truth of my former assertion, that the Chiefs of Singapoor and Johore are dependants of the Sultan [of] Rhio, etc. I can see no other reason why these Chiefs should have addressed the Rajah Mooda of Rhio, but that they knew they were accountable to him for their conduct, and had reason to dread his vengeance as much as that of the Hollanders.

"*16th March.*

"Since writing the above, a despatch-prow has brought me another letter from Major Farquhar, dated 6th instant, reporting, as the Board may see, that Captain Ross of the Honourable Company's Marine has given him information of the Dutch Governor of Malacca having strongly recommended the Government of Java to send up a force and seize the party at Singapoor, and requiring therefore a reinforcement of troops to enable him to maintain his post against a hostile attack on the part of the Netherlanders.

"It must be notorious that any force we are able to detach to Singapoor could not resist the overpowering armament at the disposal of the Batavia Government, although its presence would certainly compel Major Farquhar to resist the Netherlanders even to the shedding of blood, and its ultimate and forced submission would tarnish the national honour infinitely more seriously than the degradation which would ensue from the retreat of the small party now at Singapoor.

"Neither Major Farquhar's honour as a soldier nor the honour of the British Government now require him to attempt the defence of Singapoor by force of arms against the Netherlanders, as he knows Sir Stamford Raffles has occupied that island in violation of the orders of the Supreme Government, and as he knows that any opposition from his present small party would be a useless and reprehensible sacrifice of men, when made against the overwhelming Naval and Military force that the Dutch will employ. Under these circumstances I am satisfied that Major Farquhar must be certain that he would not be justified in shedding blood in the maintenance of his post at present.

"The question then is, Shall this Government reinforce Major Farquhar, and invite him to a violent opposition against the Netherlanders? or shall it recommend him rather to evacuate the Post Sir S. Raffles has so injudiciously chosen, than shed a drop of human blood in its defence?

"After the knowledge we possess of the views and present policy of the

Governor-General; after the information we have obtained of the means used by Sir Stamford Raffles to obtain the Island of Singapoor; and after the intelligence we have received of the Dutch right to that territory, admitted as it is, by the secret correspondence of the Chiefs there, I am decidedly of opinion that this Government will not be justified in reinforcing Major Farquhar and inciting him to resist the Hollanders by force of arms.

"I had fully stated the possibility of a hostile attack from the Dutch to the worthy Major, when he first lost sight of his usual prudence, and allowed himself to be seduced and made a party in Sir Stamford Raffles's proceedings, as it appeared to me upon the receipt of that gentleman's letter of the 1st of January, and although my advice was then little attended to, yet my duty, as well as a considerable portion of personal regard, will not now permit me to withhold from offering it to him again, accompanied as it may be with much responsibity to myself.

"I beg, then, that the accompanying reply be returned to that officer by the despatch-prow, together with copies of the different papers alluded to therein; and I further propose that the accompanying temperate and firm remonstrance be immediately addressed to Mr. Timmerman Thyssen, by means of which I hope any projected violent measures of his Government will be deprecated, without affecting in the slightest degree the national honour and credit.

"I also beg to recommend, as no opportunity will probably occur for several weeks, and as Major Farquhar would in the meantime be exposed to inconvenience, that one of the transports taken up for the conveyance of the relief be sent to Singapoor, with another European officer and a further supply of six thousand dollars. This last I am, however, surprised to learn that he should require so soon, for his small detachment has not been forty days at Singapoor before it appears to have expended so large a sum as 15,000 dollars which was taken with it.

"In proposing to send this transport to Major Farquhar, I have another object in view. I have just had reason to believe that the *Ganges* and *Nearchus* (the only two vessels now at Singapoor) are quite incapable of receiving on board the whole of the detachment there, in the event of Major Farquhar's judgment deciding that a retreat from the Post would be most advisable. If, therefore, one of the transports is victualled equal to one month's consumption for two hundred and fifty men, and sent to Singapoor, with authority given to Major Farquhar to employ her should her services be requisite, that officer will then have ample means for removing, whenever indispensably necessary, not only all his party, but such of the native inhabitants as may fear the Dutch vengeance, and whom it would be most cruel to desert.

"This arrangement, the Board knows, may be executed without any additional expense and without much inconvenience, as the transport is now lying idle in this harbour, and as the instructions of the Governor-General respecting Singapoor will certainly arrive before she can be probably required. I desire, therefore, the Secretary to Government may issue the necessary directions to the proper departments, and also address the accompanying letter to Major Farquhar.

"I must here fairly acquaint the Board that this measure of despatching a transport to Major Farquhar will subject us to one serious imputation, *i.e.* that *we* held out inducements and furnished means to that officer to withdraw the Establishment from Singapoor, which he otherwise would not and could not have done.

"The necessity of sending another officer and more money to Major Farquhar must be allowed to be urgent, indispensable, and immediate; and as to the expediency of placing within his power means, and British means, for withdrawing from a Post whence a Dutch force may, in the first instance, induce him to consent retreat, and then compel him to embark on board one of their ships, my conscience tells me is equally indispensable and proper, and calculated to save the national character from a very great portion of disgrace. I confess the mortification to me would be infinitely aggravated if I saw Major Farquhar and his detachment brought into this port under the Dutch flag. If the Netherlanders visit him, I certainly think they will never allow him to wait for any reference to this Government for a vessel, but insist upon his immediately embarking the Establishment on board of their ships.

"Under every view of the case, therefore, I think it is our undoubted duty to furnish Major Farquhar with means for removing the Establishment in an English vessel if such a measure becomes indispensable.

"However invidious the task, I cannot close this Minute without pointing out to the notice of our superiors the very extraordinary conduct of the Lieutenant-Governor of Bencoolen. He posts a detachment at Singapoor under very equivocal circumstances, without even the means of coming away, and with such defective instructions and slender resources that, before it has been there a month, its commander is obliged to apply for money to this Government, whose duty it becomes to offer that officer advice and means against an event which Sir Stamford Raffles ought to have expected, and for which he ought to have made an express provision in his instructions to that officer.

"My letters of the 15th and 17th February will prove that upon his return from Singapoor I offered him any supplies he might require for the detachment he had left there, and also earnestly called upon him to transmit instructions to Major Farquhar for the guidance of his conduct in the possible event of the Netherlanders attempting to dislodge him by force of arms. Did he avail himself of my offer and state what further supplies Major Farquhar would require? or did he attend to my appeal and send the requisite instructions to that officer? No. He set off for Acheen, and left Major Farquhar to shift for himself. In fact he acted (as a friend of mine emphatically observed) like a man who sets a house on fire and then runs away. J. A. BANNERMAN."

On the concluding paragraph of this remarkable Minute it will be sufficient to observe that it was of course no part of Raffles's duty to instruct an English soldier not to lower the English flag to any one, or to provide against the pusillanimous reluctance of an English Governor to send to Singapore the military support which the Supreme Government of India had taken for granted, as Lord Hastings sets forth in his despatch of the 8th of April 1819, would be rendered if any sufficient emergency arose. Moreover, Raffles, who perhaps knew him best, had anticipated that Mynheer would indulge in "a paper war," rather than in anything so alarming to Colonel Bannerman and his emphatic friend as "shedding blood"; and these anticipations proved correct.

That Minute, however, reveals Governor Bannerman at the height of his imaginary triumph. The sense of victory was brief, and his discomfiture the more complete, because he had deemed it to be impossible.

On the 20th of February the Governor-General wrote: "If the post had not been obtained," Raffles was to desist from the attempt to found it; but, three weeks before the words were written, and six weeks before they reached Colonel Bannerman, Singapore had been founded. When the Governor of Penang's Minute, and his correspondence of effusive complaisance to the Dutch Governor of Malacca, reached Calcutta, Lord Hastings had received the official intimation that Raffles had secured the desired position, and he may have recollected that he himself had written a despatch to Colonel Bannerman, not many months before, stating that "the proceedings of the Netherlandish Agents" "have marked in a manner not to be misunderstood the real character and objects of the present policy of the Dutch." Yet it was to those agents that Colonel Bannerman extended his sympathy and approbation when another English officer applied to him for succour against a threatened attack. The combination of the two circumstances —the accomplished fact in the matter of the Post, and the desertion by Penang of a garrison established on the chosen site wherever it might be, by the Governor-General's authority, fixed the determination of Lord Hastings. Whatever course might finally be taken, he would extend no further toleration to the jealousy and spite of Colonel Bannerman. On the 8th of April of 1819 he accordingly addressed him the following despatch; and its severity will not be deemed excessive:—

"With regard to Singapore, we [the Governor-General in Council] say that we think your Government entirely wrong in determining so broadly against the propriety of the step taken by Sir Thomas Raffles; 'the opposition of the Dutch' *was not of the nature which we had directed to be shunned under the description of collision.* The ground on which Sir Thomas Raffles stood was this, that Singapore was never mentioned in the Treaty between the Sultan of Johore and the Dutch.

The supposition that it was included in the general term of dependencies is one of those gratuitous assumptions which merit no consideration. We fear you would have difficulty in excusing yourselves should the Dutch be tempted to violence against that Post. The jealousy of it, should misfortune occur and be traceable to neglect originating in such a feeling, will find no tolerance with Government, who must be satisfied (which is not now the case) that perseverance in maintaining the Post would be an infraction of equity, before they can consent to abandon it."

Lord Hastings was a finished master of the style of official reprehension. He never had a more appropriate opportunity for displaying it than in this censure on the blind and blundering proceedings of Colonel Bannerman, proceedings which might well have entailed the very collision that Hastings and Raffles desired to avoid. On receiving the censure of the Supreme Government, Colonel Bannerman sent two hundred troops on the *Mary Anne*, with 6000 dollars in specie, to reinforce Major Farquhar at Singapore; but, as six weeks had elapsed between the original request and their departure, the reinforcement would have been too late, if the Dutch authorities of Batavia had endeavoured to treat Major Farquhar at Singapore as they had treated Captain Salmond at Palembang.

In the meantime Raffles had kept the Governor-General supplied with constant information, and with hints as to how the Dutch might be answered with suitable arguments in the paper war which he anticipated. When the Dutch first drafted their Protest, they relied on a Treaty with the Sultan of Johore, Pahang, Rhio, Lingen, and their dependencies, dated the 26th of December 1818; but Major Farquhar had signed a Convention with the same individual, as Sultan of Rhio, three months earlier, viz. on the 19th of August 1818. On the 30th of March 1819, Raffles wrote a despatch to the Governor-General, in which occurs the following passage:—

"This Dutch Treaty is a daring violation of the very right on which they claim respect from other Powers; because they had a perfect knowledge of the commercial treaty concluded by us with Rajah Mooda of Rhio on 19th August 1818. The basis on which our Treaty [*i.e.* the new one, concerning Singapore] rests, is perfectly independent of that of the Dutch, being made with an independent prince, who was *no* party to the Dutch Treaty, and whose right to the throne is universally and indisputably admitted. . . . It is difficult to look seriously on such a document, and ridiculous to maintain the validity of an instrument which bears on its face so much insincerity and absurdity."

Raffles's justification for our occupation of Singapore was based on the following points:—Firstly, that subsequent to the death of Sultan Mahomed, which happened about the year 1810, there had been no regular installation of a successor, nor had any chief been acknowledged as such with the essential forms required by the Malay custom. Secondly, that the Regalia (the possession of which is considered essential to sovereignty) still remained in the custody of Tunku Putrie, widow of the deceased Sultan. Thirdly, that the Rajah of Lingen had never exercised the authority of Sultan of Johore, and explicitly disclaimed the title. And, fourthly, that the prince whom we supported was the eldest son of the late Sultan, and was intended for the succession; that he was acknowledged by one at least, if not both, of the constituting authorities of the empire, and that he himself stood in no way committed to the Dutch "when I formed the Treaty with him."

While Raffles had to cope with the open opposition of the Penang Government, and to keep the Governor-General firm in purpose by the success of the measures he had taken at Singapore, and by showing how easily what had been acquired could be legitimately retained, he had also to experience the frowns of the Court in London. The Secret Committee, the inner council of the East India Company, were not sparing in their denunciation of Raffles and all his works. The mere mention of his name sufficed to call forth a torrent of detraction and abuse, which was the more freely uttered because expressed in the closest secrecy and under the seal of confidence, but was, none the less, extraordinary and misapplied in the case of a man filling a difficult and responsible position. When they heard of the Governor-General's decision to send Raffles eastward, they wrote a despatch, dated the 22nd of May 1819, disapproving of the step, and of the employment of Raffles on any mission which would bring him to close quarters with the Dutch. "We express," they wrote, "our decided disapprobation of the extension in any degree to Eastern islands of that system of subsidiary alliance which has prevailed, perhaps too widely, in India."

But the language of this despatch was mild in comparison with that written on the 14th of August 1819, when the news reached London of the occupation of Singapore. Far from receiving the intimation with satisfaction, they described the Post as one that could only be retained at the hazard of war; and they then proceeded to pour the vials of their wrath on the head of Raffles, of whom it was said, "Any difficulty with the Dutch will be created by Sir Stamford Raffles's intemperance of conduct and of language." They would, however, await the further explanations of Lord Hastings "before retaining or relinquishing Sir Stamford Raffles's acquisition at Singapore." England is clearly not indebted to the policy of the East India Company for that possession. All the authorities were, in fact, against it. Even Lord Hastings wavered, and would have recalled his emissary if he could have done so; but the fateful step had been taken. Among the high authorities who were entitled to express a decision on the matter, the opinion was unanimous that the measure was solely due to Raffles's conception and execution. Let no one attempt to rob him of the credit which he alone deserves for an achievement that has rarely, if ever, been surpassed in the importance of its consequences.

In accordance with his instructions and his own wish —for at this time not a cloud had come over their relations—Sir Stamford Raffles appointed Major, soon afterwards promoted to be Colonel, Farquhar to be Resident at Singapore; while Lord Hastings had arranged that his scale of pay and allowances should be those he had formerly enjoyed at Malacca. "On reaching Penang," writes Lady Raffles, "he [Sir Stamford] found that this officer had already engaged his passage to England, in a vessel which was to sail in a few days. Colonel Farquhar was, however, prevailed upon to alter his arrangements," and, accepting the prospective appointment, "allowed himself," in the words of Colonel

Bannerman, "to be seduced and made a party in Sir Stamford Raffles's proceedings." It was, however, understood that he had only postponed his departure on furlough, and that he accepted the post temporarily, with a view to giving the new settlement a good start. The rapid progress made by Singapore as a place of commerce soon altered Farquhar's views. At the end of 1820 he wrote: "Its trade already far exceeds what Malacca could boast of during the most flourishing years of its long continuance in our possession;" and, at the same time that he made this interesting communication, he sent this personal statement, that "as the same urgent call no longer exists for my proceeding to Europe on furlough, I desire to postpone departure till season of 1821–22." It is necessary to note that Colonel Farquhar's salary and allowances were framed on a very generous scale, and one considerably in excess of what the revenues of Singapore could properly meet. Economy was necessary in the expenditure; and Raffles, with the approval of the Governor-General, drew up a new scheme for the administration, the head of which was to receive a much lower remuneration than Farquhar did. In anticipation of his vacating the office, Mr. John Crawfurd was appointed to succeed him at Singapore; and, in accordance with Raffles's own wish and suggestion, Singapore was to be dependent on the Supreme Government alone.

In consequence of these necessary steps Farquhar's intentions had to be ascertained; and on the 1st of May 1821, Raffles's secretary wrote, asking him to define the period of his departure. In September 1821, Farquhar replied that he was not ready to do so; and it was not until after Raffles went to Singapore, in the latter part of the year 1822, that a notification was made to Colonel Farquhar in January 1823, that, as the accounts of the place were to be transferred from Bencoolen to Calcutta, and as Mr. Crawfurd was about to leave Bengal, a termination would have to be put to "his temporary and dependent appointment." Farquhar refused to resign or to recognise Raffles's authority, and, on the 21st of March 1823, he was summarily removed by an official notification, intimating that his resignation, dated and tendered as far back as the 23rd of October 1820, had been accepted.

This was a regrettable ending for the relations between the Founder and the first Resident of Singapore; but Raffles could not have acted otherwise than he did, or have shown greater forbearance to an old colleague. In this matter Lord Hastings not only supported Raffles, but issued his own orders. The Governor-General declared that the necessary "degree of firmness, decision, and general efficiency" could not be expected from Colonel Farquhar, whose "measures had been unfortunate when they had departed from your [Raffles's] instructions."

In the next chapter it will unfortunately be necessary to examine the reckless and injudicious statements Colonel Farquhar made after his return to England; but here his evidence, recorded after the first year of the occupation, viz. on the 31st of March 1820, as to the value of the place may be given:—

> "Nothing can possibly exceed the rising trade and general prosperity of this infant colony; indeed, to look at our harbour just now, where upwards of *twenty* junks, three of which are from China, and two from Cochin China, the rest from Siam and other quarters, are at anchor, besides ships, brigs, prows, etc. etc., a person would naturally exclaim, Surely this cannot be an establishment of only a twelve months' standing! One of the principal Chinese merchants here told me, in the course of conversation, that he would be very glad to give five hundred thousand dollars for the revenues of Singapore five years hence. Merchants of all descriptions are collecting here so fast that nothing is heard in the shape of complaint but the want of more ground to build on. . . . In short, this settlement bids fair to become the emporium of Eastern trade, and in time may surpass even Batavia itself."

Before that letter could possibly have reached Raffles, the latter had written, on the 3rd of April 1820, from Bencoolen:—"Singapore, I am happy to say, continues to thrive beyond all calculations. . . . The exports and imports, even by native boats alone, exceed four millions of dollars in the year." Under cover of this letter he enclosed one from Mr. Charles Grant, a director of the East India Company, showing that a change of view was taking place in England. Mr. Grant wrote: "The acquisition of Singapore has grown in importance. The stir made here lately for the further enlargement of the Eastern trade fortified that impression. It is now accredited in the India House;

of late, in an examination before a Committee of the House of Lords, I gave my opinion of the value in a moral, political, and commercial view, of a British establishment in the locality of Singapore under the auspices of the Company."

The Marquis of Hastings had also been brought round to appreciate fully the value of Signapore, and to take a firmer position against Dutch encroachments. In one despatch home he wrote: "It was obvious we could not but expect that in the event of securing a station, which would baffle the injurious policy of our neighbours, they would not fail to impugn our right to take possession of such a spot by advancing some prior title to it."

In the autumn of 1822 Raffles left Bencoolen for Singapore, with the intention of placing the administration of the new settlement on a firm and lasting basis; for, by this time, it was known that the place would not be surrendered. The Dutch had endeavoured to support their case against the British occupation of Singapore by producing an earlier treaty of 1784 made with Johore, and containing a clause which prohibited other Europeans from being admitted to the ports of Johore and Pahang; but these exclusive pretensions had at last become out of date and were past endurance. The Dutch position in Java had also again become one of financial embarrassment, due partly to the cost of excessive enterprise and of costly expeditions to Palembang and Rhio. Moreover it was known in the East that the discussions with a view to the eventual exchange of Bencoolen for Malacca had been carried to a stage assuring the conclusion of the arrangement between the two Governments. Raffles, whatever doubt he continued to feel about the treatment he would himself receive, had no longer any anxiety on the score of the retention of Singapore. It was at this period that he wrote as follows to the Duke of Somerset:—

"BENCOOLEN, *February* 28, 1822.

"My settlement of Singapore continues to prosper. By the returns of shipping and native vessels arrived since it has been in our possession the following results appear:—

"The total tonnage arrived in two years and a half has been upwards of 161,000 tons, and the estimated value of imports and exports, 8,000,000 dollars, or £2,000,000. Considering all the disadvantages under which Singapore has been placed, the want of confidence in its retention even for a month, the opposition of the English settlement at Penang, and of the Dutch, a stronger proof of its commercial importance could hardly be afforded. It is my intention to go round to Singapore in about three months, and to remain there until I have made the necessary arrangements for establishing the place on a proper and lasting foundation."

In October of the same year, Raffles arrived at Singapore. His recent domestic losses in Sumatra invest with peculiar pathos the following apostrophe to Singapore, "my almost only child," penned at that place on October 11th, 1822:—

"We landed yesterday, and I have once more established my headquarters in the centre of my Malayan friends. The coldest and most disinterested could not quit Bencoolen, and land at Singapore, without surprise and emotion. What, then, must have been my feelings, after the loss of almost everything that was dear to me on that ill-fated coast, after all the risks and dangers to which this my almost only child had been exposed, to find it grown and advanced beyond measure, and even my warmest anticipations and expectations, in importance, wealth, and interest—in everything that can give it value and permanence? Rob me not of this my political child, and you may yet see me at home in all my wonted spirits, and with an elasticity about me which will bear me up against all that party spirit can do to depress me."

The following extract from Raffles's correspondence with his cousin, Dr. Raffles, will show what he thought of his colony four years after he had occupied it. Writing from Singapore on the 12th of January 1823, he says:—

"The progress of my new settlement is in every way most satisfactory, and it would gladden your heart to witness the activity and cheerfulness which prevails throughout.

Every day brings us new settlers, and Singapore has already become a great emporium. Houses and warehouses are springing up in every direction, and the inland forests are fast giving way before the industrious cultivator. I am now engaged in marking out the towns and roads, and in establishing laws and regulations for the protection of person and property. We have no less than nine mercantile houses (European); and there is abundant employment for capital as fast as it accumulates. I cannot help thinking the soil of Singapore also opens a fine field for European speculation, and that some hundreds of our countrymen, with a very small commencement, might soon realise a handsome independence; but more of this when we meet, which, I hope, will be e'er long—that is to say, within a year after you receive this, as my determination is, God willing, to quit this country, at all events by the end of the present year. . . .

"The death of my friend, Dr. Milne of Malacca, has, for a time, thrown a damp on missionary exertions in this quarter; but I expect Mr. Morrison, of China, to visit this place in March, and I hope to make some satisfactory arrangement with him for future labours. The two missionaries who are here are not idle; Messrs. Milton and Thomson, the former in Chinese and Siamese, and the latter in Malay and English printing.

"I have selected a spot for my intended college, and all I now require is a good headmaster or superintendent. It is my intention to endow it with lands, the rents of which will cover its ordinary expenses. I am also about to commence upon a church, the plan of which is already approved, etc. etc., T. S. R."

The differences with Colonel Farquhar, in respect to his relinquishing the Residentship, have been described. In the six months during which Raffles resided at Singapore, prior to his final departure from Asia, he may be said to have laid the foundations of the modern city. He wrote to one of his correspondents dwelling on the care he took in the wording of the grants of land; and he went on to say that "My time is at present engaged in remodelling and laying out my new city, and in establishing institutions and laws for its future constitution; a pleasant duty enough in England, where you have books, hard heads, and lawyers to refer to, but here, by no means easy, where all must depend on my own judgment and foresight. Nevertheless I hope that, though Singapore may be the first capital established in the nineteenth century, it will not disgrace the brightest period of it." The reader may recollect what Raffles said to Abdulla at Malacca about a Malay school. He now had the opportunity of giving effect to his wishes. He selected a good site, and endowed the institution with a sufficient quantity of land to keep it in a flourishing condition. He also secured the co-operation of that able and enlightened missionary and pundit, Dr. Morrison of China, in establishing this college "for the cultivation of Chinese and Malayan literature, and for the moral and intellectual improvement of the Archipelago and the surrounding countries."

Among the more noticeable acts of Raffles in establishing a settled order of things at Singapore was the abolition of slavery, a measure which Colonel Farquhar strongly opposed and bitterly resented, as it affected his own property. Raffles also put down gaming-houses and cock-fighting, which the same officer had sanctioned and encouraged. His declaration of Singapore as a free port, open to the ships of all nations, was also a remarkable measure, promulgated, too, at a moment when the Company was fighting hard to preserve its last commercial privilege, the monopoly of the China trade. But certainly the most original and remarkable piece of work he performed was the framing of a short code of laws and regulations for the preservation of peace and good order in this rapidly growing port, frequented by sailors and traders of every colour and creed. During the period of doubt, which closed with Crawfurd's appointment, the Supreme Government had left Raffles to act as seemed best to him, at the same time freeing themselves of responsibility should anything turn out wrong. His code was simplicity itself; and it was carried into effect by the Resident and twelve magistrates, selected from the merchants of the place. The juries were to be either five Europeans, or four Europeans together with three natives of admitted respectability. As in Java, Raffles made recourse to the Courts of Law simple, cheap, and secure.

The Bengal Government, in the formal resolutions it passed on the 29th of March 1823, did justice to Raffles's rule at Singapore, saying, "On the occasion of relieving Sir Stamford Raffles from the superintendence of Singapore, the Governor-General in Council deems it an act of justice to that gentleman to record his sense of the activity, zeal, judgment, and attention to the principles prescribed for the management of the settlement, which has marked his conduct in the execution of that duty." Those on the spot knew better than the authorities in India and England all that Raffles had done for Singapore. Their discernment, as well as their gratitude, dictated the tribute to his merit and his work, which found expression in the following address on the occasion of his departure from the place in June 1823:—

"To Sir T. S. RAFFLES,
"Lieutenant-Governor of Fort Marlborough.

"HONOURABLE SIR,—The period of your approaching and final departure is one of peculiar interest to the commercial community of this place, and we, the undersigned members of it, gladly seize the opportunity which it affords us of indulging in the expression of those feelings towards your person, which the occasion is so well calculated to excite.

"At such a moment we cannot be suspected of panegyric, when we advert to the distinguished advantages which the commercial interests of our nation at large, and ourselves more especially, have derived from your personal exertions. To your unwearied zeal, your vigilance, and your comprehensive views, we owe at once the foundation and maintenance of a settlement unparalleled for the liberality of the principles on which it has been established—principles, the operation of which has converted, in a period short beyond all example, a haunt of pirates into the abode of enterprise, security, and opulence.

"While we acknowledge our own peculiar obligations to you, we reflect at the same time with pride and satisfaction upon the active and beneficent means by which you have promoted and patronised the diffusion of intellectual and moral improvement, and we anticipate with confidence their happy influence in advancing the cause of humanity and civilisation.

"We cannot take leave of the author of so many benefits without emotion, or without expressing our sorrow for the loss of his protection and his society. Accept, sir, we beseech you, without distinction of tribe or nation, the expression of our sincere respect and esteem, and be assured of the deep interest we shall ever take in your own prosperity, as well as in the happiness of those who are most tenderly related to you.—We remain, with the deepest respect, your most obedient servants.

(Signed by the European and Native Merchants of Singapore.)

"SINGAPORE, *June* 5, 1823."

Less than ten days later, when he had left Singapore for the last time, he wrote to Dr. Raffles as follows:—

"At Sea, off the Coast of Borneo,
"14*th June* 1823.

"MY DEAR COUSIN,—We left Singapore on the 9th, and are thus far on our return to Bencoolen, with the intention of touching at Batavia on the way. My time was so fully occupied while closing my administration at Singapore that I really had it not in my power to sit down, as I ought to have done, to thank you most sincerely for your letter announcing the arrival of our dear little Ella. It was the first account we received, and I need not attempt to express the joy and gladness which it diffused throughout our domestic circle. . . . I am sorry that I have been obliged to leave Singapore before the printing of the papers on the formation of the Singapore Institution was completed. Printing in this country is indeed most tedious and expensive work. I have left orders that several copies be sent to you by the very first opportunity; and you will perceive that I have put your name down as a Trustee. I laid the foundation-stone of the buildings three days before I embarked. Mr. Crawfurd is now the Resident of Singapore; and, in anticipation of my return to Europe at the end of the year, I have resigned all further charge of the place. It is a most promising settlement, and is fast realising my most sanguine views regarding it. I have had a great deal of trouble and annoyance in the details owing to the imbecility and obstinacy of the local Resident,

Colonel Farquhar; but as Crawfurd has relieved him, and all my measures and plans are approved of and supported by the higher authorities, I have had great reason to be satisfied with the result upon the whole. T. S. R."

Raffles formed the highest anticipations of the future of Singapore. It was to be the emporium of the East. Suffice it to say that it has realised his hopes. It is the key of British commercial supremacy in Asia.

Sixty-four years after the address from its merchants just quoted, Singapore erected to the memory of its founder the long-projected statue which now adorns its Esplanade. On the occasion of the unveiling of that statue, the Governor, the late Sir Frederick A. Weld, delivered the following eloquent address, containing the words—"In Raffles England had one of her greatest sons." The unveiling of the statue formed, it may be stated, the principal feature of the ceremonies celebrating the Jubilee of Her Majesty the Queen at Singapore in 1887:—

"YOUR HIGHNESSES, LADIES AND GENTLEMEN,—I stand here on the occasion of the celebration of the 50th anniversary of the reign of Her Most Gracious Majesty the Queen and Empress, to unveil the statue of an illustrious administrator and statesman, whose sagacious foresight laid foundations upon which have been built up a great centre of commerce, a focus from which British influence, carrying with it the light of civilisation, radiates far around, and which has not only been a blessing to thousands, but has added directly or indirectly in no inconsiderable measure to the extent and resources of that vast Empire over which Her Majesty rules.

"A most auspicious occasion, therefore, is this on which I have the great and long-wished-for pleasure of inaugurating and unveiling the statue of my great predecessor, Sir Stamford Raffles, a statue worthy in every way of the genius of Mr. Woolner. Had not the other celebrations of this day prevented my delivering a lengthened and carefully prepared oration, I should have wished to have sketched the career of Sir Stamford as a great and typical Englishman, to have pictured him as an administrator, as a philanthropist in a true and manly sense, as a promoter of science, and as a far-seeing statesman. I should have desired to have shown him grappling with difficulties, undismayed by reverses, unspoiled by successes—but time and opportunity is wanting, and his life speaks for itself.

"Look around, and a greater monument than any that the highest art or the most lavish outlay can raise to him is visible in this, that his name is still held in affectionate veneration by all our races, that all acknowledge the benefits that have resulted from his wise policy. See that crowd of splendid shipping in the harbour in front of his statue. Cast a glance at the city which surrounds it, on the evidences of civilisation—churches, public buildings, and offices—law courts, educational establishments, in the vicinity of this spacious recreation-ground on which we stand and near which he landed. Were this all, it would still be sufficient to say, '*Si monumentum quæris, circumspice.*' But this is only a small part of the monument. Look for it in other parts of the colony. Look for it in the Native States. I have a rough draft in my possession, in Sir Stamford's own handwriting, of a large and extended Residential programme for neighbouring countries. Look for it in the constantly increasing influence of the British name in these parts, and you will say with me that IN RAFFLES ENGLAND HAD ONE OF HER GREATEST SONS.

"I cannot but express the pleasure that I feel in seeing near me their Highnesses the descendants of the Malay Potentates who made the concession of Singapore. To them also we must express a debt of gratitude.

"It only remains for me to read to you a telegram that I have received from the Raffles family. It was as a voice from another world,—'Prosperity to Singapore, Raffles.' I now unveil the statue. Long may it remind men that 'in our fair island story the path of duty is the way to glory.'"

The reader will be interested in learning that the sender of the telegram, "Prosperity to Singapore, Raffles," which was as a voice from another world, was the Rev. R. B. Raffles, then enthusiastically engaged in the search for, and collection of, those materials about his cousin's life, which I have been allowed to use in this biography.

I cannot close this chapter, telling the story of the most complete, striking, and successful episode in the life of Sir Stamford Raffles, more appropriately, or with greater effect, than by inserting the following description of Singapore, from the pen of the sender of that significant and sympathetic telegram :—

The circumstances of the case were typical. No well-considered and steadily-pursued design of the authorities at home has been the leading force in the colonial expansion of Great Britain. That force has emanated from the adventurous spirit of her sons abroad. And in the occupation of the island which Raffles, with a statesman's foresight, added to her empire, and, in spite of cold encouragement and opposition, retained with English pertinacity, the story of the growth of Greater Britain is, in part, epitomised. Nor is it only fancy which finds some striking resemblances between the mother-country and her miniature representative in the Eastern seas. Each, while vastly exceeded in extent of territory and population by neighbouring or rival dominions, is the island-junction of great ocean-highways, and thus attracts to itself, the one in European and the other in Asiatic waters, a preponderating share of the world's shipping. From the anxieties and dangers of the continents to which each of them is adjacent, both are alike protected by a narrow streak of water, which, in the case of the island of Singapore, winding along its northern coast-line opposite the mainland of Johore, is narrowed down in many places to a width of barely half a mile. The low hills which, averaging from 70 to less than 400 feet, vary the surface of the Eastern island, and only once, to the north-westward of the city, attain a height of 519 feet, may recall to an Englishman's recollection the subdued and gentle scenery of our home and midland counties. Here the comparison must cease; for England's prosperous colony at the southern end of the Malay Peninsula, the gate-house to the Straits of Malacca and the China Sea, the watch-tower looking southward, past clustering islets, down the sunny waters between Sumatra and Borneo, towards the lost Java, is but a tiny island of twenty-seven miles in length from east to west, and an extreme breadth of fourteen miles. Its rivers, never exceeding six miles in length, and only swollen to importance by an unusual rainfall, stole, when Raffles landed, through forests and jungles; which, since 1837, have given place to thickets of palms and plantains, limes and orange-trees, delighting in the warm and liquid air, and forming, with the ferns and orchids that cluster in their shade, a favourite haunt of monkeys and squirrels, sloths, wild-hogs, and deer, and an occasional hunting-ground for stray tigers from the peninsula.

Lying like an emerald in the bright waters not quite a degree north of the equator, with seventy little islands gathered under the protection of the British flag at distances of less than ten miles off its southern and western shores, Singapore enjoys an equable and smiling climate, in which the temperature ranges from 70° to 90° Fahr., the night-time is cool, and the rain falls gently and throughout the year, rather than in torrents during a few weeks; while, if it were not for the short, sharp, purifying squalls of the south-west monsoon, itself erratic in its strength and continuance, the air that enwraps the island is but little troubled by the north-easterly winds prevailing from November to April, or by the treacherously refreshing and unhealthy breezes of the Java winds in May and June.

Opposite the site where Raffles marked out his new city the sea is not many fathoms deep; and the harbour, affording a commodious anchorage, is easily reached by any ordinary navigator from any quarter, while its waters and those of the surrounding deep are scarcely rocked by the waning swell of storms that have spent their fury in the neighbouring oceans.

"Rob me not of this my political child," wrote Raffles of Singapore in 1822: and neither time nor envy, neither opposition close at hand, nor the want of sympathy in council-chambers far away, have robbed him. With its population risen from one hundred and fifty natives at the hour of its foundation to more than a thousand times that number in the present day; with its six long miles of busy frontage facing seaward, and its harbour brightened by the coming and the going of the stateliest, swiftest shipping, and the quaintest, in the world; with its streets, and squares, and markets, humming to the tongues and feet of its residents of many nations, and its welcomed visitors from many lands; with its cathedral-churches, roomy buildings, pleasant gardens, and the noble institutions that retain his very name; with its freedom and its justice, Singapore remains, as enduring as the earth on which it stands, a monument to the wisdom, courage, and beneficence of the often jealously impeded, sometimes almost ruined, but indomitable Englishman who founded it.

CHAPTER XI

THE LAST RETURN HOME

THE regulation of affairs at Singapore, and the transference of its control from Bencoolen to the Supreme Government of India, ended Raffles's public work in the East. But he had still to wind up matters at Bencoolen, and, on leaving Singapore in June 1823, he proceeded to that station. From the first days of his residence in Sumatra, Raffles had devoted himself to the collection of objects of natural history. During his stay in London in 1817, he had discussed with Sir Joseph Banks a plan for establishing in London a zoological collection and museum, which should interest and instruct the public. Sir Joseph Banks warmly supported the proposition; and, in a letter from him to Dr. Horsfield, there occurs this interesting passage: "We are all here delighted with the acquaintance of Governor Raffles; he is certainly among the best informed of men, and possesses a larger stock of useful talent than any other individual of my acquaintance." Some of the Directors, no doubt, sympathised with, and encouraged Raffles's desire to increase scientific and general knowledge; but the East India Company as a body had no such concern; and when, in March 1820, Raffles sent home the first half of a valuable collection illustrating the natural history of Sumatra, he received in reply a coldly worded despatch, remonstrating with him on his extravagance, and forbidding him to expend any of the Company's funds in such directions. This collection was sent by the ship *Mary* to Sir Joseph Banks, and he forwarded "a duplicate, and even more complete sets, of the quadrupeds and birds" by a later vessel, the

London. Besides the specimens intended for public purposes, he remembered also to send some for his friends; and, in one of his lists, Prince Leopold figures as the destined recipient of "a dried specimen of the Tapir."

It was arranged that Sir Stamford Raffles should return with his wife to England on board a ship called the *Fame*, early in December 1823; and he had gathered together all his property, including the second portion of his natural history collection; a perhaps incomparable assortment of Malay manuscripts; and, what was even more irreplaceable, a full set of all the official papers relating to Java, and his administration preliminary to his final departure from the East. The *Fame* was more than two months after her time in arriving at Bencoolen, and Raffles had actually begun to embark his property on another ship, when, unfortunately as it proved, the *Fame* arrived. Apart from the official and historical documents, Raffles placed, at a moderate computation, £25,000 worth of property on board that vessel; and, as there was no possibility of insuring at Bencoolen, the whole was shipped at the owner's risk. In a letter, dated two days after the now historical catastrophe which followed, Raffles wrote: "We embarked on the [2nd] February 1824, in the *Fame*, and sailed at daylight for England, with a fair wind, and every prospect of a quick and comfortable passage. The ship was everything we could wish; and, having closed my charge here much to my satisfaction, it was one of the happiest days of my life. We were, perhaps, too happy; for in the evening came a sad reverse." What followed cannot be better told than in Sir Stamford's own narrative:—

"Sophia had just gone to bed, and I had thrown off half my clothes, when a cry of 'Fire! fire!' roused us from our calm content, and in five minutes the whole ship was in flames! I ran to examine whence the flames principally issued, and found that the fire had its origin immediately under our cabin. 'Down with the boats.' 'Where is Sophia?' 'Here.' 'The children?' 'Here.' 'A rope to the side.' 'Lower Lady Raffles.' 'Give her to me,' says one. 'I'll take her,' says the captain. 'Throw the gunpowder overboard.' 'It cannot be got at; it is in the magazine close to the fire.' 'Stand clear of the powder.' 'Skuttle the water-casks.' 'Water! water!' 'Where's Sir Stamford?' 'Come into the boat, Nilson! Nilson, come into the boat!' 'Push off—push off. Stand clear of the after part of the ship.'

"All this passed much quicker than I can write it. We pushed off, and as we did so, the flames burst out of our cabin-window, and the whole of the after part of the ship was in flames. The masts and sails now taking fire, we moved to a distance sufficient to avoid the immediate explosion; but the flames were now coming out of the main hatchway; and seeing the rest of the crew, with the captain, still on board, we pulled back to her under the bows, so as to be more distant from the powder. As we approached, we perceived that the people on board were getting into another boat on the opposite side. She pushed off; we hailed her: 'Have you all on board?' 'Yes, all save one.' 'Who is he?' 'Johnson, sick in his cot.' 'Can we save him?' 'No, impossible.' The flames were issuing from the hatchway. At this moment the poor fellow, scorched, I imagine, by the flames, roared out most lustily, having run upon the deck. 'I will go for him,' says the captain. The two boats then came together, and we took out some of the persons from the captain's boat, which was overladen; he then pulled under the bowsprit of the ship, and picked the poor fellow up. 'Are you all safe?' 'Yes, we have got the man; all lives safe.' 'Thank God!' 'Pull off from the ship. Keep your eye on a star, Sir Stamford. There's one scarcely visible.'

"We then hauled close to each other, and found the captain fortunately had a compass, but we had no light except from the ship. Our distance from Bencoolen we estimated to be about fifty miles in a south-west direction. There being no landing-place to the southward of Bencoolen, our only chance was to regain that port. The captain then undertook to lead, and we to follow, in a N.N.E. course, as well as we could; no chance, no possibility being left, that we could again approach the ship; for she was now one splendid flame, fore and aft; and aloft, her masts and sails in a blaze, and rocking to and fro, threatening to fall in an instant. 'There goes her mizzen-mast; pull away, my boys! There goes the gunpowder. Thank God! Thank God!'"

For a graphic picture of that appalling incident, a fire at sea, it would be hard to surpass this description. The fire was caused by "the shameful carelessness of the steward going with a naked light to draw off brandy from a cask, which took fire." The survivors, although without provisions or water, and with scarcely any clothes, succeeded in making their way back to Bencoolen. What Raffles had lost on board may be given in his own words:—

"The loss I have to regret beyond all, is my papers and drawings,—all my notes and observations, with memoirs and collections, sufficient for a full and ample history, not only of Sumatra, but of Borneo, and almost every other island of note in these seas;—my intended account of the establishment of Singapore;—the history of my own administration;—Eastern grammars, dictionaries, and vocabularies;—and last, not least, a grand map of Sumatra, on which I had been employed since my arrival here, and on which, for the last six months, I had bestowed almost my whole undivided attention.

This, however, was not all;—all my collections in natural history—all my splendid collection of drawings, upwards of *two thousand* in number—with all the valuable papers and notes of my friends Arnold and Jack; and, to conclude, I will merely notice that there was scarce an unknown animal, bird, beast, or fish, or an interesting plant, which we had not on board; a living tapir, a new species of tiger, splendid pheasants, etc., domesticated for the voyage; we were, in short, in this respect, a perfect Noah's Ark."

Such was the bitterly disappointing catastrophe that befell Raffles immediately after his departure for England. All his property was lost, and most of it could never be replaced. In his letter to the Court of Directors he stated:—

"In a pecuniary point of view, my loss has not been less extensive, as may be perceived by the annexed statement, in which I have assumed the actual cost of the principal articles which have been sacrificed. [The statement gives the total loss at £30,000.] Most of them are what no money can replace; such as the service of plate presented to me by the inhabitants of Java; the diamonds presented to my family by the captors of Jojocarta; the diamond ring presented to me by Princess Charlotte on my embarkation for India, a week before her death. These, and many other tokens of regard, friendship, and respect, during an active and varied life, can never be replaced. Money may compensate perhaps for other losses, but no insurance was, or could be, effected from home. It rests solely and exclusively with the Court to consider in how far my claims on account of services may be strengthened by the severity of misfortune which has latterly attached itself to my case."

The very next morning after the return of passengers and crew, Raffles gave one more proof of his self-possession, by commencing a fresh sketch of the map of Sumatra, and by taking steps to form a new natural history collection. Some delay took place in obtaining another ship; and it was not until the 10th of April that Raffles finally sailed from Bencoolen on board the ship *Mariner*. The passage to the Cape was retarded by violent gales. For some weeks the passengers were unable to leave their berths for several days at a time; the sea often poured through the decks into the cabin; and "we resigned ourselves," wrote Raffles in his diary, "to the feeling that our pilgrimage in this world was soon to close." The rest of the voyage presents no further occasion for remark, beyond the fact that at St. Helena Raffles received tidings of his mother's death. On the 22nd of August he landed at Plymouth. From Plymouth he proceeded to Cheltenham, where his wife's relations were then residing; and, for the first few months after his return, he made that place his headquarters. He took "a snug house, No. 2 Wellington Place"; decided to "give the waters a fair chance"; and paid one or two flying visits to town, where "the feeling seems very general in my favour, and I trust that before Christmas something will be done by those in power to acknowledge my past services, and remunerate me for my losses." In the letter to Dr. Raffles, from which these extracts are taken, he also wrote: "I have delivered in a short statement to the Court, and shall await their decision with patience. I have not appealed to them *in formâ pauperis*, though it would be affectation in me to say that my future plans do not materially depend on the assistance I receive from them."

In a letter to the Duchess of Somerset, written immediately after his arrival, he thus sketched his future wishes and plans:—"I confess that I have a great desire to turn farmer, and have the vanity to think I could manage about two hundred acres as well as my neighbours. With this, I suppose, I should in time become a country magistrate, an office of all others which I should delight in; and, if I could eventually get a seat in Parliament without sacrifice in principle, I should be content to pass through the rest of my life without aiming at anything further, beyond the occupation of my spare time in promoting, as far as my humble means and talents admitted, the pursuits of knowledge and science, and the advancement of philanthropic and religious principles."

While Sir Stamford Raffles thus looked forward with the eye of hope to the generous treatment he might expect at the hands of the East India Company, he was also turning his thoughts to a Parliamentary career; and he consulted the same cousin as to the chance he might have at Liverpool. Dr. Raffles replied, giving him a good deal of local information, stating that the Liverpool merchants were tired of the sitting member, and suggesting that "Bristol or Liverpool might solicit him to stand, on account of his unequalled commercial knowledge." Raffles also consulted the Duke and Duchess of Somerset on the subject; and Lancaster, where the Duchess's brother, the Duke of Hamilton, had influence, was also mentioned as a suitable constituency. No doubt, if Raffles had lived, he would have returned to public life as a member of the House of Commons; but his early death put an end to all such projects.

On the 17th of November 1824, Raffles took up his residence in town at 104 Piccadilly—a house that was pulled down only a few years ago to make room for a club. The "house, though well situated, is by no means equal to our demands," he wrote, "and I fear we shall have, e'er long, to move to another." In a few months he did remove to 23 Lower Grosvenor Street, the house of his friend, Sir Humphry Davy, from whom he purchased its lease for a remaining period of thirty years. Some time after this he bought, as a country residence, Highwood at Hendon, for which he paid altogether the sum of £20,000, and he hoped to get 3 per cent. for the investment. For some time he hesitated between this place and one in "the beautiful and romantic country round Godalming"; but the fact that his friend, William Wilberforce, had taken the adjoining residence decided him in favour of Highwood. The house had one hundred and twelve acres attached to it, and Raffles threw himself into the pursuit of farming with keen delight. It became his boast that everything for the consumption of the family, with the exception of groceries and spices, was produced on the estate.

He resumed his acquaintance with his old friends; and he made new ones. He gained the esteem of the Marquis of Lansdowne; and his friendship with the Earl and Countess Harcourt became more intimate even than it had been in 1817. As a prominent Fellow of the Royal and Antiquarian Societies, President of the Royal Asiatic Society, and a member of other learned bodies, he was associated with the leading men of science of the day; and between him and Sir Humphry Davy in particular there was a close alliance. In the political world, William Wilberforce was on cordial terms with one who had already proclaimed the emancipation of slaves in three regions of Asia. Nicholas Vansittart, afterwards Lord Bexley, espoused his views and interests; while, above all, George Canning, one of whose letters has already been quoted, took him into his favour. Raffles went to see Canning on the 30th of November 1824; and, in describing the interview, he wrote to Dr. Raffles: "Mr. Canning detained me so long yesterday evening, that I was precluded from attending the Royal Society. He received me most cordially, and promised me the most friendly support in all my plans. We parted under the understanding of becoming better known to each other, and I think I may fairly calculate on his influence, as far as I may require it." In one of his letters he also speaks of the second Earl of Minto as "a warm friend."

Raffles had a great fondness for animals of nearly every description. He was seldom without pets of several kinds; and he is said to have treated one of these, a favourite bear, with champagne when it was ill. He also intended to write its biography in a Natural History he was contemplating. One of the first and most important subjects to which he turned his attention after his arrival in England, was the foundation of the Zoological Society, which he had originally contemplated in 1817. The following extracts from his correspondence with Dr. Raffles, in the first half of 1825, give some new particulars about its inception:—

"I am much interested at present in establishing a Grand Zoological collection in the Metropolis, with a Society for the introduction of living animals, bearing the same relations to Zoology as a science that the Horticultural Society does to Botany. The prospectus is drawn out, and, when a few copies are printed, I will send some to you. We expect to have 20,000 subscribers at £2 each, and it is further expected we may go far beyond the Jardin des Plantes at Paris. Sir Humphry Davy and myself are the projectors, and, while he looks more to the practical and immediate utility to the country gentlemen, my attention is more directed to the scientific department. More of this, however, hereafter. . . .

"The few copies of the Zoological plan which were struck off were soon dispersed, and I did not think of sending some to you until I found that I had not *one* left for myself. Some idea has been entertained of throwing the prospectus into a new form, and at this very time I am a little at issue with Sir Humphry Davy as to the share which science is to have in the project. As soon as I have a copy of the plan resolved upon I will send it to you, and, in the meantime, I shall take the liberty, *sans permission*, of placing your name with the *honourables* who support it. . . .

"I sent you by the coach of Saturday a few copies of the prospectus of the Zoological Society. It is a subject on which much has been said, and more might be written, but it has been thought best, in the present state of the speculation, to confine the notice to a few words. The names are coming in fast, and I shall be happy to receive a list of any of your friends at Liverpool who may be desirous of becoming subscribers. The amount of the sum will not ruin them, neither will they find themselves in bad company, and no pecuniary call will be made until the plan is advanced, and we can show them something for their money. It is proposed to have a general meeting of the subscribers who may be in town in the course of the present month [June], in order to appoint a committee and proceed to business. We expect to have at least five hundred members to begin with, and that Government will provide us with ground, etc."

The prospectus of the new Zoological Society was drawn up and issued on the 20th of May 1825. It was very short and to the point. The society was to have the same relation to zoology that horticulture bears to botany. Its aim was twofold. It was to introduce, by means of a public establishment, new varieties, breeds, or races of living animals, such as quadrupeds, birds, fishes, etc., which might be judged capable of application to purposes of utility, either in our farmyards, woods, wastes, ponds, or rivers. In the second place, it was to assist this establishment, and the general study of zoology, by a museum of prepared specimens. Sir T. Stamford Raffles, a bust of whom adorns the lion-house of the Society's gardens in Regent's Park, was the first President of the Society; and, "on his lamented death," the Marquis of Lansdowne was elected his successor. A selection from Sir Stamford's collection was made after his death, by the permission of Lady Raffles, for the museum of dried specimens. The conditions attached to the gift—which was announced by Dr. Raffles, who, after his cousin's death, had been elected a member of the Council, in order to represent the interests of the Raffles family—were, that it should be kept separate; that it should not be responsible for any of the society's debts; and that it should revert to the family if the society were at any time broken up.

Dr. Raffles's reminiscences throw some light on the relations between two such illustrious friends of the anti-slavery cause as Wilberforce and Raffles. I make the following extract from them:—

"Wilberforce and Sir Stamford were friends, and at length came to be next-door neighbours, dividing Highwood Hill, near Barnet, between them. The village at the top of the hill was also pretty equally divided between them, Sir Stamford owning one half and Wilberforce the other. Each portion had a public-house in it, and he used to laugh and say, 'Wilberforce has the "Crown," and I the "Rising Sun."' Each had an excellent house, unpretending, but very convenient. My cousin's amount of land was about one hundred and twenty statute acres, yielding enough for all purposes, with a considerable amount for sale. In fact the family lived upon it—house and stables. Lady Raffles told me that she bought nothing but wine and fish. She fed her own mutton and veal and poultry, and exchanged with the butcher for beef. . . .

"He used to treat his friends occasionally with rare and curious delicacies. I remember that, on one occasion, when I was staying in Grosvenor Street, he had a few friends to dinner, amongst whom was Sir Everard Home, the King's physician and great comparative anatomist; and before we began dinner, when just seated at the table, Lady Raffles said, 'Now, I shall not tell you what the soup is till you have partaken of it.' It was handed round, and all, on tasting it, exclaimed, 'How delicious! What can it be?' 'Well,' she said, 'that soup is made of Chinese snails;' and, indeed, so exquisite was it, that, ordering dinner the next morning, I requested that, if, perchance, any of that soup remained, we might have it that day. It was not likely that I should ever taste it again. Another most delicious, but very expensive, soup is made of the edible birds' nest of Java. Sir Stamford told me he gave Queen Charlotte a sufficient quantity of it to make a small tureen of soup; but that, small as it was, he said it was worth eight guineas. How great is the power of prejudice! Had we been told what the snail soup really was, the probability is that we should none of us have touched it!

"But I am forgetting Wilberforce. Before he came to reside at Highwood, he left the laying out of the grounds contiguous to the house to the taste of Sir Stamford. He took me in with him on one occasion to show me what he was doing; and I well remember the glee with which he said, taking me to a long mound which he had raised and planted with shrubs and flowers, 'There, I have raised this mound that the little man may enjoy his daily walk, sheltered by it from the north winds, which would otherwise be too severe for him.' Alas! How brief was the period allowed for the happy intercourse he thus anticipated! Wilberforce had scarcely got settled there when Sir Stamford died. Wilberforce did not long survive him; and, as they were, when death parted them, living beside each other, so their statues are now, and will long remain, side by side, in close juxtaposition, amongst the illustrious dead in Westminster Abbey."

With one more extract, of a different character from that just quoted, I may take my leave of these vivid first-hand glimpses of the man whose career we are following to the goal he has so nearly reached. The final picture I select shows Stamford Raffles dilating on the advantages of Java—the Java which had been lost. Dr. Raffles writes:—

"I shall never forget the scene, which I witnessed at Mr. Wilberforce's, confirmatory of the statement of the gross ignorance which prevailed respecting the islands given up to the Dutch. Wilberforce at that time resided at Kensington Gore, in a house which was afterwards inhabited by the celebrated Countess of Blessington. I breakfasted with him [Sir Stamford] there one morning, when a deputation from the Asiatic Society met him, by appointment, to present him with the congratulations of the society on his return from the East, and their thanks for his noble conduct in the abolition of slavery in the islands which he had governed. They were naturally anxious to obtain information from him concerning those islands, their people, and their produce; and great was their astonishment when, kneeling before the maps placed against the back of a sofa, they bent over him as he pointed them out, and they listened to the interesting and astonishing details which he gave concerning them. There was Java, an island of rice; and Borneo, an island of gold; and Banca, an island of tin; and the Celebes, islands of spice—enough, as he said, to supply the rest of the world for ages, all recklessly abandoned to the Dutch by a Government that knew neither *why* or *what* they were giving. Alas for Sir Stamford! he lived too soon. It was a *war* administration in that day; as for the commerce of the country, Lord Castlereagh, whose Ministry it was, neither knew nor cared anything about it."

At the end of the year 1824 the attention of Sir Stamford Raffles was drawn away from parliamentary and literary subjects by an attack on his proceedings at Singapore, and by a serious attempt to rob him of the credit of having originated the occupation of that settlement. In the last chapter the true history of the affair has been given, without bestowing an unnecessary word on the alleged inspiration which Raffles is stated, in some geographical gazetteers and similar books of reference, to have received from various officers of the royal and mercantile navies; while the rival claims of Colonel Farquhar have been reserved for consideration under the date when they were first advanced. As Colonel Farquhar was the Resident at Singapore during the first four years of its existence, a claim made by himself to be regarded as its founder would, on the face of it, deserve attention, and could not fail to obtain a certain amount of credence. I am assured that the myth of Farquhar, and not Raffles, having been the true founder of Singapore, is still the faith of some persons; and that those who accept statements without examining the basis on which they rest have conceived that they had found an easy way out of the difficulty of deciding between Raffles and Farquhar in this matter by dividing the honours between them. This sort of verdict is neither satisfactory nor just.

Fortunately the evidence is too clear to admit of any doubt or misconception; and Colonel Farquhar's Memorial, which was drafted in order to rob Sir Stamford Raffles of his "political child," and the memory of which certainly induced some of Raffles's detractors to cast a slur on its parentage, has provided the means of proving more conclusively than ever that Singapore was the discovery of Sir Stamford Raffles, and that it owed far less to Colonel Farquhar's care in the early stage of its existence than had been generally supposed. To those who recollect how Colonel Bannerman attacked Raffles alone, merely referring to poor Colonel Farquhar as being seduced and led astray by his superior in office and in intellect, further evidence on the subject might seem unnecessary. At Penang the view held about Singapore was, that it was "the Post which Sir Stamford Raffles had so injudiciously chosen." Nothing was known in Calcutta of the pretensions of Colonel William Farquhar. From one end of the correspondence to the other, the affair is treated as the work of Raffles alone. It was Raffles who founded it; it was Raffles who gave the instructions for its government on February 6th, 1819, and again, for its reorganisation and remodelling in 1823; it was Raffles who combated the Dutch view and supplied the case and arguments which eventually constituted the policy of Great Britain and carried the day. From one end of the correspondence to the other there is not a line, not a word, that gives Farquhar a tittle of credit, or a tithe in the act of founding Singapore. The whole and the sole praise, mingled with blame and the attachment of responsibility, is given to Raffles by Lord Hastings, who only partly shared Sir Stamford's views, but who admitted, in his despatch to the Court of the 14th of May 1819, that "the position of Singhapura appears to be well selected for the protection of our commerce in those seas, and, therefore, we consider it to be a valuable post, which it is desirable to retain." The credit is also given to Raffles by inference, in the unhesitating denunciations pronounced upon him by those who termed its occupation injudicious and calamitous. It is not out of place to repeat that Farquhar's plan was "the occupation and settling of the Islands of Carimon," and that the Supreme Government, in November 1818, wrote "that there were considerations which would incline it to hesitate to sanction that scheme, apart from the fact *that it would be entirely superseded by the result of Sir Stamford Raffles's mission.*"

With these preliminary observations, Colonel Farquhar's Memorial may now be given, or, rather, the complete portion of it relating to Singapore, for I find that to quote the whole document, with Sir Stamford's reply, would fill nearly a fourth of this volume; but, with a view to preventing misapprehensions, I would state that the whole of these documents (33,000 words) from the Records of the Government of India have been carefully read and considered by me with such an intention. Colonel Farquhar's Memorial reached Raffles's hands on the 27th of December 1824.

"THE MEMORIAL OF WILLIAM FARQUHAR, LIEUTENANT-COLONEL IN THE HONOURABLE COMPANY'S SERVICE, LATE RESIDENT AT SINGAPORE, ETC.

"To the HONOURABLE THE COURT OF DIRECTORS
OF THE EAST INDIA COMPANY.

"*Sheweth*,—

"*That* from the year 1819 to the month of April 1823, he was employed as Resident [at] Singapore, a settlement *formed at his own suggestion and matured under his personal management*, and which, though originally made dependent upon Fort Marlborough, under the superintendence of Sir Stamford Raffles, the late Lieutenant-Governor, has within the above-mentioned period acquired such importance as to be brought into immediate connection with the Supreme Government at Fort William. . . .

"Under a deep sense of the injury he has received as a high public functionary and as a soldier, your Memorialist throws himself upon your Honourable Court, and he solicits your patient attention while detailing at some length a series of acts of the most flagrant injustice and tyranny on the part of the late Lieutenant-Governor of Fort Marlborough, contrasted, as he flatters himself, by a forbearance on the part of your Memorialist, even in cases of strict right, where he felt that personal considerations might interfere with a paramount interest of the Company. . . .

"This brings your Memorialist to the formation of the Settlement of Singapore, a Settlement the importance of which is now so fully estimated, that it would be idle to occupy the attention of your Honourable Court upon that point. It will, however, be necessary for him to go back shortly to trace his connection with the origin of that settlement.

"So early as the year 1816, the disadvantage to the interest of the Honourable Company likely to attend the cession of Malacca, and particularly in respect to the China trade, had induced your Memorialist to make a representation upon the subject to the Honourable Mr. Petrie, then Governor of Prince of Wales's Island, in which his attention was invited to the subject by the following paragraph:—

"'In the event of Malacca being delivered up to the Dutch, I think it would be extremely desirable if a new British Settlement could be formed in some convenient spot near the south-east entrance of the Straits, so as to be as nearly as possible in the way of shipping passing to and from China and the Eastern

Archipelago.' 'The port of Rhio, formerly a dependency of Malacca, would, if not repossessed by the Dutch, be a very desirable place for us to occupy, being at present a Settlement of considerable trade, and, although properly appertaining to the Rajah of Lingen, arrangements might be made, without much difficulty, I conceive, for the transfer of the Government to us. Rhio is indeed rather out of the way of ships passing to China through the Straits of Singapore, but not so far as to cause any material delay in touching there ; this Settlement would certainly be preferable to any new one, as it would fully pay its own expenses, and be the means of preserving to us a share, at least, of that influence over the Malay which, by the restitution of Malacca, will most undoubtedly fall entirely into the hands of the Dutch.'

"When the time approached for surrendering Malacca, the importance of this measure became more sensibly felt, and in the year 1818 your Memorialist was selected by the Honourable Colonel Bannerman, who had succeeded Mr. Petrie as Governor of Prince of Wales's Island, to proceed on a public mission to the States of Siack, Rhio, Lingen, and Pontiana, for the purpose of endeavouring to establish commercial treaties with such of the Malay powers as were at the time considered to be independent.

"In the short space of six weeks your Memorialist completed the objects of his mission. . . .

"During the negotiations which took place with the commissioners of the King of the Netherlands upon the surrender of Malacca, your Memorialist discovered that it was the intention of the Dutch Government to establish a factory at Rhio, and to extend their influence to the utmost of their power among the neighbouring States so soon as the British force should be withdrawn ; and as the circumstances would allow no delay, your Memorialist, on his own responsibility, despatched an agent to the Rajah Mudah, or Viceroy of Rhio, to represent to him the advantage which would be derivable from the formation of a British establishment at the Carimon Islands, in the Straits of Malacca, and your Memorialist succeeded in obtaining permission to surveying the Carimon Islands for the purpose of forming a British Settlement. . . . Your Memorialist had obtained permission to be absent on a visit to Europe for three years, and on his return to Penang after the surrender of Malacca at the close of the year 1818, as above mentioned, he was making his arrangements for availing himself of this permission, when Sir S. Raffles arrived at Penang as Political Agent to the Governor-General. . . .

"Having surveyed the Carimon Islands, which did not afford advantages for the settlement, it was resolved to proceed to Johore, but on the way, at the suggestion of your Memorialist, they stopped on the 19th January at Singapore, then the residence of a native prince called the Tumung'gong of Johore, and the local advantages afforded by it being immediately discovered, your Memorialist on the following morning proceeded to Rhio, where he succeeded in obtaining the sanction of the Government in the formation of a British Settlement at Singapore. On the 5th of February your Memorialist returned to Singapore, and on the morning of the 6th the British flag was formally displayed. On the following day Sir Stamford Raffles left the Settlement, after having placed your Memorialist in charge as Resident and Commandant, leaving with him a letter of general instructions. . . .

"Your Memorialist has already stated that he surrendered Malacca to the Dutch in the year 1818, and, in the ordinary course, he might then have availed himself of the above permission to visit England ; but before any plans were arranged, he received instructions from the Supreme Government to proceed with Sir Stamford Raffles to take charge of the intended Settlement in the Eastern Seas, and he need only call the attention of your Honourable Court to the terms of the request in that letter, to show that his stay in India was at that time considered important, still he had not abandoned his intention of returning to Europe; but circumstances occurred, occasioned by this delay, which rendered it less an object of importance to him, and, on the 23rd of October 1820, he addressed the Governor [-General] at Fort William, stating, that as the same urgent call for his proceeding to Europe on furlough did not then exist, he was desirous of postponing his departure from India until the ensuing season of 1821–22, and in the meantime to continue in charge of Singapore, or otherwise as the Governor [-General] in Council should be pleased to direct. No answer was received from the Supreme Government to this letter, but from the [Lt.-] Governor of Fort Marlborough he received an answer, dated the 1st May 1821, requesting him to specify, for the information of the Lieutenant-Governor, the period for which he was desirous of remaining in the charge of Singapore; and your Memorialist, on the 19th September, replied to that letter, that he should wish to defer coming to any fixed determination on the point, until definitive arrangements should be made respecting the permanent retention of Singapore by the Company; and your Memorialist is assured that your Honourable Court will well appreciate those feelings of interest excited in his mind in regard to a Settlement selected and founded by himself, and which he was anxious not to quit until he was assured of its permanent prosperity.

"In the month of October 1822, Sir Stamford Raffles visited the Settlement of Singapore, and though in the commencement he expressed high approbation of the measures of your Memorialist, and satisfaction with the state of the Settlement, it was not long before, finding his opinion clash with that of your Memorialist, in various local questions, he commenced a course of conduct which, to an officer of your Memorialist's rank and experience in the affairs of the Company, could not fail to be in the highest degree offensive.

"Your Memorialist has been thus minute, because he cannot acquiesce in the justice of the charges made against him by the Lieutenant-Governor on any of these points. But your Memorialist has no claim to an exemption from the common infirmities of human nature. He may have been mistaken in point of fact, he may have erred in point of judgment, but he may confidently say that he must have been more than man who, placed for four years in an arduous command, where his acts were reported to the Supreme Government by (to say the least) no friendly medium, and with little or no opportunity afforded of explanation on his part, could have avoided giving some excuse for complaint; but the sweeping charge of incompetence, now for the first time brought against your Memorialist, is one the services in which he has been engaged and the opinions of those under whom he has acted for a series of years forbid him to concede.

"The facts are obvious, the explanation which would carry conviction upon the subject is long and complicated, and requires a painful degree of attention. Your Memorialist feels that the only mode of restoring that credit and reputation of which he has been thus unjustly deprived, is by allowing him to return, with the sanction and approbation of your Honourable Court, to that command from which he was improperly removed."

Before quoting the principal passages of Sir Stamford's rejoinder, I would note one or two points of general interest in connection with this Memorial. The first point is that Colonel Farquhar thrusts into the background his own suggestion, repeatedly pressed on Raffles, as well as on the Bengal and Penang Governments,—which was in favour of the Carimons. There is no doubt of Farquhar's advocacy of that scheme up to the very eve of the occupation of Singapore, but it would obviously have been indiscreet for him to introduce it into a claim to be the suggester and true founder of the latter post. When Farquhar proceeds to details, he declares that it was on his suggestion they—that is to say, Raffles and Farquhar—stopped at Singapore on the 19th of January. But on that day Raffles was still at Penang, and Farquhar was not with him,—so that Farquhar's statement is false on the face of it. His pretension is also refuted by Raffles's letter to Mr. Marsden, of the 12th of December 1818; by Raffles's despatch of the 1st of January 1819, to Colonel Bannerman; as well as by the despatch from Raffles to the Supreme Government, quoted in the last chapter, showing that Raffles had fully decided on Singapore by the 16th of January. It is also advisable to state that when Raffles reached Penang on the 1st of January, that is to say, after his two first written testimonies had been recorded in favour of Singapore, he had not seen Farquhar for six or seven years, and had held, so far as can be traced, no correspondence with him. Finally, the concluding decision as to the unsuitability of the Carimons was not arrived at until the 25th or 26th of January, after Raffles had met Farquhar returning to Penang from Rhio. In another passage, Farquhar accuses Raffles of being unfriendly long before the date of his supersession. On that particular I may refute Farquhar's statement out of his own words. In a letter to "My dear Raffles," from Singapore, March 31, 1820, he wrote: "We are, as you may suppose, most anxious to hear from you again. I hope you have long ere this reached Bencoolen in safety. Pray present my best wishes to Lady Raffles, and give your dear little ones a kiss each on my account.—Believe me, ever yours, W. Farquhar." There is a pencil note on Farquhar's Memorial in the India Office, opposite the paragraph asking for permission to return, of one word—"Impossible." The writing is said to be that of the Chairman of the East India Company.

We have also clear evidence as to what Raffles himself thought of the measures he had been compelled to take against Colonel Farquhar twelve months before that officer presented his Memorial. Writing to a friend from Bencoolen on November 1st, 1823, he said, "God knows, I have had but one object in view—the interests of Singapore,—and if a brother had been opposed to them, I must have acted as I did towards Colonel Farquhar, for whom I ever had, and still do retain, a warm personal affection and regard. I upheld him as long as I could, and many were the sacrifices I made to prevent a rupture, but when it did take place, I found it necessary to prosecute my cause with vigour and effect." The following is Sir Stamford Raffles' reply:—

"To the HONOURABLE THE COURT OF DIRECTORS OF THE EAST INDIA COMPANY.

"HONOURABLE SIRS,—I beg to return my acknowledgments for the opportunity which your Honourable Court have been pleased to afford me of perusing the statement made by Lieutenant-Colonel Farquhar, in which I am charged with a 'series of acts of the most flagrant injustice and tyranny,' a charge which cannot but have had the effect of creating an unfavourable impression towards myself, and which has been presented at a moment of all others the most likely to prejudice my interests with reference to the appeal which I have had occasion to make to your Honourable Court.

"I lament that Lieutenant-Colonel Farquhar should have been advised to adopt this course, because it compels me to advert to points which necessarily involve the character of that officer in the discharge of his duty at Singapore, and which, from motives of personal consideration towards him, I preferred leaving to the judgment and decision of the Supreme Government.

"Much of Lieutenant-Colonel Farquhar's statement relates to services and questions long antecedent to the period at which he became connected with me in the establishment of Singapore. Our connection in that duty will be found to have commenced in the year 1818, when his services were placed at my disposal by the Supreme Government.

"The statement of Lieutenant-Colonel Farquhar is so diffuse and violent that it is difficult to trace the exact grounds on which he prefers his charge, but it may perhaps be resolved into the three following heads, on each of which I beg to offer explanations:—

"First, the credit assumed by him for having suggested, nurtured, and matured the Settlement of Singapore to its present state of unexampled prosperity;

"Secondly, the acts of flagrant injustice and tyranny with which he so unreservedly accuses me; and—

"Thirdly, his removal from the charge of Singapore.

"On the credit assumed by Lieutenant-Colonel Farquhar for having suggested the establishment of Singapore, I will observe that THIS IS THE FIRST TIME I EVER HEARD OF THE CIRCUMSTANCE, AND THAT ON REFERENCE TO THE PUBLIC RECORDS I FIND NOTHING TO SUPPORT IT. THE CIRCUMSTANCES UNDER WHICH THE SETTLEMENT WAS ESTABLISHED WILL FULLY APPEAR IN MY CORRESPONDENCE WITH THE SUPREME GOVERNMENT AT THE TIME, AND I CAN HARDLY SUPPOSE THAT A SERIOUS REFUTATION OF THIS PART OF COLONEL FARQUHAR'S STATEMENT CAN NOW BE NECESSARY. The selection of Singapore is admitted to have been judicious, and God forbid that I should deprive Colonel Farquhar of any just credit which may be due to him in the establishment of it, but a regard to truth compels me to deny in broad terms that Colonel Farquhar ever suggested, or, to my knowledge, knew or stated anything with regard to the formation of a Settlement at Singapore, until I communicated to him the authority with which I was invested, to form a Settlement there. It is true he had suggested to Colonel Bannerman the advantage of a settlement at the Carimons; but when I arrived at Prince of Wales's Island, the unanimous and unqualified sentiment of the Penang Government was against the possibility of the British Government in India executing any advantageous political arrangements with the Malay States. 'Rhio and Lingen, they say, being in the possession of the Dutch, the southern entrance of the Straits of Malacca were considered as hermetically sealed against us; the execution, therefore, among these States of any political arrangement as a counterpoise to the influence of the Dutch, it is needless to disguise, is now beyond the power of the British Government in India.'

"With regard to the Carimon Islands, when, out of deference to the opinion of Colonel Farquhar, I proceeded to examine them, they were proved to his own conviction to be altogether unfit for the proposed establishment, and this fact is admitted in his present statement.

"Lieutenant-Colonel Farquhar would infer that our Settlement at Singapore arose out of the measures adopted by him at Rhio, and his negotiation there.

"So far from this being the case, it must be notorious to every one who knows anything of the matter, that Singapore was not taken possession of by me under any authority or negotiation with the Chief of Rhio, but in *direct opposition and altogether independent of that State*, and had Colonel Farquhar adverted to the terms of the Treaty with the Sultan and Tumung'gung of Singapore, and to the main argument in our subsequent discussions with the Netherlands authorities, viz. *that Singapore was independent of Rhio*, he might have avoided this mistake. The following extract from the Governor-General in Council to the Netherlands authorities at Batavia, under date the 25th June 1819, will, at any rate, show how distinct the occupation of Singapore was kept from any proceedings at Rhio:—

"'Para. 10. Sir Stamford Raffles, on his arrival at Prince of Wales's Island, found that the agent of your nation had anticipated him at Rhio; he therefore very properly avoided that port.

"Para. 11. He proceeded to Singapore, and there formed a Treaty with a Chief, whom he describes as the rightful Sovereign of Johore, as well as with the local Government, which he represents as being independent of that established at

Rhio. A copy of the Treaty we have the honour to enclose for your Excellency's information.'

"Lieutenant-Colonel Farquhar has further taken great credit to himself for his management of the Settlement and its progressive advancement. On this point I should be sorry to detract in any way from his just due. I have always been ready and anxious to acknowledge the assistance he rendered to me on the first establishment of the Settlement, but when Lieutenant-Colonel Farquhar goes further, I must beg leave to refer to the sentiments of a higher authority on the subject :—

"'Indeed, the instructions which you furnished to that officer for the formation of the Settlement seem to have been generally well suited to the circumstances of the place, and the arrangements adopted by the Resident (Colonel Farquhar) would appear to be injudicious in proportion as he deviated from your directions.'

"On the second head, viz. the series of acts for which I am accused by Lieutenant-Colonel Farquhar of flagrant injustice and tyranny, I request to observe that I am not aware of having had any personal question with that officer. He can therefore only advert to the public acts of my administration ; and as these are to be found on the Public Records, I appeal to them in refutation of the charge. I am satisfied it will thence be found that, so far from my treatment of that officer being unjust or tyrannical, I deferred to him the utmost personal consideration which a sense of public duty and the paramount interests of the public admitted.

"In support of this assertion I entreat your Honourable Court will do me the justice to peruse the correspondence which took place between Lieutenant-Colonel Farquhar and myself, and the reports and proceedings of the Governor-General in Council thereon, from the first establishment of the Settlement until the period of Lieutenant-Colonel Farquhar's departure for England.

"Not to detain your Honourable Court with minor questions, in which I had occasion to complain of the maladministration and imbecility of Lieutenant-Colonel Farquhar, I shall confine myself to the following points :—

"His irregularity in the construction of public buildings and appropriation of the ground expressly reserved for public purposes for the benefit of a few favoured individuals, which added to the mode followed in the disposal of lands generally, in contravention of his instructions and to the manifest injury of the rights of Government, whereby the whole plan and order of things directed on the first establishment of the Settlement were so far deranged as to render it indispensable that his proceedings should be disavowed, that the town should be removed, and that the whole of the land should be resumed at great expense to Government and no less loss to individuals.

"'It is from such an error on the part of Lieutenant-Colonel Farquhar that the Governor-General in Council now finds himself under the necessity of incurring a considerable expense, which, under the present circumstances of the Settlement, he was naturally anxious not to incur, or of allowing the public service to continue exposed to, serious inconvenience and embarrassment for an indefinite period of time.'

"I will only add on this subject, that it became my unpleasant duty to undo almost everything Lieutenant-Colonel Farquhar had done, and this under circumstances of no ordinary difficulty. I had certainly a right to expect that after the subject had been deliberately viewed in all its bearings, and all that Lieutenant-Colonel Farquhar had to say in his justification had been considered, and the orders under which I was bound to act were peremptory, I should at least have had the advantage of his personal assistance and support, in remedying the evil which had been occasioned by his departure from my instructions; but in this, I am sorry to say, I was disappointed. On communicating to Lieutenant-Colonel Farquhar the instructions for new modelling the town, etc., and for the establishment of a more regular police, above alluded to, for his corrections or suggestions, that officer returned the draft to me without an envelope, declining to have any personal communication on the subject; and from this period I may date the commencement of a course of opposition to every measure which I deemed it my duty to carry into effect for the general benefit of the Settlement.

"The establishment of gaming and cockfighting, contrary to the most express and positive orders which he had received on the first establishment of the Settlement, and which, after much opposition and discussion on his part, I felt it my duty to abolish. The following is the reply of the Supreme Government to my reference on the subject, enclosing the correspondence with Lieutenant-Colonel Farquhar on the occasion:—

"'I am directed to acknowledge the receipt of your letter of the 22nd April last, with its enclosures, and in reply to inform you that the Governor-General in Council fully concurs in the sentiment expressed by you, and highly approves your determination to abolish the gaming farms at Singapore.'

"The recognition and admission of the slave-trade at Singapore.

"On this point I certainly did not give any particular instructions to Colonel Farquhar, because I never could have supposed that a British officer could have tolerated such a practice in a Settlement circumstanced like Singapore, and formed after the promulgation of the Act of Parliament declaring it to be felony.

"I need therefore hardly say how much I was shocked in hearing the cries of a female, shortly after my landing in Singapore in 1822, proceed from a vessel in the river, whose principal cargo was female slaves for the market of Singapore.

"On so serious a subject, however, it was my most anxious desire to proceed in a manner that would least involve Lieutenant-Colonel Farquhar, who, in the opinion of many, seemed to have exposed himself to the penalties of the law against the slave-trade; and my sentiments on the subject being well known, few or no subsequent importations took place during my residence. It was not, therefore, until a public appeal was made to me by the magistrates of Singapore for instructions how to act in cases which came before them, that I took up the subject publicly. To this representation, and to the correspondence which passed with the Resident at Singapore on the subject generally, I must request to make particular reference, because it will at once show the different views which I was induced to take on the subject from those entertained by Lieutenant-Colonel Farquhar.

"I will not detain your Honourable Court by going into further particulars. I have said enough to show that the conduct of Lieutenant-Colonel Farquhar was called in question on many of the most essential parts of his local administration, and a perusal of the correspondence will prove that he was afforded every opportunity of explaining and justifying it. In every case his own statements were transmitted to Bengal, and, if an unfavourable judgment has been passed, he can in no way complain of unfairness on my part.

"In conclusion, I beg to express my regret that I should have had occasion to trespass on your Honourable Court with such a lengthened statement, in which, I trust, it will appear that, in the outset of my mission to the Eastward, I maintained the character of Lieutenant-Colonel Farquhar against the opinion of the authority under whom he had previously so long acted;—that whilst I have acknowledged the zeal of Lieutenant-Colonel Farquhar in the aid which he afforded me in the prosecution of my mission, I have at the same time shown that his claim to the credit of having suggested the formation of the Settlement of Singapore, or its ultimate acquisition, has no foundation;—that in the administration of the affairs of that Settlement most of the measures which he adopted were at variance with the instructions which he had received for his guidance, and that consequently many were reversed by order of the Supreme Government, at a considerable cost to the East India Company and detriment of the Settlement; whilst others were denounced as unworthy the character and rank of an officer in his station;—that so far from my having any personal hostility towards Colonel Farquhar, it must be evident to your Honourable Court that in every step I took to remedy the inconvenience occasioned by his measures, much personal trouble and annoyance was occasioned to myself, whilst every disposition was shown to carry the same into effect with consideration to Lieutenant-Colonel Farquhar's feelings;—that upon each point my views and proceedings were supported by the Bengal Government;—and that, lastly, whilst that authority questioned the necessity for my taking upon myself the temporary direction of the Settlement without their previous authority, they had already appointed a successor to Lieutenant-Colonel Farquhar, upon the ground that a reference to his measures 'indicated, to say the least, a degree of facility and want of discretion not calculated to inspire any confidence in the administration of Lieutenant-Colonel Farquhar, when left without a local controul.'

"I have the honour to be, with the greatest respect, honourable sirs, your most obedient, humble servant, T. S. Raffles.

"London, *25th January* 1825."

On the following 2nd of April Colonel Farquhar made a brief rejoinder, but as he entirely omits all reference to Singapore, or to the claim he had put forward on that score, it is unnecessary to reproduce it. He seems, indeed, to have had no other object in advancing that pretension than the desire to irritate Sir Stamford Raffles. Farquhar knew that he could not hit his opponent on a more tender place, and he tried to take his revenge for having been removed from a profitable and prominent post with quadruple allowances, by claiming what Raffles most cherished. It was the handiest weapon to throw at his enemy, or, that worst of supposed enemies, a lost friend. It would be inaccurate to compare it to the spear of Priam,—*telum imbelle sine ictu*,—for it proved a boomerang to its author, by revealing in still clearer characters "the incapacity and imbecility," which made him unequal to the task of Resident at Singapore. Farquhar posing at the expense of Raffles as the originator of Singapore, resembles one of Napoleon's lieutenants claiming his victories; but Farquhar has no valid pretension even to that minor contributory part, which would be allowed to Kellermann for Marengo, and Lannes for Austerlitz.

Even his routine administrative work as Resident had to be undone or done over again. If the British Empire had been dependent on Colonel Farquhar for a settlement to the Eastward, then, since time was of vital importance to its acquisition, we should have obtained nothing, because at the crucial moment Farquhar was proceeding to England to enjoy three years' leisure!

CHAPTER XII

CLOUDS AND DEATH

RAFFLES had never been physically a strong man, and the little strength he possessed had been so sapped by the sustained and indefatigable labours which he undertook in the course of his public duty, that it is not surprising to find that his health was bad, and a constant source of anxiety to his relatives after his final return in 1824. He had never complained, at the time, of the effect of that climate which proved fatal to his first wife, his children, and his best friends—one after another; but, none the less, it told its tale on him. It was not merely in repeated attacks of illness that this was shown, but in the difficulty of writing. His hand became cramped, and he suffered from pains in the head. His active and comprehensive mind was full of great schemes, but he had not the physical strength to carry them out. In his desk was found, after his death, a memorandum on a projected work to be entitled "Notes on the Eastern Islands," including an account of the establishment of Singapore; and he was also intent on publishing, in conjunction with Dr. Horsfield, a Natural History.

There is no doubt that Sir Stamford Raffles was a man of a delicate and sensitive mind, as well as of a precarious constitution. The Farquhar attack had touched his deepest feelings more severely than any other ordeal through which he had passed. With regard to Singapore, he felt secure and convinced that none could deprive him of the credit of an achievement in accomplishing which he had borne alone the heat and burden of the day. To effectually dispose of the arguments of an adversary, to smash a rival and preposterous case, is agreeable, but there are some matters in which the mere putting forward of a rival plea has the effect of shaking one's self-confidence, and of introducing an element of doubt into all one's calculations. To a highly-strung temperament, such as Raffles's was, the blow was not the less injurious because so effectually parried that it only damaged the man who dealt it. If Raffles had been strong in health, the impression would have been only transitory; but his health was gone in the service of his country, and as fortune inflicted on him a succession of the most cruel blows, the diminished strength left by unmerited adversity was unequal to the task of repelling bodily ailment.

The story of the last eighteen months of the life of Sir Stamford Raffles is a sad one; and there has seldom, if ever, been a case of a man, who had done so much for his country, passing away under such a cloud of varied misfortunes as befell him, without a contributory act of his own. His courage and eagle spirit would no doubt have enabled him to bear up under these trials, and to have triumphed, as he had done before, over all opponents; but successive attacks, premonitory of the malady that killed him, sapped his vigour, and exhausted, with each fresh effort, the remaining powers of his body.

The following extracts from his correspondence with Dr. Raffles will show the reader how much he suffered during the last year of his life. On the 24th of May 1825 he wrote:—"Thank God I can return a tolerably satisfactory answer to your kind inquiry by saying, that though still rather weak and nervous, I am again getting about. My attack was sudden and unexpected, but fortunately was not apoplectic, as was at first feared. I was inanimate for about an hour, but, on being bled, got better, and have had no return"; and again, on June 6th, he wrote: "This last attack has so shaken my confidence and nerves, that I have hardly spirit at the present moment to enter upon public life, and prudence dictates the necessity of my keeping as quiet as I can until I completely re-establish my health." On the 10th of November, in the same year, he wrote:

"I have been confined to my bed the whole of the day with one of my most violent headaches"; and on the 7th of February 1826 he said: "I have, upon the whole, very much improved in my general health, and am at present, barring occasional attacks, in better health than I have enjoyed since my return to England. . . . I have, however, had, and still have, a good many annoyances and inquietudes, which have occasionally disturbed my peace of mind, owing to the misconduct and distresses of friends; but I hope these will soon be over."

The more serious matters which, during the whole of this period, agitated the mind of Sir Stamford Raffles, related to his pecuniary claims on the East India Company. These were of several kinds, and must be duly set forth. In the first place, Raffles had, from Bencoolen, on the 22nd of March 1818, presented a Memorial to the Court asking for early decision on the merit of his administration in Java, and begging that, if his measures "shall generally be proved to have been proper, and such as the circumstances in which the colony was placed called for, the Court will award him such consideration as he is entitled to expect with reference to the general scale of his services and pretensions." That Memorial was shelved and ignored during the six years that intervened between its despatch and Sir Stamford's return home. After his return, he renewed the application for a final pronouncement on the part of the authorities as to his administration in the East, adding to the list of his services the record of what he had done in Sumatra and at Singapore. He was also a petitioner for compensation on account of the losses he had suffered in and through the *Fame*, since, in addition to the original loss, a new passage and outfit had cost him £3000; and, although he would not sue *in formâ pauperis*, he threw himself on the generosity of the Company he had served in the East during almost twenty eventful years. These were the greater matters, but one at least of the lesser claims was interesting. The cost of the passage of himself, his family, and staff, to Bencoolen in 1817, had been £1500. He had actually paid that sum out of his pocket, and had drawn on Government for the amount. Of all his claims on the Company, this was the only one absolutely settled in his lifetime. The Court refused to allow more than £1000 for the passage, and Raffles was required to refund the difference. That comparatively small matter was settled while Raffles was still in Sumatra; and, with regard to the other points, he entertained, down to the beginning of the year 1826, a reasonable amount of hope that they would be decided in his favour. On one occasion, in November 1825, he wrote: "What the East India Company may do is uncertain; but if their liberality keeps pace with their delay, I ought to expect something handsome; though I confess I do not look for much." With the new year the matter took a more definite turn, and on the 7th of February 1826 the following letter to Dr. Raffles gives Sir Stamford's view of the situation:—

"The East India Company are now talking of taking up my case and granting me an annuity; but I fear it will be very moderate, and £500 a year is the largest amount I hear of. This, had I the means of living independent of them, I should not be inclined to accept; but necessity and consideration for my family must predominate, and I must e'en be content with what I can get. I have, unfortunately, been a considerable loser by the cession of Bencoolen—some thousands. My bankers have failed here, and altogether my prospects are not as comfortable as they were; but the pressure is, I hope, only temporary, and I trust all will be right again, and that I shall not be obliged to seek a tropical clime again in search of *filthy lucre*—for nothing else would I think, tempt me to venture."

It has now to be shown how even these moderate views were to be disappointed. The mode in which the East India Company conducted the pecuniary transactions with its servants was at this time marked by many anomalies, and was not free from an arbitrary tendency. In the main its policy was generous, and it dealt with the more favoured and highly placed of its servants in a lavish fashion, and with a large-handedness that obtained their enthusiasm by stimulating their hopes. But, if this was the general policy, there were many individual cases in which the Court adopted another course, criticising every item of account with the keenness of a professional auditor, and asserting its supreme authority by the reduction, and even the dismissal, of claims which deserved at least as much consideration as those that were freely admitted. There was another characteristic of the Court's decisions. They were often not given for years after the transactions to which they referred; so that, when adverse, they fell with a double harshness on those who had imagined that long silence meant approbation and sanction. In proof of this, I would recall to the reader's mind what occurred in connection with the extra pay accorded to Raffles, when Secretary at Penang, by the local authorities. Raffles was not relieved by the Court from the responsibility of possibly refunding the amount he had received, until the 30th of April 1817, or more than seven years after the transaction. It also took four years to get a settlement of the item as to his passage-money to Bencoolen. These facts will explain how it was that, when the Company made the claim on Raffles which has now to be described, several of the matters related to a period nine years earlier. It is not surprising that Raffles should have regarded them as settled, and as points that were beyond dispute.

Attention has been called in an earlier part of this book to the parsimonious spirit in which the Company regarded the establishment on the West Coast and in the Straits, as compared with its treatment of Indian matters. It was parsimonious, because its ledger showed nothing but losses in that direction, and its interest waned as it became clearer that Bencoolen would be resigned to the Dutch. Raffles could not hope to combat these facts; and no doubt it would have been more discreet if he had not brought into play the energy that characterised all his proceedings when coming before the Court as a suitor, not for favours, but for money.

Raffles was also unfortunate in the moment of his claim. The finances of the Company were embarrassed by the long and costly wars of Lord Hastings. An agitation was in progress against the China monopoly, and the shareholders were beginning to feel anxious as to the security of their dividends. But of far more immediate significance, and the cause of pressing fear, was the marked decline that had taken place in the value of the rupee. When Raffles arrived at Bencoolen, and for some time afterwards, the rupee seemed fixed on a proud eminence—being worth two shillings and threepence; but very shortly after his arrival it fell to two shillings, and for some periods it was even fractionally lower. This was the state of affairs when Raffles came as a suppliant to the Court, representing that he had a heavy claim against the Company, not only for services rendered, but for losses incurred either in its cause, or under such unavoidable circumstances as gave him some right to expect recompense. It was one of those moments when the less generous side of the old Company was made evident, and when claims were settled on the criticism of the auditor's department, and not in accordance with the large and lavish views expressed in the public Court.

On the 7th of February 1826, Sir Stamford Raffles expected an annuity of £500 a year. At that moment the auditor was analysing his accounts with rigid scrutiny, stimulated, no doubt, by the discovery on the very surface of the matter, that Raffles claimed the loss he had suffered by discount on the paper money in which he had been paid his last year's salary in Java, when the order to hand over charge to Mr. Fendall compelled him to realise at the market rate. His successor and colleagues were allowed full value for their paper. There were other points to which the auditor took exception. It will be recollected that Lord Minto had appointed Raffles, in 1813, to the Residency of Bencoolen as a place of retreat, and that this reserved appointment was to take effect from the date of his leaving Java, the allowances commencing at the same time. Raffles, therefore, considered, very naturally, that the pay of that post began after his leaving Batavia in the spring of 1816, although it was on the lower scale of a Resident, until the Court, as "a peculiar mark" of its favour, raised him in the spring of 1817 to the rank of a Lieutenant-Governor. In this opinion, Raffles drew his salary for the year 1816–17 on the minor scale of about £3000 a year, and for the year 1817–18 on the higher scale of £3750; and those items appeared duly set forth in the accounts of Fort Marlborough. But during those two years Raffles was either at home or on the sea. In those days the East India Company, as a general rule, only paid for the period its servants were actually at their posts. The civilian had then none of the luxuries of leave to Europe, on full or half pay. The Court was not, however, absolutely consistent in the enforcement of this rule. It frequently made exceptions, and Raffles seems to have thought that his quasi-public work in London in 1816–17, in connection with Java and the situation in the Archipelago, would have brought him under the favoured clause. There was at least no reason why he should not claim them, and he accordingly put them down in the first accounts from Fort Marlborough sent to Calcutta and London in the year 1819. He was perfectly aware that these claims might be disallowed, and, as will be seen, he took precautions accordingly. The accounts themselves reached London before the end of 1819, and from that moment until March 1826 not the smallest objection had been raised to the charges; and after an interval of over six clear years Raffles was, not unnaturally, satisfied that they had been passed. He had also been eighteen months in London, and not a word had been said to him on the subject.

Such was the position when, on the 12th of April 1826, Raffles received from the Company a formal demand to refund the large sum of £22,272, based on the items set forth in the following claim:—

CLAIM OF THE EAST INDIA COMPANY.

	Rupees.	Pounds Sterling.
Salary as Lieutenant-Governor at Bencoolen, February 1817 to March 1818 . . .	36,284	
Interest, at 5⅛ per cent. . . .	4,959	
	41,243	3,864
[In the original claim the rupees are worked out into sicca-rupees. Here this is unnecessary.]		
Loss in respect of discount	31,435	
Interest, at 5 per cent. . . .	3,929	
	35,364	3,313
Carry forward, . . .		7,717

	Rupees.	Pounds Sterling.
Brought forward, .	. .	7,717
Salary as Resident, 1816–1817 . . .	30,687	
Interest, at 4½ per cent. . . .	1,413	
	32,100	2,919
Commission on exports	73,792	6,914
Extra charges at Acheen and Singapore .	49,840	4,670
Total		£21,680
Add balance of proceeds of spice, per Borneo .		592
Grand Total		£22,272

The receipt of so large a demand made in peremptory language against a man who was expecting satisfaction for claims of his own, could not fail to be a terrible shock. I have shown the reader what was the state of Raffles's health while he was still buoyed up with the hope that the Company would treat him with more or less generosity. All his expectations in that direction were now shattered; and, at the same time, he was summoned to hand over a large sum of money on account of items of salary—some of which the lapse of time justified him in regarding as definitely settled in his favour—and of public expenditure in connection with the founding of Singapore and his mission on behalf of the Governor-General to Acheen. Not only did the Company claim the principal, but also the interest worked out with arithmetical accuracy. This blow was quickly succeeded by another. The claim of the East India Company had hardly reached him when the news arrived from India of the failure of the great house of Palmer, of Calcutta and Hyderabad, by which Raffles lost at a stroke the sum of £16,000. It may be as well to state that his only relations with that firm were that his agents in Bengal had purchased, in the course of business, one of their bills for remittance to London.

At this stage Sir Stamford Raffles may be left to speak for himself. The following letter, dated the 29th of April 1826, is addressed to Joseph Dart, Esq., Secretary to the Honourable East India Company:—

"Sir,—I have the honour to acknowledge the receipt of your letter of the 12th inst., and to request that you will assure the Honourable Court that I should have lost no time in complying with the requisition it contains, had not a most distressing and unlooked-for event, which occurred at the moment, deprived me of the means.

"The event to which I allude is the insolvency of the house in India, which was intrusted with the remittance of my property to this country, by which I have suffered a loss exceeding £16,000, with little or no chance of recovering any part. For the particulars of the calamity I request to refer to Messrs. Fairlie, Bonham, & Co., my agents in this country, through whom the remittance was to have been made. Thus circumstanced, I have no alternative but to place the Honourable Court in possession of the fact, and to throw myself on their liberality.

"I have already stated to the Honourable Committee of Correspondence that I was prepared to meet the two first and most important items by giving an immediate order on the Accountant-General and Sub-Treasurer in Bengal, to the extent of the Government securities deposited in their hands, with an order on my agents for the balance, and I trust that, as the money was placed there for the especial purpose of meeting this emergency, the Honourable Court will not, under my present circumstances, object to this arrangement.

"On the third and next important item, viz. the amount drawn as commission on exports, while I express my readiness to bow to the decision of the Honourable Court, and to abide by it without demur, I beg respectfully to offer the following explanation:—

"It may naturally be asked why in this case I did not take the same precaution as I did in the former, by placing the amount in deposit pending the reference to Europe. To this I reply that, considering the length of time which had elapsed, the ground of the Bengal Government having sanctioned it, subject to the approval of the Honourable Court, and the non-expression of the Court's dissent to the sums drawn, I was led to infer the same was not objected to by them.

"I will only add that the delay in the Court's decision on the question has subjected me to a total loss of the amount by the present failure of my agents; for, had the Court's definitive reply reached me while at Bencoolen, I then had the funds at hand awaiting their orders.

"I would not urge this explanation with a view to any evasion of the orders now received, but simply to account for not having made any provision to meet the present contingency, and as a ground on which I may venture to hope that, if still insisted upon by the Honourable Court to its present extent, I may be allowed the indulgence of time to enable me to raise the sum necessary. At present I have no other means of doing so but by disposing of my India Stock, and the sale of the little property I had set apart as a provision for my family after my death. In making this appeal to the Court, I do so in the hope that they take into consideration a life actively and most zealously devoted to their service."

In a second letter, of greater length and importance, Sir Stamford Raffles gives a fuller answer to the Company's claim, and this document should be carefully read in comparison with the several items constituting the claim. The following is its text, and it is also addressed to the Secretary of the Company, Joseph Dart, Esq.:—

"LONDON, 16*th May* 1826.

"SIR,—As it may be more regular that the explanations referred to in my last letter should be forwarded to you instead of the auditor, I have now the honour to submit them.

"In explanation of the sums drawn as extraordinary charges at Acheen and Singapore, amounting to Rs.49,840, I request to observe on the first item, viz. 'In 1819–20, charge as Agent to the Governor-General, Rs.27,766.'

"This disbursement was incurred and charged under the authority, and consistently with the orders, of the Supreme Government, and independent of the personal allowances of the Resident of Bencoolen.

"It occurred under the following circumstances:—Inconvenience had arisen from the mode in which former Residents had drawn their personal expenses, and it was on my suggestion directed that in future I should be allowed to draw monthly the average of the former charges on this account, reference being at the same time had by the Supreme Government to the increased expenses which must necessarily be incurred by me as Agent to the Governor-General, and otherwise in moving from place to place. It was proposed by the civil auditor that I should be authorised to draw at the rate of Rs.5000 per month on account; but it was finally determined that the amount to be in the first instance drawn should be limited to the average expenses of Bencoolen, viz. about Rs.3700, and that any excess incurred beyond that sum should be separately drawn, and accounted for as Durbar charges. The disbursement in question, and the charges now referred to, were for such expenses incurred during the mission to Acheen and Singapore, and for the period from my quitting Calcutta till my leaving Singapore to return to Bencoolen.

"A regular account of these expenses was kept by my Acting Secretary, Captain Cropley, of the Bengal Establishment, and on my return to Bencoolen, where a similar account had been kept of the Government House Establishment expenses, which had also been kept there by Captain Travers, the second assistant, the two amounts were added together, and the aggregate was found to exceed the average of the Resident's usual expenses by the sum stated. This excess was consequently charged in a separate account, and, this being duly certified according to the regulation provided in such cases, forwarded to the civil authorities in Bengal, the receipt of it was duly acknowledged, and, some further explanation having been subsequently furnished, no further notice was taken of it, and I of course concluded that it had been regularly carried to account.

"At all events, this item may be considered, if not already carried to account, at any rate under audit in Bengal. I request to claim the benefit of that audit, and, in the meantime, it may perhaps be satisfactory to the Honourable Court to observe how much the sum actually drawn by me fell short of the amount which, according to the calculations of the civil auditor, I might have been expected to have drawn.

"On the principle adopted by former Residents, I migh have drawn the actual expense on honour, without limitation as to the amount, and it was only at my request, and to simplify the accounts, that any change in form was made. It was arranged that the amount regularly drawn and carried to account should be limited to an average of what had been formerly drawn in ordinary times, and that what was incurred on extraordinary occasions should be drawn in a separate account, and according to a prescribed form. The extraordinary case did occur in the mission to Acheen and Prince of Wales's Island, and in the establishment of Singapore; and that such an extra charge should be incurred in excess of the ordinary charge at Bencoolen will be satisfactorily explained when it is considered that at Bencoolen there was a Government House and paid establishment and a regular succession of expenses consistent with the nature and duties of that establishment; and that it became my duty not only to provide for our establishment and its expense, entirely independent of these, while employed on foreign service, on a distant mission on distinct and political authority, as was the case on the mission to Acheen and Singapore; and, moreover, had not only to provide for the whole of the paid establishment at Bencoolen during my absence, but to pay and entertain an extra establishment while in the Straits of Malacca and Singapore, hired only for the time, and consequently at high rates.

"On the second item, viz. 'In 1822–23 charges at Singapore, Rs.17,785.'

"I beg to state that these must have been charges on the Public Account, and can in no way be connected with the amount drawn by me for personal expenses, which, on the occasion of my second visit to Singapore, when I had time to make arrangements to limit the charge, did not exceed the ordinary average of the Bencoolen Resident, and were charged and carried to account accordingly, without any excess.

"On the third item, viz. 'House rent at Singapore,' I trust that a few words will be sufficient.

"I have already stated that during my last visit to Singapore, during which the charge was incurred, I drew no additional sum for personal expenses beyond the ordinary charge of Bencoolen, but I had, of course, to be provided, while I resided at Singapore, with a house and accommodation for myself and establishment. There was no house belonging to the Government, and I did not intrude on the accommodation of the Resident, who occupied his own quarters. The most reasonable that offered was the upper part of a house occupied by the master attendant, which was engaged at 150 dollars per month, and for the most part occupied by the writers and servants of the establishment, and latterly entirely as an office, at which I attended daily when my health admitted,—my indisposition during the latter months compelling me to sleep on the hill, where I occupied a temporary bungalow.

"This charge was as necessarily incurred as every other public charge at Singapore, and I am at a loss to know on what principle it can be charged against me personally—why it is now disputed. That it should be an extraordinary charge accounts for itself, and that it was actually incurred cannot be questioned; and I know not how it was to be avoided, unless I had paid the money out of my own pocket, which could not be expected.

"The sum authorised by the Honourable Court, under the head of Deputation Allowances, I consider to be a compensation or remuneration for extra duty; and, although the largest portion of it was actually expended by defraying my personal expenses, it could not be expected that such a charge as an official house and office to the chief authority was to form part of these expenses.

"In explanation of the amount of £592, 5s. 10d. which the Court has called upon me to pay, as the balance due on account of the proceeds of spices per Borneo in 1822, I request to refer to the adjustment made by me previous to my leaving Bencoolen, and then submitted in my despatch to the Honourable Court, and to express a hope that, under the circumstances, the Court will still be inclined to consider it in the light of a remittance, as it was expressly intended and declared to be, and that, instead of my being subjected to a loss on the commercial speculation, the accounts may be adjusted on the principle of a fair rate of exchange between the money paid into the Bencoolen treasury in rupees and the amount sterling paid by the Honourable Court in England to my agent. In this case it only remains to be decided whether the adjustment made at Bencoolen, at the rate of 2s. 3d. the rupee, was a fair rate or not, and if not, I shall be ready to pay any difference that may arise by substituting any other rate of exchange that may be determined upon.

"Should any further explanation be required, in addition to my former statements respecting the commission drawn by the first assistant and storekeeper, I shall be happy to afford it on being permitted to refer to the Bencoolen Books; but as the same are entirely unconnected with the present call which has been made upon me, and cannot in the remotest degree apply to me personally with any pecuniary reference, it may not be necessary that I should swell this letter with further detail respecting them.

"Having now submitted to the Honourable Court such explanations and observations respecting the several items contained in your letter, I request to recapitulate them as follows, for the convenience of reference:—

"First.—The amount drawn as arrears of salary from March 1816 to March 1818, Rs.98,226·19 (*pencil note*, Rs.98,435·19). [This sum is the amount of the first three items in claim.] For these amounts, calculated with interest and converted into sterling money by the auditors, I have requested payment may be received in Calcutta, where the funds are deposited for the purpose.

"However serious the repayment of so large an amount may be, I have no right to complain, as the express condition on which the sums were provisionally drawn was their being subject to the confirmation of the Honourable Court, which has been denied. It will, however, appear that with regard to the first and most important item, viz. the arrears of salary, it could not have constituted a claim but from the circumstances of my removal from Java, and the tenor of my appointment to Bencoolen by the Earl of Minto; and as my appeal to the Honourable Court on that question, viz. my removal from Java, is still before the Honourable Court, and it remains to be decided upon how far my unfortunate recall was merited by my conduct, I trust that if it shall appear, on the general review of my administration, that such recall occurred under partial and defective information, which has been since supplied, and that subsequent inquiry has proved that such administration was, upon the whole, sound and creditable to myself and my employers, I may still look to the Honourable Court's liberal consideration of the heavy pecuniary loss to which I was subjected on the occasion, and of which this item forms a part. Had I been allowed to remain until the transfer to the Dutch, and proceeded to Bencoolen direct, I should at any rate not have lost two of the most important years of my life by the necessity of proceeding to England.

"The other item, viz. the loss by discount on paper, being an actual abstraction from the amount of my salary as Lieutenant-Governor, will, I hope, also be considered with reference to the small amount of that salary, and to the loss being occasioned by my sudden recall at a moment no less injurious to my character than pecuniary interests, for had I remained till the transfer, I should have derived the advantage of the notes being all at par and paid off.

"Second.—The amount drawn as commission on exports, Rs.73,791, 15a. 8p., left for the final decision of the Honourable Court under the explanation I have offered.

"Third.—Extraordinary charges at Acheen and Singapore, Rs.49,840. These being actual disbursements, cannot be supposed to have afforded me any pecuniary advantages, and, at all events, should the explanations offered not be sufficient, I claim the benefit of the audit in Bengal on such amounts as may be before that Government.

"Fourth.—The balance on account of a remittance in spices of £592, 5s. 10d. This I have requested may be adjusted on the principle of a remittance as it was intended, at any rate the Court may give.

"The commission drawn by the Assistant to the Resident and Storekeeper can have no reference to myself personally.

"In conclusion, I have to apologise for any accidental error that I may have been led into from the want of any documents to refer to, the whole of my papers and accounts having been destroyed, and my being under the necessity of making these explanations from memory.—I have the honour to be, sir, your most obedient, humble servant, T. S. RAFFLES."

The claim of the East India Company was therefore divisible into the following heads:—

1. Salary for the years 1816–18	£6,783
2. Discount on his paper money, received as salary, when realised on his removal in 1816 from Java . . .	3,313
3. Commission on exports at Bencoolen	6,914
4. Extra charges on Singapore and Acheen Missions . .	4,670
And the minor disputed point about the remittance in spices	592
	£22,272

On the first point Raffles contended that he was entitled to the sum; but, as there was some doubt in the matter pending a final sanction from the Court, he had deposited the money in Bengal, for the purpose of refunding it if desired. The evidence, as well as a sense of justice, points conclusively to his being entitled to that salary; for the Earl of Minto stated in his letter to Raffles of June 22nd, 1813, that he had formally appointed him to Fort Marlborough, "the allowances to commence from the time of your departure from Java."

On the second point, viz. the discount, being an actual abstraction from his salary, he claimed generous treatment.

On the third point, he bowed to the decision of the Court, although the lapse of time tended to justify his thinking that it had been sanctioned, while the failure of the bankers led to his total loss of that sum and more. If the Company had decided with reasonable promptness, the funds were then at his disposal to discharge the claim. As it was, he was a double loser through no fault of his own, and he consequently begged for the indulgence of time.

On the fourth and last point, for the fifth is trivial, he showed that the expenditure was on Public Account, and that he could not be expected to defray the cost of the Mission to Singapore and Acheen out of his own pocket. In fact Raffles gave a complete and satisfactory answer to the more serious side of the Company's claim, by showing in each and every case that he was entitled, from his point of view and in accordance with official procedure, to make the charges; that the Supreme Government had in every case sanctioned his steps; and that, where the sanction of the Court was necessary, he had set aside the funds to discharge the liability, should an adverse decision be given. There is no doubt that, so far as his honour was involved, Raffles met the case fully; and that his frank and explicit explanations satisfied the Court that he had not deviated from the path of official rectitude, although he put forward pretensions with which they refused to comply. How far the Court was justified, and within the strict letter of its rights, I will not stop to inquire. How far it was generous in its treatment the reader will have no difficulty in deciding for himself. It had in the first place, and before he explained it, disparaged his work in Java, and cast such reflections on his procedure that he had to come to England to vindicate that work as well as his own character. In return, the Company mulcted him of two years' salary, while, of all the English officials connected with Java, he alone was not allowed to receive par value for his paper. Lastly, the Court insisted on his defraying out of his own pocket charges for the Singapore Mission, which was undoubtedly the affair of the Company.

It seems indisputable that, if Raffles had lived to fight his own battle, some of these items would have been withdrawn, and it might even have been that the Court would have granted him some equivalent compensation for his own losses and services. His premature death unfortunately ended the possibility of contesting the Company's claim, by reference either to Bengal or to the larger views with which the Court treated those of its servants who had rendered signal services.

But as the reader will wish to know the end of this matter, I record the arrangement effected after his death. The Court did not withdraw its claim, but, under all the circumstances, accepted on the 7th of March the £10,000 offered by Lady Raffles in February 1827 as a settlement of the matter; and ordered the Board's solicitor to prepare a bond of mutual release. I append Lady Raffles's letter, making the offer of the payment of this sum :—

[No date given, but about *26th February* 1827.]

"SIR,—I am naturally anxious to bring the subject of the demands of the East India Company against Sir Stamford Raffles to a final settlement.

"After defraying the claims brought against the estate, it appears by the Statement of Property laid before you, sir, that there is little more than £10,000 to meet the demands of the East India Company.

"I therefore beg to offer to transfer to the Company six thousand pounds now in Bengal, together with the India Stock, amounting now to about two thousand four hundred and fifty pounds, and Consols one thousand one hundred and fifty, which will leave a balance of between five and six hundred pounds to make up the ten thousand, and which balance shall be made good on the first realisation from the estate.

"I beg to apologise to you for trespassing upon your personal kindness, through which I hope the matter may be finally concluded.—I have the honour to be, sir, your most obedient servant, SOPHIA RAFFLES.

"JOSEPH DART, Esq."

In this manner came to an end the petition of Raffles—first made in 1818, repeated by him on the 15th of September 1824, and on the 3rd of November in the same year, and finally advanced by him on the 23rd of March 1826—for compensation at the hands of the authorities. They ignored the whole of his request so far as it related to money, and they came down upon him for a sum exceeding £20,000. The nature of that claim has been set forth. The persistence with which Raffles pressed his petitions for justice was matched by theirs in insisting on the repayment of the sums they claimed with less justice than technical right. Even death did not soften their hearts. They extracted from the widow the £10,000 which constituted the balance of his estate. It is not by referring to that page of its records that the East India Company can claim a character for generosity towards its deserving servants—a character which on many other occasions it must be allowed to have fully merited.

Although the Company ignored Raffles's claims for compensation, it at last passed its final award on the subject of the merit of his administration in the East. On the 12th of April 1826 it put forward its claim as described; and, on the same day, it formulated the following decision about Sir Stamford Raffles's administration and political services in the Archipelago. Considering the opposition which the authorities, and especially the Secret Committee, of the Company had offered to some of the more important of the measures he had advocated and carried through, the tenor of the award must be regarded as extremely favourable to Raffles's public reputation. It is only natural to suppose that this award was announced on the 12th of April with the intention of softening the effect of the claim made on the same day, and of showing that the claim itself carried with it no intended or implied aspersion against Sir Stamford's honour. The text of the Court's decision reads as follows:—

"*Of Java.*—The Court admit, that the success of the expedition to Java was promoted by the plans and information of Sir Stamford Raffles. That the representation of Sir Stamford Raffles as to the financial embarrassment of Java on the outset of his government is correct.

"That those financial difficulties were enhanced by the inevitable hostilities with Palembang and Jojocarta.

"That of the measures introduced by Sir Stamford Raffles for the removal of the financial embarrassments; viz. the sale of lands, withdrawal of Dutch paper currency, and a new system of land revenue;

"The sale of lands is considered to have been a questionable proceeding.

"The entire series of measures for the reform of the currency are conceded to have been well adapted to their object.

"With regard to the system of revenue introduced by him, the Court state that they would have been inclined to augur favourably of the success of his measures, and consider it highly probable that the colony would have soon been brought at least to liquidate its own expenses by the lenient and equitable administration of Sir Stamford Raffles's system.

"The regulations for reform in the judicial department and police, the Court consider entitled, both in their principles and in their details, to a considerable degree of praise.

"On the measures respecting Borneo, Banca, and Japan, the Court remark, that, under a permanent tenure of Java, and a different system of policy, the measures in question (promoting intercourse and enlarging the British power) would have been valuable service.

"*Sumatra.*—The measures of internal reform introduced by Sir Stamford Raffles are generally approved.

"In his political measures he incurred the strong disapprobation of the Court; but the motives by which he was actuated were unquestionably those of zealous solicitude for the British interests in the Eastern seas, and form a part of a series of measures which have terminated in the establishment of Singapore.

"*Singapore.*—It is allowed that Sir Stamford Raffles developed the exclusive views of the Dutch, and the measures ultimately carried into effect are to be attributed to his instrumentality, and to him the country is chiefly indebted for the advantages which the Settlement of Singapore has secured to it. The Court consider this to be a very strong point in Sir Stamford Raffles's favour, and are willing to give him to the full extent the benefit of their testimony respecting it.

"His administration of Singapore has been approved by the Bengal Government."

The Court's opinion with regard to the general services of Sir Stamford Raffles is summed up in the following terms:—

"The government of Sir Stamford Raffles appears, with sufficient evidence, to have conciliated the good feelings of, at least, the great majority of the European and native population; his exertions for the interests of literature and science are highly honourable to him, and have been attended with distinguished success; and although his precipitate and unauthorised emancipation of the Company's slaves, and his formation of a settlement at Pulo Nias, chiefly with a view to the suppression of a slave traffic, are justly censured by the Court, his motives in those proceedings, and his unwearied zeal for the abolition of slavery, ought not to be passed over without an expression of approbation."

There is an indirect reference to the affair in the following letter to Dr. Raffles, the last of the long series from which I have drawn so much fresh information. It will reveal its writer still serene under his many shocks, and not without hope for the future:—

"HIGHWOOD, MIDDLESEX, 15*th June* 1826.

"MY DEAR COUSIN,—I have just received your welcome letter of the 12th, and should send this immediate acknowledgment to Liverpool, if it did not appear that I should best ensure its delivery and meet your arrangements by forwarding it to Highbury Place.

"We are here, thank God, once more out of the trammels and disorders of a London life. We came down last week, and, looking forward to the hope of remaining some time, we have nearly dismantled the house in Grosvenor Street, so that I fear you would find but poor accommodation *there*. *Here* we cannot have you too much with us, and from the nature of the house you can best judge the accommodation we can afford.

"We have the same dread of the measles that you appear to have. Neither of the children have had it, and as they have had a sad bout, and are only just recovering from the whooping-cough, which I caught from them, we cannot be too particular. As to my engagements for the next three weeks, I know but of one or two likely to interfere with any arrangement we can make for being together as much as possible while you are in the vicinity of London. We are daily waiting a summons from Lady Harcourt to go to St. Leonards, where we have promised to take the children for a week. We are also under the necessity of going into Essex after the midsummer holiday to put Charles [his nephew] to school, and spend a few days with Sotherby, the poet, and our friend Mr. Hamilton. With these exceptions the coast is clear.

"You don't say the time that Mrs. Raffles proposes coming to town, but I hope you will arrange for her coming to us when she does come; and that, at all events, we may be able to make a comfortable family circle previous to your trip to Hamburgh. Let me have a line from you when you reach

Highbury, should you not stop by the way at Barnet, and first look in upon us. I generally go into town once a week, and we must lose no time in meeting. I have had a good deal to annoy me since I saw you last, but it is a worldly affair, and I trust will [not] materially affect our happiness. Sophia is quite well, and desires her kindest love.—Yours affectionately,

"T. S. RAFFLES."

"We suffer a little from the heat, but as we hope to make our hay in the course of next week, I don't complain. Highwood is now in its best dress, and will, I am sure, please you. My neighbour, Mr. Wilberforce, takes possession to-morrow, and will previously spend the day with us."

This last glimpse of Sir Stamford Raffles, little more than a fortnight before his death, shows that to his long succession of illnesses, losses, and worries, had now to be added an attack of whooping-cough, which no doubt further diminished his remaining strength. To those who appreciate the effect which the mind exercises on the body, it will not seem an extreme conclusion to draw that the disappointment he had experienced in his relations with the East India Company must have caused him a severer strain than even bodily ailments. His cousin came and visited him at Highwood, and then proceeded to Hamburg, leaving Sir Stamford engrossed in country pursuits and in getting in his hay. There was then no reason to suppose that his course was nearly run, or that the cares of a public position and the pleasures of English country life were both for him on the eve of closing.

While Dr. Raffles was in Hamburg, Sir Stamford Raffles died suddenly, and the first intimation the former received of the sad occurrence was given in the following letter:—

"MY VERY DEAR DOCTOR,—The last time I had the pleasure to see you, you said upon your return you should stay only a few hours in London, and should avail yourself of the first conveyance for Liverpool.

"An event has, however, taken place which I am persuaded would occasion you to alter your mind—an event in which I most feelingly sympathise. It is nothing less than the death of Sir S. Raffles, which took place on Wednesday last at his country seat.

"Knowing how much the chances might be against your seeing a newspaper containing the information in a foreign country, and supposing that Lady Raffles at the moment of her distress might be at a loss to direct to you, I have thought it my duty as a friend to apprise you of the event—an event I most sensibly and feelingly deplore.—I am, truly yours, J. A. COLLINS.

"*July* 8, 1826."

In conveying the news to his wife at Liverpool, Dr. Raffles wrote: "When I last saw it [Highwood about ten days earlier], it appeared like an earthly paradise; happiness and peace reigned in its mansion; but what a change has a few days made! It is now the scene of death, and all is agony and gloom."

The *Gentleman's Magazine*, for July 1826, gives the following particulars of Sir Stamford's death, which occurred early in the morning of the 5th of that month, the day before his forty-fifth birthday:—"He had passed the preceding day in the bosom of his family, and, excepting a bilious attack under which he had laboured for some days, there was nothing in his appearance to create the least apprehension that the fatal hour was so near. Sir Stamford had retired to rest on the Tuesday evening [4th July] between ten and eleven o'clock, his usual hour when in the country. On the following morning at five o'clock, it being discovered that he had left his room before the time at which he generally rose, six o'clock, Lady Raffles immediately rose, and found him lying at the bottom of a flight of stairs in a state of complete insensibility. Medical aid was promptly procured, and every means resorted to, to restore animation, but the vital spark had fled. The body was opened, under the direction of Sir Everard Home, the same day, who pronounced his death to have been caused by an apoplectic attack, beyond the controul of all human power. It was likewise apparent that the sufferings of the deceased must, for some time past, have been most intense." In the course of an appreciative notice the writer concludes as follows:—"Considered as a whole, the character of the late Sir T. Stamford Raffles displays little, if anything, to censure, and much to applaud. His name will live in British history, not among warriors, but among the benefactors of mankind, as a philanthropist and statesman of the very first eminence."

Among the panegyrics passed on Sir Stamford Raffles at the time of his death and since, I will only quote one, viz. the tribute paid to his work and character by his friend and associate, Sir Humphry Davy, in his Presidential Address for the year to the Royal Society:—

"Sir T. Stamford Raffles was not a contributor to your *Transactions* directly, yet he was the occasion of many discoveries in zoology, botany, and physiology. His disinterested promotion of every branch of natural history; his sacrifice of his fortune and his time to collections in this department of knowledge; the readiness with which he laid them open to scientific men, claimed the highest admiration. Occupying high situations in our Empire in the East, he employed his talents and his extensive researches, not in the exercise of power, or the accumulation of wealth, but in endeavouring to benefit and to improve the condition of the natives, to found liberal institutions, and to establish a permanent commercial intercourse between the Colonies, where he presided, and the mother-country, which, whilst it brought new treasures to Europe, tended to civilise and to improve the condition of the inhabitants of some of the most important islands of the East. Neither misfortune nor pecuniary losses damped the ardour of his mind in the pursuit of knowledge. Having lost one splendid collection by fire, he instantly commenced the formation of another, and, having brought this to Europe, he made it not private, but public, property, and placed it entirely at the disposition of a new association, for the promotion of zoology, of which he had been chosen president by acclamation. Many of the fellows of this Society can bear testimony to his enlightened understanding, acute judgment, and accurate and multifarious information; and all of them must, I am sure, regret the premature loss of a man who had done so much, and from whom so much more was to be expected, and who was so truly estimable in all the relations of life."

Sir Stamford was buried in Hendon Parish Church, but, owing to differences with the vicar, a member of a slave-owning family, no monument was erected at the time, and the actual site of the grave has not been ascertained. Sir Stamford, who had interested himself in the building of a chapel-of-ease at Mill Hill, not far from Highwood, in writing to Dr. Raffles on February 7th, 1826, throws some light on the causes of those differences :—

"We have not yet come to any conclusion, and the difficulty seems to rest with our vicar, who is of a very peculiar character, and on bad terms with most of his parishioners. Mr. Wilberforce, being Evangelical, is a great stickler for Mother Church, so that I anticipate we shall not be able to proceed without the aid of the Bishop and our ecclesiastic local. . . . My recommendation is to set about building the chapel at once, and discuss the government of it afterwards. I . . . will only add how happy it would make us were we within that sort of reach of you, that we could partake of your pastoral care and exhortation,—your blessing we always shall have."

The exact position of the grave of this illustrious man remains unknown, and there was no memorial even to show that his body lies in Hendon Church, until the Rev. R. B. Raffles, in 1887, associating with his own the practical counsels of his brother, erected out of his slender means a brass tablet on the wall of the church, with the following inscription :—

IN MEMORY OF

SIR THOMAS STAMFORD RAFFLES, F.R.S., LL.D.,

STATESMAN, ADMINISTRATOR, AND NATURALIST,

FOUNDER OF THE COLONY AND CITY OF SINGAPORE, 29TH JANUARY 1819 ;

BORN 5TH JULY 1781, DIED AT HIGHWOOD, MIDDLESEX, JULY 5TH, 1826,

AND BURIED NEAR THIS TABLET.

ERECTED IN 1887 BY MEMBERS OF THE FAMILY.

This tablet, the statue in Westminster Abbey, the statue at Singapore, Chantrey's bust in the Raffles Institution in that city of his own creation, and the duplicate of it in the Zoological Gardens—are among the public and private memorials to his greatness. They are more than enough; for, if none of them existed, the name of Stamford Raffles could still never be removed from the list of England's great statesmen.

Thus closed suddenly, and under the shadow of ill-health, pecuniary losses, and personal disappointment, the career of Sir Stamford Raffles. In years he had only just entered the period of middle life, and the work he had performed, as well as the experience he had gained, would have entitled him to take a further prominent part in the affairs of the East. Had his life been prolonged, there can be little doubt that he would have won fresh fame as a statesman on the floor of the House of Commons, or as an administrator in some new station beyond the seas. He had done enough, however, in his brief and almost meteoric career, to obtain a place among the few great intellects and brave spirits that have pointed out for this country the path to empire in Southern Asia. Opposition, prejudice, calumny during his lifetime, and since his death, forgetfulness, and the haste which prevents our realising that our Empire came to us by inheritance from our forefathers, have not undone his work or diminished his reputation. Stamford Raffles is a name we need not fear to place in the same class with Robert Clive and Warren Hastings, with Wellesley and Dalhousie.

What was his work? Let the reader throw back his mind and consider all that Raffles had done, written, and inspired in the twenty-one years between the day on which he left the home-country, a young man, serious but hopeful, half-educated, he said in his modesty, but employing his time on ship-board in learning Malay, resolute to succeed by his own merit, but still more resolute to promote the interests of England,—and that early summer morning when his wife found him dead by the foot of the stairs at Highwood. His rise in the official service of the Company was extraordinarily rapid. Six years after he reached Penang, the Government, with the fullest powers, of a large island and its dependencies, recently invaded and only partially subdued, was intrusted to this young man of thirty summers, whose training had been in an office, and who had not possessed an opportunity or a friend except those made by his own exertions. Who would not have predicted failure for such an experiment? Who can wonder that his seniors in the service, the men of powerful connections and recognised families, were, at first, scornful of this unknown and youthful ruler whose ignominious failure they anticipated, and, then, jealous and resentful when they found that he was successful, and superior to their malice and opposition? The marvel is that his detractors were so few; and great must have been the merit, subtle must have been the charm of manner, that at that period disarmed the enmity of the privileged ranks of the services and made so many of them his friends and admirers. His success, the resolution with which he carried his own views and policy into effect, were the more remarkable, because he never put on the hollow aspect of humility, so often used as a screen for ambition. He deferred to no one, he formed his own view of every situation, and he carried through his plans with a vigour, determination, and skill that could not be surpassed. He was no mild and cringing disputant, seeking to disarm his adversary by feigning weakness, or ready with some plausible excuse for turning his other cheek to the smiter. He may not have gone out of his way to court strife, but he certainly never shirked it. He stood up to his most formidable antagonist, and he gave blow for blow. Whether it was a Government or an individual, he fought out the case in the spirit of Squire Widdrington at Chevy Chase, and he endeavoured to dispose of his adversary, to use his own words, "with vigour and effect."

Such was the spirit in which he accomplished his life's mission. Sanguine in temperament, quick in his judgment, fixed in his resolutions, courageous in the execution of his plans, and undaunted in the face of difficulty, Raffles revealed on all critical occasions those qualities which are essential to the man of action, whether he be a statesman or a soldier. The merit of his work was not fully appreciated in his own time, because the region in which he laboured was too remote from the public gaze, and too distasteful, from its association with pecuniary loss, in the eyes of the Company. India monopolised attention, and China had not yet arisen above the horizon as a possibly vast field for enterprise and trade. Raffles's labours in the intermediate zone appealed to a later generation than his own. They are valued now, because we know the importance and value of Singapore for our Far Eastern trade and communications. But the full force of his political wisdom and work in the Archipelago will not be appreciated until the Australias have fifty millions, instead of five, stretching forth their grasp over the islands that Raffles so exhaustively described and so admirably governed.

The founding of Singapore was a great achievement—great by reason of the method and the attendant conditions of its accomplishment. It was also a definite and concrete performance which everyone can see and understand. But, after all, this single act was not the real claim of Stamford Raffles to rank in the front group of English statesmen. His claim is based on his long struggle with the Dutch, of which that measure was the concluding incident. It is to him, and to him alone, that we owe the overthrow of the exclusive system maintained in those seas by the Dutch for two centuries after the massacre of Amboyna. When we evacuated Java, we left them in a stronger and improved position to carry out and continue their old policy. Had the anxiety of the Governor-General and the home Government to avoid a collision with the Dutch, had the craven spirit of Colonel Bannerman prevailed, England would have finally lost her position in this quarter; Rhio, or perhaps Singapore, would have been the Antwerp and not the Malta of the East; and our trade would to this hour be fettered by the suspicious and grudging competition of the Dutch, just as it had been by Batavia alone in the two hundred years before Raffles threw himself single-handed in their path, and at last accomplished their discomfiture. His great work, then, was that he beat the Dutch, as Clive beat the French; and, as a statesman should achieve his ends, he beat them without firing a shot.

But if Raffles triumphed over the Dutch, his good work in Java, his struggle for the native races, has not passed into oblivion. Many Dutch writers have paid him a tribute of admiration and respect. The colonists still preserve the recollection that the golden age in their beautiful island, all too brief as it proved, was due to the efforts of its English Governor. In the native courts of Suracarta and

Jojocarta there still survive memories of that Governor Raffles who made himself equally loved and feared. Nor is this tradition altogether sentimental and devoid of practical value. The Dutch colonists are attached to Holland, and the tie between them and their parent State will not be broken by their own act. But should events in Europe place the Netherlands in the possession of a stronger continental Power, as was the case in the beginning of this century, the recollection of Raffles's wise and beneficent rule will serve to direct Dutch colonial opinion, so that it may seek that sure haven of British protection, freedom of trade, and of institutions which it found in the days of Minto and his representative, rather than again become subject to a military despotism. This is no random statement or hasty thought. Not so many years ago there was a spasm of fear in Holland and throughout her colonies that they might be absorbed in the German Empire; and I have high authority for saying that, when that apprehension reached the colonies, the Governor of the Dutch East Indies declared that as soon as the Black Eagle was hoisted at the Hague he would run up the Union Jack at Batavia. It is to Raffles that we should owe what I will venture to call the moral reversion to Java by the free action of its inhabitants, whenever violence or ambition shall snap the link with Holland.

There is only one point more. Raffles suffered much in pocket and in calumny because there were no telegraphic or rapid postal communications in his day. But, on the other hand, he owed to the same deficiencies the opportunities which enabled him to achieve his ends for the advantage of the country and the discomfiture of her foes. Had there been cables, or even steamers, the several financial questions that covered in settlement periods of many years, the misrepresentations of Gillespie and Blagrave would have been brought at once to a final and satisfactory settlement. But if in that sense Raffles would have been the gainer, in every other respect he would have been the loser, and so would England. Two illustrations will suffice to bring the significance of this point before the reader. George Canning would have recalled him in the first heat of rage for the protest against the Dutch proceedings at Palembang; Lord Hastings would have annulled his commission on hearing of the Dutch seizure of Rhio; and Singapore would have had to wait for its Columbus.

We may well ask ourselves, in conclusion, whether, in these days of checks and counter-checks upon individual initiative, when democratic institutions and interdependent councils combine with the telegraph to render it difficult to fasten responsibility on any one short of some ill-defined central authority, it is possible for such men as Stamford Raffles to obtain and to turn to account the opportunities that fall to their lot for the national aggrandisement. And if the individual statesman and soldier cannot obtain the chance, how is this Empire to be carried on, how are the triumphs of the past to be repeated in the future history of the world? With, however, the example and career fresh in our minds of this great man, this buoyant English statesman, who would have said, in the words of Shakespeare, "Come the three corners of the world in arms, and we shall shock them," doubt and fear would be out of place. Not of such as Raffles was Tennyson's mind full when he wrote the lines—

> "Pray God our greatness may not fail
> Through craven fears of being great."

INDEX OF SUBJECTS